THE REGULATION OF THE STATE IN COMPETITIVE MARKETS IN THE EU

This book looks at the changing role and nature of the regulation of State

interve

It exa

Europe

provid

togeth

the Eu

Individ

sible rc

of the

and the controversial application of Articles 81 and 82 EC to the state. chapters examine the processes of privatisation and liberalisation with case studies on the postal sector, utilities and telecommunications.

Modern Studies in European Law: Volume 11

Modern Studies in European Law

The Regulation of the State in Competitive Markets in the EU

Erika Szyszczak

·HART·
PUBLISHING

OXFORD AND PORTLAND, OREGON
2007

Published in North America (US and Canada) by
Hart Publishing
c/o International Specialized Book Services
920 NE 58th Avenue, Suite 300
Portland, OR 97213-3786
USA
Tel: +1 503 287 3093 or toll-free: (1) 800 944 6190
Fax: +1 503 280 8832
E-mail: orders@isbs.com
Website: www.isbs.com

Hart Publishing, 16C Worcester Place, OX1 2JW
Telephone: +44 (0)1865 517530 Fax: +44 (0)1865 510710
E-mail: mail@hartpub.co.uk
Website: http://www.hartpub.co.uk

British Library Cataloguing in Publication Data
Data Available

ISBN: 978-1-84113-497-0 (hardback)

Typeset by Columns Design Ltd, Reading
Printed and bound in Great Britain by
TJI Digital, Padstow, Cornwall

For Richard

'Just dancing in the dark'

Preface

THE INTERNAL MARKET programme of the European Union created a geo-political space where national boundaries are intended to have little economic significance. Over time the legitimate role of state intervention in the market became a prominent question in the formulation of national and EU policy, and, since the 1990s a body of law and regulation has emerged on this topic, covering procurement policy, competition policy, industrial policy and the free movement (Internal Market) rules.

Underpinning these developments are a number of issues relating to the relationship between the state and the market. These include: the relationship of the state with its citizens (and non-citizens) in the provision of traditional public services, the responsibility of the private sector, and non-state bodies, in providing universal service obligations, the role of citizenship in a market without frontiers, the challenges of liberalisation and the new economy, the relationship between market integration, competition policy and regulatory policy choices and the role to be played by different levels of government and institutions. Analyses of these issues tend to be fragmented. Therefore the aim of this book is to address this wide range of issues by organising them around the theme of the regulation of state intervention in competitive markets.

The changing terminology of the European Union and re-numbering of the Treaty Articles is a challenge for modern writers. Throughout I have used the most recent numbering of the EC Treaty. Unusually I have used the term EC Commission to distinguish this Institution from other 'Commissions' which have grown up in Europe since 1957. I have also adopted the modern term of the European Union to describe the supra-national political structure of European integration, with occasional lapses into the use of the term Community, for example, Community law, where it seemed appropriate.

The genesis of this book was a lunch with two colleagues, Marise Cremona and Leo Flynn, in a Turkish restaurant in Covent Garden, London, in 1997. We were frustrated with the rigid structures of the typical LLM programme which did not provide the flexibility to absorb the rapid political, legal and economic changes which were taking place in Europe during the 1990s. Issues of liberalising markets, regulating public procurement, the control of state aids and public monopolies were consigned to the margins as the focus on the liberalisation of the four economic freedoms of the Internal Market and economic and monetary union took centre stage. Competition law courses tended to concentrate upon the regulation of *private* economic power, centred around Articles 81 and 82 EC and the Merger Regulation. Our belief that the control of public and new forms of hybrid public/private economic power was an equally important dimension of the future economic and social structure of Europe led us to create a new course which we hoped would complement the traditional LLM courses. I am indebted to Professor Ross Cranston QC for his support and encouragement at the start of this project.

Leo never fulfilled his ambition of teaching the course; he was enticed to a référendaire post at the Court of Justice and now works in the Legal Service of the EC Commission. It was a pleasure to teach the London LLM course with Marise and with Anna Mörner; many of the ideas, and the structure of this book, are the result of our conversations, alongside those with students at London, Nottingham and Leicester Universities, colleagues in Warsaw, Ljubljana, Udine and the ERA in Trier. Everyone provided enthusiasm and insights which made the study of the subject challenging.

Richard Hart has the patience of a saint. It took time to liberate my thoughts from the computer. The book would never have been finished without the help of Vinaeet Budhiraja and would not be as complete without the editing skills of Kate Elliott and Lorna Day. Thanks to Jamie, Larissa and Will for providing pleasant distractions and preventing me from sliding into social and digital exclusion by keeping me up to date with modern technology, language and music. Richard Disney has been (fairly) tolerant in giving robust and assertive answers to my various questions, providing insights on how economists view the world.

Temple, London and Leicester
January 2007

Contents

Table of Cases

Cases Before the Court of First Instance

Cases Before the German Courts

1

The Changing Role of State Intervention in Markets

THE POST-war reconstruction of Europe accepted a positive role for the state in rebuilding the devastated economies of Western Europe. At the time of the Treaty of Rome, 50 years ago (1957), the state, directly or indirectly, intervened in a large part of the national economy. Often goods were provided through state monopolies, in fields such as defence industries, energy and raw materials production. A variety of rationales were provided for state monopolies: that, in the absence of state provision, the private sector would abuse monopoly power arising from barriers to entry such as economies of scale; that 'essential services' or the 'national interest' required public production of goods and services; and that economic efficiency required extensive state regulation of prices and trading conditions. State subsidies were also seen as a tool of national economic policy. The tolerance of state intervention in the market was recognised in what was originally Article 222 EC, now Article 295 EC:

> The Treaty shall in no way prejudice the rules in the Member States governing the system of property ownership.

The original EEC Treaty was seen as reflecting an essentially agnostic approach to state ownership and extensive regulation of the private market. By the 1990s the emergent economic constitution of the EU embodied a growing orientation towards private market provision and a growing affinity with the concurrent liberal market approach of greater privatisation and reduced tolerance of public provision. As these new trends have evolved, the European Courts have interpreted Article 295 EC as imposing restrictions on the specific methods and form of regulation that a Member State may choose when it intervenes in the economy.

That state intervention in the market may distort competition, as well as affect inter-state trade was recognised in the EEC Treaty. There were legal tools for regulating state intervention in the market, for example, measures to control state monopolies and the review of state aids, but these addressed only the extreme versions of state economic activity and were fragmented and under-used. The ECSC Treaty included provisions regulating interference with the conditions of competition and also regulated government subsidies which foreshadowed the rules on state aid in the EEC Treaty. However, the EC Commission was cautious in using the competition rules against politically sovereign states.

State intervention in the market continued to be an under-regulated area of economic activity until the EC Commission's White Paper of 1985.[1] By then the use of the core economic freedoms had made extensive inroads into the sovereignty of the Member States, leading Lenaerts to assert, with some confidence, that 'there is no constitutionally protected nucleus of residual State sovereignty'.[2]

The 1990s saw a dramatic change of policy towards state intervention in the increasingly liberalised markets of the EU. The changes are seen in policy documents from the EC Commission, the rise in litigation in the national courts, especially against state monopolies and undertakings granted special or exclusive rights. The EC Commission created the idea that state intervention was a persistent and pervasive barrier to full market integration:

> it is felt that at the present stage of economic integration in the Community the barriers are greatest in markets currently subject to state regulation.[3]

Van Miert, the Commissioner for Competition in 1997, alleged that this fact held back the competitiveness of the European economy:

> I have already mentioned that within Europe the consensus has rejected national champions, but I cannot stress this too highly. If our firms are to compete internationally they must learn to compete at home.[4]

Thus during the 1990s the EC Commission, aided by opportunistic litigants and favourable judgments from the Court of Justice, developed a policy on regulating state intervention in the newly liberalised and competitive markets, not only for the existing Member States of the European Union, but also for the Accession States:

> As well as enforcement of the competition rules we have a key role to play in policy making. We have been instrumental in pushing the EU programme of liberalisation. For years much of European industry has been the subject of public sector monopolies. These have limited innovation, stifled competition and led in many cases to consumers paying too high a price for essential goods and services. It is clear that such a system of

---

[1] COM(85)310 final, 14 June 1985.

[2] K Lenaerts, 'Constitutionalism and the Many Faces of Federalism' (1990) 38 *American Journal of Comparative Law* 205.

[3] EC Commission, *Twentieth Report on Competition Policy* (Brussels/Luxembourg, EC Commission, 1990) at 50.

[4] K van Miert, 'Europe 2000, the Challenge of Market and Competition Policy', speech to the EUI, Florence, 26 Sept 1997, available at http://europa.eu.int/comm/dg04/speech/seven/en/sp97051.htm.

national monopolies is incompatible with an internal market based on free competition and free circulation of goods, services, people and capital.[5]

Writing in 1997, Petretto observed that:

Entry to the European Union automatically implies acceptance of the concept lying at the roots of its 'economic constitution': the developing of competition by means of widespread liberalisation processes in the industrial sectors. The aim of this process is the gaining of the advantages associated with free competition between agents—in terms of innovation, cost minimisation, price containment and a high level of quality—independently of the private or public ownership of the enterprises operating in single markets. This therefore means liberalisation, with or without privatisation, above all in the basic sectors producing public-utility services such as telecommunications, energy, transport and water supply.[6]

PRIVATISATION AND LIBERALISATION

From the 1980s onwards what had seemed to be the inexorable growth of the welfare state in Europe was questioned. Governments and private capital persuaded electorates and consumers of the capacity of markets to provide, not only private goods and services, but a range of what have traditionally been regarded as *publicly* provided goods and services. A prominent feature of the late 1980s and 1990s, therefore, was the retreat of the state from direct involvement in markets and the opening up of markets to liberalisation. The liberalisation of markets walked hand in hand with the privatisation of state ownership of assets *and* state provision of welfare services and commercial services.[7] Indeed the transfer of state assets to the private sector is viewed as the most extraordinary economic development of the latter part of the twentieth century.[8] From 1990 to 1999 the OECD estimates that some $850bn of state assets were transferred to the private sector, with some 40 per cent of these transfers taking place in Europe. However, the processes of privatisation are complex. States use different methods and employ various legal and economic tools to transfer state enterprises to private sector ownership. In particular they are often reluctant to relinquish total

---

[5] *Ibid.*

[6] A Petretto, 'The Liberalization and Privatization of Public Utilities and the Protection of Users' Rights: The Perspective of Economic Theory' in M Freedland and S Sciarra (eds), *Public Services in European Law* (Oxford, OUP, 1997).

[7] Privatisation is taken to mean the definition provided by Kay and Thompson as the various ways in which the relationship is altered between state-provided activity and the private sector: J Kay and D Thompson, 'Privatization: A Policy in Search of a Rationale (1986) 96 *Economic Journal* 18. See also S Butler, 'Privatization for Public Purposes' in W Gormley, Jr (ed), *Privatization and Its Alternatives* (Madison, Wisc, University of Wisconsin Press, 1991) at 17: 'the shifting of a function, either in whole or in part, from the public sector to the private sector'.

[8] I Mahboobi, *Recent Privatisation Trends* (Paris, OECD, 2002).

control of the enterprise in question. This in turn has created a number of regulatory challenges which are explored in this book.

While privatisation has a strong ideological base the shrinking of the state is part of a process of economic reform that has been justified in terms of efficiency gains. It is recognised that the competitive environment and management structures play an important role in the productivity of enterprises, alongside the *nature* of ownership: analysts persuaded governments that state ownership tends to lower the internal efficiency of companies in markets.[9] Privatisation was also a response to policymakers' leanings towards favouring a smaller core of activities which can be seen as legitimately, or inherently, belonging to the exercise of government.

The belief in free markets is premised on the view that not only is private enterprise more efficient than state provision, but that it may also be more responsive to consumer wishes. The change in attitude towards free markets has complemented other goals and activities being pursued by governments, not only in Europe, but globally. These activities include, by way of example, the exercise of fiscal discipline on public spending and embracing new forms of public management[10] by neo-liberal governments seeking to provide a climate in which markets can develop and flourish. As a result traditional concepts of the state have been swept aside in a number of experiments:

> The concept of the public sector is by now quite multidimensional covering a variety of phenomena which do not necessarily hang together. … decentralisation, privatisation, incorporation, de-regulation and re-regulation, the introduction of executive agencies, internal markets or the use of purchaser-provider split, as well as tendering/bidding schemes.[11]

This process has been described as not so much as a hollowing out of the state but a recognition of, and distrust in, the nationalisation processes as the most efficient way to run a national economy.[12] Today even natural monopolies and public services are perceived to be capable of delivery through private markets using the right institutional framework and degree of regulation.

---

[9]   See G Yarrow, 'Privatization in Theory and Practice' (1986) 2 *Economic Policy* 324; Kay and Thompson, above n 7; M Bishop and J Kay, 'Privatization in the United Kingdom: Lessons From Experience' (1989) 17 *World Development* 643; J Vickers and G Yarrow, 'Economic Perspectives on Privatization' (1991) 5 *Journal of Economic Policy* 111.

[10]   New forms of public management include: dividing policy formation from policy implementation, the creation of new independent regulatory agencies and experimenting with new initiatives to fund and deliver public services. See the influential work of D Osborne and T Gabler, *Reinventing Government: How the Entrepreneurial Spirit is Transforming the Public Sector* (Reading, Mass, Addison-Wesley, 1992); C Hood, C Scott, O James and T Travers, *Regulation Inside Government* (Oxford, OUP, 2000).

[11]   J Lane, *New Public Management* (London, Routledge, 2006) at 6.

[12]   G Majone, 'Paradoxes of Privatization and Deregulation' (1994) 1 *Journal of European Public Policy* 54.

During the 1990s privatisation contributed significantly to the broadening and deepening of capital markets, primarily because privatisations involved large state enterprises.[13] This in turn was intended to promote a shareholder culture within Western Europe, fuelled by the state's willingness to raise revenues as well providing the capacity for the state to divest itself of the burden of a loss-making enterprise, or invest in developing technology. Privatisation was also driven by fiscal factors as governments were increasingly responsive to limits on their revenue-raising capacity, for example, public borrowing for investment purposes.[14]

Moves towards less direct state intervention in the market have been accompanied by experimentation with various legal tools to allow states to retain some control over privatised enterprises, especially where the supply of goods and services in sensitive sectors and the provision of public services are involved. State intervention in a privatised company may allow for covert forms of state aid to be granted and the state may be able to exercise control over the foreign ownership of shares. One approach is for the state to retain some equity interest in a privatised enterprise, particularly through the use of golden shares. The privatisation of state-owned companies has stimulated the growth and development of capital markets in Europe by creating an equity culture alongside the institutional processes of the liberalisation of capital markets. This has occurred alongside the launch of economic and monetary union (EMU) and the processes of structured liberalisation of key sectors of the economy such as telecommunications, utilities and postal services.

The transfer of more responsibilities of the state to the private sector resulted in a policy debate on *how* the private sector should respond in terms of corporate governance. The acceptance of the logic, or fit, of privatisation with the Internal Market programme has not been uniform across Europe, and as a result neither the liberalisation nor privatisation of markets has been complete. Equally there are reversals of policy, where markets fail or new political parties come into power.[15] The continued state involvement in the competitive market, particularly through partial shareholdings and golden shares, hindered the emergence of a fully competitive market for corporate control. The continued involvement of the state in a privatised company not only blurs the legal status of the company, but impacts upon the competition process and the whole corporate governance regime. Many commentators have pointed out that the use of state intervention

---

[13] See P MacAvoy, W Stanbury, G Yarrow and R Zeckhauser (eds), *Privatisation and State-Owned Enterprises* (Boston, Mass, Kluwer, 1989).

[14] W Devroe, 'Privatizations and Community Law: Neutrality versus Policy' (1997) 34 *CMLRev* 268.

[15] For an historical account of the UK see J Foreman-Peck and R Millward, *Public and Private Ownership in British History 1820–1990* (Oxford, Clarendon Press, 1994).

in private companies replaces the market in corporate governance.[16] However, privatisation may also stimulate the development of new institutions that improve market operations, and there is evidence to suggest that privatisations create dynamic markets.[17]

These developments were particularly acute in the EU where the processes of liberalisation, already evident in some of the Member States, were hastened by the precise schedule set by the Internal Market Programme, arising from the EC Commission's White Paper of 1985[18] and the fiscal structures imposed by the introduction of economic and monetary union (EMU) set in train in the Maastricht Treaty of 1991. Article 4 EC, introduced by the same Treaty, stated that the EU economy was to be organised along free market principles:

> the activities of the Member States and the Community shall include, as provided in this Treaty and in accordance with the timetable set out therein, the adoption of an economic policy which is based on the close coordination of Member States' economic policies, on the internal market and on the definition of common objectives, and conducted in accordance with the principle of an open market economy with free competition.

This principle is reiterated in Article 98 EC. The Court of Justice, in *CIF*, uses Articles 4 and 98 EC as solidarity clauses:

> Moreover, since the Treaty of Maastricht entered into force, the EC Treaty has expressly provided that in the context of their economic policy the activities of the Member States must observe the principle of an open market economy with free competition (see Articles 3a(1) and 102a of the EC Treaty (now Article 4(1) EC and Article 98 EC)).[19]

However, in an earlier case, the Court had suggested that the economic principles underpinning integration are not a matter for the courts. Articles 4 and 98 EC establish a:

> general principle whose application calls for complex economic assessments which are a matter for the legislature or the national administration.[20]

---

[16]   C Graham, 'All that Glitters... Golden Shares and Privatised Enterprises' (1988) 9 *Company Law* 23; I Harden, 'The Approach of English Law to State Aids to Enterprise' (1990) 11 *ECLR* 100; T Boyle, 'Barriers to Contested Takeovers in the European Community' (1991) 12 *Company Law* 163.

[17]   M Boutchkova and W Megginson, 'The Impact of Privatisation on Capital Market Development and Individual Share Ownership' (2000) 29 *Financial Management* 67.

[18]   COM(85) 310 final, 14 June 1985.

[19]   Case C–198/01 *Consorzio Industrie Fiammiferi (CIF) v Autorità Garante della Concorrenza e del Mercato* [2003] ECR I–8055, para 47.

[20]   Case C–9/99 *Echirolles Distribution SA du Association du Dauphiné and others* [2000] ECR I–8207, para 25. See also, Case C-451/03 *Servizi Ausiliari Commercialisti Srl v Giuseppe Calafiori* [2006] ECR I-2941: 'At the outset, it must be pointed out that Articles 4 EC and 98 EC establish the fundamental principles of the economic policy of the Community system and set out the context of

As a result of these Treaty amendments the liberalisation of the public sector was viewed by one EC Commissioner, Van Miert, as an *unavoidable consequence* of the establishment of an Internal Market:

> It is obvious that a market based on competition and free circulation of goods, services, people and capital is at odds with systems based on national monopolies. Our liberalisation policy was therefore conceived as an indispensable instrument for the establishment of the internal market.[21]

And at the Lisbon European Council Meeting of March 2000 the role of competitiveness in the European economy was catapulted into greater prominence.

In contrast to the Member States' wide variety of legal means to pursue autonomous economic policies at the national level the Community/EU had more limited means to control state intervention in the market and create an industrial policy at the EU level. Subsequent chapters will reveal how, even when called upon to act in the face of alleged anti-competitive conduct by a Member State, or faced with direct complaints, the EC Commission prevaricated. Yet a shift in the attitude towards legitimate state intervention in markets came about in a relatively short space of time, triggered by individual litigation, using first the free movement of goods provisions, and then the competition provisions of the EC Treaty.[22] More recently the regulatory role of the state has been questioned, using the economic freedoms of the EC Treaty. At the centre of this process the European Courts have assumed the role of maintaining what often appears to be a fragile equilibrium between the remorseless drive of free and competitive markets and the reflexive action on the part of some of the Member States, as well as interest groups, to retain autonomy in the sphere of domestic economic policy. The EU has had to address the uneasy constitutional tensions between finding the right balance between Member State sovereignty, subsidiarity and EU versus Member State competence. The issues have been complicated by the arrival of new non-state actors capable of providing many of the traditional goods and services historically provided by the state, in a more competitive environment. At stake is not only the right balance of competing interests but also the issue of what kind of *values* are inherent in the EU legal order. These issues have been mediated through the evolution of an economic constitution.

---

which the competition rules in Articles 82 EC and 86 EC form part. In those circumstances, the reference by the national court to Articles 4 EC and 98 EC does not call for a reply distinct from that which will be given on the interpretation of Articles 82 EC and 86 EC.' (para 20).

[21] K Van Miert, 'Liberalization of the Economy of the European Union: The Game is Not (yet) Over' in D Geradin (ed), *The Liberalization of State Monopolies in the European Union and Beyond* (The Hague, Kluwer, 2000) at 1.

[22] Arts 96 and 97 EC give the EC Commission powers to intervene when laws, regulation or administrative action in Member States distort the conditions of competition in the Common Market, but these powers have been under-used.

THE EVOLUTION OF AN ECONOMIC CONSTITUTION

The shaping of the Internal Market and the role of state intervention in the market were led by individual litigants, with many of the cases raising the *interaction* of the free trade and competition rules. During a foundational period the European Court of Justice was reluctant to use the competition rules against the Member States but instead focused upon developing the canons of free movement, particularly in relation to the free movement of goods, to create a certain *idea* of an integrated Europe beyond the concept of non-discrimination, which was the language of the substantive provisions of the EC Treaty.[23] In later cases the imperative of market integration was welded by the symbiosis of the protection of the competition goal in the EC Treaty with the promotion of the free trade ambition.

Economic and Non-economic Activity of the State

At stake in the emergence of an economic constitution for the EU was the issue of competence. Member States defended their right to intervene in the market, particularly where public interests were allegedly at stake, by claiming immunity from the free market and competition rules. In the golden shares cases[24] the Member States attempted to use Article 295 EC as a buffer against encroachment of Community law into sensitive areas of domestic economic policy, but the Court was not willing to entertain such a wide role for Article 295 EC.

Over time the Court has created bright lines demarcating state *public* activity from state *economic* activity. This applies to both the competition and the free movement rules, although in his Opinion in *FENIN* [25] Advocate General Poiares Maduro suggests that there may be different outcomes according to which set of rules is applied:

> At first sight, it appears desirable to adopt the same solution in the field of the freedom to provide services and in that of freedom of competition, since those provisions of Community law seek to attain the common objective of the completion of the internal market. However, the scope of freedom of competition and that of the freedom to provide services are not identical. There is nothing to prevent a transaction involving an exchange being classified as the provision of services, even where the parties to the exchange are not undertakings for the purposes of competition law. As stated above, the Member States may withdraw certain activities from the field of competition if they

---

[23]   See M Poiares Maduro, *We the Court. The European Court of Justice and the European Economic Constitution* (Oxford, Hart Publishing, 1998).

[24]   Case C–463/00 *Commission v Spain* [2003] ECR I–4581; Case C–367/98 *Commission v Portugal* [2002] ECR I–4731; Case C–483/99 *Commission v France* [2002] ECR I–4781.

[25]   Case C–205/03P *Federación Española de Empresas de Tecnología Sanitaria (FENIN), formerly Federación Nacional de Empresas, Instrumentación Científica, Médica, Técnica y Dental v Commission,* Opinion of 10 Nov 2005, [2006] ECR I-6295.

organise them in such a way that the principle of solidarity is predominant, with the result that competition law does not apply. By contrast, the way in which an activity is organised at the national level has no bearing on the application of the principle of the freedom to provide services. Thus, although there is no doubt that the provision of health care free of charge is an economic activity for the purposes of Article 49 EC, it does not necessarily follow from that that the organisations which carry on that activity are subject to competition law.[26]

The Court of Justice has also stated that the free movement and competition rules can work independently of each other.[27]

One advantage of allowing the European Courts to demarcate the activities which are subject to Community law is that the process is dynamic and evolutionary. It is, however, a casuistic approach, dependent upon the referral of questions from the national courts using Article 234 EC. Crucial to this drawing of a bright line was the notion of an *economic* activity. However, the binary divide between economic and non-economic activities of the state is not a satisfactory classification, or indeed an appropriate methodology to delimit the competence between the Community and the Member States. Indeed other devices are also used; for example, in competition law issues the concept of an 'undertaking' is a significant legal tool[28] and the *de minimis* principle is also used.[29] In free movement cases the use of the *Cassis*-inspired mandatory requirements[30] and the growing interest in a wider range of non-state bodies with delegated powers

---

[26] *Ibid.* para 51, footnotes omitted.

[27] Case C–519/04P *David Meca-Medina and Igor Majcen v Commission of the European Communities*[2006] ECR I-6991 at para 31.

[28] Eg, individuals (RAI/UNITEL [1978] OJ L157/39), self-employed medical specialists (Joined Cases C–180 to C–184/98 *Pavel Pavlov and others v Stichting Pensioenfonds Medische Specialisten* [2000] ECR I–6451) and the liberal professions may qualify as undertakings: see Cases C–221/99 *Giuseppe Conte v Stefania Rossi* [2001] ECR I–9359, T–144/99 *EPI v Commission* [2001] ECR I–1087; C–309/99 J CJ *Wouters, J W Savelbergh, Price Waterhouse Belastingadviseurs BV v Algemene Raad van de Nederlandse Orde van Advocaten* [2002] ECR I–1577 and C–35/99 *Manuele Arduino, Diego Dessi, Giovanni Bertolotto v Compagnia Assicuratrice RAS SpA* [2002] ECR I–1529; public sector entities such as hospitals are not undertakings even though they buy large quantities of goods and services from the private sector and enjoy substantial market power, if they perform a public function: Case T–319/99 *Federación Nacional de Empresas de Instrumentación Científica, Médica, Técnica y Dental (FENIN) (FENIN)* [2003] ECR II–357, the Opinion of Poiares Maduro AG of 10 Nov 2005 and ruling of the ECJ in Case C–205/03P *FENIN v Commission*[2006] ECR I-6295. Similarly exercising powers of a public authority does not constitute an economic activity: Case C–343/95 *Diego Calì & Figli Srl v Servizi ecologici porto di Genova SpA (SEPG)*[1997] ECR I–1547. In contrast, the fact that an entity operates under official powers does not prevent the application of the competition rules: Case C–82/01 P *Aéroports de Paris v Commission* [2002] ECR I–9297. See V Louri, '"Undertaking" as a Jurisdictional Element for the Application of the EC Competition Rules' (2002) 29 *Legal Issues of Economic Integration* 143.

[29] Cf the reluctance of the Court to deploy a *de minimis* principle in the state aid arena: Case C–280/00 *Altmark Trans GmbH and Regierungspraesidium Magdeburg v Nahverkehrsgesellschaft Altmark GmbH* [2003] ECR I–7747, paras 81–82.

[30] Case 120/78 *Rewe-Zentral v Bundesmonopolverwaltung für Branntwein* [1979] ECR 649.

which may raise a public interest justification[31] are other tools used to determine the scope of application of Community law. Liberalisation processes have led to the greater use of Community law definitions of economic activities.

The partial liberalisation of many markets and the creation of new forms of hybrid, public–private power have also made the economic/non-economic divide harder to discern. The Member States continue to experiment, exploring how far they can push back the frontiers of the state. Some Member States, for example, have accepted that even the traditional duties of the state, such as revenue protection, and even the coercive powers of the state, such as immigration control, security and prison services, are subject to market testing. The reach of Community law has extended to the regulatory activity of the state, particularly in the dynamic interpretation of Articles 28 and 86 EC, the combination of Article 10 EC with Articles 86 and 82 EC and the acceptance, although reluctant use, of Articles 10 and 81 EC to question state regulatory activity.[32] While the liberalisation of a number of sectors and activities has brought more state activity into the economic domain, the Member States continue to oscillate between nationalisation and privatisation. Thus the dividing line between the reach of the market rules and the residual public sphere, or nucleus of state sovereignty, is increasingly blurred. To counter this, in the absence of a definition of economic activity in the EC Treaty, the European Courts employ a functional approach by focusing upon the *effects* on the market of state activity, rather than legal form.[33] This approach has allowed Community law to challenge the regulatory authority of the state under the free movement and competition rules.

Over time the net of Community law was cast wide. In early cases services such as education[34] and compulsory basic social security schemes based upon the principle of solidarity[35] were excluded from the scope of Community law. The explanation for this approach is given by the EC Commission in its soft law Communications on services of general interest. The state:

---

[31]   Case C–309/99 *Wouters* [2002] ECR I–1577. Sport-related cases would also fall into this category: Case 36/74 *Walrave and Koch v AUCI* [1974] ECR 1405; *The Helsinki Report*, COM (1999)644 final of 10 Dec 1999; Case C–519/04P *David Meca-Medina and Igor Majcen v Commission* [2006] ECR I–6991.

[32]   This is explored in Ch 2.

[33]   See, eg, Case C–41/90 *Klaus Höfner and Fritz Elser v Macrotron GmbH.* [1991] ECR I–1979, paras 20–22.

[34]   See the discussion in Case 263/86 *Belgium v Humbel* [1988] ECR 5365; Case C–109/92 *Stephan Max Wirth v Landeshauptstadt Hannover* [1993] ECR I–6447.

[35]   Case C–160/91 *Christian Poucet and Daniel Pistre v Assurances Générales de France and Caisse Mutuelle Régionale du Languedoc-Roussillon and Daniel Pistre Caisse Autonome Nationale de Compensation de l' Assurance Vieillesse des Artisans (Cancava)* [1993] ECR I–637. See also Case C–70/95 *Sodemare SA, Anni Azzurri Holding SpA, Anni Azzurri Rezzato Srl v Regione Lombardia* [1997] ECR I–3395.

is not seeking to engage in gainful activity but is fulfilling its duty towards its own population in the social, cultural and educational fields.[36]

Particularly in competition law the demarcation line between economic and non-economic activity of the state has been fought over where the line passes through the traditional Member State concept of public service. This battle has been fought most vigorously in the litigation using Article 86 EC, and this is discussed in Chapters 4, 5, 6 and 7. Buendia Sierra has attempted to impose some rigour on this exercise by classifying a distinction between what he calls 'diffuse' and 'specific' services of the State. Diffuse services equate with the economist's idea of a public good, and would fall outside the scope of Community law. In contrast a specific service is one where: 'the benefit obtained by each individual is easily quantifiable and therefore easy to substitute with privately contractually based services'.[37] This, however, is not an entirely workable tool because, even with diffuse services, Community law appears to recognise few boundaries beyond which it should not stray. Article 12 EC, the non-discrimination on grounds of nationality clause, has been used in recent years to create a new *tranche* of Citizenship rights. Together these two principles cut across national, solidaristic boundaries which traditional diffuse services seek to create. Poiares Maduro has argued, in his academic capacity, that the independent use of Article 12 EC makes 'it difficult to conceive of any area which is still *ratione materiae* outside the scope of Community law'.[38]

The embryonic beginnings of these ideas are seen in *Cowan*.[39] Here the Court used the free movement of services provisions as the legal basis for applying the principle of non-discrimination to an English tourist who was mugged in France, but was not allowed to claim compensation from a criminal injuries fund. More recently the Court has used Article 12 EC in conjunction with the Citizenship provision of free movement to allow access to a range of social rights, bringing with it the scope for 'welfare tourism'.[40] In *Martínez Sala*[41] a Spanish national lawfully resident in Germany was able to rely upon Article 12 EC in order to claim social assistance on the same basis as German nationals' entitlement. Subsequent cases have extended this right to subsistence allowances,[42] labour

---

[36] *Communication from the Commission Services of General Interest in Europe,* COM(2000)580 final 3, at para 29.

[37] J Buendia Sierria, *Exclusive Rights and State Monopolies Under EC Law* (Oxford, OUP, 1999) at 56.

[38] M Poiares Maduro, 'Europe's Social Self: "The Sickness Unto Death"' in J Shaw (ed), *Social Law and Policy in an Evolving European Union* (Oxford, Hart, 2000).

[39] Case 186/87 *Cowan v Trésor Public* [1989] ECR 195.

[40] See M Dougan and E Spaventa, '"Wish You Weren't Here ..." New Models of Social Solidarity in the European Union' in M Dougan and E Spaventa (eds), *Social Welfare and EU Law* (Oxford, Hart, 2005).

[41] Case C–85/96 *Maria Martínez Sala v Freistaat Bayern* [1998] ECR I–2691.

[42] Case C–184/99 *Rudy Grzelczyk v Centre public d'aide social d'Ottignies-Louvain-la-Neuve* [2001 ECR I–6193.

market access allowances[43] and student loans.[44] The EU responded by introducing Article 24(1) of Directive 2004/38/EC (known as 'The Citizenship Directive'[45]) which restricts rights of access to social welfare in the host state by placing a residence requirement on the intended beneficiary. Article 24(2) of the Directive goes further by allowing the Member States to deny social assistance during the first three months of residence and, where appropriate, require permanent residence as a condition for certain kinds of assistance, for example, maintenance aid for students.

Increasingly many of the diffuse services formerly provided by the state have been subject to liberalisation processes where national regulation has been replaced by European regulation. Chapters 5, 6 and 7 investigate these processes in greater detail. Once an activity is brought within the economic domain of Community law Member States are under a duty to remove *all* obstacles to trade which could *not* be justified. Justification of measures is assessed according to Community law catalogues and the principles of non-discrimination, effectiveness and proportionality.

These justifications in turn created a set of Community-based *values*, rather than purely national interests to be protected.[46] Thus, this idea of an economic constitution marked the Community out in a way which was fundamentally different from other free trade areas which were developing in the nascent global trade liberalising regime of the General Agreement on Tariffs and Trade (GATT).

The EEC Treaty did not intend to create, or prescribe, a particular economic regime for the Member States, and the 1957 Treaty appeared neutral in regard to the economic policies being pursued at Member State level. This is seen in the original Article 222 EEC, now Article 295 EC, discussed above. Many of the original EEC Treaty provisions condone a mixed economy, albeit within the limits set by Community law. However, the economic order of the Community is that of a *market* system, essentially based upon the concept, and process, of competition. Individual rights are guaranteed, but certain limits can be set on the *exercise* of these rights in the light of the public interest. The EC Treaty allocates competition as a principal goal of the Internal Market, with Article 3 EC creating a picture of 'an internal market characterised by the abolition, as between member States, of obstacles to the free movement of goods, persons, services and capital' and 'a system ensuring that competition in the internal market is not

---

[43] Case C–224/98 *Marie Natalie D'Hoop v Office national de l'emploi* [2002] ECR I–6191.

[44] Case C–209/03 *R v London Borough of Ealing and Secretary of State for Education ex parte Bidar* [2005] ECR I–2119.

[45] Dir 2004/38/EC of the European Parliament and of the Council of 29 Apr 2004 on the right of citizens of the Union and their family members to move and reside freely within the territory of the Member States amending Reg (EEC) No 1612/68 and repealing Dirs 64/221/EEC, 68/360/EEC, 72/194/EEC, 73/148/EEC, 75/34/EEC, 75/35/EEC, 90/364/EEC, 90/365/EEC and 93/93/EEC [2004] OJ L229/35 (correcting [2004] OJ L158/1) further corrected at [2005] OJ L197/34.

[46] O Gerstenberger, 'Expanding the Constitution Beyond the Court: The Case of Euro-Constitionalism' (2002) 8 *ELJ* 172.

distorted'. This is to take place within the context provided by Article 4 EC of 'an open market economy with free competition'. The Court has subsequently elevated competition into one of the fundamental principles of the economic constitution.[47]

The *process* of economic integration, however, favours economic liberalism over state ownership, central planning and state intervention in the market, and this is seen in the open texture of the subsequent amendments to the original Treaty in relation to economic policy. After the introduction of the 1992 Internal Market programme Ehlermann was able to assert that 'the Community has the most strongly free-market oriented constitution in the world'.[48]

The concept of the Internal Market included broader social and economic goals which were to be attained at the Community, rather than the Member State, level. These goals have subsequently been complemented with a set of values embracing notions of Citizenship, with continued emphasis upon the rule of law to implement the processes of change. This in turn has led to the juridification, proceduralisation and constitutionalisation of modern economic policy in the EU, giving the European Courts a significant role in mediating these processes.

Article 10 EC: The Tie that Binds

Article 10 EC provides a fidelity or solidarity clause which obliges the Member States to cooperate in a positive way to facilitate the objectives of the EC Treaty and, in a negative way, not to harm or hamper the attainment of the EC Treaty objectives:[49]

> Member States shall take all appropriate measures, whether general or particular, to ensure fulfilment of the obligations arising out of this Treaty or resulting from action taken by the institutions of the Community. They shall facilitate the achievement of the Community's tasks. They shall abstain from any measure which could jeopardise the attainment of the objectives of this Treaty.

---

[47] In Case C–126/97 *Eco Swiss China Time Ltd v Benetton International NV* [1999] ECR I–3055, para 36, the Court states: 'according to ... Article 3(1)(g) EC), Article 85 of the Treaty constitutes a fundamental provision which is essential for the accomplishment of the tasks entrusted to the Community and, in particular, for the functioning of the internal market. The importance of such a provision led the framers of the Treaty to provide expressly, in Article 85(2) of the Treaty, that any agreements or decisions prohibited pursuant to that article are to be automatically void'. See also Case C–453/99 *Courage Ltd v Bernard Crehan* [2001] ECR I–6297, paras 19–24. At para 20 the Court states: 'according to Art 3(g) of the EC Treaty (now, after amendment, Art 3(1)(g) EC), Art 85 of the Treaty constitutes a fundamental provision which is essential for the accomplishment of the tasks entrusted to the Community and, in particular, for the functioning of the internal market (judgment in Case C–126/97 *Eco Swiss* [1999] ECR I–3055, para 36)'.

[48] C-D Ehlermann, 'The Contribution of EC Competition Policy to the Single Market' (1992) 29 *CMLRev* 257, 273.

[49] J Temple Lang, 'The Duties of Cooperation of National Authorities and Courts Under Article 10: Two More Reflections' (2001) 26 *ELRev* 84.

Article 10 EC has been extended to apply to the Community Institutions.[50] This may prove to be important in the future as the EU recognises a range of values, particularly fundamental rights and Citizenship ideas relating to the provision of public services in the EU. For example, a new Article 16 EC charges the Member States *and* the Community to promote public services:

> Without prejudice to Articles 73, 86 and 87, and given the place occupied by services of general economic interest in the shared values of the Union as well as their role in promoting social and territorial cohesion, the Community and the Member States, each within their respective powers and within the scope of application of this Treaty, shall take care that such services operate on the basis of principles and conditions which enable them to fulfil their missions.

The Constitutional Treaty, in Article III–122, goes further stating that:

> European laws shall establish these principles and set these conditions without prejudice to the competence of the Member States, in compliance with the Constitution, to provide, to commission and to fund such services.

Article 10 EC has been at the centre of the debate on the limits to the economic sovereignty of the Member States. Applied broadly it is an effective legal tool to regulate state intervention in the market. This has contributed to the growing belief, which is addressed in the subsequent chapters of this book, that now Community law and the underpinning economic constitution contain a general *presumption of illegality* of state intervention in the market.[51] The Court of Justice consistently uses Article 10 EC in conjunction with Article 81 EC to affirm that the Member States may not maintain in force legislation that allows undertakings to infringe EC competition law because this would compromise the competition law provisions of the EC Treaty, depriving them of their effectiveness (*effet utile*):[52]

> it is appropriate to point out, first, that, although Articles 81 EC and 82 EC are, in themselves, concerned solely with the conduct of undertakings and not with laws or regulations emanating from Member States, those articles, read in conjunction with Article 10 EC, which lays down a duty to cooperate, none the less require the Member States not to introduce or maintain in force measures, even of a legislative or regulatory nature, which may render ineffective the competition rules applicable to undertakings (see Case 13/77 *GB-Inno-BM* [1977] ECR 2115, para.31; Case 267/86 *Van Eycke* [1988]

---

[50]   Case 2/88 *Imm Zvartveld* [1990] ECR 3365.

[51]   See, eg, Darmon AG's Opinion in Case C–185/91 *Bundesanstalt für den Güterfernverkehr v Gebrüder Reiff GmbH & Co KG* [1993] ECR I–5801; J Temple Lang, 'Article 5 of the EEC Treaty: The Emergence of Constitutional Principles in the Case Law of the Court of Justice' (1987) 10 *Fordham International Law Journal* 503 and 'Community Constitutional Law: Article 5 EEC Treaty' (1990) 27 *CMLRev.* 645.

[52]   This case law is analysed in detail Chs 2 and 3.

ECR 4769, para.16; Case C–185/91 *Reiff* [1993] ECR I–5801, para. 14; Case C–153/93 *Delta Schiffahrts-und Speditionsgesellschaft* [1994] ECR I–2517, para.14; Case C–96/94 *Centro Servizi Spediporto* [1995] ECR I–2883, para. 20; and Case C–35/99 *Arduino* [2002] ECR I–1529, para. 34).

The Court has held in particular that Articles 10 EC and 81 EC are infringed where a Member State requires or favours the adoption of agreements, decisions or concerted practices contrary to Article 81 EC or reinforces their effects, or where it divests its own rules of the character of legislation by delegating to private economic operators responsibility for taking decisions affecting the economic sphere (see *Van Eycke*, paragraph 16; *Reiff*, paragraph 14; *Delta Schiffahrts-und Speditionsgesellschaft*, paragraph 14; *Centro Servizi Spediporto*, paragraph 21; and *Arduino*, paragraph 35)'.[53]

A Member State may be liable in damages where harm is caused by such illegal legislation. In *CIF* [54] the Court added another layer of enforcement opportunities by stating that the Italian Competition Authority had a duty to declare unlawful and set aside a state law that facilitated, or obliged, private parties to enter into anti-competitive agreements contrary to Article 10 EC when read with Article 81 EC. The Court also held that liability in damages may be available against undertakings which act on the encouragement of such anti-competitive state legislation. It is only where the state requires such anti-competitive conduct that the private undertaking will be immune from liability. But once the national law is disapplied in a definitive manner the immunity will be lost. This remedy is part of the modernisation process of competition law generally where the EU is promoting the greater use of private enforcement of competition law as part of a policy of raising stakeholder interests in Community policies.[55]

At the legal level the Member States still retain freedom of choice to implement economic policies. They can also choose the method by which they attain the economic objectives set out in the Treaty. But that choice is now somewhat illusory, with a heavy reliance upon liberal market policies, the constraints of EMU, EC Commission policies and the European Courts' case law.

Competition Law and Policy as Means of Implementing an Industrial Policy

Competition law has played a central role in the economic constitution in fashioning an industrial policy for the EU. However, the capacity of the EU to

---

[53] Case C–198/01 *Consorzio Industrie Fiammiferi (CIF) v Autorita Garnate della Concorrenza e del Mercato* [2003] ECR I–8055, paras 45 and 46.

[54] *Ibid.*

[55] Seen more recently in the EC Commission's Green Paper, *Damages for Breach of the EC Antitrust Rules*, COM(2005)672 final; EC Commission, *EC State Aid Action Plan*, COM(2005)107 final. Cf W Wils, 'Should Private Antitrust Enforcement Be Encouraged?' (2003) 26 *World Competition* 473.

create, and develop, an industrial policy has been, and still is, limited[56] and is questioned.[57] Indeed the use of the term industrial policy is contentious in the EU. Used at its widest definition, it is a generic term to describe all acts and policies of the state which relate to industry. This embraces the various *ways* in which the state intervenes in the economy, which may be either active or passive, as well as the *instruments* used, for example, the tax policy, fiscal policy, regulation of labour markets; in fact all measures which are designed to control and influence the performance of firms within a particular economy. Passive measures may promote the liberalisation of markets, whereas active measures may be needed to correct market failure.

The original EEC Treaty in 1957 did not contain an industrial policy and, unlike the ECSC Treaty, provided no legal basis for active sectoral policies to be pursued. This fact explains why the original EEC Treaty was viewed as a liberal economic constitution, but it is more of a reflection of the limited ambitions of the founders of the Community who envisaged the Community as no more than a customs union based upon principles of negative integration. In 1957 the regulation of state intervention was not perceived to be a major problem, and it is commonly thought that the provisions relating to state aids (the old Articles 92–94 EEC) addressed the major, or extreme, problems which would arise from distortions in the market arising from state intervention. Thus industrial policy was left within the competence of the Member States and, for the most part, interventionist national policies went unquestioned. However, one of the effects of the liberalisation of trade at the global level has been to focus attention on whether strategic behaviour can alter the balance of comparative advantage where trade has developed between states with similar economic structures. Thus new ideas have emerged whereby the use of an industrial policy may play a role in altering the terms of economic competition *between* states.

A treaty base for a Community industrial policy was first introduced in the Treaty on European Union (TEU) 1991. This coincided with a greater range of aims and objectives for European integration, including ideas for social rights and citizenship. Article 3(1)(m) EC states that activities of the Community shall include 'the strengthening of the competitiveness of Community industry'. Title XVI allows the EC Commission to coordinate the Member States' actions in this field.[58] The Community and the Member States are to ensure that the conditions

---

[56] See, generally, W Sauter, *Competition Law and Industrial Policy in the EU* (Oxford, Clarendon Press, 1997).

[57] See, eg, the view that industrial policy is an 'empty-shell' concept in D Geradin and N Petit, 'La politique industrielle sous les tiers croises de la mondialisation et du droit communautaire de la concurrence', Working Paper, 2006, available at
http://www.ieje.net/fileadmin/IEJE/Pdf/Mondialisation_politique_industrielle_e_.pdf. The authors argue that there are various of dimensions to industrial policy (innovation, research and development, infrastructures) and different means to achieve it more efficiently than by sheltering industrial sectors from competition enforcement (tax law, administrative law, intellectual property law, etc).

[58] Art 157(2) EC.

necessary for the Community's industry exist. The Council may support action taken by the Member States to achieve the objectives of the industrial policy.[59] But even today express Community competence in the field of industrial policy is not evident in the EC Treaty. The EC Commission has, however, interpreted the competition policy of the EU widely. By allowing competition policy to pursue a number of objectives, for example, the promotion of integration, efficiency, the competitiveness of European industry and, albeit limited in extent, wider social objectives, competition policy has internalised an industrial policy for the EU. This goes beyond the EC Treaty base introduced by the TEU. Today, the close connection between competition policy and industrial policy is explicitly recognised. The control of private power in the market through the competition rules has led to the ideas of an economic constitution for the EU, and this is reinforced by the way in which competition policy has also been used against state intervention in the market.

The Role of Competition Law and Policy in Regulating State Intervention in the Market

Competition law provides the framework which defines the rules which economic actors, both public and private, must respect when operating in the market.[60] Competition law is distinct from the four freedoms which are viewed as tools of *negative* integration by removing barriers to trade. In contrast, competition law serves to regulate *markets*, and this is why it has assumed greater importance in the Internal Market project. It has been seen as a core regulatory policy area of European integration.[61] More recently competition law has addressed the abuse of unusual power in the market, by the state as well as non-state actors, especially in the post-liberalisation markets of telecommunications where merger and acquisitions create dominant private firms which replace the old state monopolies. A clearer explanation of *why* there is an emphasis upon competition is given by Ehlermann:

> Fair competition based on the principle of performance results in an increase in the economic efficiency of firms. It enables them to compete both within the Community and with firms outside the Community. The international competitiveness of European

---

[59] Art 157(3) EC.

[60] See P Pescatore, 'Public and Private Aspects of European Competition Law' (1987) 10 *Fordham International Law Journal* 373; H von der Groeben, *The European Community: The Formative Years. The Struggle to Establish the Common Market and Political Union (1958–66)*, European Perspectives Series (Brussels/Luxembourg, OOEPC, 1985).

[61] G Majone, *Deregulation or Regulation? Regulatory Reform in Europe* (London, Pinter, 1990).

industries is an essential pre-condition for the opening-up of the Single Market to the world market or, to put it another way, for maintaining and further developing a liberal competition-based trade policy.[62]

The diffusion of economic *power* is recognised in the competition rules, which explains, for example, the peculiar position of Article 86 EC and the state aid rules in the competition policy section, even though the use of public monopolies and state aid produce effects which may also distort free trade patterns. The Member States acknowledged that their activities may distort competition, but in the early years of the Common Market the EC Commission focus was largely upon controlling the economic power of *private* undertakings.[63]

From the late 1980s and during the 1990s onwards, competition policy has been used by individual litigants, and the EC Commission, as a tool to impose constraints on national economic policy in ways which were not envisaged when the EEC Treaty was first drafted. The focus of the competition tools has been upon market structure, not just processes of competition. This new policy for competition law is seen in the regulation of mergers having a Community dimension, the regulation and modernisation of state aids, the use of Article 10(2) EC in conjunction with Article 81 EC and the use of Article 86 EC to explore the limits of public monopolies and state regulatory power in the market. Competition policy has, therefore, been used to bring about a complementarity between competition and the Internal Market project, to shore up the nascent Community industrial policy *and* as a tool to push forward a liberalisation policy. This is seen if we examine some of the major developments in competition policy.

Merger Policy

Mergers are an important tool of industrial policy and are more likely to take place when cross-border trade as a result of integrated markets takes place.[64] Until the adoption of a regulation in 1989[65] there was no systematic approach to

---

[62]   C-D Ehlermann, 'The Contribution of EC Competition Policy to the Single Market' (1992) 29 *CMLRev* 257, 265.

[63]   For an account of the history of European competition policy see D Gerber, 'Constitutionalizing the Economy: German Neo-liberalism, Competition Law and the "New" Europe' (1994) 42 *American Journal of Comparative Law* 25, and *Law and Competition in Twentieth Century Europe. Protecting Prometheus* (Oxford, Clarendon Press, 1998). An interest in the application of competition law to state activity is scarce in these works.

[64]   Art 66 ECSC regulated mergers in the coal and steel sector because it was accepted that these sectors were strategic in the post-war economic reconstruction of Europe. See Sir Leon Brittan, *Competition Policy and Merger Control in the Single European Market* (Cambridge, Grotius, 1991) at 23.

[65]   Reg 4064/89/EC on the control of concentrations between undertakings [1990] OJ L257/13. This was reviewed at the same time as the new Reg 1/2003/EC was introduced: Council Reg 139/2004 of 20 Jan 2004 on the control of concentrations between undertakings [2004] OJ L24/1.

mergers in the EU. The ECSC Treaty had allowed the High Authority to prohibit mergers in coal and steel which allowed firms to determine prices or hinder effective competition. This recognised that these sectors were a strategic part of the post-war recovery of Europe. The EC Commission had expressed an interest in controlling what were termed 'concentrations' since the 1960s[66] but two proposals for a power to regulate mergers in 1973 and 1981 were rejected by the Council. The 1985 White Paper did not suggest that there was a need for a specific new legal provision to regulate mergers, but instead suggested that the competition provisions of the EC Treaty could be used.

In *Continental Can* the Court had accepted that Article 82 EC could be used to control a take-over of a competitor by a dominant firm which would alter the structure of the market. Although the EC Commission had failed to show that the undertaking had a dominant position in the West German container market, the Court stated:

> There may therefore be abusive behaviour if an undertaking in a dominant position strengthens that dominant position so that the degree of control achieved substantially obstructs competition, ie, so that the only undertakings left in the market are those which are dependent on the dominant undertaking with regard to their market behaviour.[67]

Later, in *BAT/Reynolds*,[68] the Court confirmed that Article 81 EC could be used in situations where, by agreement, an undertaking acquired a minority shareholding in another undertaking which allowed the holder of the new shareholding to control the commercial conduct of the acquired undertaking. The EC Commission, under the direction of Peter Sutherland, used Article 81 EC to block a number of mergers, for example, the take-over of British Caledonia by BA and the take-over of Irish Distillers by the GC & C Brands consortium.

This approach highlighted the procedural deficiencies of using the competition rules *ex post* to control mergers. It also brought the EC Commission into conflict with the Member States which wished to retain sovereignty over merger control in their territory, either to prevent too much foreign capital taking over sensitive sectors or to allow national champions to be created through mergers and take-overs. But many national decisions on mergers were seen as protectionist and were highly politicised. The Member States reacted with hostility to the idea that the regulation of mergers should be centralised through the EC

---

[66] H de Jong, 'Concentration in the Common Market: a Comment on a Memorandum of the EEC Commission' (1966–7) 4 *CMLRev* 166.

[67] Case 6/72 *Europemballage Corp and Continental Can v Commission* [1973] ECR 215, 230.

[68] Cases 142/84, 156/84 *BAT and Reynolds v Commission* [1987] ECR 4487.

Commission,[69] but they also saw the value of a procedural approach to mergers rather than allowing the EC Commission to use its discretion under Articles 81 and 82 EC.

Community competence to regulate mergers through competition law is contentious since it is arguable that mergers do not constitute anti-competitive behaviour but alter the *structure* of competition in the market.[70] Thus there has been a continuing battle between the EC Commission and the Member States over the control over mergers as a tool for an industrial policy for the EU. As a result, competence for mergers was, and still is, split between the Member States and the Community. This is achieved by setting turnover thresholds in Article 1 of the ECMR[71] and the use of the 'two-thirds rule' whereby even where the thresholds are met mergers remain within national competence where two-thirds of the aggregate turnover is achieved within one Member State. Recent energy and financial services mergers have prompted the current Commissioner for Competition, Neelie Kroes, to investigate whether the rules are still viable. Her concern is that even purely national mergers may have cross-border effects when national champions are created. These issues are discussed further in Chapter 5.

The Member States have a limited range of public interest justifications to block a merger which has a Community dimension, and some Member States continue to intervene in mergers where there are perceived national interests at stake. For example, the EC Commission has decided that the Spanish energy regulator (CNE) is in breach of Article 21 of the Merger Regulation by imposing obligations upon a proposed acquisition of Endesa, a Spanish energy company, by a German company E.on. The acquisition had been cleared in April 2006 by the EC Commission.[72]

---

[69] See, *inter alia*, S Bulmer, 'Institutions and Policy Change in the European Communities: the Case of Merger Control' (1994) 72 *Public Administration* 423; L McGowan and M Cini, 'Discretion and Politicization in EU Competition Policy: the Case of Merger Control' (1999) 12 *Governance* 175; Sir Leon Brittan, *Competition Policy and Merger Control in the Single European Market* (Cambridge, Grotius, 1991).

[70] See the criticisms of the limited references to industrial policy considerations in the original Reg: B Hawk, 'The EEC Merger Regulation: the First Step Toward One-Stop Merger Control' (1990) 59 *Antitrust Law Journal* 195; J Venit, 'The "Merger" Control Regulation: Europe Comes of Age ... Caliban's Dinner' (1990) 27 *CMLRev* 7.

[71] The Member States insisted on setting the thresholds at a high level to retain competence for an industrial policy at the national level. Subsequent attempts by the EC Commission to reduce the thresholds have been resisted by the Member States: EC Commission, *Merger Review: Comments on the Green Paper by Associations*, COM(96)313 final; EC Commission, *Report to the Council on the Application of the Merger Regulation Thresholds*, COM(2000)399 final; *Green Paper on the Review of Council Regulation 4064/89*, COM(2001)745/6 final.

[72] See also, eg, attempts by Poland and Spain to block sensitive mergers available at https://registration.ft.com/registration/barrier?referer=&location=http%3A//news.ft.com/cms/s/3b6c79e0-f5c2-11da-bcae-0000779e2340.html. Cf Case T–417/05 *Endesa SA v Commission* [2006] ECR II-18 where Endesa, a Spanish company active in the electricity sector, was subject to a public takeover bid from National Gas, a company active in the energy sector, unsuccessfully challenged a Decision of the EC Commission that there was no Community dimension to the merger and that there was no jurisdiction to intervene under the Merger Reg.

The former UK Chancellor of the Exchequer (Finance Minister), Gordon Brown, has described some recent interventions as economic patriotism:

> We have seen in the past few months restrictive practices by some of the major economies in Europe where they're blocking mergers [and] blocking takeovers. . . .They're trying to operate what are called economic patriot policies where in a sense they are restricting the growth of the single market and preventing us as British companies and us as British employees getting work from the rest of the single market.[73]

Another criticism levelled at EC Commission merger policy is the narrow emphasis upon Internal Market and competition goals of European integration when today merger issues cut across a number of other policies being pursued by the EU.[74]

State Aid

One of the main reasons for including the regulation of state aid in the Community legal system is to prevent a subsidy race. Until the TEU 1993, the regulation of state aid was the principal manifestation of the Community's limited commitment to an industrial policy for the EU. Initially the Community rules on state aid had been aimed at ensuring transparency rather than controlling national economic policy. In fact, during the recession of the 1970s general state aid schemes had grown. State aid received attention in the EC Commission's 1985 White Paper,[75] with the aims being to create an inventory of state aid and a report outlining the implications for future state aid policy. The EC Commission took a tougher stance in the run up to the SEA 1986, trying to persuade the Member States to move towards specific aid schemes. It took a tougher stance on aid to failing industries and aid for export schemes to another Member State and began to devise special rules for industries such as shipbuilding, textiles, steel and coal which were facing fierce competition from non-EU states.

The EC Commission also became increasingly concerned about the financial relationship between governments and public undertakings. This was seen in the new attention given to vetting public procurement exercises and also in the

---

[73]   Available at http://business.timesonline.co.uk/article/0,,16849-2211781,00.html. Although critics were quick to point out the inconsistencies in the UK Chancellor's approach, since at the same time he indicated that politics would play a part in the UK's attempt to block a take-over by Centrica by the Russian Gazprom: see http://business.timesonline.co.uk/article/0,,16849-2212303,00.html.

[74]   See, eg, G Durand, *Gas and Electricity in Europe: the Elusive Common Interest* (Brussels, European Policy Centre, 2005), available at http://www.theepc.be/en/pub.asp?TYP=TEWN&LV=187&see=y&t=&PG=TEWN/EN/detailpub&l=12&AI=528.

[75]   COM(85) 310 final.

introduction of the Transparency Directive[76] requiring states to provide data on the financial relationships between the state and public corporations. Some Member States opposed the introduction of this Directive, which was based upon Article 86(3) EC, but the European Court of Justice upheld the EC Commission's use of its powers.[77] The EC Commission also took action against the growing tendency for sectoral aid to take the form of state participation in the capital of a private company. Where this capital was injected on favourable terms, and below commercial rates of return, the EC Commission, supported by the Court, took the view that this was also a form of state aid.[78] The EC Commission became involved in some highly politicised cases particularly in the car industry.

The EC Commission began to insist on tighter proceduralisation of state aid, requiring it to be notified in advance, but it was not until 1989 that these procedures were formalised into a Regulation.[79] Tougher sanctions for illegal state aid were introduced with the EC Commission requirement of repayment of illegal state aid with interest.[80]

Unintelligent use of state aid is seen by the EC Commission as a waste of public money, and its use prevents the necessary restructuring and innovation which are necessary to keep the European economy competitive. Thus central regulation of state aid was seen as necessary to ensure that state aid is granted only in the interests of the Community but also to ensure a level playing field from a competitive as well as a cohesion aspect. In the absence of a central regulator wealthier regions would be able to grant state aid at the expense of poorer regions.

The EC Treaty rules on state aid relied upon cooperation between the Member States and the EC Commission. The Court of Justice reinforced this interdependence by denying the direct effect of Article 92(1) EC (now Article 87(1) EC) in *Lorenz v Germany*.[81] The consequences of this case were described by Weatherill and Micklitz as 'a politicization of the decision-making procedure'.[82] If Article 92(1) EC had been declared to be directly effective, decision-making power would have been transferred from the EC Commission to the national courts and, possibly, *via* Article 234 EC, to the Court. This was clearly something the

---

[76] Commission Dir (EEC) 80/723 on the transparency of financial relations between member States and public undertakings [1980] OJ L195/35.

[77] Cases 188–190/80 *France, Italy and the United Kingdom v Commission* [1982] ECR 2545.

[78] In Case 323/82 *Intermills v Commission* [1984] ECR 3809 the 'hypothetical private investor test' was used. This concept is discussed in Ch 6.

[79] Council Reg 659/99/EC [1999] OJ L83/1.

[80] As early as 1973 the Court held that the EC Commission was competent under Art 88 EC to decide that a Member State must give practical effect to a Decision finding state aid to be incompatible with the Common Market, and this could include an obligation to require repayment of such aid: Case 70/72 *Commission v Germany (Kohlengesetz)* [1973] ECR 813. From 1985 onwards the Court has increasingly affirmed the right to recovery: see eg, Case 52/84 *Commission v Belgium* [1986] ECR 89; Case 310/85 *Deufil v Commission* [1987] ECR 901.

[81] Case 120/72 [1973] ECR 1471.

[82] At 124.

Court did not want at this time, but in later years we see the Court taking a greater judicial interest in the proceduralisation of state aid control.

After the Single European Act 1986 the EC Commission focused state aid policy upon developing a system of control covering all aid falling within the scope of the EC Treaty, giving practical effect to the substantive legal provisions through individual decisions and using general guidelines to explain the kinds of aid which are incompatible with the EC Treaty and the conditions for exemption through Community frameworks. The EC Commission looked at the types of aid which were particularly important in practice, for example, aid to assist the regions, research and development aid, environmental protection and aid to rescue firms in difficulty. Sector specific rules were also established, covering areas such as synthetic fibres, shipbuilding, steel and motor vehicles. Ehlermann[83] argues that the twin aims of this policy reflected two concerns: first, state aid which was incompatible with the Common Market, namely a ban on operating aid which is used to maintain non-viable firms and aid which affects exports; secondly, aid which can promote Community objectives, for example, the authorisation of aid for the development of economically backward regions, restructuring of branches of industry, social objectives aid and the promotion of projects which serve the interests of the Community as a whole. The SEA 1986 introduced a number of flanking policies of the Internal Market and thus state aid could be channelled towards Community-based policies such as economic and social cohesion, research and technological development and the environment. As a consequence of the Internal Market programme the competition policies inherent within the state aid rules were extended to new areas and policy shifted from the national to the Community level.

However, the EC Commission moved cautiously on state aids, preferring to use soft law processes to develop policy.[84] One reason for this tentative approach is that state aid policy has been described as an encroachment into the economic sovereignty of the Member States since the ability to establish, finance, subsidise and fiscally influence industrial and commercial undertakings is historically fundamental to the integrity of the modern industrialised state.[85] State aids are applied with equal force to public and private undertakings, and cover all areas of the economy. The completion of the Internal Market, abolishing restrictive trade barriers, combined with EMU, left state aid as one of few remaining tools left to protect national industry, and therefore made the effective control of state aid an

---

[83]   C-D Ehlermann, 'The Contribution of EC Policy to the Single Market' (1992) 29 CMLRev 257.
[84]   G della Cananea, 'Administration by Guidelines: The Policy Guidelines of the Commission in the Field of State Aids' in I Harden (ed), *State Aid: Community Law and Policy*, (Cologne, Bundesanzeiger, 1993); M Cini, *From Soft Law to Hard Law?: Discretion and Rule-making in the Commission's State Aid Regime* (Florence, Robert Schumann Centre for Advanced Legal Studies, EUI, 2000).
[85]   S Wilks, 'The Metamorphosis of European Competition Law' in F Snyder (ed), *European Community Law, Vol 1.* (Aldershot, Wiley, 1993).

important issue for the EC Commission.[86] State aid is seen as a visible, distortive method whereby competitors *and* consumers[87] in an integrated market may be placed at a disadvantage by protectionist measures. This may explain why in recent years the Court has been willing to protect the rights of competitors in the procedural aspects of state aid control.

One aspect of the modern era of state aid control is to offer a normative dimension to the EC Commission's decision-making. It was generally thought that state aid decisions turned largely on their own facts. It is only since 1990 that the EC Commission has begun to publish, on a systematic basis, details of decisions to close its Article 88 EC procedures and allow a state aid to be granted. Thus until then it was not easy to generalise or distil the factors which prevailed in determining what kind of state aid *was* compatible with the Common Market. During the 1990s the EC Commission gained confidence to create a pro-active policy, setting out areas where state aid could be used in the Community interest.

The policy reasons for state aid control are now articulated openly in a number of modern documents in the Lisbon Process era:

> State aid distorts competition and, whether or not it has an impact on trade between member states, may damage the allocative efficiency of the European economy. In particular, it modifies economic incentives and so may cause the inefficient allocation of scarce private resources to industries receiving aid and away from others. State aid may also encourage rent-seeking behaviour and 'capture' of government by industries, and moral hazard in the case of failing industries. Like other government expenditures, the financing of State aid also raises the issue of the marginal cost of public funds, i.e. the loss of efficiency due to taxation.

> The consequences of State aid in terms of inefficient functioning of product markets imply that the European Commission's control of State aid needs to be supplemented by an effort of self-discipline on the part of the member states themselves. In view of the cross-border spill-over effects of State aid, this self-discipline can be more rigorous and politically acceptable if the efforts of the Member States are co-ordinated. To this end, since 1999 recommendations on State aid are included in the framework of the Broad Economic Policy Guidelines (BEPG).[88]

The following year, in the Ninth Survey on State Aid in the European Union,[89] these ideas are reiterated:

> A key element of Competition *policy* is Community State Aid control, the benefits of which are clear. State aid can frustrate free competition by preventing the most efficient

---

[86]   See the comments of the then EC Commissioner for Competition, K van Miert, *XXVII Report on Competition Policy* (Brussels, EC Commission, 1997) at 3.

[87]   Competition law and policy have often focused upon the impact of state aid on competitors, at the expense of analysis upon the impact upon consumers.

[88]   Lisbon European Council, Mar 2000, SN 100/1/100, pt 17.

[89]   COM(2001)403 final, para 2.

allocation of resources and posing a threat to the unity of the Internal Market. In many cases, the granting of State aid reduces economic welfare and weakens the incentives for firms to improve efficiency. Aid also enables the less efficient to survive at the expense of the more efficient. In addition to creating distortions within the Internal Market, the grant of State aid can affect trade between the EU and third countries thereby encouraging them to adopt retaliatory measures that may be a source of further inefficiency...

More recently the EC Commission has continued with this policy theme in the State Aid Action Plan:

> State aid control comes from the need to maintain a level playing field for all undertakings active in the Single European Market, no matter in which Member State they are established. There is a particular need to be concerned with those state aid measures, which provide unwarranted selective advantages to some firms, preventing or delaying the market forces from rewarding the most competitive firms, thereby decreasing overall European competitiveness. It may also lead to a build-up of market power in the hands of some firms, for instance when companies that do not receive state aid (e.g. non-domestic firms) have to cut down on their market presence, or where state aid is used to erect entry barriers. As a result of such distortions of competition, customers may be faced with higher prices, lower quality goods and less innovation.[90]

In the modern era state aid has received much harsher scrutiny as part of the Lisbon Process. A proactive policy has been set out of reducing the overall amount of state aid as well as transferring the focus of state aid away from sectors towards horizontal projects which are of greater benefit to European integration. The Stockholm European Council of 2001 agreed for the first time an objective indicator to benchmark Member States' expenditure on state aid, by expressing such expenditure as a percentage of GDP. Concurrently it has also been recognised that state aid may be necessary to meet some of the Lisbon targets, for example, aid for employment and training.

As a means of meeting the Lisbon targets new forms of economic governance were introduced. A naming and shaming process was implemented through a *State Aid Score Board*.[91] As well as analysing state aid in the Member States each update has a special focus. To provide for greater openness and transparency a *State Aid Register* was created in 2000.[92] Recently a *State Aid Weekly* e-newsletter was produced in 2006.[93] The greater openness of EC Commission behaviour allows competitors and consumers to understand where state aid is being used and also contributes to a normative understanding of how state aid decisions are made.

---

[90]   EC Commission, *State Aid Action Plan*, COM(2005)107 final, para 7.
[91]   Available at http://europa.eu.int/comm/competition/state_aid/scoreboard/.
[92]   Available at http://europa.eu.int/comm/competition/state_aid/register/.
[93]   Available at http://europa.eu.int/comm/competition/state_aid/overview/newsletter.html

State Monopolies

Integration of the market is also the objective underlying the provisions of Article 86 EC, which is directed against state measures taken in favour of public undertakings. Although it is located in the competition provisions of the EC Treaty it addresses the incompatibility of state monopolies and undertakings granted special or exclusive rights with both the competition and the Internal Market rules of the EC Treaty. Until the mid-1980s, coinciding with the SEA 1987, Article 86 EC was applied rarely. Since then it has become a key EC Treaty provision in bringing about deregulation of certain sectors as well as maintaining a balance between the equal treatment of private and public undertakings in the market. The EC Commission argued that, instead of providing a framework for a free market system, the Member States distorted the system by pursuing their own economic policies and, in some instances, furthered these policies by granting special or exclusive rights to public undertakings to conduct economic activities at the state's behest. The use of public undertakings allows the state to exercise influence directly, or indirectly, in particular sectors of the economy. The reservation of specific economic activity to one undertaking allows the undertaking, on behalf of the state, to control the whole economic activity in that area. The impact is felt not only within the Member State but also across the Internal Market.[94] As a consequence of what was regarded as the state orchestrating undue influence in the market, it was argued that the state must take responsibility for its own, and the undertaking's, actions.[95]

The political pressures surrounding the goal to complete the Internal Market by 31 December 1992 were a major factor in the EC Commission turning its attention towards the regulation of public monopolies.[96] From this grew the premise that exclusive rights and monopolies could continue to exist *only* if they furthered the goals of the Member States *and* the Community. Other factors were present, particularly rapid technological change and opposition from taxpayers who were not willing to subsidise what were often seen as inefficient, bureaucratic and sometimes unpopular monopolies;[97] sectors traditionally granted exclusive rights were in need of funds that could not be raised by the state acting as owner of the public enterprise.

---

[94] See Commission Dir 80/723 [1980] OJ L195/35; M van der Woude, 'Article 90: Competing For Competence' [1991] *ELRev Supplement (Competition Law Check List)* 60, 61.

[95] A Pappalardo, 'State Measures and Public Undertakings: Article 90 of the EEC Treaty Revisited' (1991) 12 *ECLR* 29.

[96] C-D Ehlermann, 'Managing Monopolies: The Role of the State in Controlling Market Dominance in the European Community' (1993) 14 *ECLR* 61.

[97] There is an amusing example of this culture in D Landes, *The Wealth and Poverty of Nations* (London, Abacus, 1998) at 306: '[t]he meanness of the French Post Office was notorious. Until the 1990s, airmail letters … paid a surcharge above a weight of 5 grams, stamps included. That meant using specially thin and pricey paper—a boon to the stationery industry. Even so the PO would not have a single stamp for the postage required and would combine 2 or 3 stamps to make the amount,

The EC Commission's initial use of its enforcement and legislative powers under Article 86 EC led some Member States to question the legality of the EC Commission's actions in a bid to retain national autonomy over economic policies. This position was supported by academic writers, for example Ehlermann,[98] and also Van der Woude[99] who argued that Article 86(1) EC does not control the existence of exclusive rights, but only the 'assessment of ancillary restraints' which affect competition as a result of the existence of the rights. Thus an argument was made out that Article 86(1) EC had a very narrow role to play in the EC Treaty, similar to the role of Article 31 EC.

The EC Commission had taken a broad view of Article 31 EC, arguing that monopolies needed to be structurally changed so that they could no longer engage in discrimination. In *Publico Ministero v Manghera*[100] the Court held that Article 31 EC does not require the *elimination* of state monopolies but does prevent exclusive rights for the import of goods from other states. The EC Commission also took a wider view of Article 86(1) EC: all exclusive rights should be abolished in the absence of a non-economic public-interest justification.[101] Under this approach the idea of re-structuring such monopolies inevitably led to the *abolition* of exclusive rights.

In contrast the Court's attitude has changed over time. In the early case law the Court drew a distinction between the *existence* and the *exercise* of monopoly rights. The Court established that the existence of a monopoly right for television advertisements granted by Italy[102] did not, by itself, violate the rules on the free movement of goods, particularly where the grant of exclusive rights furthered the public interest:

Nothing in the Treaty prevents Member States, for considerations of public interest, of a non-economic nature, from removing radio and television transmissions…from the field of competition by conferring one or more establishment an exclusive right to conduct them. However, for the performance of their tasks these establishments remain subject to the prohibition against discrimination and, to the extent that this performance comprises activities of an economic nature, fall under the provisions referred to in [Article 86] relating to public undertakings to which member states grant special or exclusive rights.[103]

However, the Court stresses that if the undertaking breaks the conditions of Article 86(1) EC by discriminating against foreign products, or acting in an

---

and these would tip the scale. One had to experience these exercises in petty tyranny to understand the retardive effects of bureaucratic constipation. Fortunately for the French, the European Community has imposed new standards.'

[98]   Above n 96.
[99]   Above n 94.
[100]   Case 59/75 *Publico Ministero v Manghera* [1976] ECR 91.
[101]   Cf Ehlermann, above n 96 at 67, n 17.
[102]   Case 155/73 *Giuseppe Sacchi* [1974] ECR 409.
[103]   *Ibid*, at 428–9.

anti-competitive way, then the monopoly would be in violation of the EC Treaty. In relation to the competition rules the Court held that the grant of exclusive rights was not a violation of the competition rules or Article 86 EC *per se.* This finding also extended to an *extension* of exclusive rights by the undertaking after a new intervention by the state if the rights were extended for a non-economic public interest reason. The undertaking could infringe Article 86 EC if it engaged in discrimination. Interestingly the Court ruled that the national court should determine whether the undertaking had abused its dominant position. If the national court found an abuse of a dominant position then the EC Commission would respond and remedy the infringement of Article 86 EC. Thus in *Sacchi* the Court clearly separates out *existence* from *exercise* of the exclusive rights.

The Court confirmed this approach in *Centre Belge d'Etudes de Marché-Télémarketing SA v Compagnie Luxembourgeoise de Télédiffusion SA.* Here a dominant position was created by law but was nevertheless subject to the competition rules. In looking at the exercise of the dominant position the Court found a violation of Article 82 EC in that the undertaking had extended its exclusive right, without an objective reason, into areas where there was potential competition from other undertakings capable of providing the service:

> an abuse within the meaning of [Article 82 EC] is committed where, without any objective necessity, an undertaking holding a dominant position on a particular market reserves to itself or to an undertaking belonging to the same group an ancillary activity which might be carried out by another undertaking as part of its activities, ...with the possibility of eliminating all competition from such undertaking.[104]

Thus here the Court applies the same standard to the state's original grant of exclusive rights to an undertaking as it applies to any expansion of exclusive rights.

During the 1990s, in a series of Article 234 EC rulings, the Court took a rigorous approach to the way in which state monopolies operated. The change in policy was litigation-driven from the national level. The direct effect of Article 86(1) EC led to a number of references to the Court, which in turn provided the dynamic for a number of liberalisation processes at the national level. The original idea of the drafters of the 1957 Treaty was that the Member States could no longer retain complete sovereignty in relation to the creation and mainte-nance of legal monopolies. Their economic preferences must be subject to the principles of free trade and competition.[105] Equally the 1957 Treaty recognised that there are some economic activities which cannot be properly performed by

---

[104]   Case 311/84 [1985] ECR 3261, 3266.
[105]   D Edward and M Hoskins, 'Article 90: Deregulation and EC Law. Reflections Arising from the XVI Fide Conference' (1995) 32 *CMLRev* 160. See also in the *Terminal Equipment Case* (Case C–202/88 [1991] ECR I–1272, para 22) where the Court states that Art 86 EC does *not* presuppose that all special or exclusive rights are compatible with the EC Treaty

respecting fully the rules on competition.[106] However, the subsequent case law of the Court reveals a discernable shift away from a presumption of *neutrality* towards public and privileged undertakings towards an assumption of their *illegality*, unless permitted in specific circumstances.[107] This has been described by Amato as a 'peculiarly European area of exception'. He argues that towards public monopolies and holders of exclusive rights:

> the Commission and the Court of Justice itself, are markedly severe; indeed it is only towards them that the sanction of break-up, which in Europe is not directly provided for, has indirectly been applied.[108]

The effects of this litigation are discussed in detail in Chapter 4.

Competition and the Economic Constitution

Competition law was originally conceived as a complement to the free movement rules of the EC Treaty, addressing the regulation of non-state power in the market: a mirror to the four fundamental freedoms of the Common Market, now the Internal Market. In *Walt Wilhelm v Bundeskartellam*[109] the Court articulated the unspoken objectives of competition law inherent within the EC Treaty as two fundamental aims: market integration and market efficiency. Competition was therefore:

> one of the instruments towards the fundamental goals laid out in the Treaty—namely the establishment of a common market, the approximation of economic policy...

Until recently, the two sets of EC Treaty provisions appeared to operate in separate spheres. This was because the Court did not rise to the challenges posed in the early litigation of considering the interaction and concurrent application of the competition and free movement rules. The increasing emphasis upon subjecting the state to competition law has highlighted not only the *complementary* nature of the free movement rules and the competition rules but also their *interconnectedness*.

The competition and free movement rules are seen as the basic layer of the economic constitution of Europe, further layers being economic and monetary union and the common commercial policy. This is enhanced by Article 4 EC

---

[106] Seen, eg, in the inclusion of Art 86(2) EC. See G Marenco, 'Competition Between National Economies and Competition Between Business —A Response to Judge Pescatore' [1987] *Fordham International Law Journal* 420.

[107] A Gardner, 'The Velvet Revolution: Article 90 and the Triumph of the Free Market in Europe's Regulated Sectors' (1995) 16 *ECLR* 78.

[108] G Amato, *Antitrust and the Bounds of Power. The Dilemma of Liberal Democracy in the History of the Market* (Oxford, Hart, 1997) at 88.

[109] Case 14/68 *Walt Wilhelm v Bundeskartellamt* [1969] ECR 1, paras 4–5.

which instructs the Member States and the Community to conduct their economic affairs 'in accordance with the principle of an open market economy with free competition'. The chapters in this book show that while this obligation imposes a number of substantive constraints on the policy choices available to the Member States, however, the Court has accepted that the regulation of the Member States through Article 4 EC as a legally binding principle has its practical limitations.[110]

Subsequently the European Court has declared the hierarchical superiority of free competition as a constitutional norm protected by the EC Treaty and by the Court:

> according to ... Article 3(1)(g) EC, Article 85 of the Treaty constitutes a fundamental provision which is essential for the accomplishment of the tasks entrusted to the Community and, in particular, for the functioning of the internal market. The importance of such a provision led the framers of the Treaty to provide expressly, in Article 85(2) of the Treaty, that any agreements or decisions prohibited pursuant to that article are to be automatically void.[111]

These ideas are also emphasised in *Courage v Crehan*:[112]

> It should be borne in mind, first of all, that the Treaty has created its own legal order, which is integrated into the legal systems of the Member States and which their courts are bound to apply. The subjects of that legal order are not only the Member States but also their nationals. Just as it imposes burdens on individuals, Community law is also intended to give rise to rights which become part of their legal assets. Those rights arise not only where they are expressly granted by the Treaty but also by virtue of obligations which the Treaty imposes in a clearly defined manner both on individuals and on the Member States and the Community institutions (see the judgments in Case 26/62 *Van Gend en Loos* [1963] ECR 1, Case 6/64 *Costa* [1964] ECR 585 and Joined Cases C–6/90 and C–9/90 *Francovich and Others* [1991] ECR I–5357, paragraph 31).
>
> Secondly, according to Article 3(g) of the EC Treaty (now, after amendment, Article 3(1)(g) EC), Article 85 of the Treaty constitutes a fundamental provision which is essential for the accomplishment of the tasks entrusted to the Community and, in particular, for the functioning of the internal market (judgment in Case C–126/97 *Eco Swiss* [1999] ECR I–3055, paragraph 36).

As we shall see in Chapters 2, 3 and 4 this interconnectedness between the free movement and competition rules of the EC Treaty was grasped much earlier by

---

[110]   Case C–9/99 *Echirolles Distribution v Association du Dauphiné* [2000] ECR I–8207, para 25.
[111]   Case C–126/97 *Eco Swiss China Time Ltd v Benetton International NV* [1999] ECR I–3055, para 36, my emphasis.
[112]   Case C–453/99 *Courage Ltd v Bernard Crehan* [2001] ECR I–6297, paras 19–20.

opportunistic litigants. The lawyers in many of the early cases testing the limits of Article 28 EC also raised a breach of the competition rules. The Court saw this interconnectedness:

> Articles 2 and 3 of the Treaty set out to establish a market characterised by the free movement of goods where the terms of competition are not distorted. That objective is secured *inter alia* by Article 28 *et seq.* prohibiting restrictions on intra-Community trade, to which reference was made during the proceedings before the Court, and by Article 81 *et seq.* on the rules of competition.[113]

The Court, however, chose to develop the role of Article 28 EC over the competition rules.

THE INTERACTION OF THE FREE MOVEMENT AND COMPETITION RULES

Under the EC Treaty the state is at a greater disadvantage than private economic operators since the state is subject to the cumulative operation of the competition and the free movement rules. The horizontal application of the free movement rules of the EC Treaty is under-explored in litigation.[114] As we shall see in Chapter 2, many of the early cases invited the Court to explore the *interconnection* between the free movement and competition rules. The Court preferred to choose between the application of one set of rules over another, with preference being given to the free movement rules. Similarly where the *cumulative* effect of the free movement provisions is an issue there is a tendency to apply only one of the four economic freedoms to the individual case. More recently the European Courts are being asked to recognise the role of delegated or hybrid public–private power in the market and the Courts are starting to recognise the role of private power and the restrictive effects it may have on the free market rules[115] and the competition rules.[116]

---

[113] Case 229/83 *Leclerc* [1985] ECR 1, para 9.

[114] See J Baquero Cruz, *Between Competition and Free Movement* (Oxford, Hart, 2002) ch. 7; S van den Boggaert, 'Horizontality' in C Barnard and J Scott (eds), *The Law of the Single Market* (Oxford, Hart, 2002).

[115] Case C–415/93 *Union royale belge des sociétés de football association ASBL v Jean-Marc Bosman, Royal club liégeois SA v Jean-Marc Bosman and others and Union des associations européennes de football (UEFA) v Jean-Marc Bosman* [1995] ECR I–4921; Case C–281/98 *Roman Angonese v Cassa di Risparmio di Bolzano SpA*, [2000] ECR I–4139. Cf. in relation to goods Case 311/85 *Vlaamse Reisbureaus* [1987] ECR 3801.

[116] Case C–309/99 *Wouters* [2002] ECR I–1577; Case T–193/02 *Laurent Piau v Commission* [2005] ECR II–209; on appeal: Case C–171/05 P *Laurent Piau v Commission*, Order of 23 Feb 2006 [2006] ECR I–37; Case T–313/02 *David Meca-Medina and Igor Majcen v Commission* [2004] ECR II–3291; on appeal: Case C–519/04P *David Meca-Medina and Igor Majcen v Commission of the European Communities* [2006] ECR I-6991.

Casting the Community Law Net Wide

The Court cast the reach of the free movement rules wide. In Chapter 2 we explore the use of Article 28 EC relating to the free movement of goods to capture state regulation of the market and the subsequent attempts post-*Keck*[117] to rein in what became an unruly horse. More recently litigants have turned their attention to exploring the scope of the free movement of services provisions. This litigation has provided the opportunity for litigants to challenge a number of rules relating to the state provision of social welfare services. The most notable and current example of these tactics is seen in the use of the free movement rules to challenge Member State rules which restrict or hinder patients from travelling abroad to receive medical services in another Member State. The Court has stated consistently that Community law does not limit the powers of the Member States to organise their social welfare systems.[118] Yet in a series of cases the Court has limited the autonomy of the Member States to organise their healthcare services. In *Kohll* [119] a father who was a Luxembourg national sought reimbursement of the dental treatment received by his daughter in Germany. He had taken his daughter to Germany for the treatment without obtaining prior permission from the Luxembourg authorities. The Court ruled that healthcare services fell within the scope of the free movement of services, even where, as in this case, they were provided in the context of a social security scheme: 'the special nature of certain services does not remove them from the ambit of the fundamental principle of freedom of movement'.[120]

The Court by-passed Regulation 1408/71/EEC,[121] allowing the Court to examine the compatibility of the national rules with the EC Treaty rules on the free movement of services. The Court found that the prior authorisation rules, which in this case had not been complied with, were in conflict with Article 49 EC, but

---

[117] Joined Cases C–267/91 and C–268/91 *Criminal Proceedings Against Bernard Keck and Daniel Mithouard* [1993] ECR I–6097.

[118] Case 238/82 *Duphar v Netherlands* [1984] ECR 523, para 16; Joined Cases C–159/91 and C–160/91 *Poucet and Pistre* [1993] ECR I–637, para 6; Case C–70/95 *Sodemare v Regione Lombardia* [1997] ECR I–3395, para 27; Case C–157/99 *Geraets-Smits and Peerbooms* [2001] ECR I–5473; Case C–372/04 *R on the application of Yvonne* v *Bedford Primary Care Trust Secretary of State for Health* [2006] ECR I-4325, at para 121: 'although Community law does not detract from the power of the Member States to organise their social security systems and decide the level of resources to be allocated to their operation, the achievement of the fundamental freedoms guaranteed by the Treaty nevertheless inevitably requires Member States to make adjustments to those systems. It does not follow that this undermines their sovereign powers in the field: see Case C–385/99 *VG Müller-Fauré v Onderlinge Waarborgmaatschappij OZ Zorgverzekeringen UA, and E.E.M. van Riet v Onderlinge Waarborgmaatschappij ZAO Zorgverzekeringen* [2003] ECR I–4509, paras 100 and 102.'

[119] Case C–158/96 *Raymond Kohll v Union des caisses de maladie* [1998] ECR I–1931.

[120] *Ibid*, at paras 27 and 28.

[121] [1971] OJ L149/2. The Reg has been modified a number of times and was codified and repealed by Reg (EC) 883/2004 of 29 Apr 2004 [2004] OJ L166/1. The aim of the Reg is to coordinate the basic national rules in the area of social and welfare benefits. In Case C–158/96 *Kohll* [1998] ECR I–1931 the Court held that the Reg was not intended to regulate the reimbursement by Member States of costs incurred in connection with medical treatment provided abroad.

there was the possibility of a justification for the national rules by relying upon Article 46 EC, to the extent that national measures had the objective of maintaining a balanced medical and hospital service open to all.[122] The Court also ruled that the national measure could be justified if it was necessary to ensure the financial balance of the social security scheme as an overriding reason in the public interest.[123] The Court found that neither justification could be applied here since refund of the medical treatment at home state tariffs would not affect the financial balance of the Luxembourg healthcare scheme or the quality of the medical services in Luxembourg.[124] The ruling in *Kohll* conflicted with earlier rulings of the Court[125] but later judgments[126] extended its application.

The EC Commission has also examined the way in which the restrictive practice rules of the liberal professions could be opened up to more competition, threatening the use of Article 86 EC.[127] The Council has recently adopted a Directive which aims to liberalise some services in the Internal Market.[128]

The golden shares cases are another example of how the free movement provisions have been used to regulate state intervention in the market in a sensitive area. These issues are directly related to the liberalisation processes and the continued involvement of the state in privatised enterprises through the use of equity ownership, especially in the form of special shares known as 'golden shares'. The shares give the state controlling rights over the activities of the privatised enterprise. The use of golden shares originated in Britain but they have become a central policy tool in privatisations across Europe. They are seen as a useful residual tool to influence policy, and to achieve this the scope of golden shares was not always tightly defined. Golden shares are used in enterprises which

---

[122]   *Ibid*, at para. 50.

[123]   *Ibid*, at paras. 41 and 42.

[124]   *Ibid*, at paras. 42 and 52.

[125]   This ruling is difficult to reconcile with earlier rulings of the Court in *Poucet and Pistre* and *Sodemare*, above n 118 and the later ruling in Case C–355/00 *Freskot v Elliniko Dimosio* [2003] ECR I–5263. But cf Case C–174/97P *FFSA* [1998] ECR I–1303. See also the rulings dealing with *competition law* aspects of social security schemes in Case C–67/96 *Albany International BV v Stichting Bedrijfspensioenfonds Textielindustrie* [1999] ECR I–5751, Cases C–115/97, C–116/97 & C–117/97 *Brentjens' Handelsonderneming BV* [1999] ECR I–6025.

[126]   Case C–368/98 *Abdon Vanbraekel and Others v Alliance nationale des mutualités chrétiennes (ANMC)* [2001] ECR I–5363; Case C-385/99 *Müller-Fauré v Onderlinge Waarborgmaatschappij OZ Zorgverzekeringen* [2003] ECR I–4509; Case C–157/99 *Geraerts-Smits v Stichting Ziekenfonds and Peerbooms v Stichting CZ Groep Zorgverzekeringen* [2001] ECR I–5473; Case C–56/01 *Inizan v Caisse primaire d'assurance maladie des Hauts-de-Seine* [2003] ECR I–1240;, Case C–8/02 *Leichtle v Bundesanstalt für Arbeit* [2004] ECR I–2641, Case C–193/03 *Betriebskrankenkasse der Robert Bosch GmbH v Bundesrepublik Deutschland* [2004] ECR I–9911; Case C–372/04 *R on the application of Yvonne Watts v Bedford Primary Care Trust and Secretary of State for Health* [2006] ECRI-4325. The response of the EU has been to encourage the use of the open method of coordination in an attempt to iron out some of the differences between the way health services are offered in the Member States: see E Szyszczak, 'Experimental Governance: The Open Method of Co-ordination' (2006) 12 *ELJ* 486.

[127]   See the papers at: http://ec.europa.eu/comm/competition/sectors/professional_services/ conferences/20061230/index.html

[128]   European Parliament and Council Directive (EC) 2006/123 on services in the internal market, [2006] OJ L 376/36

are viewed as national champions, or in sensitive economic or security areas. Golden shares may also be used to maintain a consensus of public interest in the private sector and also to defend public services. Until it was recognised that proper regulation is a better way of maintaining competition, state shares in privatised companies were a useful insurance against anti-competitive conduct by the privatised enterprise. Golden shares may also be justified to permit temporary measures to allow management to acclimatise to private sector activity, and to prevent a sensitive sector from being taken over by foreign capital. In many of the liberalisations taking place in Europe the national champion remained as an incumbent in the market. There was the risk that one national champion could find itself being taken over by another national champion. It was felt that public confidence would be diminished in the product or services being provided if this was allowed to happen.

Thus golden shares became a key tactic in the liberalisation programmes of Europe. This blurred the boundaries between the public duties of the state and the legitimate exercise of the economic free movement rights, especially the free movement of capital and establishment. The use of golden shares raised a basic constitutional question for Community law: where to draw the boundaries between the sovereign rights of the Member States to choose how to allocate the ownership of property in their territory and the reach of the Internal Market law.

The EC Commission's concern over the use of golden shares stretches back to the early days of privatisation.[129] Within the EC Commission there were tensions between the different Directorates, with the Internal Market Commissioner objecting to the use of golden shares and the Energy Commissioner accepting that they were justified. The EC Commission took the view that prior authorisation for the acquisition of shares beyond a certain threshold is discriminatory and contrary to the EC Treaty. But later, during the 1990s, the EC Commission went further, seeing the golden shares as a form of economic nationalism.[130] The initial legal focus of the EC Commission was the potential for golden shares to infringe the freedom of establishment rules. This was partly because of the relative under-development of the free movement of capital provisions, but also the encouragement on the scope of the free movement of establishment provisions from the Court's rulings in *Factortame*[131] and *Commission v France.*[132]

After years of threatening to take action the EC Commission finally brought three infringement actions against France, Spain and Portugal resulting in Court

---

[129]   A Verhoeven, 'Privatization and EC Law: Is the European Commission "Neutral" With Respect to Public Versus Private Ownership of Companies?' (1996) 45 *International and Comparative Law Quarterly* 27; C Graham and T Prosser, *Privatising Public Enterprises* (Oxford, Clarendon Press, 1991). *Communication of the Commission on Certain Legal Aspects Concerning Intra-EU Investment* [1997] OJ C220/15.

[130]   *Ibid*, para 7.

[131]   Case C–221/89 *R v Secretary of State for Transport, ex parte Factortame* [1991] ECR I–3905.

[132]   Case 270/83 [1986] ECR 273, para 14.

rulings in 2002,[133] and a further two infringement actions against the UK and Spain resulting in Court rulings in 2003 .[134] The Court was asked to define the limits which Community law places on the Member States when they intervene in the market as market participants, attempting to retain some control over a privatised sector. Advocate General Ruiz-Jarabo Colomer was willing to use Article 295 EC as a buffer for the Member States against the full force of the free market rules. He argued that since a state can in theory retain full control over companies through public ownership it can retain a more limited control in privatised companies through certain special rights.[135] The Court held that the application of Article 295 EC was irrelevant to the golden shares cases. The Court also chose to apply the free movement of capital rules over the freedom of establishment rules. It held that golden shares, while not illegal *per se*, could infringe the free movement of capital rules, but also extended the range of justifications for golden shares beyond those found in Article 58(1) EC to embrace a wider generic concept of overriding public interest grounds.

Recently the Court found that the golden share owned by the Dutch government in TNT was also contrary to Community law.[136] The Dutch government has held a golden share in TNT since the firm was privatised and split into two in 1998, arguing that it was necessary to guarantee a universal mail service. While the Court accepted that this could be a legitimate justification for the use of golden shares, in the Netherlands' case the justification was too general and the ambit of the golden share too wide:

> In that regard, the Court acknowledges that the guarantee of a service of general interest, such as universal postal service, may constitute an overriding reason in the general interest capable of justifying an obstacle to the free movement of capital (see, by analogy, Joined Cases C–388/00 and C–429/00 *Radiosistemi* [2002] ECR I–5845, paragraph 44).

> However, the special share at issue goes beyond what is necessary in order to safeguard the solvency and continuity of the provider of the universal postal service.

> As the Advocate General has rightly pointed out in paragraphs 38 and 39 of his Opinion, it should be noted, first, that the special rights of the Netherlands State in TPG are not limited to that company's activities as provider of a universal postal

---

[133] Case C–367/98 *Commission v Portugal* [2002] ECR I–4731; Case C–483/99 *Commission v France* [2002] ECR I–4781. See E Szyszczak, 'Golden Shares and Market Governance' (2002) 29 *Legal Issues of European Integration* 255.

[134] Case C–463/00 *Commission v Spain* [2003] ECR I–4581; Case C–98/01 *Commission v United Kingdom* [2003] ECR I–4641.

[135] See para 66 of Cases C–367/98, C–483/99 & C–503/99, above n 133 and paras 54–57 of the Opinion in *Commission v Spain* and *Commission v United Kingdom*, above n 134.

[136] Joined Cases 282/04 and C–283/04 *Commission v Kingdom of The Netherlands*, [2006] ECR-9141.

service. Moreover, the exercise of those special rights is not based on any precise criterion and does not have to be backed by any statement of reasons, which makes any effective judicial review impossible.[137]

However, the Member States continue to use golden shares. The United Kingdom and Portugal have been reminded of their duty to conform to the Court's rulings and an action against Germany is pending.[138]

These developments show that the EC Treaty rules of the Internal Market create obligations for the Member States and national authorities irrespective of whether the public authorities act in their capacity as a public authority or as an entity under private law. Where private entities undertake public functions the Court has also held that the state is acting through the private entity and therefore, as a consequence, the Internal Market rules may also apply to the private entity.[139] Thus by being subject to the Internal Market and the competition rules the Member States are subject to greater constraints when operating as market participants than the constraints imposed upon non-state undertakings in the market.

Justifications

As a balance to bringing a wide area of economic activity within the scope of Community law, the Court has also offered the state a greater opportunity to defend or justify laws and practices which run up against the free movement rules of the EC Treaty. The Court has adapted its case law from the free movement of goods arena[140] and established that there are certain mandatory requirements which protect public interests which may be raised by the state, provided that they satisfy the four criteria set out in *Gebhard*:[141]

> from the Court's case-law . . . national measures liable to hinder or make less attractive the exercise of fundamental freedoms guaranteed by the Treaty must fulfil four conditions: they must be applied in a non-discriminatory manner; they must be justified by imperative requirements in the general interest; they must be suitable for

---

[137]   *Ibid,* paras 38–40.

[138]   Case C-112/05 *Commission v Germany,* Opinion of Advocate General Ruiz Jarabo-Colomer of 13 February 2007; See I Kuznetsov, 'The Legality of Golden Shares Under EC Law' (2005) 1 *Hanse Law Review* 22, also available at: http://www.hanselawreview.org/pdf/Vol1No1Art3.pdf.

[139]   Joined Cases C-266 and 267/87 *The Queen v Royal Pharmaceutical Society of Great Britain, ex parte Association of Pharmaceutical Importers and others* [1989] ECR I-1295; Case C–16/94 *Édouard Dubois & Fils SA and Général Cargo Services SA v Garonor Exploitation SA* [1995] ECR I–2421, para 20; Case C–57/02P *Compañía española para la fabricación de aceros inoxidables SA (Acerinox)* [2004] ECR I–1477, para 24. See also Opinion of Kokott AG of 17 November 2005 in Case C–470/03 *AGM-COS.MET,* para 87, judgment of 17 April 2007.

[140]   Case 120/78 *Rewe-Zentral v Bundesmonopolverwaltung für Branntwein (Cassis de Dijon)* [1979] ECR 649.

[141]   Case C–55/94 [1995] ECR I–4165, para 37.

securing the attainment of the objective which they pursue; and they must not go beyond what is necessary in order to attain it (see Case C–19/92 *Kraus v Land Baden-Wuerttemberg* [1993] ECR I–1663, para. 32).

The case law of the Court demonstrates a sensitivity towards allowing the state to retain control of the regulation of a number of policies, particularly those policies relating to social issues.[142] For example, it is possible to identify a set of special justifications, or overriding reasons that have developed to protect health-care from the full thrust of the competitive market created by the free movement provisions. These reasons are still subject to the principles of proportionality and should be applied in an objective and non-discriminatory manner. Another idea is the use of solidarity, a concept developed under competition law and seen in use in *Sodemare*.[143] Here the Court started with the premise that a Member State may, in the exercise of the powers it retains to organise its social security system, consider what a social welfare system necessarily implies.[144] The Court then found that the measure being challenged did not result in any *discrimination* on the basis of the place of establishment of the companies seeking to provide the care facilities. Without looking to see if there was a barrier or hindrance to the right of free movement the Court found that there was no infringement of Articles 43 and 48 EC. Later cases[145] have argued that the *core* of solidarity activities must be strictly defined. *Sodemare* can be read as holding that where such activities are involved the Internal Market rules are infringed only by *discriminatory* measures and not the normal hindrance test. From the case law it appears that when core solidarity issues come into play solidarity is to be used as a reason or justification for non-discriminatory measures, as an initial balancing act, rather like the *Cassis* approach developed in relation to the free movement of goods.

Another general concept is the idea of balance and cohesion of a social security scheme in relation to healthcare provided by hospitals. This is an idea drawn from the taxation case law under the free movement provisions.[146] It comes perilously close to an economic justification, which is not recognised by the Court.[147] The Court has acknowledged that any wastage of financial, technical

---

[142] See, eg, Case C–124/97 *Markku Juhani Läärä, Cotsworld Microsystems Ltd. Oy Translatice Software Ltd. v Kihlakunnansyyttäjä (Jyväskylä) and Suomen valtio* [1999] ECR I–6067. Cf M Soriano, 'How Proportionate Should Anti-competitive State Measures Be?' (2003) 28 *ELRev* 112, who argues that the Court takes a tougher approach on the proportionality principle in relation to the free movement provisions than under Art 86(2) EC.

[143] Case C–70/95 [1997] ECR I–3395. The concept of solidarity is discussed in greater detail in Ch 4.

[144] *Ibid.* para 32.

[145] See Case C- 238/94 *FFSA* [1995] ECR I-4013; Case C-67/96 *Albany* [1999] ECR I-5751; Case C-180/98 *Pavlov* [2000] ECR I-6451.

[146] Cases C–204/90 *Hanns-Martin Bachmann v Belgian State* [1992] ECR I–249 and C–300/90 *Commission v Belgium* [1992] ECR I–305.

[147] Case 72/83 *Campus Oil v Minister for Industry and Energy* [1984] ECR 2727.

and human resources should be prevented, since such wastage is particularly damaging in the hospital sector which generates considerable costs and must satisfy increasing needs with limited resources.[148] Another general overriding reason often put forward by the Member States is the need to maintain a balanced medical and hospital service open to all. This again comes close to an economic justification.[149] Thus the Court has also categorised this objective as falling within Article 46 EC, in so far as it contributes to a high level of health protection.[150]

FUSING THE JUSTIFICATIONS

Perhaps one of the reasons why it has taken time to apply the competition rules to state intervention in the market is the fact that the Member States have very few opportunities to raise overriding public interest justifications to defend their actions. Articles 81 and 82 EC do not provide a defence for the state, although, as we shall see in Chapter 3, the Court is beginning to develop a justification to explain certain situations in which Article 82 EC would not apply. These ideas have been taken up for discussion in the EC Commission's Staff Discussion Paper.[151] Article 31 EC does not have an EC Treaty based justification written into it, but the Court has accepted that Article 86(2) EC may be read across to provide a justification where a service of general economic interest is at stake.[152] As we shall see in the subsequent chapters, Article 86(2) EC has played a pivotal role in protecting public services from the full application of the Internal Market and competition rules. But it is limited, and thus in competition law we see a tendency for the Courts to exclude certain areas of sensitive state activity from the remit of the rules where the Member State would not have the opportunity to justify its behaviour according to Community law principles.[153] This approach creates uncertainty, inconsistency and an incoherent basis for the regulation of state intervention in the market. It also leaves huge areas of state economic activity outside the scrutiny of Community law.

---

[148]   Case C-157/99 *Geraets-Smits and Peerbooms* [2001] ECR I-5473 at para 79.

[149]   See Case C-158/96 *Kohll* [1998] ECR I-1931; Case C-368/98 *Vanbraeke* [2001] ECR I-5363; Case C-157/99 Geraerts-Smits *and Peerbooms* [2001] ECRI-5473 where the Court accepted that this was a valid objective to be pursued by the Member States but would not classify it as an *overriding reason of general interest.*

[150]   See Case C-358/99 *Müller-Fauré* [2003] ECRI-4509; Case C-56/01 *Inizan* [2003]ECR I-12403;Case C-8/02 *Leichtle* [2004] ECR I-2641; Case C-193/03 *Bosch* [2004] ECR 9911.

[151]   *DG Competition Discussion Paper on the application of Article 82 of the Treaty to exclusionary abuses* (Brussels, Dec 2005) at para. 10.2.4, available at http://ec.europa.eu/comm/competition/antitrust/others/discpaper2005.pdf.

[152]   Case C-157/94, *Commission v The Netherlands (Electricity Imports)* [1997] ECR I-5699.

[153]   Case T-319/99 *FENIN* [2003] ECR II-357; Case C-205/03 [2006] ECR I-6295; Cases C-264, 306, 354 & 355/01 *AOK Bundesverband and others v Ichthyol-Gesellschaft Cordes, Hermani & Co* [2004] ECR I-2493.

The processes of liberalisation and privatisation have subjected more and more areas of state activity to the rules of the market and, concurrently, the state has handed over more areas of traditional state activity to non-state actors. The Courts and the EC Commission are attempting to clarify the circumstances in which state activity is subject to Community law using a variety of legal tools and techniques. This has resulted in a fragmented approach. One way forward for a more coherent approach is to see competition and Internal Market law as intertwined: a continuum of ideas which are consistent in their goals and their application. An argument can be made for a simpler approach to determining the application of the free movement and the competition rules to state activity: where the state or delegated public or *private* actors engages in market activity then the EC Treaty rules should apply. A generic defence/justification should be available for a breach of Community law based upon the ground that there is an overriding requirement of the general interest justifying the behaviour. The compelling argument for the adoption of this approach is seen in the uncertainty caused by the current confused state of the law and the consequences of unravelling huge areas of public finance commitments. The suggested solution fits the logic of the Internal Market, allowing for Community scrutiny, transparency and accountability of the Member States' policies.

The search for an acceptable generic public interest defence or justification for anti-competitive behaviour on the part of the state raises a major constitutional question on the regulation of state activity in the market involving delicate questions of the balance of power and determination of values within the EU. This issue has not been at the forefront of the current political governance agenda. Yet these issues are addressed, albeit sometimes tacitly, in the case law of the Court. To date the Court has concocted a number of techniques to provide relief to the Member States in deserving cases. Article 86(2) EC has been stretched to provide a derogation in state aid policy and Article 31 EC, but the weaknesses and illogical consequences of this approach have been exposed in the Opinion of Advocate General Jacobs in *GEMO*.[154] The Court has also deployed new ideas, such as the flexible use of the concept of solidarity to protect social policy programmes from the full thrust of market forces. In relation to sport and competition law the Court has held that an anti-doping rule which led to a long ban from competitive swimming for two long-distance swimmers was not incompatible with the competition rules of the EC Treaty if the rule was justified by a legitimate objective. This limitation on the swimmers' freedom of action was 'inherent in the organisation and proper conduct of competitive sport and its very purpose is to ensure healthy rivalry between athletes'.[155]

---

[154] Case C–126/01 *Ministre de l'économie, des Finances et de l'industrie v GEMO SA* [2004] ECR I–13769; Opinion of 30 Apr 2002.

[155] Case C–519/04P *David Meca-Medina and Igor Majcen v Commission of the European Communities* [2006] ECR I-6991, para 45.

What is more tantalising is the glimpse of the use of the more versatile and flexible public interest justifications found in the Internal Market rules, which provide protection for a greater range of national interests and values which can legitimately be protected in the Internal Market.[156]

Many of the EC Treaty-based justifications are outdated. The *Cassis— Gebhard* approach allows for evolution and flexibility in introducing new ideas of interests to be protected where indistinctly applicable measures are at issue.[157] A simpler solution would be to use a generic public interest justification where the regulation of state activity was at stake. Within the four freedoms' case law the Court appears to be moving towards such an approach, utilising the concept of proportionality as a flexible tool to adapt to different situations.[158] The use of a generic justification would allow the Court to adapt to new situations and new ideas of policies and values to be protected in the new constitutional order. This would provide a balance between outlawing overtly protectionist national interests and enhancing the Europeanisation of common policies and values.[159]

The second issue, currently a stumbling block, would be how far the EU should continue with the Court's case law in the area of free movement that a valid justification can only be a general interest of a *non-economic nature*.[160] In *Campus Oil*[161] the Court raised a possibility that economic interests might be protected in

---

[156] Case C–3/95 *Reisebüro Broede v Gerd Sandker* [1996] ECR I–6511; Case C–309/99 *Wouters v Algemene Raad van de Nederlandse Orde van Advocaten* [2002] ECR I–1577; See also S Weatherill, 'The EU Charter of Fundamental Rights and the Internal Market', *Francisco Lucas Pires Working Papers Series on European Constitutionalism*, Working Paper 2003/03 (Lisbon, Facudade de Direito da Universidade Nova de Lisboa, 2003).

[157] In some cases the Court does not apply a rigid distinction between justifications to a distinctly applicable and indistinctly applicable measure: Case C–2/90 *Commission v Belgium* (*Walloon Waste*) [1992] ECR I–4431; Case C–120/95 *Nicolas Decker v Caisse de maladie des employés privés* [1998] ECR I–1831; Case C–281/98 *Roman Angonese v Cassa di Risparmio di Bolzano SpA* [2000] ECR I–4139; Case C–379/98 *PreussenElektra AG v Schleswag AG* [2001] ECR I–2099.

[158] J Jans, 'Proportionality Re-visited' (2000) 27 *Legal Issues of Economic Integration* 239; M Soriano, 'How Proportionate Should Anticompetitive State Measures Be?' (2003) 28 *ELRev* 112. For a discussion of how the use of proportionality can be differentiated further see J Baquero Cruz, *Between Competition and Free Movement* (Oxford, Hart, 2002) at 161 where he suggests that a sliding scale could be implemented depending upon the degree of democratic input into the public measure under review.

[159] See O Gerstenberger, 'Expanding the Constitution Beyond the Court: The Case of Euro-Constitutionalism' (2002) 8 *ELJ* 172. An example of how environmental issues have become a Europeanised value to be protected is Case C–379/98 *PreussenElektra* [2001] ECR I-2099. For a discussion of how *competition law* is taking into account a wider range of non-economic issues see G Monti, 'Article 81 EC and Public Policy' (2002) 39 *CMLRev* 1057.

[160] Case 7/61 *Commission v. Italy* [1962] ECR 635. Case 347/88 *Commission v Greece* [1990] ECR I-4747. In relation to services see Case C–398/95 *Syndesmos ton en Elladi Touristikon kai Taxidiotikon Grafeion v Ypourgos Ergasias (SETTG)* [1997] ECR I–3091; Case C–120/95 *Decker* [1998] ECR I–1831. Cf the cases under Art 86(2) EC where *economic* reasons may be used to justify a measure which is contrary to the competition and free movement provisions: Case C–320/91 *Corbeau* [1993] ECR I–2533; Case C–157/94 *Commission v The Netherlands* [1997] ECR I–5699.

[161] Case 72/83 *Campus Oil v Ministry of Industry and Energy* [1984] ECR 2727.

other ways by the use of public policy and public security justifications.[162] This is seen also in *Kohll*,[163] a decision which takes the Court very close to the edge of where non-economic interests end.[164] Finally, a point not to be overlooked is that case law on golden shares in the area of the free movement of capital and the healthcare cases under the free movement of services provisions show that Member States may continue to have leeway in protecting national interests provided that they observe procedural rights and guarantees.[165]

MARKET GOVERNANCE THROUGH PROCEDURALISATION

Articles 86 EC and state aid rules provided the means whereby the effects of public intervention could be scrutinised, particularly by the EC Commission. The free movement, or economic freedoms, rules also provided scope for determining the normative structures of market governance, providing legal tools whereby a number of competing interests could be balanced. The increased use of infringement actions by the EC Commission, using Article 226 EC against the Member States that failed to introduce Internal Market obligations, was a form of name and shame policy in the formal sense. Post-1992 new forms of market governance emerged, seen, for example, in the use of scoreboards, indicators and benchmarking techniques, leading to the exchange of best practice. These new forms of economic governance were central tools in the Lisbon Process, which evolved from the Lisbon Summit of March 2000, using the model of the European Employment Strategy.[166] Faced with new challenges of global economic competitiveness the Presidency kick-started another cycle of integration measures with the aim of making the EU the most dynamic, knowledge based economy by the year 2010. The lesser-known Cardiff Process used the open method of coordination, bench-marking and peer pressure to improve liberalisation and productivity in product and security markets. In 2003 the EC Commission streamlined the Broad Economic Policy Guidelines with the Employment Guidelines, calling them 'an instrument for European economic governance'.[167]

---

[162] The Court missed the opportunity to re-visit this argument in Case C–157/94 *Commission v The Netherlands* [1997] ECR I–5699 where the EC Commission had used Arts 28 and 29 EC raising the possibility of invoking the Art 30 EC justification, but the Court chose the more tortuous route of finding an infringement under Art 31 EC and using Art 86(2) EC as grounds for a justification.

[163] Case C–158/96 [1998] ECR I-1931.

[164] See now, Art 137(4) EC, and A Gagliardi, 'United States and European Union Antitrust versus State Regulation of the Economy: Is There a Better Test?' (2000) 25 *ELRev* 353 who argues that the distinction between economic and non-economic interests is becoming untenable, and that a test of 'legitimate interest' would provide a generic justification for state intervention in the market.

[165] See E Szyszczak, 'Golden Shares and Market Governance' (2002) 29 *Legal Issues of Economic Integration* 255.

[166] E Szyszczak, 'The Evolving European Employment Strategy' in J Shaw (ed), *Social Law and Policy in An Evolving European Law* (Oxford, Hart Publishing, 2000).

[167] EC Commission, 'European Commission Adopts an Instrument for European Economic Governance', Press Release IP/03/508, Brussels, 8 Apr 2003.

One of the most complex issues of subjecting state intervention to Community law is the tacit recognition of the need not only to safeguard the neutrality of the Community system but also to admit a wider range of stakeholders to the political processes within the developing European polity. Thus the EU has turned its attention to issues of market governance. This in turn raises issues of how to govern or manage the Internal Market and leave room for a wider range of values which are making demands upon the integration project. These wider values include Citizenship questions as well as the policy statements emerging from the EC Commission Competition Directorate which address efficiency, consumer welfare and competitiveness as part of modern consumer–citizen values, and rights.

One battleground which is addressed in Chapters 4, 6 and 7 of this book is the continued provision of public services in the liberalised markets. Some Member States, interest groups and consumer protection lobbyists have attempted to ringfence the provision of such services in the liberalised markets. But the liberalisation processes have broken down the conceptual and psychological barriers which held that such services can best (and perhaps *only*) be provided by the state. Liberalisation has created the means, through regulation, whereby public services can also be provided closer to consumer demands by non-state actors. This in turn has created new obligations for such providers in private and consumer law.

The EU has responded by experimenting with new forms of economic governance in the competition field,[168] for example, the use of the open method of coordination, greater accountability and transparency through scoreboards, the State Aid Register and the weekly e-news bulletin. This wider dissemination of Community policy allows a greater role for private parties in the enforcement of Community law and the creation of policy.

The Court has contributed to these developments by increasing the judicial and procedural rights of stakeholders. In the healthcare cases the Court draws upon procedural ideas, which are part of the general principles of Community law, that all acts which relate to the application of Community law must be subject to judicial or quasi-judicial control.[169] The Court held that any prior administrative authorisation scheme must be based upon a procedural system which is easily accessible and capable of ensuring that the request for authorisation will be dealt with objectively and impartially within a reasonable time, and refusals to grant authorisation must also be capable of being challenged[170] in judicial or quasi-judicial proceedings.

---

[168] See E Szyszczak, 'Experimental Governance: The Open Method of Co-ordination' (2006) 12 *ELJ* 486 and 'The Regulation of Competition' in N Shuibhne (ed), *The Regulation of the Internal Market* (Cheltenham, Edward Elgar, 2006).

[169] See Szyszczak above n 165 and the Opinion of Darmon AG in Case 222/84 *Johnston v RUC* [1986] ECR 1651.

[170] Case C-3/85 *Muller-Fauré* [2003] ECRI-4509, para. 86.

In the golden shares cases we see the Court also using procedural propriety as a means of allowing the Member States the ability to use golden shares but ensuring that the exercise of the rights allowed interested parties the procedural means to review the exercise of the rights. In *Commission v Portugal* [171] the Court ruled that the Portuguese law which restricted the acquisition of shares in newly privatised companies without prior authorisation could not be justified on economic policy grounds. The Portuguese government attempted to argue that the authorisation was necessary to ensure that the investment would not jeopardise either the strengthening of the competitive structure of the market place or the modernisation of the particular sector.[172] The Court sets out criteria for a prior authorisation scheme: it must be objective, non-discriminatory in character and the criteria must be known in advance to the undertakings concerned. All persons affected by the restrictive measure must have a legal remedy available to them.

CONCLUSION

This Chapter has set the legal, political and economic scene for analysing the regulation of state intervention in markets. It has provided glimpses of the way the slow development of an EU industrial policy was enhanced by the application of the free movement (Internal Market) and competition rules to Member State economic activity, and this has led to changes in the attitude towards the Member States' direct intervention in the market. The Member States' retreat from economic sovereignty allowed new markets to emerge. These changes have been driven by the agenda of individual litigation, EC Commission policy and the role played by the European Courts in mediating the various tensions between non-State economic actors, the Member States *inter se* and the Member States and the EU. The following chapters expand upon the substantive development of these processes. The primary focus of this book is upon the application of the competition rules, since this area has been neglected at the expense of the emphasis upon the role played by the four economic freedoms in the process of the (de)-regulation of state economic and regulatory sovereignty in the Internal Market.[173] Another significant feature of these processes which is explored in the chapters of this book is the use of the new procedures offered by Community law to litigants and the national courts. This has allowed the European Courts to

---

[171] Case C–367/89 [2002] ECR I–4731, para 50.

[172] Cf the wider acceptance of public interest justification of what is *prima facie* a protective measure in Case C–452/01 *Ospelt v Schössle Weissenberg Familienstiftung* [2003] ECR I–9743.

[173] See, *inter alia*, M Poiares Maduro, *We. the Court: The European Court of Justice and the European Economic Constitution* (Oxford, Hart, 1998); S Weatherill, 'Recent Case Law Concerning the Free Movement of Goods: Mapping the Frontiers of Market Deregulation' (1999) 36 *CMLRev* 51; D Chalmers, C Hadjiemmanuil, G Monti and A Tomkins, *European Union Law, Text and Materials*, (Cambridge, CUP, 2006) Chs 11, 15,

avoid prescribing openly a particular *form* of economic policy but, instead, has shifted the political balance away from Member State sovereign power towards the rule of economic law.

2

Article 81 EC

CHAPTER 1 ARGUED THAT the interest in regulating state intervention in the economy corresponded with the development of the Internal Market programme during the 1990s. However if we analyse the legal tools of the EC Treaty that have been utilised to direct and complement the rapid political and economic adaptations of state intervention in competitive markets the underlying rationale for curbing state economic power can be found in pre-1992 decisions of the Court. In this and the next Chapter we shall analyse the application of the competition rules contained in Articles 81 and 82 EC to state measures. Chapter 4 addresses the role of Article 86 EC.

The competition rules are addressed to all kinds of *undertakings* which are economic actors on the market. Certain provisions specifically address state intervention, for example, Article 86 EC and the rules relating to state aid in Articles 87–89 EC. The competition rules of the EC Treaty are designed to encourage and maintain competition within the Internal Market by facilitating an efficient allocation of market resources among the Member States of the EU. To this end the EC Commission, the Court of First Instance and the Court of Justice have applied the competition rules to anti-competitive market *behaviour* as well as anti-competitive changes in market *structure*. This is because the competition rules of the EU serve a number of purposes, *inter alia* to facilitate economic integration, to promote efficiency and to protect consumer interests as well as pursuing public interest goals, such as the creation of employment, protection of the environment, social and regional cohesion. Until recently,[1] the

---

[1] A modernisation process is in place, which can be traced back to the modernisation of the vertical restraints Block Exemption (Reg 270/99, [1999] OJ L336/21. To date procedures relating to Arts 81 and 82 EC have been modernised in Reg 1/2003/EC [2003] OJ.L1/1. There is a DG Competition discussion paper on the application of Art 82 of the Treaty to exclusionary abuses, available at: http://ec.europa.eu/comm/competition/antitrust/others/discpaper2005.pdf. In 2007 a White Paper on damages actions for breach of the competition rules is expected to be adopted. The EC Commission also adopted a State Aid Action Plan—Less and Better Targeted State Aid: a roadmap for state aid reform 2005—2009, available at http://europa.eu/scadplus/leg/en/lvb/l26115.htm.

competition rules have survived virtually unscathed and are increasingly catego-
rised as central elements of the free market constitution of the EU.[2] The Court of
Justice has also recognised the centrality of the competition provisions of the EC
Treaty:

> Article 81 (ex 85) constitutes a fundamental provision which is essential for the
> accomplishment of the tasks entrusted to the Community and, in particular, for the
> functioning of the internal market.[3]

Articles 81 and 82 EC are designed, and have been interpreted, primarily to
control the behaviour of *private* economic actors, by *complementing* the four
freedoms of the EC Treaty. It would be pointless to remove state barriers to free
trade if private operators could partition the Internal Market along commercial
geographic boundaries. However, it was recognised in 1957, and increasingly so
today, that state intervention in the market may distort market competition as
well as having an effect on inter-state trade. Thus, the Court, responding to
opportunist litigation, has developed principles applying the competition rules of
Articles 81 and 82 EC to state regulatory measures. But the Court has taken on an
unruly horse. The Court has assumed the role of maintaining, what Bacon[4]
describes as a 'fragile equilibrium', between the remorseless drive to create a single
market based upon free competition and the reflexive action on the part of some
Member States to retain autonomy in the sphere of domestic economic policy.
However, as Sauter notes:

> More recently, strengthened by the consensus of the internal market programme, the
> competition policy of the Community has imposed increasingly strict limits on state
> intervention in the economy.[5]

At stake is not only the issue of the balance of competing interests, that is, which
law should take priority, national or Community law, but also the question of
what kind of *values* are inherent in the EU legal order.

THE TELEOLOGICAL APPROACH

When addressing the regulation of state intervention in the market the Court has
not used Articles 81 and 82 EC in isolation. Instead it has used a teleological

---

[2] See P Larouche, *Competition Law and Regulation in European Telecommunications* (Oxford,
Hart, 2000) at 119.
[3] Case C–126/97 *Eco Swiss China Time Ltd. v Benetton International NV* [1999] ECR I–3055, para
36; See also Case C– 453/99 *Courage v Crehan* [2001] ECR I–6297.
[4] K Bacon, 'State Regulation of the Market and EC Competition Rules: Articles 85 and 86
Compared' (1997) 18 *ECLR* 283.
[5] W Sauter, *Competition Law and Industrial Policy in the EU* (Oxford, Clarendon Press, 1997) at
229.

interpretation of these legal provisions by referring to the general principles upon which the EC Treaty is based, in particular Article 3(1)(g) EC and the legal duties of the Member States under the Treaty outlined in Article 10 EC.

Article 3(1)(g) EC states that:

> For the purposes set out in Article 2, the activities of the Community shall include, as provided in this Treaty and in accordance with the timetable set out therein:
>
> ..
>
> (g) a system ensuring that competition in the internal market is not distorted.

Article 3(1)(g) EC was used by the Court in *Continental Can,* [6] revealing its value as a teleological tool to stretch the Treaty provisions in order to give effect to the purposes and aims of the Treaty. In *Continental Can* the Court used Article 3(1)(g) EC to apply Article 82 EC to control changes in the *structure* of the market. Previous case law had focused upon market behaviour.

Article 10 EC is known as the 'fidelity', 'supremacy' or 'solidarity' clause of the EC Treaty.[7] Article 10 EC imposes both positive and negative obligations upon the Member States:

> Member States shall take all appropriate measures, whether general or particular, to ensure fulfilment of the obligations arising out of this treaty or resulting from action taken by the institutions of the Community. They shall facilitate the achievement of the Community's tasks.
>
> They shall abstain from any measure which could jeopardise the attainment of the objectives of this Treaty.

Article 10(2) EC is dependent upon other Treaty provisions for its application. For example, in *Banchero*[8] the Court states that:

> [Article 10] requires Member States to carry out their obligations under Community law in good faith. It is, however, settled case law that this provision cannot be applied independently when the situation concerned is governed by a specific provision of the Treaty.

---

[6] Case 6/72 *Europemballage Corporation and Continental Can Company Inc. v Commission of the European Communities* [1973] ECR 215.

[7] See J Temple Lang, 'Community Constitutional Law: Article 5 EEC Treaty' (1990) 27 *CMLRev* 646.

[8] Case C–387/93 *Criminal Proceedings Against Giorgio Domingo Banchero* [1995] ECR I–4683, para 17.

In a case concerning the relationship between national competition law and Community law, *Walt Wilhelm*,[9] the Court established the principle that the Member States must neither introduce nor retain measures capable of prejudicing the effectiveness of the EC Treaty or compromise its full and uniform application.

This wide-ranging duty has to be squared with the principle of democratic federalism. This principle embodies the idea that under a federal structure states retain all powers that are not expressly granted to the federal government. This notion of the division of competence between the EU and the Member States is expressly recognised by the Court in *Van Gend en Loos*.[10] Given that nearly every form of state regulation may, in principle, have anti-competitive effects the line must be drawn between those acts of state which harm the operation of the Internal Market and those acts which are still within the province of state competence. Otherwise, as Gagliardi points out:

> The opposite conclusion would grant federal courts the authority to second guess (i.e. to control) every state regulation of the economy...[11]

ARTICLE 81(1) EC

Article 81 EC addresses the anti-competitive effects of the behaviour of two or more undertakings. A variety of acts may be caught by Article 81(1) EC: agreements, decisions by associations of undertakings and concerted practices. The concept of an undertaking is not defined in the Treaty, but the EC Commission and the Court have given the term a wide meaning. The classic definition of an undertaking is taken from the Court's definition in a case involving the combination of Article 86(1) EC with Article 82 EC, concerning the abuse of a dominant position by the German federal public employment agency, *Höfner v Macrotron*:

> the concept of an undertaking encompasses every entity engaged in an economic activity, regardless of the legal status of the entity and the way it is financed.[12]

Two sets of issues have arisen in the litigation before the Court. The first set relates to the question of what constitutes an 'economic entity' for the purposes of the application of the competition law rules and principles. In the context of this book the most significant cases here are cases relating to public bodies which

---

[9]   Case 14/68 *Walt Wilhelm and others v Bundeskartellamt* [1969] ECR 1.
[10]   Case 26/62 [1963] ECR 1.
[11]   A Gagliardi, 'United States and European Union Antitrust versus State Regulation of the Economy: Is There a Better Test?' (2000) 25 *ELRev* 367, 369.
[12]   Case C–41/90 [1991] ECR I–1979, para 21.

the Court has argued are subject to the general rules and principles of competition law.[13] The use of contracting out by the Member States to provide a range of public services which are for the benefit of all citizens has led the Court to develop a particular jurisprudence for these kinds of activities. This has developed under Article 86 EC and is discussed in later chapters. The second set of issues relates to defining the boundaries of the undertaking: where does one undertaking end and another one begin?[14] What emerges from the Court's case law is that the concept of an undertaking has to be defined in terms of 'economic units' rather than 'legal units'.[15] These distinctions are important for our understanding of *how* the state organises economic activity and *how far* the state's organisation of such activity may be caught by the competition rules.

Where there is an act which is caught by Article 81(1) EC it must be shown that it may affect trade between the Member States. The effect on trade may be positive or negative. The act must have the 'object or effect' of preventing, restricting or distorting competition within the Common Market. A set of illustrations of agreements which will in particular infringe Article 81(1) EC is given. Article 81(2) EC makes any agreements or decisions caught by Article 81(1) EC void.

Finally Article 81(3) EC provides the possibility of an exemption from Article 81(1) EC where a restrictive agreement may have beneficial effects. Prior to Regulation 1/2003[16] the EC Commission held a monopoly on granting individual exemptions and also adopted a number of Block Exemptions. It should be borne in mind that Articles 81 and 82 EC are regarded as separate provisions, tackling different kinds of uncompetitive behaviour; conduct which is acceptable under Article 81 EC may still infringe Article 82 EC.

THE GENESIS OF THE *EFFET UTILE* DOCTRINE

In a number of the early cases brought under the competition law provisions of the Treaty the Court chose *not* to address the issue of whether state measures could be brought within the ambit of Article 81 or Article 82 EC.[17] In *Capolongo*[18] Advocate General Roemer *explicitly* ruled out the idea that Article 82 EC might apply to a state measure which created a tax benefit for a dominant firm. The Court did not address the issue.

---

[13] *Ibid.*

[14] See, eg, Case 15/74 *Centrafarm BV et Adriaan de Peijper v Sterling Drug Inc* [1974] ECR 1147.

[15] See, eg, Case 170/83 *Hydrotherm Gerätebau GmbH v Compact del Dott. Ing. Mario Andreoli & C. Sas.* [1985] ECR 3016; Case T–11/89 *Shell v Commission* [1992] ECR II–884. For further discussion see W Wils, 'The Undertaking as Subject of E.C. Competition Law and the Imputation of Infringements to Natural or Legal Persons" (2000) 25 *ELRev* 99.

[16] [2003] OJ L1/1.

[17] Eg, Case 78/70 *Deutsche Grammophon Gesellschaft mbH v Metro-SB-Großmärkte GmbH & Co. KG* [1971] ECR 497.

[18] Case 77/72 *Carmine Capolongo v Azienda Agricola Maya* [1973] ECR 611.

In *Geddo*[19] and *ENCC*[20] we see the interaction of public bodies and the competition rules. *Geddo* concerned a charge levied on purchases of paddy rice, the revenue raised being used to fund a public body carrying out research in order to raise awareness and increase the consumption of rice. One of the questions referred to the Court was whether the charge, and the use made of it, could constitute an abuse of a dominant position within the meaning of Article 82 EC. The Court held that Article 82 EC was not infringed. *ENCC* concerned a public agency which collected and redistributed duties on paper products originating from other Member States. The Court was asked to rule on whether Articles 81 and 82 EC were infringed. Here the Court ruled that the public agency was not caught by Articles 81 and 82 EC, since it was an institution of a public nature.

In exploring the use of Articles 81 and 82 EC to regulate state intervention in the market many of the early cases reveal the close interaction between the competition rules and the rules now contained in Articles 28–31 EC on the free movement of goods.[21] The starting point in the case law which led to the doctrine of Member State liability under the competition rules can be traced back to *GB-INNO v ATAB*.[22] *GB-INNO* engaged in a litigation strategy[23] to challenge a number of regulatory burdens imposed by national laws on undertakings operating within the Member State. Such litigation offends the principle of democratic federalism and representative democracy 'according to which the decisions of a constituency are binding on its members'.[24] Thus, the litigation touched the heart of national sovereignty and set in train a complex body of case law which, in principle, allowed the use of the Community free movement and competition rules to challenge national regulatory measures, designed to regulate the *national* market.

GB-INNO concerned Belgian legislation which fixed binding retail prices on tobacco. Tobacco was subject to an *ad valorem* excise duty calculated on the basis of the retail selling price plus VAT. The manufacturer or importer set the basic price of tobacco and then bought tax labels which were attached to each product before it was sent to the retailer. When purchasing the tax labels the manufacturer or importer paid excise duty and VAT. The tax label stated the retail selling price, and under Belgian law retailers were prohibited from selling the tobacco for any price other than the one stated on the tax label. A Belgian supermarket chain, GB

---

[19] Case 2/73 *Riseria Luigi Geddo v Ente Nazionale Risi* [1973] ECR 865.
[20] Case 94/74 *Industria Gomma Articoli vari, IGAV v Ente Nazionale per la Cellulosa e per la carta, ENCC* [1975] ECR 699.
[21] See *Deutsche Grammophon*, above n 17.
[22] Case 13/77 *GB-INNO v ATAB* [1977] ECR 2115.
[23] Such litigants have been described as 'professional' litigants (M Poiares Maduro, *We the Court* (Oxford, Hart, 1997) at 29) or 'repeat players' (R Rawlings, 'The Euro-law Game: Deductions From A Saga' (1993) 20 *Journal of Legal Studies* 309) or 'opportunistic' (E Szyszczak, 'Free Trade as a Fundamental Value' in K Economides *et al* (eds), *Fundamental Values* (Oxford, Hart, 2000).
[24] Gagliardi, above n 11, at 370.

Enterprises, the predecessor of GB-INNO-BM, had been selling tobacco at a price below the price stated on tax labels. ATAB arranged for a court official to record a finding that GB Enterprises was offering for sale and selling cigarettes more cheaply than the price on the specified tax label and brought proceedings before the Commercial Court for an order for the practice to be discontinued and an official decision to that effect.

The importance of this phase of the development of Community law from a constitutional perspective is noted by Poiares Maduro. He argues that in utilising Community law to create the 'European defence' to defend, but also indirectly to *challenge,* national regulation such litigation raised the possibility of developing new trends in Community law:

> On the one hand this helps the legitimacy of Community law which provides individuals with new rights *vis-à-vis* national political processes and gives them a new voice in the discourse shaping the European Economic Constitution. It may also help in promoting legislative innovation at national level and challenge national regulatory regimes dominated by special interests.[25]

Of crucial significance is the fact that *GB-INNO* raised the issue of the *interconnected* use of the competition rules *and* the free movement rules to challenge national regulatory autonomy. The early cases rely on the interaction of the competition and free movement of goods rules, but more recently a similar litigation strategy has emerged using the free movement of services provisions.

The Court addressed the issue by observing that a national court was obliged to take into account all the relevant Treaty Articles, namely: Articles 3(1)(g), 10(2), 28, 29 and 81 to 89 EC. The Court drew a clear parallel between Articles 3(1)(g), 10(2) and 82 EC and the obligations of a Member State under Article 86 EC. The Court's ruling is complicated and lacks clarity. The case reveals the Court's willingness to address the various Treaty provisions which may be infringed, but also its reluctance or inability to think through the way in which the various Treaty provisions interact.

The interconnectedness of the competition rules and the free movement of goods rules is seen much earlier and from the opposite perspective in the language of *Dassonville,*[26] when the Court gave a broad and authoritative definition of the concept of measures having an equivalent effect to quantitative restrictions in Article 28 EC as:

> All trading rules enacted by Member States which are capable of hindering, directly or indirectly, actually or potentially, intra-Community trade are to be considered as measures having a effect equivalent to quantitative restrictions.[27]

---

[25] Above n 23, at 29.
[26] Case 8/74 *Procureur du Roi v Dassonville* [1974] ECR 837.
[27] *Ibid.,* para 5.

This wide-ranging definition provided enough breadth to allow the Court to use it not so much as a rule, but as a *standard,* to keep under review actions of the Member States which might hinder intra-Community trade.[28]

In its judgment in *GB-INNO v ATAB* the Court cites the wide statement from *Dassonville*[29] on concerning the scope of Article 28 EC, but moves on to consider Articles 3(1)(g) and 82 EC. The Court also refers to Article 81 EC but dismisses its application since the referring Court had raised only the possibility of the application of Article 82 EC. Reference is made also to Article 86 EC. The Court's starting premise was a finding that, in the then current state of Community law, each Member State retained sovereignty to choose its own method of fiscal control over manufactured tobacco on sale in its territory.[30]

What is crucial in the *GB-INNO* ruling is the first reference to Article 10(2) EC which provides the *link* between Articles 81 and 82 EC and state action. At paragraph 31 the Court creates the ideas which will form the *effet utile* doctrine:

> while it is true that [Article 82] is directed at undertakings, nonetheless it is also true that the Treaty imposes a duty on member states not to adopt or maintain in force any measure which could deprive that provision of its effectiveness.

Inspired by the formulation of the questions from the national court, the Court develops a *principle* that the competition rules, designed to apply to private economic actors, can also be applied to the actions of the Member States using the conduit of Article 10(2) EC.

The *GB-INNO* case is puzzling from a number of perspectives. The criss-crossing between various Treaty Articles has attracted analytical comment from a number of commentators. Quite clearly, at this early stage of the Court's evolution, the Court had not worked out the scope of the Treaty rules and the various ways in which the Treaty provisions should interact. Hoffman[31] argues that the reference to Article 28 EC represents the 'bright line' between Member States' economic policies and the competence of the Community to create a common market. Hoffman's analysis of *GB-INNO* draws the conclusion that the Member States have not surrendered the sovereignty to regulate their own economies, but that their powers are now explicitly circumscribed or limited by the application of Article 28 EC where state action interferes with the free movement of goods between the Member States. In contrast Verstrynge[32] focuses

---

[28] W Wils, 'The Search For the Rule in Article 30 EEC: Much Ado about Nothing?' (1993) 18 *ELRev* 475.

[29] Above n 26.

[30] *Ibid,* at para 14.

[31] A Hoffman, 'Anticompetitive State Legislation Condemned Under Articles 5, 85 and 86 of the EEC Treaty: How Far Should the Court Go After *Van Eycke*?' (1990) 15 *ECLR* 1.

[32] J-F Verstrynge, 'The Obligations of Member States As Regards Competition in the EEC Treaty' in B Hawk (ed), *Annual Proceedings of the Fordham Corporate Law Institute* (New York, Fordham, 1989).

on Article 86 EC, arguing that this Article is used to give extra weight to the fidelity clause of Article 10(2) EC when the specific conditions of Article 86 EC have been satisfied.

It was not until eight years later that the new doctrine came into its own in another case, *Leclerc v Au Blé Vert*[33] which involved criss-crossing between various Treaty provisions. In the intervening period the Court was asked to address issues of the compatibility of state laws which involved price fixing but was unwilling to apply Articles 10(2) and 81 EC. 35 In some cases, for example, *Duphar*,[34] the Court is adamant that Articles 81 and 82 EC are applicable to undertakings and are *not* relevant for determining whether national legislation is in conformity with Community law. Similarly in *Van de Haar and Kaveka de Meern*[35] the Court distinguishes the objectives of Article 28 EC and the competition rules. In some cases during this period Article 28 EC was found to be infringed.[36] In *Van Tiggele*[37] the Court links squarely the loss of a competitive advantage enjoyed by imported goods to a market where a state has retail price maintenance laws. This is seen as a form of discrimination bringing into play Article 28 EC.[38] The classification of such cases as discrimination cases is difficult to justify, since often the national measures are being attacked by nationals of the Member State for the simple reason that the regulatory control hinders their commercial freedom to trade on their own terms. Equally, in order to show that there is discrimination there should be evidence that imported goods are at a disadvantage as a result of the national regulation. Thus, while Article 28 EC is used as the legal basis to strike down the national law, arguably competition law principles are the underlying rationale for finding the measures to be contrary to the EC Treaty.

Explanations for this case law can be made by viewing the cases purely from the internal logic of the development of the Court's role in economic integration as a result of the ruling in *Cassis de Dijon*[39] which, together with the *Dassonville*[40] ruling, gave an expansionist role to Article 28 EC. *Cassis* itself was a test case organised and brought on behalf on various interest groups in the alcohol

---

[33] Case 229/83 [1985] ECR 1; See also Case 254/87 *Syndicat des libraires de Normandie v L'Aigle distribution SA* [1988] ECR 4457.

[34] Case 238/82 *Duphar BV and Others v The Netherlands* [1984] ECR 523. See also Joined Cases 177 and 178/82 *Criminal Proceedings Against Jan van de Haar and Kaveka de Meern BV* [1984] ECR 1797.

[35] *Ibid*, at paras 11–12.

[36] See, eg, Case 82/77 *Ministère public du Kingdom of the Netherlands v Jacobus Philippus van Tiggele* [1978] ECR 25; Case 181/82 *Roussel Laboratoria BV and Others v The Netherlands* [1983] ECR 3849.

[37] Case 82/77, above n 36.

[38] See L Gormley, 'Actually or Potentially, Directly or Indirectly? Obstacles to Free Movement of Goods' (1990) 15 *Yearbook of European Law* 197.

[39] Case 120/78 *Rewe-Zentralfinanz AG v Bundesmonopolverwaltung für Branntwein* [1979] ECR 649.

[40] Case 8/74 *Procureur du Roi v Dassonville* [1974] ECR 837.

industry.[41] In the hands of the Court the authority and impact of Community law had grown enormously, paradoxically at a time when political commitments to economic integration were waning and losing direction. In contrast to the Member States' resistance to integration the Court had not shied away from subjecting national policies to a European discipline, using market-building objectives based upon the guaranteed economic freedoms contained in the Treaty.

THE *EFFET UTILE* DOCTRINE

The *Leclerc v Au Blé Vert*[42] litigation took place in the context of a litigation strategy employed by a French supermarket chain challenging resale price maintenance legislation in France. A group of booksellers had tried to prevent the supermarket chain from undercutting the set resale price for books. The Court of Appeal in Poitiers referred a number of questions on the compatibility of the French law with Community competition law. In his Opinion, Advocate General Darmon did not consider Article 28 EC. He was of the view that Articles 3(1)(f), 81 and 82 EC would *not* apply unless it was shown that the resultant restriction on competition substantially compromised the application of Articles 81 and 82 EC. The Advocate General focused particular attention on Article 82 EC, combined with Article 3(f) and 10(2) EC. The Member State's legislation might possibly encourage behaviour prohibited by Article 82 EC by conferring on a single importer the power to fix retail prices of books published in another Member State. The case is significant in that it established a general principle[43] and a two-limb test to be applied in order to ascertain whether a Member State's regulations or legislation were in breach of Community law. The general principle is enunciated as:

> whilst it is true that the rules on competition are concerned with the conduct of undertakings and not with national legislation, member states are none the less obliged under the second paragraph of [Article 10] of the Treaty not to detract, by means of national legislation, from the full and uniform application of Community law or from

---

[41] See K Alter, and S Meunier-Aitsahalia, 'Judicial Politics in the European Community—European Integration and the Pathbreaking *Cassis de Dijon* Decision' (1994) 26 *Comparative Political Studies* 535.

[42] Case 229/83 *Association des Centres distributeurs Édouard Leclerc and Others v Sàrl 'Au Blé Vert' and others* [1985] ECR 1.

[43] This classification of a general principle, and what she labels 'two prongs', is used by U Neergaard, *Competition and Competences The Tension Between European Competition Law and Anti-Competitive Measures By the Member States* (Copenhagen, DJØF, 1998).

the effectiveness of its implementing measures; nor may they introduce or maintain in force measures, even of a legislative nature, which may render ineffective the competition rules applicable to undertakings...[44]

The Court then applies the two-limb test. First, in order for the competition rules *not* to apply it must be shown that the legislation challenged does not require agreements to be concluded or results in other behaviour which might be caught by Article 81 EC. Secondly, it must be shown that the national legislation rendered corporate behaviour of the type prohibited by Article 81 EC superfluous by making the undertaking responsible for fixing retail binding prices. This would detract from the effectiveness of Article 81 EC and would be contrary to Article 10(2) EC.

One question which emerges from this early case, and remains unanswered to this day, is the issue of whether a Member State can justify legislation found to lead to an infringement of the competition rules. Under the free movement of goods provisions there is a margin of discretion in the application of Article 28 EC where there is a valid justification for a measure which is restrictive of trade. A Member State may also be able to protect a restriction on trade, either by using justifications contained in the Treaty (Article 30 EC), or by reference to the mandatory requirements doctrine developed from *Dassonville* [45] and *Cassis*. [46] Such justifications are interpreted restrictively and are subject to the principle of proportionality. Under the freedom to provide services the EC Treaty also offers some fixed justifications for state activity which is contrary to the free movement provisions, and over time the Court has expanded these ideas to embrace a generic public interest justification.[47]

Article 81(3) EC offers the scope for an exemption, which initially could only be granted by the EC Commission, to private undertakings whose behaviour infringes Article 81(1) EC.[48] Technically, there is no scope for the justification of an abuse of a dominant position under Article 82 EC, but the CFI and the Court have indicated that they will find that certain behaviour is *not* an abuse of a dominant position where it can be justified.[49] Article 86(2) EC opens up the possibility of a derogation from the Treaty rules and, in particular, the competition rules for undertakings performing services of 'general economic interest' or

---

[44] Case 229/83 *Association des Centres distributeurs Édouard Leclerc and Others v Sàrl 'Au Blé Vert' and others* [1985] ECR 1, para 14.

[45] Case 8/74 *Procureur du Roi v Dassonville* [1974] ECR 837.

[46] Case 120/78 *Rewe-Zentralfinanz AG v Bundesmonopolverwaltung für Branntwein* [1979] ECR 649.

[47] See Case C–55/94 *Gebhard* [1995] ECR I–4165.

[48] See Case C–250/92 *Gottrup-Klim e.a Grovvareforeninger v Dansk Landbrugs Grovvareselskab AmbA* [1994] ECR I–5641.

[49] The burden of proof is on the dominant undertaking: Case T–203/01 *Michelin v Commission* [2003] ECR II–4071, paras 107–109. For a discussion of the case law see EC Commission, *DG Competition Discussion Paper on the Application of Article 82 to Exclusionary Abuses*, 5.5 'Possible Defences: Objective Justifications and Efficiencies' Dec 2005.

having the character of a revenue producing monopoly where the application of the Treaty rules would obstruct the performance of these tasks. However, there is a proviso: '[t]he development of trade must not be affected to such an extent as would be contrary to the interests of the Community'.

In *Au Blé Vert* France argued that the purpose of the legislation was to protect the book market. This was seen as an important objective since books were viewed as instruments of culture. Unfettered price competition would affect the diversity and cultural level of book publishing. The EC Commission had also argued the need for special national rules to apply to the book market. Neither justification was considered by the Court, since it found that neither Article 10(2) EC nor Article 81 EC was specific enough to preclude a Member State from enacting resale price maintenance legislation for books provided that such legislation was compatible with other specific Treaty provisions, in particularly the rules relating to the free movement of goods. In applying Article 28 EC the Court was being asked to deal with an indistinctly applicable rule: the measure applied to books published in the Member State and to foreign books. There is no reference to discrimination occurring in relation to the foreign books.[50]

Poiares Maduro[51] points out that this case, alongside *GB-INNO-BM*, was not concerned with imports, but addressed national regulatory burdens placed on national undertakings. Thus what is at stake in these cases is the general restriction imposed on *access* to the market and *competition* on the market. The state's interest is in regulating the market in pursuit of public interest goals other than economic protectionism. The Court engages in a test, balancing the cost benefits of a certain national provision against the principles of free market competition, thus making the Court responsible for defining the appropriate regulatory policy.

In relation to the justification offered under Article 30 EC the Court reiterated the established principle that the free movement of goods was a fundamental right of the Treaty, and therefore any derogation from such a fundamental right must be interpreted strictly and cannot be extended to cover objectives not expressly enumerated. Neither the safeguarding of consumer interest nor the protection of creativity and cultural diversity in publishing was mentioned in Article 28 EC.[52]

The case has been the subject of much analysis and critical comment. Joliet notes that the logical reasoning and application of the Court's tests would have

---

[50]   See the thesis of Marenco who argues that in this period the decisions of the Court which address 'measures having an equivalent effect to quantitative restrictions' can be united under a theory that there is discrimination against foreign products as a result of the Member States' measures: G Marenco, 'Pour une intérpretation traditionelle de la notion de mesure d'effet equivalent à une restriction quantitative' (1984) *Cahiers de Droit Européen* 291.

[51]   M Poiares Maduro, *We the Court* (Oxford, Hart, 1997). at 63.

[52]   Case 229/83 *Association des Centres distributeurs Édouard Leclerc and Others v Sàrl 'Au Blé Vert' and others* [1985] ECR 1, para 30.

led to an application of the competition rules.[53] Hoffman suggests that this was perhaps the first conclusion drawn by the Court, but it then reconsidered the enormity of applying the competition rules to state regulation and that it chose a different solution by applying the free movement of goods provisions instead.[54] Neergaard[55] plays down the alleged innovative approach of *Au Blé Vert*. She argues that the general principle had already been established in *GB-INNO*,[56] albeit in relation to Articles 82 and 86 EC. She argues that what is important about *Au Blé Vert* is that it introduced the second limb of the test for applying the competition rules to state action. She argues that the first limb could already be found in the Court's previous case law, in particular the *Buys*[57] case. Neergaard describes the second limb of the test as the 'Community's balance of competences', that is, the Court was determining whether it was the Community or the Member State which had the power to legislate in the field in question. In *Au Blé Vert* there was no common policy in the field and the competence was not yet occupied by the EU. The competence was therefore still within the realm of Member States' jurisdiction.

THE APPLICATION OF THE *EFFET UTILE* DOCTRINE

During 1985 a series of cases followed swiftly in the footsteps of *Au Blé Vert*. The leading case, *Cullet*,[58] concerned French legislation fixing minimum prices for fuel. France defended the legislation to guarantee the supply of fuel and protect small petrol stations from larger competitors. Members of the Leclerc supermarket chain were selling fuel at petrol stations attached to the supermarkets at prices below those set in the French legislation and were prosecuted. In its ruling the Court repeated and applied the general principle and the first limb of the *Au Blé Vert* test. The Court again found that the French legislation did not intend to compel suppliers and retailers to conclude agreements or to take any action which would be contrary to Article 81(1) EC and therefore the legislation did not to deprive the competition rules of their effectiveness. The Court did not apply the second limb of the test. It did find that the French law was a measure equivalent to a quantitative restriction within the meaning of Article 28 EC since

---

[53] R Joliet, 'National Anti-competitive Legislation and Community Law' (1989) 12 *Fordham International Law Journal* 172.

[54] A Hoffman, 'Anticompetitive State Legislation Condemned Under Articles 5, 85 and 86 of the EEC Treaty: How Far Should the Court Go After *Van Eycke*?' (1990) 15 *ECLR* 1.

[55] U. Neergaard, *Competition and Competetnces The Tension Between European Competition Law and Anti-Competitive Measures By the Member States* (Copenhagen, DJØF, 1998).

[56] Case 13/77 [1977] ECR 2115.

[57] Case 5/79 *Procureur Général v Hans Buys, Hans Pesch, Yves Dullieux and Denkavit France Sarl* [1979] ECR 3203.

[58] Case 231/83 *Henri Cullet and Chambre Syndicale des réparateurs automobiles et détaillants de produits pétroliers v Centre Leclerc Toulouse and Centre Leclerc Saint-Orens-de-Gameville* [1985] ECR 305.

imports could not benefit fully from lower cost prices in the country of origin. Both the Advocate General VerLoren Van Themaat and the Court rejected the French government's defence of the measure under the public policy ground of Article 30 EC. The French government had argued that in the absence of price control there would be civil disturbances, blockades and violence.

The ruling in *Cullet* was followed by a number of rulings concerning price fixing policies endorsed or encouraged by the various Member States.[59] While the Court recognises the general principle that a Member State's actions may infringe Articles 81 and 82 EC when read with Article 10(2) EC , in each case the Court does not find a breach of the principle.

One case which is of note is *Bulk Oil (Zug) AG v Sun International Limited and Sun Oil Trading Company* [60] which concerned a *policy* of the United Kingdom government restricting the export of crude oil to non-EC countries. The policy had not been translated into legislation or any other kind of legally binding measure. Although the policy did not infringe Community law, the case reveals the Court's willingness to extend the review of Member States' intervention in the market to *policies* of the Member States.

In contrast, in a case decided the day after the *Cullet* ruling, *BNIC v Clair*,[61] the Court found a price fixing agreement contrary to the competition provisions of the Treaty where it was based upon Member State regulation. Clair had bought cognac from a number of wine producers at prices lower than those permitted under an agreement negotiated within the framework of the BNIC, a trade organisation established by ministerial orders for the cognac and wine industry. The BNIC was composed of members of trade organisations for the industry, a Government Commissioner and an independent Chairman, all appointed by the Minister for Agriculture. Minimum prices for the wine and cognac industry were set by an agreement within BNIC pursuant to a law of 1975. The French government approved the prices and the BNIC agreement was made binding by an Order issued in 1980. The Court of Justice found the BNIC agreement to be in violation of Article 81 EC. BNIC had argued that the minimum price fixing agreement was not binding and that its role was merely to advise the French government. Only the Ministerial Orders had binding effect. The Court dismissed this defence. The case did not address the fact that the BNIC agreement was based upon a Member State's legislation and actively encouraged by the French government. This issue was not raised by the referring national court and not considered by the Court of Justice. Two years later, however, a production quota system agreed within the framework of BNIC was found to be contrary to

---

[59] See, *inter alia,* Case 11/84 *Procureur de la République v Christian Gratiot* [1985] ECR 2907; Case 34/84 *Procureur de la République v Michel Leclerc* [1985] ECR 2915; Joined Cases 79 & 80/84 *Procureur de la République v Claude Chabaud and Jean-Louis Rémy* [1985] ECR 2953.

[60] Case 174/85 [1986] ECR 559.

[61] Case 123/83 *Bureau national interprofessionnel du cognac v Guy Clair* [1985] ECR 391.

Article 81 EC, and also the Ministerial Order, making the agreement binding, was found to be contrary to the Member States' obligations under Articles 10(2) and 81 EC.[62]

AN ECONOMIC DUE PROCESS CLAUSE?

This early case law led to allegations that the Court was developing an economic due process clause by the use of Article 28 EC and the competition rules to review state intervention in the market. The role of Article 28 EC in the process of European integration is addressed by Advocate General Tesauro in his Opinion in the later case of *Hünermund* when he asks:

> Is Article [28] of the Treaty a provision intended to liberalise intra-Community trade or is it intended more generally to encourage the unhindered pursuit of commerce in individual Member States?[63]

Poiares Maduro[64] argues that the concept of an economic due process clause leads to a recognition that the Treaty rules are, and can be, used not just to address discrimination or protectionism against imported goods, but can also further a concept of a free market, open competition and a particular view of the *kinds* of regulation that are acceptable. Judicial review of state intervention in the market facilitates this process. However, as Poiares Maduro points out, the scope granted to Article 28 EC was so wide that it was this Article that controlled, and continues to control, the application of competition values to challenge national regulations.[65] This in turn led to much academic and judicial disquiet over the role Article 28 EC was being asked to perform.[66]

THE SUCCESSFUL CASES

Vlaamse Reisbureaus[67] is the first case which linked a contested state measure to an infringement of Article 81(1) EC. The case concerned a number of Belgian

---

[62] Case 136/86 *Bureau National Interprofessionnel du Cognac v Yves Aubert* [1987] ECR 4789.

[63] Case C–292/92 *Ruth Hünermund and others v Landesapothekerkammer Baden-Württemberg* [1993] ECR I–6787, para 1.

[64] M Poiares Maduro, *We the Court* (Oxford, Hart, 1997).

[65] *Ibid*, at 76.

[66] See, eg, E White, 'In Search of the Limits to Article 30 of the EEC Treaty' (1989) 26 *CMLRev* 235; J Steiner, 'Drawing The Line: Uses and Abuses of Article 30 EEC; (1992) 29 *CMLRev* 749; K Mortelmans, 'Article 30 of the EEC Treaty and Legislation Relating To Market Circumstances: Time to Consider a New Definition' (1991) 28 *CMLRev* 115; D Chalmers, 'Free Movement of Goods Within the European Community: an Unhealthy Addiction to Scotch Whisky?' (1993) 42 *International and Comparative Law Quarterly* 269.

[67] Case 311/85 *VZW Vereniging van Vlaamse Reisebureaus v VZW Sociale Dienst van de Plaatselijke en Gewestelijke Overheidsdiensten* [1987] ECR 3801.

laws which prohibited the transfer of travel agents' commission to customers. The association of Flemish travel agencies accused the Sociale Dienst (which acted as a travel agent for public service employees) of giving rebates to its clients who booked holidays with it. The rebates constituted the amount of commission which would normally have been paid to travel agents. The Court interpreted one of the questions referred by the national court as whether the laws were compatible with Articles 3(g), 10(2) and 81 EC. In this ruling there is a new formulation of the tests which focuses upon activities taking place *prior* to the enactment of the national measures.

In relation to the first limb, whether the evidence produced disclosed the existence of agreements, decisions or concerted practices, the Court ruled that this can be satisfied merely by proving the *existence* of such agreements. The Court found that there was a system of agreements both between travel agents *inter se* and between travel agents and tour operators. The Court found that the agreements had the object and effect of restricting competition between travel agents and that such agreements could affect trade between the Member States.

In relation to the second limb of the test, whether the provisions of the Belgian laws were intended to reinforce the effects of such agreements, decisions or concerted practices, the Court found the Belgian laws 'as contrary to fair commercial practice[68] and incompatible with the competition rules. The Court applied, with some clarity and rigour, a number of criteria. It looked to see whether an original contractual prohibition was transformed into a permanent legislative restriction which the parties could no longer alter, whether the legislation contained any legal remedies which allowed the cartel members to enforce compliance with the rules and, finally, whether there were other sanctions which could be used against non-compliant undertakings.

The judgment also attracted comment. Neergaard[69] argues that the second limb of the test is not new, but can be traced back to the earlier case of *Asjes*.[70] The latter case concerned French legislation setting minimum prices for airline tickets. Although the Court held that the sector of air transport remained within the competence of the Member States it introduced the idea that where a Member State reinforced the effects of anti-competitive agreements it would be liable under Article 81 EC. At paragraph 72 of the judgment in *Asjes* the Court argued that the competition rules would be infringed:

> in particular, if a member state were to require or favour the adoption of agreements, decisions or concerted practices contrary to [Article 81 EC] or reinforce the effects thereof.

---

[68]   *Ibid*, at para 24.
[69]   U Neergaard, *Competition and Competences The Tension Between European Competition Law and Anti-Competitive Measures By the Member States* (Copenhagen, DJØF, 1998) at 62.
[70]   Joined Cases 209–213/84 *Ministère public v Lucas Asjes and others, Andrew Gray and others, Jacques Maillot and others and Léo Ludwig and others* [1986] ECR 529.

In contrast to Neergaard, Joliet[71] points to the wide language used in *Vlaamse Reisbureaus*, arguing that the general terms of 'legislative provisions or regulations' gives the case a wide impact.[72] The impact of *Asjes* is described by Van der Esch as prohibiting a Member State from legitimately building a house of state intervention on a cartel basement.[73]

The ruling in *Vlaamse Reisbureaus* was followed very quickly by the ruling in *Aubert*.[74] As in *Clair*,[75] the facts concerned the production of cognac in France. While the *Clair* case had focused upon the *agreement*, *Aubert* focused upon the *state measure*. In this case the United Kingdom government in its submissions had specifically asked for clarification of the roles of Article 10(2) and 81 EC in their application to state regulations. BNIC had established a quota system which had been made binding by a Ministerial Order and a Law. Aubert had exceeded his quota and was penalised by BNIC pursuant to the Ministerial Order and the Law. The Court reformulated the questions to inquire whether the BNIC quota violated Article 81(1) EC and whether the Ministerial Order, which made the quota system binding, infringed Articles 3(g), 10(2) and 81(1) EC. The Court found that the *agreement* established by BNIC infringed competition rules because it penalised increases in production, thus preventing a producer from improving his position on the market. In applying the first limb of the *Vlaamse Reisbureaus* test the Court also addressed the question whether trade between the Member States was capable of being affected and found this to be the case. The Court then moved on to address the Ministerial Order reinforcing the agreement. After repeating the general principle, the Court addressed the second limb of the *Vlaamse Reisbureaus* case, finding that the Ministerial Order made the BNIC agreement binding, and thereby reinforced the effects of an agreement which was itself contrary to Article 81(1) EC.

A new dimension is raised in this case: the application of Article 81(1) EC to the acts of the state raises the issue of whether a Member State may rely upon Article 81(3) EC to justify the measure. BNIC argued that the measures were adopted to compensate for declining sales and over-production. The Court's response was terse. It replied that the justifications raised provided undertakings with no more than the basis for an application to the EC Commission for an individual exemption under Article 81(3) EC which BNIC could have applied for. BNIC had not wanted to apply for such an exemption since so doing was an admission that Article 81 EC applied to the agreement. The Court seems to suggest that only the undertaking, and not the Member State, can apply for an

---

[71] R Joliet, 'National Anti-competitive Legislation and Community Law' (1989) 12 *Fordham International Law Journal* 186.

[72] See also Case 174/85 *Bulk Oil v Zug* [1986] ECR 559.

[73] B van der Esch, 'Anticompetitive State Measures in the EEC and EEC Competition Policy and Enforcement' in B Hawk, (ed), *Annual Proceedings of the Fordham Corporate Law Institute* (New York, Fordham, 1989).

[74] Case 136/86 *BNIC v Yves Aubert* [1987] ECR 4789.

[75] Case 123/83 *BNIC v Clair* [1985] ECR 391.

exemption under Article 81(3) EC. BNIC did not want to apply for an exemption since it argued that it was a public body and that the agreement was not contrary to Article 81(1) EC.

Ahmed Saeed [76] concerned price fixing in the airline industry. Pressure had been brought to bear on the EC Commission to investigate alleged anti-competitive conduct by national champions. An action was brought by ZBW, an association campaigning against unfair competition, arguing that travel agencies were selling airline tickets at prices below those set by the Federal Minister in accordance with a German law. ZBW's argument was that the undercutting of approved tariffs was anti-competitive, since other travel agents who obeyed the German law were legally bound to sell at the approved tariff. The Court found an infringement of Article 81 EC, holding that the bilateral and multilateral agreements were void:

> It must be concluded as a result that the approval by the aeronautical authorities of tariff agreements contrary to [Article 81(1) EC] is not compatible with Community law and in particular [Article 10] of the Treaty. It also follows that the aeronautical authorities must refrain from taking any measure which might be construed as encouraging airlines to conclude tariff agreements contrary to the Treaty.[77]

Ahmed Saeed [78] is the only case where the Court gives any indication of what it understands to be the meaning of 'favouring'. It understands the nature of the problem when it states that the national authorities should 'refrain from taking any measure which might be construed as encouraging airlines to conclude a tariff agreement contrary to the Treaty'.

The Court also found that the existence of bilateral and multilateral agreements may, in certain circumstances, constitute an abuse of a dominant position where an undertaking in a dominant position has succeeded in imposing on other carriers excessively high or low tariffs or the exclusive application of only one tariff on a given route. The Court also examined the application of Article 86(1) EC, raising the possibility that the German laws could be justified under Article 86(2) EC. This is a rare example of the Court applying Articles 81(1) and 86 EC together. In theory it is difficult to bring the grant of an exclusive right within the scope of Articles 81 and 86 EC since Article 81 EC deals with agreements between two or more *undertakings*. In *Bodson* [79] the Court held that the grant of an exclusive right does not fall within the scope of Article 81 EC since it links the state with either a public or a private undertaking. But, as Buendia

---

[76] Case 66/86 *Ahmed Saeed Flugreisen and Silver Line Reisebüro GmbH v Zentrale zur Bekämpfung unlauteren Wettbewerbs eV* [1989] ECR 803.

[77] *Ibid*, at para 49.

[78] *Ibid*.

[79] Case 30/87 [1988] ECR 2512, para 18.

Sierra[80] points out, one can envisage a situation where a public or private undertaking is obliged or induced by the state to grant an exclusive right to another undertaking, and that the subsequent chain of exclusive rights could be analysed in the light of Articles 86(1) and 81 EC. Furthermore, Advocate General van Gerven in his Opinion in *Port of Genoa*[81] discusses the possibility of Articles 81 and 86 EC applying to state measures which induce vertical agreements that restrict competition.

CONSOLIDATION OF THE CASE LAW

The *Van Eycke*[82] case is an important milestone in the Court's application of the competition rules to Member State action. In this case the Court pulled together many of the unresolved issues from previous decisions and established a new test, now consisting of three limbs.[83] The case concerned vigorous competition in the Belgian banking sector which had led to high interest rates being offered to encourage investments. Various financial institutions had in 1985 entered into self-regulatory agreements which set a maximum rate for interest on savings. This self-regulation did not work, and therefore the Belgian government issued a decree in 1986. A dispute arose between Van Eycke and a financial institution, ASPA NV. ASPA NV had offered attractive interest rates, but when Van Eycke attempted to open an account he was informed that due to a new Belgian Royal Decree of 1986 the terms could no longer be offered. Van Eycke brought proceedings against the bank arguing that because the Decree was contrary to Article 81(1) EC the bank could not rely upon the Decree to defend its actions.

The Court, first of all, adds the fidelity clause of Article 10(2) EC to the national court's limited question asking whether the law is contrary to Article 81(1) EC. The Court repeats the 'general principle' and, at the same time, states that Articles 81 and 82 EC *per se* only concern the conduct of *undertakings*. The Court then sets out a three-limb test which can be summarised as follows. National legislation would be void if a Member State were to require or favour the adoption of agreements, decisions or concerted practices contrary to Article 81 EC; *or* to reinforce the effects of such agreements; *or* to deprive its own

---

[80] J-L Buendia Sierra, *Exclusive Rights and State Monopolies Under EC Law* (Oxford, OUP, 1999) at 290.

[81] Case C–179/90 [1991] ECR I–5889, para 23.

[82] Case 267/86 *Pascal Van Eycke v ASPA NV* [1988] ECR 4769.

[83] Hoffman (A Hoffman, 'Anticompetitive State Legislation Condemned Under Articles 5, 85 and 86 of the EEC Treaty: How Far Should the Court Go After *Van Eycke*?' (1990) 15 *ECLR* 1) considers the third limb of *the Van Eycke* case to be new, whereas both Neergaard (U Neergaard, *Competition and Competences The Tension Between European Competition Law and Anti-Competitive Measures By the Member States* (Copenhagen, DJØF, 1998)at 69 and L Gyselen, 'State Action and the Effectiveness of the EEC Treaty's Competition Provisions' (1989) 26 *CMLRev* 54) see *Van Eycke* as a mere restatement and consolidation of the Court's previous case law.

legislation of its official character by delegating to private traders responsibility for taking decisions affecting the economic sphere.

Applying this new three-limb test the Court found the Belgian legislation to be compatible with the competition rules. In relation to the first test, the Court found that the Belgian law did not, and was not intended to, require or favour the adoption of new restrictive agreements or the implementation of new restrictive practices. This was so even though restrictive agreements did exist before the adoption of the law. In applying the second limb, the Court notes that the legislation could be regarded as intending to reinforce the effects of pre-existing agreements only if it incorporated, wholly or in part, the terms of the agreements concluded between undertakings and required or encouraged compliance on the part of those undertakings. The Court concluded that there was a sanction, in that a preferential tax rate treatment would be lost which would induce compliance with the legislation, but decided that the national court should investigate further whether the legislation merely confirmed pre-existing methods of restricting yields of deposits and the level of maximum rates adopted under pre-existing agreements, decisions or practices.

Finally, applying the third limb, the Court found that the legislation was not deprived of its official character. The authorities reserved to themselves the power to fix maximum rates on savings deposits and did not delegate that responsibility to private economic actors.

By consolidating the Court's case law, we can distinguish four categories of state measures which may infringe the obligations contained in Articles 3(g), 10(2), 81 and 82 EC:

— Member States imposing restrictive agreements;
— Member States facilitating the conclusion of restrictive agreements;
— Member States reinforcing the effects of such agreements;
— Member States delegating to private economic actors the responsibility for decisions regarding the parameters of competition, thereby divesting the state's regulation of its public character.

From *Van Eycke* it is unclear whether these are merely illustrations or an exhaustive list of state measures which could infringe the competition rules.[84] In a subsequent case, *Alsthom Atlantique,* the Court extends the *Van Eycke* principles to scrutinise the case law in France.[85] In this case, and in the three cases decided after *Van Eycke* but before the 'November Revolution' of 1993, the Court applies

---

[84] Cf Buendia Sierra's analysis of the later case of *Meng* (discussed below, n 107, where he describes the Court's formal approach to these four categories: '[t]he judgment in *Meng* converts into a closed list what in previous cases had only been examples': J Buendia Sierra, *Exclusive Rights and State Monopolies Under EC Law* (Oxford, OUP, 1999) at 265.

[85] Case C–339/89 *Alsthom Atlantique SA v Compagnie de construction mécanique SulzerSA* [1991] ECR I–107.

the three-limb test, confirming its adherence to the principles set out, although in each case the Court finds the state's measures to be in conformity with Community law.[86]

THE 'NOVEMBER REVOLUTION' 1993

In a series of cases decided in plenary session during November 1993 the Court of Justice drew in the reins of the far-reaching principle it had developed whereby the issue of Member State autonomy to take economic regulatory decisions was capable of being challenged by individual traders. The most pressing factor which influenced the Court's decisions was the fact that the bright line between the requirements of the Internal Market and the protection of standards to be assured by the Member States in the absence of Community legislation had become less fluid. A number of opportunist litigants had jumped upon the bandwagon using Articles 28, 81 and 86 EC to challenge national regulatory laws; the case law of the Court had shifted the balance away from the Member States' autonomy and more towards the imperatives of the Internal Market. Striking down too may national laws would create regulatory gaps which could not be plugged by the adoption of Community level regulation.

In two references from a French criminal court, two managers of French supermarkets were charged with infringing a French law prohibiting resale at a loss. In defence, the managers argued that the French legislation infringed Article 28 EC.[87] The case was initially heard before the second Chamber of the Court and transferred to the Full Court because of its importance. Advocate General Tesauro had delivered two Opinions, but in fact the Court drew upon another Opinion delivered in the *Hünermund*[88] case where the same Advocate General criticised the Court's inconsistency in its application of Article 28 EC. The criticisms were levelled at the application of Article 28 EC to situations relating to national market regulation where imported products were not being treated differently from home produced goods. As Roth pointed out:

> [Article 28] of the Treaty is an instrument to protect interstate trade in goods, and not to ensure the commercial freedom of traders as such.[89]

But the Court had struggled to find a formula to keep national rules which were not designed to regulate inter-state trade outside the scope of Article 28 EC. In

---

[86] Case C–332/89 *Criminal Proceedings Against André Marchandise, Jean-Marie Chapuis and Trafitex SA* [1991] ECR I–1027; Case C-260/89 *Elliniki Radiophonia Tileorassi AE v Dimotiki Etairia Pliroforissis and Sotirios Kouvelas* [1991] ECR I–2925; Case C–60/91 *José António Batista Morais* [1992] ECR I–2085.

[87] Joined Cases C–267/91 & C–268/91 *Keck and Mithouard* [1993] ECR I–6097.

[88] Case C–292/92 *Ruth Hünermund* [1993] ECR I–6787.

[89] W-H Roth, 'Joined Cases C–267 and C–268/91 *Bernard Keck and Daniel Mithouard*; C–292/92 *Ruth Huenermund et al v Landesapothekerkammer Baden-Wuerttemberg*' (1994) 31 *CMLRev* 845, 851.

Keck the Court repeated the *Dassonville*[90] formula but restricted the scope of the *Cassis de Dijon*[91] doctrine by arguing that the French legislation did not have the purpose of regulating trade in goods *between* Member States. Although it was recognised that the legislation might deprive traders of a method of sales promotion, it was not a sufficient reason to characterise the measure as having an equivalent effect to a quantitative restriction on imports. The Court then went on to argue that it was necessary to re-examine and clarify its case law:

> in view of the increasing tendency of traders to invoke Article [28] as a means of challenging any rules whose effect is to limit their commercial freedom even when such rule are not aimed at products from other Member States.[92]

The Court attempted to curtail the perceived abuse of Article 28 EC by drawing a distinction between *product requirement* rules which would continue to be caught by the *Cassis* doctrine and *selling arrangements* which would not normally be caught by the *Cassis* doctrine.[93] There was a proviso: the legislation or regulations must apply to all affected traders operating within the national territory and they should affect in the same manner *in law and in fact* the marketing of domestic products and those from other Member States. In *Keck* the Court could not find such discrimination in the application of the prohibitions of resale at a loss, and therefore the French legislation fell outside the scope of Article 28 EC.

It has been argued that, at a practical level, *Keck* should not lend itself to mechanical application. In his Opinion Advocate General van Gerven pointed out that there are conceivable situations where seemingly neutral state regulations may have a potential deterrent effect on intra-Community trade. For example, in the *Keck*-type situation, a ban on selling at a loss may affect imported products seeking to establish new markets, or where retail outlets are situated close to a national border where retail outlets in another Member State may engage in competitive selling arrangements. From an economic and political integration perspective Poiares Maduro argues that the formality of the *Keck* approach does not lend itself to an enquiry as to whether the importing state has given sufficient weight to foreign interests in its decision-making processes and leaves little room for those interests to be taken into account in a formal application of the rule.[94]

---

[90]   Case 8/74 [1974] ECR 837.

[91]   Case 120/78 *Rewe-Zentralfinanz AG v Bundesmonopolverwaltung für Branntwein* [1979] ECR 649.

[92]   Case C–292/92 *Ruth Hünermund* [1993] ECR I–6787, para 14.

[93]   The Court adopted an approach set out in an article by an EC Commission official: E White, 'In Search of the Limits of Article 30 of the EEC Treaty' (1989) 26 *CMLRev* 235. Cf K Mortelmans, 'Article 30 of the EC Treaty and Legislation Relating to Market Circumstances: Time to Consider a New Definition' (1991) 28 *CMLRev* 115.

[94]   M Poiares Maduro, 'Reforming the Market or the State? Article 30 and the European Constitution: Economic Freedom and Political Rights' (1997) 3 *ELJ* 51.

Keck has also been interpreted as an attempt at docket control: limiting the opportunities for traders to invoke Community law to challenge Member States' national laws, for example the Court refers to 'the increasing tendency of traders to invoke [Article 28]....'.[95] But Weiler dismisses pure docket control as simplistic, and credits the Court with re-thinking the very merits of the *Dassonville* doctrine which had been in place for 20 years. He argues that *Keck* reveals a willingness on the part of the Court openly to acknowledge that its judicial doctrines are rooted in a socio-political and economic reality which changes over time and which calls for revision even of the most hallowed canons.[96] In contrast, Torgersen points out that in fact:

> the great number of cases being reversed by this judgment had ultimately been found to be justified, it was obviously not the results as such the Court was concerned about, but rather the number of cases where Article 28 was invoked.[97]

Keck was important in drawing the outer limits of the reach of Article 28 EC and thereby defining the elusive boundaries, or division of competence, between the Community and the autonomy of the Member State. But viewed from the perspective of freedom to trade as a central tenet of the European economic constitution it was a curious response from the Court. Reich[98] argues that the concept of 'selling arrangements' was a new and obscure concept and the Court did not elaborate upon it in the judgment. The Member States can circumvent Article 28 EC by couching restrictive laws and regulations in a manner which is not a 'selling arrangement'. Ross[99] makes a profound observation that *Keck* does not offer up a coherent approach to balancing free trade against other values in the economic constitution. Product requirements are subject to a balancing and proportionality test as to whether they are necessary to meet a public interest requirement (the *Cassis* test), whereas selling arrangements appear to be subject to a discrimination test. Little wonder, then, that Reich was critical of the Court for failing to give clarification and legal certainty to the scope of Article 28 EC.

The ruling in *Keck,* and its application in later cases, has been subject to vigorous criticism on other counts. For example, in contrast to the case law on the application of the competition rules the Court does not consider a *de minimis*

---

[95] Joined Cases C–267/91 & C–268/91 [1993] ECR I–6097, para 14.

[96] J Weiler, 'The Constitution of the Common Market Place: Text and Context in the Evolution of the Free Movement of Goods' in P Craig and G de Búrca (eds), *The Evolution of EU Law* (Oxford, OUP, 1999).

[97] O-T Torgersen, 'The Limitations of the Free Movement of Goods and Freedom to Provide Services- in Search of Common Approach' (1999) 9/10 *European Business Law Review* 371, 375.

[98] N Reich, 'The "November Revolution" of the European Court of Justice–*Keck, Meng* and *Audi* Revisited' (1994) 31 *CMLRev* 459.

[99] M Ross, 'Keck: Grasping the Wrong Nettle' in A Caiger and D Floudas (eds), *1996 Onwards* (Chichester, John Wiley, 1996).

doctrine.[100] Another criticism is that the Court has adopted a *per se* approach to the issue of whether the national measures under challenge affect market access. A more trenchant criticism is that while the Court is focusing upon market access as the crucial issue, the test adopted by the Court emphasises *discrimination* as the relevant criterion. Given the aims of the Internal Market to establish a single market for goods, discrimination is not the issue. Indeed adopting a discrimination approach actually leads to fragmentation of the Internal Market since traders can only compare the treatment of their goods with the treatment of domestic goods in each Member State. The adverse effect on trade in terms of *access* to the Community market is the real issue. As a result various alternative tests have been suggested. One of the clearest and boldest statements of an alternative test is found in the Opinion of Advocate General Jacobs in *Leclerc Siplec.*[101]

Keck has not stemmed the flow of litigation, and this has led academic commentators to attempt to refine the test for the application of Article 28 EC to indistinctly applicable rules which may hinder intra-Community trade. One of the most fundamental criticisms of the test in *Keck* stems from the fact that trading rules may be equal in the formal sense but nevertheless *in practice* may inhibit or deter *market access* to foreign products.[102]

In *De Agostini and TV-Shop*[103] the Swedish Consumer Ombudsman brought an action against a publisher for breaching Swedish laws which restricted the advertising of goods to children under the age of 12 against a TV station for broadcasting misleading advertising. In defence it was argued that the Swedish advertising regulations were in breach of Article 28 EC. The Court accepted that even an outright ban on advertising fell outside the scope of Article 28 EC unless it could be shown than the ban discriminated against products from other Member States. It was left to the national court to decide whether this was the case.

In a second reference from Sweden a provoked attack on the Swedish alcohol monopoly allowed the Court to re-examine selling arrangements in the context of licences sold by the Swedish alcohol monopoly.[104] The measure was very restrictive of trade, particularly in relation to restrictions on wholesale licences, since these might limit the volume of foreign drinks which are available on the domestic market. There was also evidence in this case that the Swedish monopoly operated in a discriminatory way since a low number of licences was granted

---

[100] See, eg, Case C–126/91 *Schutzverband gegen Unwesen in der Wirtschaft eV v Yves Rocher GmbH* [1993] ECR I–2361.

[101] Case C–412/93 *Société d'Importation Edouard Leclerc-Siplec v TFI Publicité SA* [1995] ECR I–179.

[102] See especially S Weatherill, 'After *Keck*: Some Thoughts on How to Clarify the Clarification' (1996) 33 *CMLRev* 885.

[103] Joined Cases C–34/95 & C–36/95 *Konsumentombudsmannen (KO) v De Agostini (Svenska) Förlag AB (C-34/95) and TV-Shop i Sverige AB* [1997] ECR I–3843.

[104] Case C–189/95 *Criminal proceedings against Franzén* [1997] ECR I–5909.

with almost all the licences awarded to traders established in Sweden.[105] Thus the regulation did not satisfy the principle of proportionality.

A further reference from Sweden concerned another action brought by the Consumer Ombudsman where a magazine was in breach of the Swedish ban on advertising drinks which contained more than 2.25 per cent alcohol. The Court does not engage with an analysis of whether the Swedish restriction affects trade, and indeed evidence was presented to show that the sales of foreign alcohol had actually increased at the expense of domestically produced alcohol. The Court merely noted that without the ban the sales of foreign alcohol might have been higher. The Court's reasoning appears to focus on the overall effect restrictions on advertising may have on all alcohol markets. Ultimately new entrants to the market would be affected to a greater extent than the established producers on the market. Thus the competitive balance of the market is affected. In this respect the *Cassis, Keck* and *Franzén* case law is a significant curb on the power of the Member State to regulate its own market. *Cassis* protects a right to *access* a market, subject to the protection of mandatory requirements tempered by a principle of proportionality. In this respect the right to trade is not absolute. The *Franzén* approach goes further, since it seeks to regulate at the EU level the competitive nature of the market and how this may affect both home-produced and foreign goods. In this respect, competition law principles are emerging in the post-*Keck* case law.

Two parallel cases decided before *Keck,* on 17 November 1993, concerned the relationship of the competition rules and Member States' regulatory powers. *Meng* [106] concerned a German regulation prohibiting insurance intermediaries from passing on to their clients commission received from insurance companies for selling health and legal aid policies. Meng had passed on his commission in breach of the German regulations. In defence Meng argued that the German regulations were contrary to Articles 3(g), 10(2) and 81 EC. The case was again transferred from a chamber to a plenary hearing of the full Court. What is unusual about this case is that the Court took what Bach[107] describes as a 'drastic and unprecedented' step of reopening the oral hearings and asked a set of questions of the parties and the Commission. The Court then chose to ignore the answers to these questions in its subsequent ruling where it applied the general principle and the three-limb test of *Van Eycke.* None of the limbs of this test was satisfied and the Court held that the German legislation was not contrary to the competition rules.

---

[105]   See also Case C–254/98 *Schutzverband v TK Heimdienst-Sass* [2000] ECR I–151 in relation to a restriction in the retail trade which was found to be in breach of Art 28 EC.

[106]   Case C–2/91 *Criminal Proceedings Against Wolfgang Meng* [1993] ECR I–5751.

[107]   A Bach, 'Annotatation Case 185/91, *Bundesanstadlt für den Güterfernverkehr v Gerbruder Reiff GmbH & Co KG*; Case C–2/94, *Meng*; Case 245/91, *OHRA Schadeverzekeringen NV*' (1994) 31 *CMLRev* 1357.

Reich argues that the *Meng* ruling is less controversial than the *Keck* ruling since the task of the Court was 'simply to restate and to clarify [the ruling in *Van Eycke*] in opposition to a broader reading suggested in other case law, especially the *Leclerc/Au Blé Vert* case'.[108] There is, however, controversy over the application of the second limb of the *Van Eycke* test in *Meng*. The Court had found that the German legislation at issue was not preceded by any agreement in the sectors to which it related (namely, health insurance, indemnity insurance and legal expenses insurance). Since there was no pre-existing agreement the Court did not have to analyse whether it was reinforced by the legislation. But the EC Commission and Advocate General Tesauro had referred to a number of pre-existing agreements and one agreement made in 1978, after the German legislation had been enacted. Furthermore, Bach[109] argues that the wording in the various agreements covering the different sectors is virtually identical and that all agreements had a common spirit. The facts of *Meng* are very similar to those of *Vlaamse Reisbureaus*,[110] the difference in outcomes turning on the fact that in *Vlaamse Reisbureaus* the Court did find the pre-existing agreements were reinforced by the Member State's legislation.

The approach in *Meng* is praised by Reich who argues that the case:

> eliminates the somewhat speculative doctrine of *effet utile* of competition law, and links it with specific state action in relationship to anti-competitive practices of undertakings.[111]

A positive aspect of *Meng* was the fact that it did not make the implementation of Articles 81 and 82 EC dependent upon the *manner* in which the supervision of economic activity at the national level is organised. The case has been criticised, however. The Court had ordered the re-opening of the oral proceedings where it asked to hear argument on whether Articles 3(g), 10(2) and 81 EC should, despite the non-existence of agreements between undertakings, be interpreted as prohibiting any state measure which would make such agreements superfluous and would affect competition within the Common Market. High expectations had been placed upon the outcome of the case, with the hope that the Court's ruling might clarify its earlier jurisprudence on this sensitive issue, but this did not occur. A second point which needed clarifying, and was not clarified, was whether a Member State can justify measures which are *prima facie* contrary to the competition rules. Despite raising the question, the Court declined to provide the answer in its ruling.

---

[108]   Above n 107, at 468.

[109]   Above n 107.

[110]   Case 311/85 *VZW Vereniging van Vlaamse Reisebureaus v VZW Sociale Dienst van de Plaatselijke en Gewestelijke Overheidsdiensten* [1987] ECR 3801.

[111]   N Reich, 'The "November Revoultion" of the European Court of Justice–*Keck*, *Meng* and *Audi* Revisited' (1994) 31 *CMLRev* 459, 472.

Reiff [112] concerned the fixing of tariffs for road haulage through the use of tariff boards. The facts of this case are similar to those of the *Clair* ruling, where the Court had found that the behaviour of a tariff setting body infringed Article 81 EC. The members of the boards were independent but were representatives from the relevant branches of each road haulage sector, proposed by their sectors and appointed by the Federal Minister. If the Federal Minister agreed with their decisions then he would publish the tariffs by means of a Ministerial Order. Reiff had paid a tariff lower than the one fixed by the tariff board, and proceedings were taken against him for the recovery of the difference between the two tariffs.

The Court of Justice stated the general principle and applied the three-limb test of *Van Eycke*. In relation to the first limb the Court found that the tariff experts were independent and were obliged to fix tariffs taking into account a wider set of interests such as the economically weak regions and the agriculture sector. The second limb of *Van Eycke* was not considered. In relation to the third limb, the Court found that the public authorities had not delegated their powers to private economic operators. The Federal Minister could substitute his own decisions if he felt that the tariffs set by the boards did not take into account the public interest.

The final case, *Ohra,*[113] was concerned with Dutch measures which prohibited insurance companies from granting any kind of rebate or other financial advantage to their clients. Ohra was prosecuted for infringing these measures. The Court again applied the general principle and the three-limb test of *Van Eycke*. As with *Meng,* the Court did not find an infringement of the competition rules.

EFFET UTILE: AN AWKWARD CONCEPT

The *effet utile* doctrine represents what Bengoetxea[114] has described as a dynamic aspect to the Court's reasoning processes. The doctrine provided the *conceptual basis* for applying Articles 81 and 82 EC to state regulation, but it was not without criticism,[115] some commentators going as far as asserting that it was conceptually flawed. The first limb of the *Van Eycke* test is regarded as superfluous. Gyselen[116] argues that it is unnecessary to refer to a link between a state measure and an agreement between undertakings and, therefore, the concept of *effet utile* is redundant. A state measure which purports to legalise conduct prohibited by

---

[112]　Case C–185/91 *Bundesanstalt für den Güterfernverkehr v Gebrüder Reiff GmbH & Co KG* [1993] ECR I–5801.

[113]　Case C–245/91 *Criminal Proceedings Against Ohra Schadeverzekeringen NV* [1993] ECR I–5851.

[114]　J Bengoetxea, *The Legal Reasoning of the European Court of Justice* (Oxford, Clarendon Press, 1993).

[115]　See J Buendia Sierra, *Exclusive Rights and State Monopolies Under EC Law* (Oxford, OUP, 1999) 265: '[t]he behaviour doctrine is bordering on the infantile in its formalism'.

[116]　L Gyselen, 'State Action and the effectiveness of the EEC Treaty's Competition Provisions' (1989) 26 *CMLRev* 33, 36.

Article 81(1) EC is directly contrary to Article 81(1) EC and consequently automatically void by virtue of the pre-emptive effect of this provision. Therefore it is unnecessary to show that an agreement has been formed as a result of the state measure. In relation to the second limb of the test, the case law of the Court reveals that in the cases where there has been an infringement of Article 81(1) EC the necessary link to a pre-existing agreement has been tenuous. For example, in the *Vlaamse Reisbureaus*[117] ruling the Court did not ascertain whether the previous agreement was still operative. It merely held that the existence of such an agreement had been the origin of the state measure.

The second limb of the *Van Eycke* test has been criticised for undermining the conceptual basis of the first limb. This delegation of powers test relates to the situation in *Leclerc*[118] and *Inno v ATAB*[119] where manufacturers and importers were authorised to fix unilaterally the retail selling price of goods. Such a measure does not require, favour or reinforce an agreement. Advocate General Tesauro points out at paragraph 18 of his Opinion in *Meng* and *Ohra* that the basis of the challenge to the state measure is that it produces the same effects as would an agreement/cartel in the sector. The same proposition must also form the basis for the prohibition of state measures such as those found in *Vlaamse Reisbureaus*. Here the state measures effectively replace, and thus render superfluous, agreements/cartels in the sector.[120] Despite these conceptual flaws, the Court has adhered to the formal application of the *effet utile* tests. In each case the Court sees *Van Eycke* [121] as setting out a general principle.[122]

The Court has found few infringements of Articles 81(1) EC and, to date, has never found a state measure to infringe Articles 3(g), 10 and 81 EC without there being an independent breach of Article 81(1) EC by the undertakings in question. The parallel application of the principles applied to Article 81 EC to satisfying an independent breach of Article 82 EC has also rendered the test virtually impossible to satisfy, as we shall see in the next chapter. The formalism of the tests developed in *Van Eycke* has been criticised, most aggressively by Buendia Sierra who argues that:

> The behaviour doctrine is bordering on the infantile in its formalism. According to this doctrine Articles 3, 10 and 81 are only breached if the behaviour of undertakings contrary to Article 81 exists either before or after the introduction of the state measure. However, it is clear that in the vast majority of cases the adoption of a State measure

---

[117]   Case 311/85 [1987] ECR 3801.

[118]   Case C–412/93 [1995] ECR I–179.

[119]   Case 13/77 [1977] ECR 2115.

[120]   See *Leclerc*, above n 118, at para 15.

[121]   Case 267/86 [1988] ECR 4769.

[122]   Reich (N Reich, 'The "November Revolution" of the European Court of Justice–*Keck, Meng* and *Audi* Revisited' (1994) 31 *CMLRev* 459) argues the opposite. He maintains that the formal, legalistic approach in the November Revolution cases implies a departure by the Court from the doctrine of *effet utile* of Community law.

makes such behaviour totally unnecessary. It is sufficient to draft the national regulation with a minimum of care to avoid prohibition and obtain identical results.[123]

The German Constitutional Court in its judgment of 12 October 1993 on the constitutionality of the Maastricht Treaty had implicitly charged the Court with a wide abuse of the *effet utile* doctrine[124]

The November Revolution rulings are important and controversial. Far more attention has been placed upon the *Keck* ruling than the other rulings which address the competition aspects of state regulation of markets. The Court appears to be restraining its own *effet utile* doctrine, and instead substitutes a more formal test arguing that only where there is a strong link between a private agreement and a state measure or where measures delegate decisional powers to private actors will the Member State be found to be in breach of the competition rules. Reich argues that legal formalism holds out the promise of legal certainty. The use of *effet utile* had created uncertainties in the relationship between Community and Member State law.[125]

Keck, Meng, Reiff and *Ohra* represent a watershed, a definitional shift of power from the Community to the Member States. In the years following the cases we see a distinctive retreat in the Court's case law from the interconnected use of the free movement of goods rules and competition rules.[126] It is only in relation to exclusive rights of distribution granted to monopolies under Article 86(1) EC that the Court has continued to regard such behaviour as an infringement of Article 28 EC unless justified under Article 30 EC or the mandatory requirements doctrine.[127] Gagliardi[128] is critical of the Court's jurisprudence since it has left open the possibility that measures which are anti-competitive but are not regarded as discriminatory may fall outside the ambit of Community law altogether. This in turn may go against the purpose of competition law, the

---

[123] J Buendia Sierra, *Exclusive Rights and State Monopolies Under EC Law* (Oxford, OUP, 1999) at 265.

[124] Cases 2 BvR 2134/92 and 2159/92 *Manfred Brunner and Others v The European Union Treaty* [1994] 1 CMLR 57, 105.

[125] N Reich, 'The "November Revolution" of the European Court of Justice–*Keck, Meng* and *Audi* Revisited' (1994) 31 *CMLRev* 459 at 470.

[126] Case C–379/92 *Criminal Proceedings Against Matteo Peralta* [1994] ECR I–3453 paras 19–22; Case C–412/93 *Leclerc v TF 1 Publicité* [1995] ECR I–179, paras 25–27; Case C–387/93 *Criminal Proceedings Against Domingo Banchero* [1995] ECR I–4663.

[127] See Cases C–277, 318–319/91 *Ligur Carni Srl and Genova Carni Srl v Unità Sanitaria Locale n. XV di Genova and Ponente SpA v Unita Sanitaria Locale n. XIX di La Spezia and CO.GE.SE.MA Coop arl (Ligur Carni)* [1993] ECR I–6621; Case C–323/93 *Société Civile Agricole du Centre d'Insémination de la Crespelle v Coopérative d'Elevage et d'Insémination Artificielle du Département de la Mayenne.* [1994] ECR I–5107, para 29. See also the electricity and gas monopoly infringement actions: Case C–157/94 *Commission v Netherlands* [1997] ECR I–5699; Case C–158/94 *Commission v Italy* [1997] ECR I–5789; Case C–159/94 *Commission v France* [1997] ECR I–5815; Case C–160/94 *Commission v Spain* [1997] ECR I–5851. Note the Advocate General in these cases took the view that the ruling in *Keck* did not apply to exclusive distribution monopolies.

[128] A Gagliardi, 'United States and European Union Antitrust versus State Regulation of the Economy: Is There a Better Test?' (2000) 25 *ELRev* 367.

efficient allocation of market resources without even the necessity of examining whether the Member State has a legitimate interest to protect. In the area of free movement of goods the post-*Franzén* case law goes some way to address this issue.

Various explanations have been put forward for the Court's apparent change of position. The 1991 Maastricht intergovernmental conference and the difficulties in ratifying the subsequent Treaty on European Union revealed some differences and disquiet over the future direction of European integration. Reich[129] points to the fact that the cases came at a time when the principle of subsidiarity written into Article 3B of the TEU came into force on 1 November 1993. But, as Reich notes, the principle of subsidiarity does not apply to areas within the exclusive jurisdiction of the Community and leaves untouched the *acquis communautaire* and rules on free movement and competition.

A different dimension is drawn out by Weiler. He argues that from the late 1980s there was greater scope for majority voting in the Council as a result of the Single European Act 1987. This re-focused the competence issue, from a political to a constitutional battle ground. The wide ambit of *Dassonville* brought many areas of Member State competence into the reach of the Community legislator, now working under the qualified majority vote system of the old Article 100a EC (now Article 95 EC). Weiler argues that by taking such matters outside the scope of Community competence the Court:

> In *Keck,* knowingly or otherwise, … made a major contribution to a more limited form of Community governance, very much the *Geist* of the times.[130]

Another explanation may be that the Advocates General and the Court wanted to acknowledge the hostility towards the opportunist litigation which the broad *Dassonville* formula had generated. The consequence of this litigation resulted in cherry picking at national laws creating the potential for the disintegration at the Member State level of national values. The November Revolution cases came at a time when the Court and its Advocates General were beginning to appraise the future direction of European integration and the role Community law was to play in it. By 1993 the economic and political climate of Europe had changed dramatically. As Weiler points out, conditions existed for a more relaxed, more mature, doctrinal framework. The commitment to an Internal Market had been internalised by national administrations and while:

---

[129]   N Reich, 'The "November Revoultion" of the European Court of Justice–*Keck, Meng* and *Audi* Revisited' (1994) 31 *CMLRev* 459.

[130]   J Weiler, 'The Constitution of the Common Market Place: Text and Context in the Evolution of the Free Movement of Goods' in P Craig and G de Búrca (eds), *The Evolution of EU Law* (Oxford, OUP, 1999) at 228.

the reflexive habits of intra-Community protectionism had not disappeared, perhaps, but were certainly not presumptive.[131]

The harmonisation process was successful and therefore there was less need for judicial activism. The maturing of economic thinking is seen in the 'New Approach' to harmonisation,[132] which paradoxically emerged from the *Cassis* ruling, and was tolerant of regulatory diversity which did not impact upon *access* to the market, and which heralded a new aspect of the European integration process involving the necessity, in some instances, of regulatory competition.

Reich[133] suggests another way of explaining these cases in that they are not so revolutionary, but part of the Court's contradictory tendency to draw broad generalised principles but to limit their application by tighter formal criteria. Until *Keck* the autonomy of Community law was based upon a concept of trade liberalisation coupled with specific areas of intervention; the idea of an autonomous Community economic constitution was far from being realised. This reflects the divergence and uncertainty between the Member States as to what Reich describes as the 'future shape of the Community order'.[134] The November Revolution might be viewed as creating new *standards* rather than new rules for Community intervention in the Member States' ability to intervene in their own markets. The cases are a good illustration of the 'integration paradox hypothesis' developed by Weiler, who argues that there is always an inherent tension between the expansion of Community jurisdiction and the anxiety of the Member States to retain their sovereignty.[135]

COMMITTEES

Member States often use committees to recommend or implement decisions at a sub-state level.[136] This allows interest groups and experts to take informed decisions in particular sectors of the economy. This raises the issue whether the actions of such committees may infringe the competition rules. The issue for competition law is whether such committees are capable of creating, and behaving as a cartel, whether they are acting independently and/or autonomously or whether their decisions are in fact delegated decisions on behalf of the state. The

---

[131] J Weiler, 'The Constitution of the Common Market Place: Text and Context in the Evolution of the Free Movement of Goods' in P Craig and G de Búrca (eds), *The Evolution of EU Law* (Oxford, OUP, 1999) at 226.

[132] EC Commission, *Enhancing the Implementation of New Approach Directives*, COM(2003) 240.

[133] N Reich, 'The "November Revoultion" of the European Court of Justice–*Keck, Meng* and *Audi* Revisited' (1994) 31 *CMLRev* 459.

[134] *Ibid*, at 482.

[135] J Weiler, 'The Transformation of Europe' (1991) 100 *Yale Law Journal* 2403 and 'Journey to an Unknown Destiny' (1993) 31 *Journal of Common Market Studies* 417.

[136] N Fenger and P Broberg, 'National Organisation of Regulatory Powers and Community Competition Law' (1995) 16 *ECLR* 365.

significance of these cases is that the principles they create may be relevant to national or Community[137] bodies established to oversee the regulatory nature of some of the liberalised sectors of the EU. The Court will not bring the action of such committees within the remit of the competition rules where such committees are composed of honorary members, fixing prices or tariffs with the public interest in mind, and where they are not representatives of industry asked to negotiate prices. In applying the general principle derived from *Van Eycke,* only the first and third tests are applied.

The starting point of the case law is in 1993, in *Reiff,*[138] which concerned the fixing of road tariffs for the carriage of goods. The EC Commission and Reiff, saw the system of fixing road haulage tariffs in Germany as a price cartel. The Court applied the *Van Eycke* test. In looking to see if there was an agreement within the meaning of Article 81 EC the Court placed emphasis upon the fact that the tariff experts were independent and were under an obligation to fix the tariffs in accordance with the interests of economically weak regions and the agricultural sector.[139] Thus the members of the tariff boards could not be regarded as representatives of the undertakings from the road haulage sector and could not be said to be concluding price agreements contrary to Article 81 EC.[140]

The Court did not address the second limb of the *Van Ecyke* test but looked to the third limb. The public authorities had not delegated their powers to private economic operators. The Federal Minister had competence to participate in the meetings of the tariff boards and to fix tariffs himself (in conjunction with the Federal Minister for the Economy) where the tariffs set were not compatible with the public interest. However, as Bach[141] notes, the tariff commissions did not just submit proposals to the Minister but were empowered to take decisions on tariffs for road transport. For the 10 years preceding the ruling in *Reiff* the Minister had not promulgated any tariffs other than those decided by the tariff commission.

The facts of this case are similar to those in *Clair.*[142] In *Clair* the members of the relevant committee were appointed by the Minister of the government and by trade organisations directly concerned by the regulation. Thus the Court drew

---

[137] The Court of Justice has ruled that the Community Institutions are also bound by the fidelity/solidarity clause of Art 10 EC: Case C–2/88 *Imm Zvartveld* [1990] ECR I–3365. In addition the Court has also recognised that there are competing interests within the EU and will not necessarily apply the imperatives of the Internal Market as dominant values: Case C–341/95 *Gianni Bettati v Safety Hi-Tech srl* [1998] ECR I–4355; Case C–25/02 *Katharina Rinke v Ärztekammer Hamburg* [2003] ECR I–8349.

[138] Case 185/91 [1993] ECRI-5801.

[139] Cf the EC Commission's statement in its *Rapport d'audience,* where it is stated that the commission for long distance road haulage was composed of owners and employees of undertakings directly affected by the tariffs with the exception of some representatives of trade associations of the transport industry.

[140] Cf the contrary view of Bach who argues that although officially composed of individual experts, the tariff commissions were in fact controlled by those regulated: (1994) 31 *CMLRev* 1357, 1360.

[141] *Ibid.*

[142] Case 123/83 *Bureau national interprofessionnel du cognac v Guy Clair* [1985] ECR 391.

the conclusion that the members of the committee 'must be regarded as in fact representing those organisations in the negotiation and conclusion of the agreement'.[143]

A crucial difference drawn by the Court was that the members of the organisations were appointed on an honorary basis and were to act independently. Neergaard[144] argues that the inspiration for this important factor, which takes regulation of the state outside of the ambit of the competition rules, may be derived from United States' antitrust law.

United States' antitrust law takes a different approach, in that the Supreme Court *exempts* conduct authorised by federal states which, if carried out by private parties, would violate antitrust law.[145] Gagliardi summarises the United States test as follows:

> When dealing with state regulations 'in restraint of trade among several states' the Supreme Court test asks (i) whether the challenged restraint is clearly articulated and affirmatively expressed as state policy and (ii) whether the policy is actively supervised by the state itself. If the answer to these questions is affirmative then the antitrust challenge to the regulation is defeated.[146]

There is no mention of the United States' jurisprudence in the cases but the Court uses some of the language of the United States case law, for example, safeguarding 'the public interest' and the role of 'independent experts' to justify the non-application of the competition rules. The view of the Court is that financially interested actors cannot be trusted to decide which restrictions on competition advance the public interest; only publicly accountable actors can.[147]

The methodology of the *Reiff* case is followed and applied in *Delta*.[148] The German law on inland waterways traffic specified that official tariffs for the

---

[143]   *Ibid*, at para 19.

[144]   U Neergaard, *Competition and Competences The Tension Between European Competition Law and Anti-Competitive Measures By the Member States* (Copenhagen, DJØF, 1998).

[145]   There is an extensive literature analysing and often comparing and contrasting the United States' case law with that of the Court of Justice: see, *inter alia*: P Pescatore, 'Public and Private Aspects of Community Competition Law' (1987) *Fordham International Law Journal*; G Marenco, 'Government Action and Antitrust in the United States: What Lessons for Community Law?' (1987) 14 *Legal Issues of European Integration* 1; D Ehle, 'State Regulation Under United States Antitrust State Action Doctrine and Under E.C. Competition Law: A Comparative Analysis' (1998) 19 *ECLR* 380; Y Ichikawa, 'The Tension Between Competition Policy and State Intervention: the EU and US Compared' (2004) *European State Aid Law Quarterly* 555; See also U Neergaard, *Competition and Competences The Tension Between European Competition Law and Anti-Competitive Measures By the Member States* (Copenhagen, DJØF, 1998), ch 5, 10 and 13.

[146]   A Gagliardi, 'United States and European Union Antitrust versus State Regulation of the Economy: Is There a Better Test?' (2000) 25 *ELRev* 353, 354.

[147]   See G Marenco, 'Government Action Antitrust in the United States: What Lessons For Community Law?' (1987) 14 *Legal Issues of Economic Integration* 2; R Elhauge, 'The Scope of Antitrust Process' (1991) 104 *Harvard Law Review* 668.

[148]   Case C–153/93 *Bundesrepublik Deutschland v Delta Schiffahrts- und Speditionsgesellschaft mbH* [1994] ECR I–2517.

transport of goods should be determined by freight commissions. The commissions were composed of equal representatives of shipping companies and shippers. The representatives were appointed by a public authority acting on recommendations from professional associations. If the commissions could not agree there was provision to expand the commission with a chair and two assessors. All the members of the commissions were honorary and acted independently. But all decisions of the commissions had to be approved by the Federal Minister for Transport who had the power to act in the public interest and fix different tariffs. The tariffs were issued by the Minister as an Order and such Orders were binding on all companies. If any companies charged a price other than the tariff set, then the difference was payable by the Federal government. Delta had transported goods at a price lower than the prescribed price.

The Court states the general principle and the three-limb test from *Van Eycke*, but the test is redefined and not applied fully. The Court appears to ask whether the existence of an agreement, decision or concerted practice within the meaning of Article 81 EC can be inferred from the contested measure. A negative answer was given since the members of the commissions were not representatives of the professional associations; they were honorary members and independent, and tariff-setting had to take into account a wider set of issues such as the agricultural sector, medium-sized businesses and economically weaker areas. The second limb of the *Van Eycke* case was not considered.

In relation to the third part of the *Van Eycke* test the Court found that the public authorities had not delegated their powers in relation to tariff fixing to private economic operators. The Minister was entitled to fix the tariffs himself where the tariffs were not satisfying the public interest. Thus the contested arrangements did not infringe Articles 3(g), 10(2) and 81 EC.

As in *Reiff* the Court places emphasis on the *formal* independence of the representatives. However the situation differed in *Delta.* and Neergaard argues this might indicate a softening in the Court's approach.[149] The members of the tariff commissions were not experts in tariff matters and the Minister was not entitled to sit on the commissions. There was no investigation as to whether the Minister actually did take a different decision.

In *DIP*[150] an Italian law stated that the opening of any new shops was subject to the obtaining of a licence from the local mayor, who received guidance from a municipal committee which followed criteria set out in a commercial development plan.[151] The mayor could deviate from the committee's guidance only where a commercial development plan had not been drawn up. The committees

---

[149] U Neergaard, *Competition and Competences The Tension Between European Competition Law and Anti-Competitive Measures By the Member States* (Copenhagen, DJØF, 1998) at 103.

[150] Joined Cases C–140/94, C–141/94 & C–142/94 *DIP SpA and others v Commune di Bassano del Grappa and Commune di Chioggia* [1995] ECR I–3287.

[151] P Caputi Jambrenghi, '"Creating A Level Playing Field" in the Italian Retail Distribution Market: The Use of EC Law and the Role of the Italian Anti-trust Authority' (1996) 17 *ECLR* 189.

were composed of a *majority* of representatives appointed by traders' associations and a *minority* of representatives appointed by traders' associations. The four applicants had been refused permission to open new shops by the local mayor. The national court asked the Court to rule on the compatibility of the Italian measures with Articles 81 and 82 EC. In its ruling the Court invokes Articles 3(g) and 10(2) EC and confirms the general principle from *Van Eycke.*

In relation to Article 81 EC the Court places emphasis upon the fact that the representatives of the traders' organisations were put upon the committees as experts on the sectors concerned, *not* to represent their individual interests. The representatives were only in a minority and had to take into account public interest factors. In relation to the third limb of the *Van Eckye* case the Court observed that the purpose of the general development plan was to provide the best possible service for consumers and to create a balance in trading establishments. The committees only expressed an opinion, which was not binding, except where a plan had not been drawn up. Thus there was no infringement of the competition rules.

Finally, in the litigation concerning an Italian law establishing and conferring autonomous power on the Italian National Council of Customs Agents, CNSD, a defence was raised that CNSD derived its status from public law and that Article 81 EC should not be applicable. The CFI and the Court dismissed this defence.[152] The Courts also found that the members of CNSD could not be characterised as independent experts. Applying the principles derived from *Reiff, Delta Schiffahrts* and *DIP* the Courts found that CNSD was not required under the law to set tariffs taking into account the interests of undertakings or associations of undertakings in the sector or the general interest of users of the services. The members of CNSD were the representatives of professional customs agents, and there was nothing in the Italian legislation to prevent them from acting in the exclusive interests of the profession. The members of the CNSD could only be registered customs agents since they were elected from among the members of the Departmental Councils on which only customs agents can sit. The Director General of Customs had not acted as Chairman of the CNSD since a law of 1992. The Italian Minister for Finance who was responsible for the supervision of the professional organisation could not intervene in the appointment of the members of the Departmental Councils and the CNSD. The CNSD was responsible for setting the tariff for the professional services of customs agents on the basis of proposals from the Departmental Councils. Thus there was no protection in the national legislation obliging, or even encouraging, the members of the CNSD or the Departmental Councils to take into account public interest criteria.

---

[152] Case C–35/96 *Commission v Italian Republic* [1998] ECR I–3851, para 40; Case T–513/93 *Consiglio Nazionale degli Spedizionieri Doganali (CNSD) v Commission* [2000] ECR II–1807, paras 39–40.

REGULATORY BODIES IN THE LIBERALISED SECTORS

In Chapter 5 we see the growth of national regulatory authorities (NRAs) to oversee the liberalisation of a number of sectors which had previously been in state ownership and regulation. NRAs are mandated through the EU legislation liberalising each sector and are given specific tasks. Generally it is for the national legal system to decide whether each NRA should also apply competition law, for example, Article 22 of the Postal Services Directive[153] states that the NRA *may* also be charged with ensuring compliance with the competition rules in the postal sector. NRAs are often under a duty to ensure that competition is not restricted as well as the promotion of competition in the liberalised sectors. For example, Article 8(2)(b) of the Framework Directive in the telecommunications sector states that NRAs shall:

> promote competition in the provision of electronic communications networks, electronic communications services and associated facilities and services, by ... ensuring that there is no distortion or restriction of competition in the electronic communications sector.[154]

Similarly, in the electricity and gas sectors NRAs are under a duty to monitor the level of competition and are responsible for ensuring effective competition. The earlier liberalisation directives contained general principles that sector specific regulation at the EU level was without prejudice to the rules of competition, and this idea is also seen in Article 16 EC which is intended to promote services of a general economic interest.

NRAs are under a positive duty to observe the competition rules. The *Ahmed Saeed*[155] ruling is an early example of the interface between sector specific legislation and the competition rules. The Court ruled that where there is sector specific secondary legislation which leaves the Member State free to encourage mutual consultations between operators:

> the Treaty nevertheless strictly prohibits them from giving encouragement, in any form whatsoever, to the adoption of agreements or concerted practices with regard to tariffs contrary to [Article 81(1) or [Article 82], as the case may be.[156]

NRAs may, for example, encourage operators to share elements of a network to reduce start up costs of rolling out a new service. NRAs are increasingly asked to take into account a range of factors, for example, protection of the environment, promotion of public health, in carrying out their duties. In this respect NRAs

---

[153]   Dir 97/67/EC, [1997] OJ L 15/14.
[154]   Dir 2002/21/EC [2002] OJ L108/33.
[155]   Case 66/86 *Ahmed Saeed Flugreisen and Silver Line Reisebüro GmbH v Zentrale zur Bekämpfung unlauteren Wettbewerbs eV* [1989] ECR 803.
[156]   *Ibid*, at paras32–33.

may encourage facilities and property to be shared to reduce the duplication of similar facilities at a cost to the environment, for example, masts, cables.[157] Such forms of agreements run the risk of infringing Article 81(1) EC, yet NRAs are not included in the network of national competition authorities which can work with the EC Commission on the application of competition law in the Member States and NRAs do not have the capacity to ask the ECJ for a preliminary ruling on the scope of such agreements. However, in *CIF* [158] the Court reinforces the obligation not to apply any national laws or regulations which conflict with EC law, and this would apply to NRAs.

DEFENCES AND JUSTIFICATIONS FOR PRIVATE UNDERTAKINGS

The Court has consistently held that Articles 81 and 82 EC only concern the anti-competitive behaviour of undertakings acting on their own initiative.[159] The possibility of excluding certain anti-competitive behaviour from the ambit of Article 81(1) EC because it has been imposed upon undertakings by national legislation or regulation, thus eliminating the possibility of competitive behaviour on their part, has been applied restrictively. The clearest statement of the principles underpinning liability of undertakings under Articles 81 and 82 EC is to be found in an appeal against a ruling of the CFI in *Ladbroke*.[160] The Court directs the EC Commission to evaluate whether national legislation prevents undertakings from engaging in autonomous conduct which prevents, restricts or distorts competition with the idea that private undertakings may be able to obtain immunity from liability under Articles 81 and 82 EC if their anti-competitive behaviour has been required or authorised by a Member State measure. The crucial question is whether the undertakings are capable of behaving autonomously. This ruling reinforces the need to hold Member States liable under Articles 81 and 82 EC. To decide otherwise would create a loophole whereby anti-competitive conduct on the part of private undertakings in compliance with national law could not be sanctioned. The *Ladbroke* ruling was applied in *CIF*.[161]

---

[157] See the EC Commission's observations on network infrastructure sharing in Commission Decision COMP/38.370, *O2 UK Ltd/T-Mobile UK Ltd*, 30 Apr 2003 [2003] OJ L200/59 and Commission Decision COMP/38.369, *T-Mobile Deutschland/VIAG Interkom*, 16 July 2003; Commission Press Release IP/03/1026, 16 July 2003.

[158] Case C–198/01 *Consorzio Industrie Fiammiferi (CIF) v Autorita Garante della Concorrenza e del Mercato* [2003] ECR I—8055.

[159] Case 41/83 *Italy v Commission* [1985] ECR 873, para 55; Case 262/88 *GB-INNO-BM* [1990] ECR I-667;para 20; Joined Cases C–359/95P & C–379/95P *Commission of the EC and French Republic v Ladbroke Racing Ltd* [1997] ECR I–6265, para 33.

[160] *Ibid.*

[161] Case C–198/01 *Consorzio Industrie Fiammiferi (CIF) v Autorita Garante della Concorrenza e del Mercato* [2003] ECR I–8055.

The increasing use made of self-regulation by professional bodies, especially the professions and sport-related regulation, has raised the issue of whether such bodies should be subject to the EC Treaty rules and, if so, whether special justifications or exemptions can be made out for them.[162]

DEFENCES AND JUSTIFICATIONS FOR THE STATE

One major problem of applying Articles 81(1) EC and 82 EC to actions of the state is the scope for a defence or justification of the state's actions. Bacon argues that a Member State must be able to defend an alleged anti-competitive state regulation on public interest grounds.[163] One argument is that if private undertakings can apply for an exemption under Article 81(3) EC then, *mutatis mutandis,* so should the Member State.[164] Equally the concept of free trade is not an absolute value of the Internal Market. The Member States are able to raise justifications which meet reasonable or compelling needs under either Article 30 EC or the 'mandatory requirements' doctrine found in paragraph 8 of the ruling in *Cassis de Dijon:*[165]

> Obstacles to movement in the Community resulting from disparities between the national laws in question must be accepted in so far as those provisions may be recognised as being necessary in order to satisfy mandatory requirements relating in particular to the effectiveness of fiscal supervision, the protection of public health, the fairness of commercial transactions and the defence of the consumer.

This list of 'mandatory requirements' is not exhaustive, and more recently the Court has leaned towards empowering the national courts with the task of assessing the justifications raised by the Member States.[166] Similarly in the field of free movement of services the Court has recognised a generic overriding public interest justification. This is an important aspect of allowing for local preferences to be taken into account in the process of market-building. However, as Weatherill[167] points out, even with the availability of such defences, the trader challenging state measures is at a tactical advantage since the burden rests with the

---

[162] See E Szyszczak, 'Competition and Sport' (2007) 32 *ELRev* 95; cf J Szoboszlai, 'Delegation of State Regulatory Powers to Private Parties—Towards An Active Supervisory Test' (2006) 29 *World Competition* 73.

[163] K Bacon, 'State Regulation of the Market and E.C. Competition Rules: Articles 85 and 86 Compared' (1997) 18 *ECLR* 283.

[164] See L Gyselen, 'State Action and the Effectiveness of the EEC Treaty's Competition Provisions' (1989) 26 *CMLRev* 54.

[165] Case 120/78 *Rewe-Zentrale AG v Bundesmonopolverwaltung für Branntwein (Cassis de Dijon)* [1979] ECR 649.

[166] See, eg, Case C–368/95 *Vereinigte Familiapress Zeitungsverlags-und Vertriebs GmbH v Heinrich Bauer Verlag* [1997] ECR I–3689.

[167] S Weatherill, 'Recent Case Law Concerning The Free Movement of Goods: Mapping The Frontiers of Market Deregulation' (1999) 36 *CMLRev* 53.

regulating state to show that its rules are justified and the hurdle of satisfying the proportionality principle 'frequently trips up national action that in principle may pursue a recognised objective'.

In *Aubert*[168] and in *BNIC v Clair*,[169] BNIC had argued that the national provisions did not infringe Article 81(1) EC because they were made by a public body which was not subject to the competition rules, as well as justifying the measures in that they were intended to compensate for declining sales and overproduction. The Court held that such factors would only be a basis for an application to the EC Commission for an exemption under Article 81(3) EC but does not suggest that recourse to Article 81(3) EC might also be an option for the state as well.

In fact recourse to Article 81(3) EC may be of little use as a justification for a Member State's anti-competitive conduct since it is concerned with protecting the competitive integrity of the market. It is rare for the EC Commission to have taken other values and policies into account when granting an exemption under Article 81(3) EC.[170] In later cases the Court has resorted to creating new exceptions, for example when competition policy may be in conflict with social values of the EC Treaty, the competition rules will not apply to certain kinds of agreements. This idea is applied in the context of collective agreements in *Brentjens*.[171] In *Wouters*[172] a challenge was made to the regulations of the Dutch Bar which prohibited multidisciplinary partnerships. The Court held that Article 81(1) EC did not apply because the restriction on competition was necessary to ensure the proper practice of the legal profession. This principle was applied in *Meca-Medina* to rules governing sport.[173]

The lack of an available defence to an infringement of Articles 81 and 82 EC may explain the Court's reluctance to find infringements of these Articles and the greater recourse to Article 28 EC in the early case law. This unease is shown in the Opinion of Advocate General Jacobs in *Pavlov*.[174]

---

[168] Case 136/86 *Bureau national interprofessionnel du cognac v Yves Aubert* [1987] ECR 4789.

[169] Case 123/83 *Bureau national interprofessionnel du cognac v Guy Clair* [1985] ECR 391.

[170] Case 26/76 *Metro-SB-Großmärkte GmbH and Co. KG v Commission* [1977] ECR 1875; Case 42/84 *Remia BV and others v Commission* [1985] ECR 2545; *Synthetic Fibres* [1984] OJ L207/17; *Ford/Volkswagen* [1993] OJ L20/14. See further G Monti, 'Article 81 EC and Public Policy' (2002) 39 CMLRev 1057.

[171] Joined Cases C–115/97, C–116/97 & C–117/97 *Brentjens' Handelsonderneming BV v Stichting Bedrijfspensioenfonds voor de Handel in Bovwmaterialen* [1999] ECR I–6025.

[172] Case C–309/99 *Wouters v Algemene Raad van de Nederlandse Orde van Advocaten* [2002] ECR I–1577.

[173] Case C–519/04 P [2006] ECR I-6991. Cf Case C-250/03 *Giorgio Emanuele Mauri v Ministero della Giustizia and Commissione per gli esami di avvocato presso la Corte d'appello di Milano* [2005] ECR I-1267.

[174] Joined Cases C–180/98 to C–184/98 *Pavel Pavlov and Others v Stichting Pensioenfonds Medische Specialisten* [2000] ECR I–6451, para 163.

In *Ahmed Saeed*[175] the Court addresses the idea of a justification for the Member State through the application of Article 86(2) EC. This 'reading over' of a justification for anti-competitive behaviour is also seen in the area of state aids. It is not an ideal solution since, as we shall discover in Chapter 4, Article 86(2) EC has a narrow ambit providing an exemption from the Treaty rules where a service of 'general economic interest' cannot be provided in accordance with the full play of the competition and free market principles. In many of the cases the legitimate justification for a Member State's intervention in the market may be for reasons other than providing a service of general economic interest.

Bach[176] is critical of the Court's approach, arguing that the Court could have started from the premise that competition, as a structured principle of the Internal Market, has to be protected against Member States and undertakings. Such a protection can be based on Article 10 EC and translated into a proportionality test applied to measures which eliminate or restrict competition. As the legal basis of the obligation is Article 10 EC the Member States' competence to enact economic legislation would remain unaffected, but equally the Community imperatives introducing limits to the exercise of this competence would be safeguarded.

The Court of Justice has had to struggle with its own limitation that justifications for restrictions on the free movement rules may only relate to non-economic reasons.[177] As Gagliardi[178] points out, many state regulations may serve a dual purpose. He gives as an example a Member State's decision to fix the price of drugs. This could be perceived as an economic measure to reduce national health budgets or as a social measure to provide health care for the lowest earners. Gagliardi argues for a middle way to be found whereby state anti-competitive regulations may be justified for both economic and non-economic reasons, and only those regulations with *a clear protectionist intent* are caught automatically by the competition rules. The difficulty with this approach is that it may raise issues about motive which are hard to prove when a Member State is arguing that the impact upon inter-state trade is an inadvertent effect of national policies.

Further answers to these issues may be found as a result of the litigation which is emerging testing the interaction of the competition rules with the free

---

[175]   Case 66/86 *Ahmed Saeed Flugreisen and Silver Line Reisebüro GmbH v Zentrale zur Bekämpfung unlauteren Wettbewerbs eV* [1989] ECR 803.

[176]   A Bach, 'Annotatation Case 185/91, *Bundesanstadlt für den Güterfernverkehr v Gerbruder Reiff GmbH & Co KG* ; Case C–2/94, *Meng,* Case 245/91, *OHRA Schadeverzekerings NV'* (1994) 31 *CMLRev* 1358.

[177]   Case 72/83 *Campus Oil v Minister for Industry and Energy and others* [1984] ECR 2727.

[178]   A Gagliardi, 'United States and European Union Antitrust versus State Regulation of the Economy: Is There a Better Test?' (2000) 25 *ELRev* 353, 373.

movement of services.[179] The Court has developed a mandatory requirements doctrine, similar to the *Cassis* idea, which may generically be described as 'overriding reasons relating to the public interest' which may be raised by the Member States to defend national regulations.[180] Given the new tendency to test the interaction of free movement of services and the competition rules the Court may be able to create a public interest justification from ideas of overriding public interest which may be used to justify restrictions which have consequences for the competition and free movement rules.

In *Arduino*[181] a challenge was made to the rules drawn up by the Italian Bar Association setting out maximum and minimum fees for lawyers' services. The Court repeated the general principle of Member State liability under the competition rules, but did not find a breach of the competition rules since Italy had not delegated regulatory powers to the Bar Council. Following on from this ruling two Italian courts referred questions to the Court on whether the fixing of out-of-court fees and a private agreement derogating from the fixed fee scale are contrary to Community law, invoking the free movement of services and the competition rules.[182] Advocate General Poiares Maduro finds the Italian rules to be compatible with Community competition law provided that the state is able to supervise the application of the fee structure and that national courts interpret the rules according to Community law. However, when examining the free movement of services the Advocate General points out that the Italian fee scales apply to all lawyers wishing to offer services in Italy. Minimum fees constitute a restriction on providing services because they neutralise the competitive advantage which may be enjoyed by lawyers established outside Italy who may want to offer legal services at competitive rates. Italian nationals wishing to engage a foreign lawyer are also denied the opportunity of this competitive advantage. The Advocate General could not find an overriding reason protecting a public interest to justify the restriction on providing legal services in Italy. It was not apparent how the fixing of minimum fees would fall within, say, the proper regulation of the legal profession in Italy. The Court held that Articles 10, 81 and 82 EC do not preclude a Member State from adopting a legislative measure which approves, on the basis of a draft produced by a professional body of members of the Bar such as the National Council of the Bar, a scale fixing a minimum fee for members of the legal profession from which there can generally be no derogation in respect of

---

[179] Eg: Case C–70/99 *Commission v Portugal* [2001] ECR I–4845; Case C–18/93 *Corsica Ferries Italia Srl v Corpo dei Piloti del Porto di Genova* [1994] ECR I–1783; Case C–381/93 *Commission v France* [1994] ECR I–5145. EC Commission, *The State of the Internal Market for Services*, COM(2002) 441, paras 6–7.

[180] Case C–55/94 *Gebhard v Consiglio dell'Ordine degli Avvocati e Procuratori di Milano* [1995] ECR I–4165.

[181] Case C–35/99 *Criminal proceedings against Manuele Arduino* [2002] ECR I–1529.

[182] Cases C–94/04 & C–202/04 *Federico Cipolla v Rosaria Fazari, née Portolese and Stefano Macrino, Claudia Capodarte v Roberto Meloni* , Opinion of 1 Feb 2006; judgment of 5 Dec 2006 (not yet reported). Cf Case C–250/03 *Mauri*, Order of 17 February 2006.

either services reserved to those members or those, such as out-of-court services, which may also be provided by any other economic operator not subject to that scale. However, legislation containing an absolute prohibition on derogation, by agreement, from the minimum fees set by a scale of lawyers' fees, such as that contested in this case, for services which are court services and reserved to lawyers constitutes a restriction on freedom to provide services laid down in Article 49 EC. It is for the national court to determine whether such legislation, in the light of the detailed rules for its application, actually serves the objectives of protection of consumers and the proper administration of justice which may justify it and whether the restrictions it imposes do not appear disproportionate having regard to those objectives.

THE USE OF ARTICLE 81 EC BY THE EC COMMISSION

In addition to the Court's hesitation to use Articles 81 and 82 EC against a Member State we see that the EC Commission had little enthusiasm for the *effet utile* doctrine. There is one EC Commission Decision of note.[183] This is a decision taken in June 1993, before the November Revolution cases. The EC Commission had received several complaints from industrial, commercial and transport businesses concerning an Italian law which granted relative decision-making power to the National Council of Customs Agents (CNSD). CNSD was a body governed by public law, composed of nine members elected by a secret ballot by the customs agents who were eligible to vote by being entered on the various departmental registers. The CNSD elected a chair from amongst its members. The CNSD was responsible for setting the tariff for services provided by customs agents on the basis of proposals from Departmental Councils. The tariff was compulsory and any customs agents disobeying the tariff could face disciplinary measures.

The EC Commission received a number of complaints from industrial, commercial and transport operators in the EU concerning the fixing of the rate of customs tariffs by the CNSD. The CNSD had agreed to a new tariff in 1988 and this was approved by the Italian Minister of Finance by a Decree of 6 July 1988. The cause of the complaint was that an increase in the tariff rates, together with changes in categories for classifying goods and the introduction of a new obligation to invoice both the sender and the Italian consignee separately for

---

[183] Cf D Ehle, 'State Regulation Under United States Antitrust State Action Doctrine and Under E.C. Competition Law: A Comparative Analysis' (1998) 19 *ECLR* 380, who argues that the EC Commission has *never* used Arts 81 and 82 EC against a Member State and J Buendia Sierra, *Exclusive Rights and State Monopolies Under EC Law* (Oxford, OUP 1999) at 263, who also argues that '[t]he Commission made hardly any use of this doctrine. All the cases which reached the Court were references from national courts: not one single action was brought by the Commission against a Member State for failure to fulfil its obligations under Articles 3, [10] and [81] or [82]', and 'it is not surprising that following *Meng* not one single national regulation has been held to be contrary to Articles 3, 10 and 81', at 265.

customs clearance the new charges had allegedly paralysed the activity of couriers by increasing the time and expenditure involved in their activities to make their work uneconomic. It was possible for undertakings to avoid the new tariff by negotiation and individual derogation.

The EC Commission instituted three separate sets of proceedings against the activities of the CNSD and the Italian legislation confirming its decisions. On 24 March 1992 the Commission applied to the Court for a Declaration that Italy had infringed Articles 23 and 25 EC by approving the tariff. The Court dismissed the claim on the ground that there was no obligation on the importer to have recourse in all circumstances to the services of a professional customs forwarding agent.[184] On 30 June 1993 the EC Commission adopted Decision 93/438/EEC[185] which was addressed to CNSD. In this Decision the Commission argued that the CNSD was an 'association of undertakings' and found that the tariff constituted an infringement of Article 81(1) EC because it restricted competition by setting fixed rate tariffs and compulsory invoicing. Even though there was the possibility for individual derogations this did not mitigate the restrictive nature of the CNSD. Trade between the Member States was affected substantially since the cost and complexity of customs operations were increased by the CNSD's actions. The CNSD had not notified the decision to the EC Commission but, in any event, there was no possibility of an individual exemption under Article 81(3) EC where there was concerted fixing of prices and the setting of minimum prices in particular.

CNSD brought an action for annulment of Decision 93/438/EEC.[186] The EC Commission also commenced a second infringement action against Italy alleging that the *national legislation* infringed Articles 10 and 81 EC.[187] In the light of the second infringement action the CFI decided to postpone its consideration of the annulment of Decision 93/438/EEC until the Court had delivered judgment in the second infringement action.

In the second infringement action,[188] Italy raised an objection of inadmissibility, arguing that the EC Commission could not initiate a second infringement action without first withdrawing its allegations in the first infringement action. Italy's contention was that the practices complained of consisted in *either* the imposition of a tax *or* the conclusion of an agreement by an association of undertakings ratified by the Member State, but could not constitute both at the same time. Italy argued that the second infringement action was incompatible with the first and that its rights of defence had been infringed, since it was obliged to defend itself simultaneously in two cases founded on the same facts. The Court rejected these arguments, pointing out that the EC Commission, as

---

[184] Case C–119/92 *Commission v Italy* [1994] ECR I–393.
[185] [1993] OJ L203/27.
[186] Case T–513/93 *CNSD v Commission* [2000] ECR II–1807.
[187] Case C–35/96 *Commission v Italy* [1998] ECR I–3851.
[188] *Ibid.*

custodian of the EC Treaty, has the discretion to decide whether it is expedient to take action against a Member State and to judge at what time to bring an infringement action. If the EC Commission finds that there are further breaches of the EC Treaty it has no option but to commence another infringement proceeding. On the substance of the action the Court found an infringement of Article 81 EC:

> By adopting the national legislation in question, the Italian Republic clearly not only required the conclusion of an agreement contrary to [Article 81] of the Treaty and declined to influence its terms, but also assists in ensuring compliance with that agreement.[189]

The Italian law required the CNSD to compile a compulsory, uniform tariff for the services of customs agents and the national legislation wholly relinquished to private economic operators the powers of the public authorities as regards the setting of tariffs. CNSD was a representative of the professional customs agents, and nothing in the Italian legislation prevented the CNSD from acting in the exclusive interest of the profession.

The defence raised by Italy was that independent customs agents were not undertakings, and therefore CNSD could not constitute an association of undertakings within the meaning of Article 81 EC. Italy argued that while customs agents exercise a liberal profession (like lawyers, surveyors, interpreters) they are independent workers providing services of an intellectual nature. The customs agents' profession required authorisation and compliance with certain regulatory provisions. Furthermore there was an indispensable organisational factor missing which was necessary to show that an undertaking existed: the combination of human, material and non-material resources permanently assigned to the pursuit of a specific economic goal. The Court rejected this argument by referring to its established case law[190] that the concept of an undertaking covers any entity engaged in an economic activity, regardless of its legal status and the way in which it is financed. The activity of customs agents had an economic character: they offered, for payment, services and assumed financial risks.

A second point was that CNSD was acting in a public law capacity as a professional body and could not therefore be considered to be an 'association of undertakings'. Applying its previous case law from *BNIC v Clair*,[191] the Court reiterated the point that Article 81 EC applies to agreements between undertakings and decisions by associations of undertakings:

---

[189]   *Ibid*, at para 55.
[190]   Case 41/90 *Höfner and Elser* [1991] ECR I–1979, para 21; Case C–244/94 *Fédération Française des Sociétiés d'Assurances and Others v Ministère de Agriculture et de la Pêche(FFSA)* [1995] ECR I–4013, para 14; Case C–55/96 *Job Centre coop .arl* [1997] ECR I–7119, para 21.
[191]   Case 123/83 [1985] ECR 391, para 17.

Accordingly, the legal framework within which such agreements are made and such decisions are taken and the classification given to that framework by the various national legal systems are irrelevant as far as the applicability of the community rules on competition, and in particular Article 85 of the Treaty, are concerned ...[192]

The Court found that there was nothing to prevent the CNSD from acting in the *exclusive* interest of the customs agents' profession.

The CFI also held that the uniform, compulsory tariff set by CNSD restricted competition and was capable of affecting trade between the Member States. The tariff set by CNSD was mandatory and set the price for customs agents' service, creating minimum and maximum prices with various scales based upon the value or weight of the goods to be cleared through customs or the specific types of goods or services. In relation to the effect on intra-Community trade the Court stated:

it need merely be pointed out that an agreement extending over the whole of the territory of a member state has, by its very nature, the effect of reinforcing the compartmentalisation of markets on a national basis, thereby holding up the economic inter-penetration which the Treaty is designed to bring about...[193]

Given that the nature of the agreement under scrutiny directly affected import and export operations, often involving transit arrangements through a non-Member State, the impact upon trade was appreciable.

In applying Article 81 EC in conjunction with Article 10 EC the Court had no hesitation in applying its previous case law which:

requires the Member States not to introduce or maintain in force measures, even of a legislative nature, which may render ineffective the competition rules applicable to undertakings...[194]

The Court then went on to find that:

By adopting the national legislation in question, the Italian Republic clearly not only required the conclusion of an agreement contrary to [Article 81 EC] and declined to influence its terms, but also assists in ensuring compliance with that agreement.[195]

An Italian law of 1960 required the CNSD to compile a compulsory uniform tariff for the services of a customs agent. The national law wholly relinquished to private operators the powers of the public authorities in relation to the setting of tariffs.and expressly prohibited the registered customs agents from derogating

[192] *Ibid*, at para 40.
[193] *Ibid*, at para 48.
[194] *Ibid*, at para 53.
[195] *Ibid*, at para 55.

from the tariff with the penalty of exclusion, suspension or removal from the register of customs agents. Although there was no legal obligation, or indeed power, for the Minister of Finance to approve the tariff set by CNSD the Decree issued by the Minister gave the appearance of public regulation since it was published in the Official Gazette. This publication gave rise to a presumption of knowledge of the tariff on the part of third parties, which would not be the official position of the CNSD decision. The official character also facilitated the application by customs agents of the prices it set and deterred customers from challenging the contested prices demanded by customs agents.

The CFI heard the appeal challenging the EC Commission's Decision against CNSD and gave its ruling on 30 March 2000. The CFI endorsed the Court of Justice's ruling in the 1998 infringement action, finding that the CNSD was an association of undertakings and that its public law status did not prevent the application of the competition rules to its activities. The CFI went on to investigate whether the restrictive effects on competition were attributable solely to the operation of the national legislation or whether the CNSD had any scope for independent action. The CFI found that while the Italian law required the CNSD to adopt a tariff it was silent as to the level of charges: there was no maximum level or criteria imposed for the setting of the tariffs. The Italian law did not determine the way in which charges were to be applied or insist that a separate charge must be made for each operation. It was shown that the CNSD had applied substantial increases to the tariffs in force and this curtailed the freedom of organisation enjoyed by customs agents, preventing them from offering more competitive rates. The CNSD also enjoyed a large measure of discretion to grant a derogation and indeed could have adopted a different approach to the setting of tariffs which would not have restricted competition. Thus the CFI concluded that in practice the nature and scope of competition were shaped by the decisions taken independently by the CNSD. Given that customs duties were still obligatory for various intra-Community trade transactions the tariff affected trade between the Member States.

CNSD is an important case of principle.[196] Like the *Ahmed Saeed*[197] case, it tackles the situation where tariffs are set by private operators and has implications for regulatory bodies which are given delegated or self-regulatory powers or powers of sectoral regulation under privatisation processes. More recently, on 15 July and 23 December 2005 the EC Commission adopted five decisions[198] under Council Regulation (EC) No 847/2004 on the negotiation and implementation of air service agreements between Member States and third countries.[199] Relying

---

[196] Cf U Neergaard, 'State Action and the Competition Rules: A New Path?' (1999) 6 *Maastricht Journal* 380.

[197] Case 66/86 *Ahmed Saeed Flugreisen and Silver Line Reisebüro GmbH v Zentrale zur Bekämpfung unlauteren Wettbewerbs eV* [1989] ECR 803.

[198] Commission Decisions C(2005)2667 and C(2005)2668 of 15 July 2005; Commission Decisions C(2005)5736, C(2005)5737 and C(2005) 5740 of 23 Dec 2005.

[199] [2004] OJ L 157/7.

upon *Matra SA v Commission*[200] the EC Commission states that when using its discretion under the Regulation it cannot authorise a result which would be contrary to EU law. A fair proportion of bilateral air service agreements require or encourage air carriers to agree or coordinate tariffs or the capacity they operate. The EC Commission found these to infringe Articles 10 and 81 EC when read together and gave the Member States 12 months in which to bring the agreements into conformity with Community law.

Thus, although there are few positive decisions of the EC Commission or the European Courts this chapter reveals the far-reaching potential of Article 81 EC to apply to the actions of the Member States and regulatory bodies with delegated powers. The next chapter examines the more limited application of Article 82 EC, standing alone, to Member State economic activity.

---

[200] Case C–225/91 [1993] ECR I–3203, para 16.

3

Article 82 EC

RTICLE 82 EC ADDRESSES the *abuse* of market power. In contrast to Article 81 EC it has been relatively under-used, and only recently has the EC Commission turned attention to analysing ways in which it might be modernised. Although Article 82 EC has been used selectively it has been a flexible tool and has adapted to recognise new concepts, particularly the rapid changes in market structure through mergers and acquisitions in the liberalised markets and the changing role of incumbents who both provide public service obligations and engage in commercial activities in the liberalised markets. Although the Court had accepted that Article 82 EC could apply to changes in market *structure* as well as abusive market *behaviour* the Court and the EC Commission were aware of the problems of applying Article 82 EC *ex post* to structural changes to the market.[1] Mergers which may lead to an abuse of market power are now dealt with under a separate procedure.[2] Article 82 EC applies to one or more dominant undertakings which abuse market power in a way which is incompatible with the Common Market and which may affect trade between the Member States. A list of illustrations of *how* market power may be abused is given. Unlike with Article 81(3) EC there is no possibility of obtaining an exemption from the application of Article 82 EC. In addition to structural changes to the market as a result of a dominant position the Court has been hesitant to apply Article 82 EC to oligopolistic markets. In *Hoffmann-La Roche v Commission*[3] the Court recognised that undertakings in an oligopolistic market may act and react in a similar ways on the market and that in the absence of explicit collusion, which of course could also be tackled under Article 81 EC, the Court was not willing to apply Article 82 EC. More recently the EC Commission and the Courts have addressed the idea of joint dominance in the market.[4] The

---

[1] Case 6/72 *Europemballage Corporation and Continental Can Company Inc v Commission of the European Communities* [1973] ECR 215.
[2] Council Reg (EC) No 139/2004 of 20 Jan 2004 on the control of concentrations between undertakings (the EC Merger Regulation) [2004] OJ L24/1.
[3] Case 85/76 [1979] ECR 461.
[4] See below.

Court has recognised the principle that undertakings in a dominant position owe a special responsibility towards the market:

> the Court points out that, according to a consistent line of decisions, an abuse is an objective concept referring to the behaviour of an undertaking in a dominant position which is such as to influence the structure of a market where, as a result of the very presence of the undertaking in question, the degree of competition is already weakened and which, through recourse to methods different from those governing normal competition in products or services on the basis of the transactions of commercial operators, has the effect of hindering the maintenance of the degree of competition still existing in the market or the growth of that competition (Case 85/76 *Hoffmann-La Roche* v *Commission* [1979] ECR 461, paragraph 91; Case 322/81 *Michelin* v *Commission* [1983] ECR 3461, paragraph 70; Case C–62/86 *AKZO* v *Commission* [1991] ECR I–3359, paragraph 69; and Case T–228/97 *Irish Sugar* v *Commission* [1999] ECR II–2969, paragraph 111).[5]

The actual scope of the special responsibility imposed on a dominant undertaking must be considered in the light of the specific circumstances of each case which shows a weakened competitive situation.[6] These developments in the Courts' case law led Amato to comment:

> Market power, just because it is conceptually accepted, is thus loaded with the burdens and limits which, according to the general principles more of public than of private law, bear upon whoever holds power.[7]

There is thus some fluidity between the idea that under competition law principles private undertakings are taking on public duties of responsibility towards the market and the state, when acting in a regulatory and a commercial capacity, is subject to the same obligations as private power in the market.

When Article 82 EC has been applied to Member State activity, it has usually been applied in conjunction with Article 86 EC. Briefly, Article 86(1) EC has the same effect as Article 3(g) EC in conjunction with Article 10 EC, in the specific context of *public* undertakings and *undertakings granted special or exclusive rights*. The undertakings are subject to the Treaty rules, unless they can show a special derogation in that they are providing a service of a general economic interest, or are revenue producing monopolies. Nevertheless the general Treaty rules apply to such bodies unless the Member State can show that the application of the Treaty rules, particularly those relating to competition, would obstruct the performance

---

⁵ Case T–203/01 *Michelin* v *Commission* [2003] ECR II–4071, para 54.

⁶ See, eg, Joined Cases C–395/96P & C–396/96 P *Compagnie Maritime Belge Transports SA, Compagnie Maritime Belge SA, Dafra Lines A/S* v *Commission* [2000] ECR I–1365, para 24. In this case Fennelly AG coined the phrase 'super dominant' but the Court merely repeats the accepted formula of the special responsibility of dominant firms.

⁷ G Amato, *Antitrust and the Bounds of Power. The Dilemma of Liberal Democracy in the History of the Market* (Oxford, Hart, 1997) at 66.

of the undertakings in law and in fact. In *GB-INNO v ATAB* [8] the Court explains that Article 86 EC 'is only a particular application of certain general principles which bind the member states'. This chapter examines whether Article 82 EC can be applied to state measures which fall outside the remit of Article 86 EC. That is where public undertakings are not the subject matter of the state's intervention but where laws and regulations are made which allow or encourage private undertakings to abuse a dominant position. Applying the general principle developed by the Court, any state measure which purports to legalise practices which constitute an abuse of a dominant position would infringe Article 82 EC; however, the Court has not addressed the issue squarely. In *France v Commission (Terminal Equipment)* [9] the Court states that:

> [Article 86 EC] confers powers on the Commission only in relation to state measures ... anti-competitive conduct engaged in by undertakings on their own initiative can be called into question only by individual decisions under Articles [81 and 82] of the Treaty.

This was a case where the EC Commission's legislative powers under Article 86(3) EC were being called into question. Nevertheless, this statement is relied upon in the later case of *RTT v GB-INNO* [10] when the Court states that Article 82 EC applies only to anti-competitive conduct carried out by undertakings on their own initiative; where a state measure is involved, then Article 86 EC comes into play. Conversely, in a number of cases involving Article 86 EC the Court has stressed that the application of Article 82 EC is not precluded where the existence of a dominant position is the result, not of the activities of the undertakings, but of state acts. [11] In a number of cases following *Höfner v Macrotron* [12] the Court has found that the existence *and* abuse of the dominant position may coincide as a result of the state's action. [13]

The turning point, which brought about the conceptual and practical limitation of using Article 82 EC on its own against acts of the Member States, came in *Spediporto*. [14] Here a dispute over alleged excessive road haulage charges led to a reference to the Court. The road haulage charges in dispute were fixed compulsorily according to an Italian law. The exercise of road haulage was subject to entry on a register and the grant of a permit by the public authorities. The

---

[8] Case 13/77 *NV GB-INNO-BM* v *Vereniging van de Kleinhandelaars in Tabak (ATAB)* [1977] ECR 2115, para 42.

[9] Case 202/88 [1991] ECR 1223, para 55.

[10] Case 18/88 [1991] ECR I-5941, para 20.

[11] Case 30/87 *Bodson v Pompes funèbres des régions libérées* [1988] ECR 2479; Case 311/84 *CBEM v CLT* [1985] ECR 3261.

[12] Case C–41/90 [1991] ECR I–1979.

[13] See, *inter alia*, Case C–258/98 *Criminal Proceedings against Giovanni Carra and others* [2000] ECR I–4217; Case C–55/96 *Job Centre Coop arl* [1997] ECR I–7119.

[14] Case C–96/94 *Centro Servizi Spediporto Srl v Spedizioni Marittima del Golfo Srl* [1995] ECR I–2883.

register was maintained by a central committee composed of 17 representatives of the public authorities and 12 representatives of road hauliers' associations appointed by the Minister of Transport and Civil Aviation. In addition to maintaining the register, the committee was responsible for proposing tariffs to the minister, who enacted them by a decree after approval. We see the Court applying the general principle but then dividing the issue into an investigation, first, of the applicability of Articles 10(2) and 81 EC and, then Articles 10(2) and 82 EC.

Looking first at Article 81 EC the Court found that in applying the tests of *Van Eycke*[15] the committee's proposals were not capable of being agreements, decisions or concerted practices between economic agents which had been imposed by the public authorities. There were 17 representatives of public authorities and only 12 representatives of the road hauliers' associations. The committee was obliged to take into account a variety of public interest factors under the law. In applying the third limb the Court found that the public authorities had not delegated their powers to private economic agents. The Minister had the competence to approve, reject or amend the proposed tariffs as well as to consult the regions and representatives of the economic sectors concerned, and there was also the possibility of derogation from the tariffs.

In *Spediporto*, as with *Reiff*[16] and *Delta*,[17] the Court places importance upon the question whether a responsible Minister was able to substitute his decision for that of the committees. Another way of looking at the issue is whether the contested measure stems from genuine state regulation. When looking at the interaction of Articles 3(g), 10(2) and 82 EC the Court establishes a new test or set of criteria to be fulfilled. The first issue was whether the national measures created a dominant position. The Court uses its traditional test normally applied to private undertakings:

> [Articles 3(g), 10 and 82] of the Treaty could only apply to legislation of the kind contained in the Italian Law if it were proved that the legislation concerned placed an undertaking in a position of economic strength enabling it to prevent effective competition from being maintained on the relevant market by placing it in a position to behave to an appreciable extent independently of its competitors, of its customers and ultimately of the consumers.[18]

In *Spediporto* the issue arose as to whether the companies were in a joint dominant position. From the facts the Court concluded that the legislation did *not* put the undertakings in a joint dominant position, which would be characterised by the absence of competition between them, and therefore there was no

15   Case 267/86 [1988] ECR 4369.
16   Case C–185/91 [1993] ECR I–5801.
17   Case C–153/93 [1994] ECR I–2517.
18   *Ibid*, at para 31.

infringement of Article 82 EC. The case is important since the Court stresses *twice* (at paragraphs 31 and 34) that there must be a *link* between the national measure being attacked and the abuse of a dominant position. Thus the Court has drawn similar principles across the application of Articles 81 and 82 EC to state activity.

The separation of Articles 81 and 82 EC is followed in the case law. For example, in *DIP*[19] the Court follows the same methodology. Again the absence of competition between the relevant economic agents is regarded as the crucial factor in deciding whether there is an abuse of a (joint) dominant position:

> National rules which require a licence to be obtained before a new shop can be opened and limit the number of shops in the municipality in order to achieve a balance between supply and demand cannot be considered to put individual traders in dominant positions or all the traders established in a municipality in a collective dominant position, a salient feature of which would be that traders did not compete against each other.[20]

The *Spediporto* test is applied in *Sodemare*.[21] Here a Luxembourg company sought to challenge an Lombardy law which allowed only non-profit-making companies to be reimbursed by the public authorities for the costs of providing residential care. The Court was asked whether this rule was precluded by Articles 3(g), 10(2), 81 and 82, and 86 EC. The Court begins with the general principle and then applies the V*an Eycke* test and then the *Spediporto* test. The Court finds that there is no evidence to suggest that the national measures infringe the competition rules of the EC Treaty.

JOINT DOMINANCE

Sediporto uses the traditional analysis of the Court's case law to establish an abuse of a dominant position, but there is a novel element to the case. Where a link is established between the companies in the group there is a hint at the concept of *joint dominance* being caught by Article 82 EC. In *Spediporto*, and in *DIP SpA*, there is the suggestion that it is possible to establish a joint dominant position by the adoption of parallel conduct on the market as a result of state regulations.

The idea of joint dominance is drawn from the actual wording of Article 82 EC

---

[19] Joined Cases C–140/94, C–141/94 & C–142/94 *DIP SpA and Others v Comune di Bassano del Grappa and Commune di Chioggia* [1995] ECR I–3287.

[20] *Ibid*, at para 27.

[21] Case C–70/95 *Sodemare SA, Anni Azzurri Holding SpA, and Anni Azzurri Rezzato Srl v Regione Lombardia* [1997] ECR I–3395.

which refers to the behaviour of 'one or more undertakings'.[22] Whish[23] points out that this language can be read in a narrow way merely to embrace the idea of the conduct of different legal entities within the same corporate group being caught by Article 82 EC. Such was the situation in *Commercial Solvents v Commission*.[24] A wider definition would embrace bringing the conduct of legally and economically independent undertakings within the scope of Article 82 EC, but this would bring with it the problem of distinguishing between rational market behaviour, particularly where there is an oligopolistic market, and behaviour which can be sanctioned as abusive. Thus, as a legal concept, the idea of joint dominance has taken time to evolve.[25]

The starting point for the judicial acceptance of a notion of joint dominance was the appeal against the EC Commission's Decision that three Italian producers of flat glass had a collective dominant position which they had abused.[26] The conduct of the flat glass producers had also been found to infringe Article 81 EC: there was evidence of concerted practices on what was a narrow oligopolistic market. The CFI would not uphold the EC Commission's Decision on the application of Article 82 EC. Working on the premise that Articles 81 and 82 EC must be applied on their own distinctive terms the CFI found that the EC Commission had merely recycled the facts of its findings under Article 81 EC. In order to apply Article 82 EC it should prove that there were dominant positions on the relevant product and geographic markets in order to establish the abuse of a dominant position. But the CFI did accept the idea of collective dominance between independent legal entities:

> There is nothing in principle, to prevent two or more independent economic entities from being, on a specific market, united by such economic links that, by virtue of the fact, together they hold a dominant position vis-à-vis the other operators on the same market. This could be the case, for example, where two or more independent undertakings jointly have, through agreements or licences, a technological lead affording them the power to behave to an appreciable extent independently of their competitors, their customers and ultimately of their consumers (judgment of the Court in *Hoffmann-La Roche...*, paragraphs 38 and 48).

The concept of 'collective dominance' receives judicial approval but with little clarity as to its component elements. This raises the issue of what was the function of collective dominance under Article 82 EC, when similar behaviour

---

[22]   In the case law the terms 'collective dominance', 'joint dominance' and 'oligopolistic dominance' have been used interchangeably by the EC Commission, Advocates General and the Court of Justice.

[23]   R Whish, 'Collective Dominance' in D O'Keeffe and M Andenas (eds), *Liber Amicorum for Lord Slynn* (The Hague, Kluwer, 2000).

[24]   Joined Cases 6/73 & 7/73 *Società Italiana Vetro SpA v Commission* [1974] ECR 223.

[25]   See T Soames, 'An Analysis of the Principles of Concerted Practice and Collective Dominance: A Distinction Without A Difference?' (1996) 17 *ECLR* 24.

[26]   Cases T–68, T–77 & T–78/89 *Società Italiana Vetro SpA, Fabbrica Pisana SpA and PPG Vernante Pennitalia SpA v Commission* [1992] ECR II–1403.

could also be caught under Article 81 EC. One of the crucial questions which needed answering from *Italian Flat Glass* was the question whether formal links between the undertakings were necessary. The phraseology of the Court's judgment suggests that it was merely creating illustrations of the kind of formal links which would establish collective dominance on the market. In a subsequent case, *Almelo*,[27] the Court of Justice confirmed the concept of collective dominance, and along with the CFI, but perhaps more clearly, held that the establishment of a *link* between the dominant firms was a necessary condition of the application of the principle.[28]

Whish[29] suggested that there must be a link between the undertakings which are the focus of the allegation of collective dominance and that the link allows the undertakings to adopt the same conduct on the market. It was for the national court to decide whether the link was 'sufficiently strong' for there to be a collective dominant position. Whish argues that *Almelo* is an improvement upon *Italian Flat Glass* in that it suggests an economic rationale for the concept of joint dominance. The significance of 'links' suggested that the Court was adopting an economic approach to Article 82 EC and would be willing to discover abuse of a dominant position where there was tacit coordination of activity. But, as Whish points out, the Court does not go any further and explain more precisely what the links should be. The *Almelo* ruling is followed in a number of EC Commission Decisions and upheld by the CFI in the appeal against the Decision in *Cewal*.[30]

More recently, the Court has ruled that the necessity for *structural links* to be established between two or more undertakings is merely an *illustration* of how collective dominance might be established. In *Gencor/Lonrho*[31] the EC Commission blocked a concentration under the Merger Regulation that would have created or strengthened what is described as a 'dominant duopoly position' in the Common Market. The contemplated merger was to take place in South Africa between two undertakings which would result in the control of the platinum group metals market. One of the grounds of challenge to the EC Commission's Decision was the allegation that the EC Commission had not established that there were structural links between Gencor and Lonrho as required from the ruling in *Italian Flat Glass*. The Court states:

---

[27] Case C-393/92 *Municipality of Almelo and others v NV Energiebedrijf Ijsselmi* [1994] ECR I-1477.

[28] *Ibid*, at para. 42.

[29] Whish, above n 23.

[30] [1993] OJ L34/2; Joined Cases T-24/93 to T-26/93 & T-28/93 *Compagnie Maritime Belge Transports and Others v Commission* [1996] ECR II-12015; Joined Cases C-395 & C-396/96P *Campaigne Maritime Belge Transport SA, Campaigne Maritime Belge SA and Dafra-Lines A/S v Commission of European Community* [2000] ECR I-1365.

[31] Case IV/M.619 [1997] OJ L11/30.

In its judgment in the *Flat Glass* case, the Court referred to links of a structural nature only by way of example and did not lay down that such links must exist in order for a finding of collective dominance to be made.[32]

Structural links such as agreements or licences are but mere examples of structural links; other *economic* links may also be established:

> there is nothing, in principle, to prevent two or more independent economic entities from being united by economic links in a specific market and, by virtue of that fact, from together holding a dominant position *vis-à-vis* the other operators on the same market. [The Court] ... added (in the same paragraph) that that could be the case, for example, where two or more independent undertakings jointly had, through agreements or licences, a technological lead affording them power to behave to an appreciable extent independently of their competitors, their customers and, ultimately, of consumers.

> Nor can it be deduced from the same judgment that the Court has restricted the notion of economic links to the notion of structural links referred to by the appellant.[33]

The CFI appears to take a fluid approach to what kind of links in the market may facilitate tacit coordination. Of significance is the broad interpretation given to the idea of economic links: such links may arise merely as part of the conditions of the market itself.

The EC Commission has continued to use the concept of joint dominance, finding two ferry companies that fixed common rates and co-ordinated timetables and marketed their services jointly to be in a dominant position.[34] A decision which adds a novel twist to the concept is the finding of *vertical dominance* between Irish Sugar and a distributor of sugar, Sugar Distributors Ltd (SDL).[35] There was no finding of *de facto* control of the distributor. There was, however, sufficient evidence of direct economic ties, derived from Irish Sugar's equity holding in SDL and the structure of policy-making, creating channels of communication between the two undertakings. The CFI upheld the finding of a *vertical* dominant position.[36]

In *Spediporto and DIP* the feature of joint dominance is the absence of competition between the undertakings. If the Court had found collective dominance in *Spediporto*, then a number of small operators would be found to hold a position of collective dominance. The question remains, however, whether on a differently structured market state action could result in an infringement of

---

[32]   Case T-102/96 *Gencor v Commission* [1997] II-753, para 273.

[33]   *Ibid*, at paras 274–275.

[34]   *Port of Rødby* [1994] OJ L95/1. Cases T–191/98, T–212/98 to T–214/98 *Atlantic Container Line AB and Others v Commission* [2003] ECR I–3275.

[35]   [1997] OJ L258/1.

[36]   Case T–228/97 *Irish Sugar plc v Commission* [1999] ECR II–2969, para 63.

Article 82 EC by creating collective dominant positions. In *Italian Flat Glass*[37] the CFI held that a collective dominant position might be established where two or more independent undertakings concluded agreements which gave them the power to behave to an appreciable extent independently of their competitors, and ultimately of their consumers. Bacon[38] points out that if a price-fixing agreement were brought within this definition then the state regulation of prices might be sufficient to put the undertakings covered by the price-fixing regulation in a dominant position. It would have to be shown that an abuse of a dominant position has occurred, for example, an excessive, unfair, or discriminatory pricing policy. Bacon argues that some behaviour which the Court has found to be compatible with Article 81 EC[39] could be exposed to scrutiny under Article 82 EC. In *Tetra Pak*[40] the Court confirmed that behaviour which may fall outside the scope of Article 81(1) EC or may be exempted under Article 81(3) EC or a Block Exemption, may still be caught by Article 82 EC. These are now issues which the national courts must address as a result of Regulation 1/2004.[41]

In *Italian Flat Glass* [42] the CFI supports the EC Commission's finding that the publication of identical price lists within a short period of time, identical discounts and identical classification of customers qualifying for particular terms amounted to the elimination of price competition on the market. The CFI also gives as an example of a collective dominant position a liner conference where a group of carriers providing international liner services for the carriage of cargo agree certain terms, for example, to operate under uniform or common freight rates. In *Ahmed Saeed*[43] the Court suggests that the elimination of price competition among airlines serving a particular route could place the airlines in a collective dominant position. In *Sodemare*[44] the Court repeats the criteria from *Almelo*[45] but concludes that the legislation under scrutiny does not create the conditions for a dominant position or create sufficiently strong links between undertakings to give rise to a collective dominant position.[46]

---

[37] Cases T–68, T–77 & T–78/89 *Società Italiana Vetro SpA v Commission* [1992] ECR II–1403.

[38] K Bacon, 'State Regulation of the Market and E.C. Competition Rules: Articles 85 and 86 Compared' (1997) 18 *ECLR* 283.

[39] For e.g, Case C–2/91 *Criminal Proceedings Against Wolfgang Meng* [1993] ECR I–5751; Case C–245/91 *Criminal Proceedings Against Ohra Schadeverzekehringen NV* [1993] ECR I–5851.

[40] Case T–51/89 *Tetra Pak Rausing SA v Commission (Tetra Pak I)* [1990] ECR II–309. See also Case 85/76 Hoffmann-La Roche & Co AG v Commission [1979] ECR 461.

[41] [2003] OJ L1/1.

[42] Above n 37.

[43] Case 66/86 [1989] ECR 803.

[44] Case C–70/95 [1997] ECR I–3395.

[45] Case C–393/92 [1994] ECR I–1477.

[46] *Ibid,* at para 47.

CONCLUSION

The majority of the cases studied in Chapters 2 and 3 are Article 234 EC rulings. The cases have arisen largely as a result of provoked prosecutions under national law. A number of the litigants are opportunistic, well-known or repeat player litigants who have had an important effect on the development of the Court's jurisprudence. By challenging diverse, and allegedly neutral, national rules the cases show the inter-relationship of the free movement and competition law provisions of the EC Treaty and their *potential* to create an economic constitution through the use of an economic due process role in the Community legal order. In practice the Court has declined to adopt a general economic due process clause and has tempered its declarations of general principle with a preference for using Article 28 EC over the competition rules. Arguably this allows for the division of competence between national interest and Community/EU interests to be achieved. It provides scope for specific pleading on the part of each Member State, to protect legitimate national interests even when there is a perceptible impact on inter-state trade. The post-*Keck* test for Article 28 EC allows a greater margin of manœuvre for the Member States to regulate their internal economy and focuses Article 28 EC mainly upon inter-state trade issues, rather than allowing it to protect the commercial freedom of traders over democratic choices of the Member States. Only recently has the Court moved the focus of Article 28 EC to address the competitive structure of the market, beyond market access issues.

The adoption of the principle that Articles 81 and 82 EC apply to a Member State's regulatory autonomy is not illogical. The Court's case law on Article 81 EC is well established: each economic operator on the market must determine its policy on the market independently.[47] The underlying purpose of the Court's approach:

> is to determine the degree of the state's intervention necessary to condemn private parties' anti-competitive conduct as being contrary to antitrust law…[48]

The Court's requirement of a link between the state measure and the anti-competitive conduct of undertakings, while attracting criticism, is not therefore entirely illogical.[49] It may create loopholes. Gagliardi argues that Member States

---

[47] This case law has developed largely in relation to the concept of concerted practices: Cases 40–48/73, 50/73, 54–56/73, 11/73 & 113–114/73 *Cooperatiëve Vereniging Suiker Unie UA v Commission* [1975] ECR 1663, para 73.

[48] A Gagliardi, 'United States and European Union Antitrust v State Regulation of the Economy Is There a Better Test?' (2000) 25 *ELRev* 353, 354.

[49] The Supreme Court of the United States has followed a similar path, with the exception of one ruling: *California Retail Liquor Dealers v Midcal Aluminium*, 445 US 97 (1980). Here a Californian statute required all wine producers and wholesalers to lodge fair trade contracts or price schedules with the state. Such producers and wholesalers could not then sell wine at a price other than the one lodged with the state. The prices were set autonomously by the producers/wholesalers and the state

are still able to displace competition by carefully creating economic policies which by-pass the intervention of private parties or by establishing supervisory schemes the mere function of which is to approve private parties' anti-competitive decisions.

Another way of rationalising the application of Articles 81 and 82 EC to state intervention in the market is to argue that the Court, through its case law, has extended the logic of Article 86 EC to cases not coming within the scope of that provision.[50] But, as Gagliardi argues and we shall discover in the next chapter, the Court has not subjected the application of Articles 81 and 82 EC to Member State intervention in the market to the same conditions of substantive review as it has applied under Article 86 EC, where it recognises that the Member States are big economic players. Equally the Court's reticence in applying Articles 81 and 82 EC to the Member States' regulation of the economy has brought with it inconsist-encies between Articles 81 and 82 EC on the one hand and the application of Articles 28 and 86(1) EC on the other. Gagliardi's solution is to suggest that the Court, in future cases, should abandon its case law under Articles 10, 81 and 82 EC and examine all future cases questioning state regulation under Article 86(1) EC. The rationale for this approach is to further the economic integration project: the inclusion of *all* anti-competitive regulations within the test would stimulate the debate over the harmonisation of state economies in the Common Market since state measures fixing the price of goods or services inevitably create distortions that prevent the free movement of goods and services. According to Gagliardi:

> The fact that in some instances these measures are not subject to antitrust scrutiny, keeps the debate concerning the harmonisation of state economies out of the reach of the federal government, the only location in which democratic discussion involving representatives of all states could take place. The threat of antitrust litigation could boost the harmonisation discussion forcing states to agree with each other on how they want to plan their economic policies.[51]

Arguably this discussion over the harmonisation of economic policies is now taking place at the EU level as a result of the Broad Economic Guidelines created under Article 98 EC and the new soft law governance processes created through the Lisbon Process. What Gagliardi seems to miss is the inherently *undemocratic* nature of private interest litigation.[52]

---

did not examine them. Nevertheless the Supreme Court found that the state's control over the wine retail price 'destroys horizontal competition as effectively as if wholesalers 'formed a combination and endeavoured to establish the same restriction ... by agreement with each other' (at 105).

[50] See J Buendia Sierra, *Exclusive Rights and State Monopolies Under EC Law* (Oxford, OUP, 1999) at 267.

[51] Above n 48, at 373.

[52] E Szyszczak 'Free Trade as a Fundamental Value' in K Economides, L Betten, J Bridge, V Shrubsall and A Tettenborn (eds), *Fundamental Values* (Oxford, Hart, 2000).

There are other problems with this idea. As we shall see in the next chapter, Article 86(1) EC applies only to the narrow situation where the state has granted 'special or exclusive rights' to an undertaking. Gagliardi deals with this problem in a footnote by suggesting:

> This requirement may be superseded if state regulations depriving Article 81 E.C. of its effectiveness are automatically considered the equivalent of a state grant of special or exclusive rights.[53]

The Community interest would be found where a state measure had an effect on inter-state trade, as described by the Court under Article 86(2) EC in *Müller*.[54] This is much narrower than the concept of inter-state trade applied under Articles 81 and 82 EC and should take into account the interests of the EU as a whole, including the objective of general economic policy pursued by the other Member States under the supervision of federal authorities. One reason Gagliardi seems to prefer this route is to allow for a 'legitimate interest' defence which, he argues, may involve a mixture of economic and non-economic considerations, as well as exclusively non-economic reasons, with the idea that only measures with a clear protectionist intent should be struck down.

In the pragmatic political climate of European integration, with an acceptance of subsidiarity and further moves towards flexibility and differentiated integration with decentralisation and private enforcement of EU competition law firmly on the agenda, the use of Articles 81 and 82 EC against state intervention in the economy is a controversial principle, and one which is difficult to sustain. This in part is due to the EC Commission's reluctance to initiate investigations against Member States under Articles 81 and 82 EC, thus denying the EU the opportunity to build up a case system of precedents which has been the basis for the legitimacy of the application of Articles 81 and 82 EC to private undertakings. These factors perhaps explain the Court's formal application of the competition rules to the Member States and its greater willingness to apply Article 28 EC with the possibility of justifications to a wide variety of situations. The domination of Article 28 EC over Articles 81 and 82 EC in this litigation has in fact been beneficial. By allowing the competition rules to play a subordinate role in controlling national regulatory processes their purpose and legitimacy in such a role, while open to criticism and question, have not been directly challenged and remain intact. As the rulings against Italy[55] reveal, they remain a potential weapon in the armoury of the EU, to ensure that a Member State does not overstep the boundaries of national competence with measures which may

---

[53]   Above n 48, at 369, fn 79.
[54]   Case 10/71 *Ministère Public of Luxembourg v Müller* [1971] ECR 723.
[55]   Case C–119/92 *Commission v Italy* [1994] ECR I–393; Case C–35/96 *Commission v Italy* [1998] ECR I–3851; Case C–198/01 *CIF* [2003] ECR I–8055.

threaten the operation and competitive structure of the Internal Market. However, as Chapter 5 shows, the competition rules, particularly Article 82 EC and the merger rules, have a significant role to play in the liberalised markets of Europe.

4

The Regulation of State Monopolies

THE POSITION OF STATE MONOPOLIES IN THE EC TREATY

ARTICLE 295 EC ALLOWS the Member States to determine the extent and the internal organisation of their public sectors. However, *all* economic actors are governed by the same rules, except where the EC Treaty permits a derogation. The objective of the Treaty of Rome 1957 was to establish a common market. While the elimination of various forms of trade barriers used by the Member States, such as customs duties, quotas and restrictive trading rules, were identifiable targets for Community law to control, the role of public monopolies was problematic. The restrictive trade effects of public monopolies were often justified by reference to the objectives of national economic policy, but not all of the Member States resorted to the use of public monopolies.[1] Thus a balance had to be drawn not only between the treatment of public and private undertakings *within* the Member States but also *between* the Member States which favoured intervention in the market through public monopolies and those Member States which did not. The compromise was the inclusion of what are now Articles 31 and 86 EC which address specifically the regulation of state monopolies in the EU. In *IGAC v ENCC* the Court held that Articles 86 and 31 EC belong to a wider group of 'provisions relating to infringements of the normal functioning of the competition system by actions on the part of states'.[2]

The intention of the drafters of the Treaty of Rome 1957 was to have a common rule relating to public monopolies, but the final draft of the Treaty located the two Articles in different parts, with very differently worded provisions which have subsequently been utilised in very different ways. Article 31 EC is located in Part Three (Community Policies), Title I of the EC Treaty relating to the free movement of goods. Initially it was thought that Article 31 EC cannot be used where a state monopoly is infringing one of the other economic freedoms of

---

[1] The division was between the Benelux countries, which did not have any public monopolies, and France, which had 7, Italy, which had 5, and Germany, which had 2 public monopolies.

[2] Case 94/74 [1975] ECR 699. The complex drafting of Art 31 EC is acknowledged by the Court in Case 6/64 *Costa v ENEL* [1964] ECR 1164 and by Colliard, who refers to the 'obscure clarity' of Art 31 EC: C Colliard, 'L'obscure clarité de l'article 37' (1964) *Dalloz* Ch. XXXVII 263.

the Treaty (persons, services, capital);[3] resort must then be had to Article 86 EC. However, the Court has accepted that Article 31 EC may apply to monopolies in the energy sector which provide goods and services.[4]

In contrast, Article 86 EC is located in Title VI (Common Rules on Competition, Taxation and Approximation of Laws), Chapter 1 (Rules on Competition), Section 1 (Rules Applying to Undertakings) of the EC Treaty. The awkward position of Article 86 EC is justified by the fact that, while it is addressed to Member States[5] and seeks to bring competition principles to bear on the role of state intervention in the market, the main justification for its position in the EC Treaty is to apply similar *competition* rules and principles to private *and* public undertakings. Yet many of the integration problems created by state monopolies are linked to free movement issues. Thus, Buendia Sierra labels Articles 31 and 86 EC as 'reference rules':

> This means that when they are applied in conjunction with the Community rules on free movement of goods, the free movement of services, the freedom of establishment or competition, they prohibit the maintenance of those monopolies whose restrictive effects are capable of affecting trade between Member States. This means that the study of Articles 31 and 86 actually takes one on a journey through a large part of the Community legal system.[6]

It can be argued that the combination of Articles 31 and 86(1) EC envisaged not only an *adjustment* of public monopolies to the conditions of a common market but also a gradual decrease in the use of commercial trading monopolies by limiting their powers. Indeed in the early years of the EEC the EC Commission closely monitored the state monopolies, and there was a significant amount of litigation using Article 31 EC.[7] In contrast, Article 86(2) EC does not contemplate the disappearance of undertakings supplying a service of general economic interest and fiscal monopolies which raise revenue for the state.

Read with Articles 3(f) and 10 EC, Articles 31 and 86 EC suggest that the Member States have extremely limited competence to intervene in the market

---

[3] Case 155/73 *Giuseppe Sacchi* [1974] ECR 429, para 10; Case 271/81 *Société coopérative d'amélioration de l'éle vage et d'insémination artificielle du Béarn v Lucien J.M. Mialocq and others* [1983] ECR 2072, para 8; Case 30/87 *Corinne Bodson v SA Pompes funèbres des régions libérés* 3 [1988] ECR 2479, para 10; Case C–17/94 *Criminal Proceedings against Denis Gervais, Jean-Louis Nougaillon, Christian Carrad and Bernard Horgue* [1995] ECR I–4353, para 35.

[4] Case C–393/92 *Almelo* [1994] ECR I–1477, para 28; Case C–158/94 *Commission v Italy* [1997] ECR I–5789.

[5] See P Schindler, 'Public Enterprises and the EEC Treaty' (1970) 7 *CMLRev* 57, 57–8, who argues that since Art 86 EC imposes an obligation exclusively upon Member States Art 86 EC is misplaced in the EC Treaty.

[6] J-L Buendia Sierra, *Exclusive Rights and State Monopolies Under EC Law* (Oxford, OUP, 1999), Preface, p v.

[7] See M Ross, 'Art. 37—Redundancy or Reinstatement' (1982) 7 *ELRev* 285; F Wooldridge, 'Some Recent Developments Concerning Article 37 of the EEC Treaty' (1979) 1 *Legal Issues of Economic Integration* 120.

through monopolies and undertakings with special and exclusive rights, especially in a manner which limits competition and restricts the operation of the non-discrimination and free movement principles. The initial focus of litigation was upon Article 31 EC, with Article 86 EC almost a dormant provision of the EC Treaty. Greater interest in controlling the behaviour of state monopolies emerged only after the EC Commission's White Paper of 1985,[8] and it was not until the 1990s that a significant change of policy occurred towards public monopolies.

There is no longer an assumption that the provision of public goods and services through monopolists, whether state or privately owned, is the most effective way to deliver certain goods or services. Ideas of natural monopolies in sectors such as the networked industries have also been challenged by the liberalisation processes in Europe. Yet a range of economic activity still remains within the control or remit of such monopolies since neither Article 31 EC or Article 86 EC requires the *abolition* of state monopolies. What has changed is that the process of elaborating a role for the public provision of goods and services has shifted away from the Member State level towards regulation using Community-based ideas.

This shift in thinking has been orchestrated by the EC Commission using powers granted under Articles 86(3) and 226 EC, encouraged and consolidated by rulings of the Court, using Article 234 EC, at the instigation of private litigation at the national level. Thus the extent to which the *laissez-faire* tolerance of the mix between public and private ownership within the Member States which Article 295 EC allows has rested in the rulings of the Court. In recent years it has been argued that many of these rulings are capable of undermining, if not obliterating, state reservation of exclusivity in many sectors at the behest of non-state operators who may rely on the direct effect of Article 86 EC in order to gain access to hitherto uncontested markets.

Thus, within the last two decades, the issue of the balance between state intervention in markets and competition in markets has been transferred into a regulatory issue. While there are definite shifts to reduce the *amount and proportion* of public involvement in the provision of goods and services in the EU, the *exact scope* of the role state monopolies are allowed to play in the national economies is not an academic question. A number of the recent Accession States retain and defend their belief in allowing some areas of economic life to be run by state monopolies.[9] Thus the scope and the parameters of the regulation of state monopolies under Community law is a central regulatory issue for the EU.

---

[8]   EC Commission, *Completing the Internal Market*, COM(85) 310 final.
[9]   See EC Commission, White Paper on the preparation of the associated countries of Central and Eastern Europe for integration into the internal market of the European Union, COM(95) 163 final.

ARTICLE 31 EC: STATE MONOPOLIES OF A COMMERCIAL CHARACTER

Article 31 EC is located in the free movement of goods section of the EC Treaty and applies to state monopolies enjoying exclusive rights in the procurement and distribution of goods, but not services.[10] Article 31 EC does not apply to regulatory activities of the state, for example, licensing, and applies only to activities intrinsically connected with the specific business of a commercial monopoly.[11] The aim of Article 31 EC is the adjustment of national monopolies so as to eliminate the exclusive right to import from other Member States and to eliminate discrimination between *nationals*[12] of the Member States in the way in which goods are procured and marketed.[13] In *Manghera*[14] the Court established the principle that exclusive rights to import were discriminatory *per se* and therefore contrary to Article 31 EC. This led to the EC Commission attacking a number of exclusive import and marketing rights in the energy sector,[15] which eventually forced the Member States to consider liberalising measures over which they had more control. These are examined in the case study in the next chapter.

A weakness in the drafting of Article 31 EC is that it does not contain any explicit exceptions or derogations whereby a Member State may justify a measure which is in the public interest. Article 30 EC, which is the justification for the free movement of goods provisions of Articles 28 and 29 EC, explicitly refers only to Articles 28 and 29, with no mention of Article 31 EC. However in *SAIL*[16] the EC

---

[10]   Although in Case 155/73 *Sacchi* [1974] ECR 409 it was recognised that a monopoly over the provision of services may have an indirect influence on the trade in goods. See also Case 271/81 *Mialocq* [1983] ECR 2072, para 10; Case 30/87 *Bodson* [1988] ECR 2511, para 10; Case C–17/94 *Gervais* [1995] ECR I–4353, paras 36–37.

[11]   Case 118/86 *Nertsvoederfabriek Nederland BV* [1987] ECR 3883; Case 86/78 *SA des grandes distilleries Peureux v directeur des Services fiscaux de la Haute-Saône et du territoire de Belfort* [1979] ECR 897.

[12]   Cf Case C–189/95 *Franzén* [1997] ECR I–5909 where the Court applied Art 31 EC to discrimination between different national *products*.

[13]   Para (1) of Art 31 EC was held to have direct effect from the end of the transitional period in Case 59/75 *Pubblico Ministero v Flavia Manghera* [1976] ECR 91; para (2) of Art 31 EC was held to have direct effect from the date of entry into force of the EEC Treaty in Case 6/64 *Costa v ENEL* [1964] ECR 585. The Court has affirmed that Art 31(1) EC is still in force even though the transitional period has ended: Case C–387/93 *Banchero* [1995] ECR I–4663. The Treaty of Amsterdam 1997 repealed paras (3), (5) and (6) of the original Art 31 EC (ex Art 37 EEC). For a detailed analysis of the operation of Art 31 EC see J Buendia Sierra, *Exclusive Rights and State Monopolies Under EC Law* (Oxford, OUP, 1999) ch 3.

[14]   Case 59/75 *Manghera* [1976] ECR 91.

[15]   See the EC Commission's opposition to the exclusive rights to import natural gas in Belgium: *XIII Report on Competition Policy 1983*, para 291; Case C–347/88 *Greek Oil Monopoly* [1990] ECR I–4789; Case C–159/94 *Commission v France* [1997] ECR I–5815; Case C–158/94 *Commission v Italy* [1997] ECR I–5789; Case C–57/94 *Commission v The Netherlands* [1997] ECR I–5699; Case C–160/94 *Commission v Spain* [1997] ECR I–5699.

[16]   Case 82/71 *SAIL* [1972] ECR 119. The EC Commission also suggested that Art 30 EC could apply to justify the Swedish and Finnish retail alcohol monopolies provided that the proportionality principle was met: EC Commission, *XXV Report on Competition Policy* (Brussels/Luxembourg, EC Commission, 1995 para 126. See also Case C–189/95 *Criminal Proceedings Against Harry Franzén* [1997] ECR I–5909; Case C–394/97 *Criminal Proceedings Against Sami Heinonen* [1999] ECR I–3599.

Commission and Advocate General Roemer had supported the idea that Article 30 EC could apply to Article 31 EC.[17] In *Greek Oil Monopoly*[18] the Court also accepted the idea but appeared to demand a high level of proof. The Greek government argued that 'public security', that is ensuring a consistent supply of oil, was the reason for the state monopoly. However the Court dismissed this claim since the Greek government had not explained *why* exclusive rights in the form of a monopoly were necessary. The ruling shows that the government should explain why alternative, less restrictive, methods would not meet the stated objectives. In the energy infringement actions[19] the Court allowed Article 86(2) EC to be used to disapply Article 31(1) EC if its application would interfere with the provision of a service of general economic interest.

THE STRUCTURE OF ARTICLE 86 EC

Article 86 EC is regarded as one of the most complicated and politically controversial provisions of the Treaty. It is located in the provisions of the EC Treaty relating to the application of the *competition* rules to *undertakings*. Yet Article 86(1) EC clearly identifies its application to state monopolies where there is *any* infringement of the EC Treaty rules, not just competition policy. State monopolies may affect the fundamental economic freedoms in the areas of goods, persons, services, establishment and capital. Chung[20] argues that Article 86 EC performs a dual role: as a *lex specialis* for the application of the competition rules to the public sector and as a *lex generalis* for delimiting the scope of the EC Treaty principles, in particular free competition as against state intervention in the market. On this interpretation Article 86 EC applies both to state undertakings and to the *policies* of the Member States.

Article 86(1) EC states:

> In the case of public undertakings and undertakings to which Member States grant special or exclusive rights, Member States shall neither enact nor maintain in force any measure contrary to the rules contained in this Treaty, in particular to those rules provided for in Article 12 and Articles 81 to 89.

---

[17] Note, however, that it would be extremely difficult for the *Cassis de Dijon* 'mandatory requirements' to apply to Art 31 EC since these should be applied only to non-discriminatory measures Case 120/78 *REWE-Zentrale v Bundesmonopolverwaltung für Branntwein (Cassis de Dijon)* [1979] ECR 649.

[18] Case C–347/88 *Greek Oil Monopoly* [1990] ECR I–4789.

[19] Above n 15.

[20] C-M Chung, 'The Relationship Between State Regulation and EC Competition Law: Two Proposals for a Coherent Approach' (1995) 16 *ECLR* 87.

In the *Sacchi*[21] case the Court is clear that Article 86(1) EC is a permission. In the *Terminal Equipment*[22] case the Court also makes the point that not all special or exclusive rights are compatible with the EC Treaty. As a result of the EC Commission's strategy and the European Courts' interpretation of Article 86(1) EC there is a discernible move towards assumption of illegality of special or exclusive rights unless the Member State can show the necessity of such rights.[23]

Article 86(2) EC provides a limited derogation or justification for not applying the full force of the Treaty rules:

> Undertakings entrusted with the operation of services of general economic interest or having the character of a revenue-producing monopoly shall be subject to the rules contained in this Treaty, in particular to the rules on competition, in so far as the application of such rules does not obstruct the performance, in law or in fact, of the particular tasks assigned to them. The development of trade must not be affected to such an extent as would be contrary to the interests of the Community.

Article 86(2) EC protects services of general economic interest and revenue raising monopolies from the full thrust of the Treaty rules. The focus has been on services of general economic interest, and the aggressive attacks upon public monopolies from the 1990s onwards has created a new discourse on how such services can be protected in liberalised markets.[24] This issue is discussed in more detail in Chapter 7. The interaction of Article 86(1) and (2) EC is a complicated process; Marenco[25] has described Article 86(1) and (2) EC as 'two extraneous bodies forced to live under the same roof'.

Finally, Article 86(3) EC grants special supervisory powers to the EC Commission:

> The Commission shall ensure the application of the provisions of this Article and shall, where necessary, address appropriate directives or decisions to Member States.

The interpretation of Article 86 EC by the EC Commission and the European Courts has attracted criticism. At the outset it is important to impose a structure upon Article 86 EC. This chapter explores the boundaries and parameters of Article 86 EC by examining first of all what kind of activity falls *outside* its scope. It will then assess the parameters of Article 86 EC by examining what *kind* of activity performed by state monopolies falls within Article 86 EC. This will include an examination of the interaction between Article 86(1) and (2) EC, since activities performed by undertakings carrying out services of general economic interest may fall within the scope of Article 86(1) EC but are granted an

---

[21]   Case 155/73 *Giuseppe Sacchi* [1974] ECR 409.
[22]   Case 202/88 *French Republic v Commission (Terminal Equipment)* [1991] ECR 1223.
[23]   See A Gagliardi. 'What Future for Member States' Monopolies?' (1998) 23 *ELRev* 371.
[24]   See T Prosser, *The Limits of Competition Law. Markets and Public Services* (Oxford, OUP, 2005).
[25]   G Marenco, 'Public Sector and Community Law' (1983) 20 *CMLRev* 505.

exemption or derogation from the application of the Treaty rules. The Court has not always followed a rigorous approach; sometimes it balances Article 86(2) against Article 86(1) EC in order to find that Article 86(1) EC is inapplicable.

The Court plays lip service to the fact that a derogation from fundamental EC Treaty provisions must be interpreted restrictively and according to the principle of proportionality. On closer analysis we discover the Court is not so rigorous in applying a restrictive approach and, in particular, in its application of the proportionality principle is more generous towards the Member States than is normally the case where derogations and justifications are involved. Here I have used the conventional interpretation of Article 86(2) EC, where it is seen as a *derogation* from Article 86(1) EC. This is seen, for example, in the Opinion of Advocate General Jacobs in *Albany:*

> Article 86(2) seeks to reconcile the Member States' interest in using certain undertakings as an instrument of economic or social policy with the Community's interest in ensuring compliance with the rules on competition and the internal market. (Case C–157/94 *Commission v Netherlands* [1997] ECR I–5699, para 39). Since it is a provision permitting derogation from the Treaty rules, it must be interpreted strictly. (*Commission v Netherlands*, para 37).[26]

However, later in this chapter and in Chapter 7, I discuss an alternative version of Article 86(2) EC, provided by Baquero Cruz, where he describes Article 86(2) as a 'binary' or 'switch' rule.[27]

THE SCOPE OF ARTICLE 86(1) EC

The Court and the EC Commission have used a number of techniques to determine when state activity is caught by the EC Treaty.[28] In relation to the competition rules it must be shown that there is an *undertaking* engaging in economic activity. The Court often conflates the two criteria. The classic definition of the term is given in *Höfner*. As we have seen, the notion of an undertaking is a functional one:

> The concept of an undertaking encompasses every entity engaged in an economic activity, regardless of the legal status of the entity and the way in which it is financed.[29]

---

[26]   Case C–67/96 *Albany* [1999] ECR I–5751, para 436.
[27]   J Baquero Cruz, 'Beyond Competition: Services of General Interest and European Community Law' in G de Búrca (ed), *EU Law and the Welfare State* (Oxford, OUP, 2005).
[28]   See E Szyszczak, 'State Intervention in the Market' in T Tridimas and P Nebbia (eds), *EU Law for the 21st Century: Rethinking the New Legal Order Volume 2* (Oxford, Hart, 2004).
[29]   Case C–41/90 *Höfner and Elser v Macrotron GmbH* [1991] ECR I–1979, para 21.

'Economic activity' is defined by the Court as 'an activity consisting in offering goods and services on a given market'.[30] Later cases have stressed the economic risk borne by an undertaking:

> [undertakings] bear the financial risks attaching to the performance of those [economic] activities since, if there should be an imbalance between expenditure and receipts, they must bear the deficit themselves.[31]

Inherent in the idea of an open market economy with free competition is the belief that the competition rules apply only to behaviour which is, in the widest sense, of an *economic* nature. This explains the philosophy of the Court outlined in the previous chapters and why the Court is willing to take certain regulatory behaviour of the state out of the scope of Article 86(1) EC. In *Spediporto*[32] the Court held that national rules which merely determine the conditions governing access to the market and certain aspects of the conduct of undertakings, in this case, as regards prices, without turning the affected undertakings into public undertakings granting them special or exclusive rights or entrusting them with services of a general economic interest are *not* contrary to Article 86 EC. Certain activities of the state are considered to be non-economic because there is no market for the goods or services supplied. This is the case where the state has exclusive competence in the regulatory sphere, such as the issue of licences or the prerogative to issue passports. The Court has placed an express limit on 'public authority activities' which do not fall within the scope of Article 86(1) EC, where the body is pursuing traditional *ius imperii* activities, for example, the activities of the judiciary, diplomacy, the representation of the state in foreign relations.[33] The extent of this concept embraces bodies which carry out a number of public control and regulatory functions of the modern state.[34] For example, in *Eurocontrol*[35] a public body was charged with the maintenance and improvement of air navigation safety, collecting route charges levied on users of airspace. These were considered to be the activities of public authorities; the international organisation (Eurocontrol) was not considered to be an undertaking for the purposes of competition law. At paragraph 20 the Court observes:

---

[30] Case C–35/96 *Commission v Italy* [1998] ECR I–3851, para 36. See also Cases C–180/98 to C–184/98 *Pavlov and others* [2000] ECR I–6451, para 75 and Case C–222/04 *Ministerio dell'Economica e delle Finanze v Cassa di Risparmio di Firenze SpA, Fondazione Cassa di Risparmio di San Miniato, Cassa di Risparmio di San Miniato SpA* [2006] ECR I–289, para 108.

[31] Case C–35/96 *Commission v Italy (CNSD)* [1998] ECR I–3851, para 37; Case C–309/99 *Wouters* [2002] ECR I–1577, para 48.

[32] Case C–96/94 *Centro Servizi Spediporto Srl v Spedizioni Marittima del Golfo Srl* [1995] ECR I–2883.

[33] J González-Orús, 'Beyond the Scope of Article 90 of the EC Treaty: Activities Excluded From the EC Competition Rules' (1999) 5 *European Public Law* 387.

[34] Cf the exercise of official authority by customs officers: Case C–35/96 *Commission v Italy (CNSD)* [1998] ECR I–3851; and lawyers: Case C–309/99 *Wouters* [2002] ECR I–1577.

[35] Case C–364/92 *SAT Fluggesellschaft mbH v Eurocontrol* [1994] ECR I–43.

it is in the exercise of that sovereignty that the states ensure … the supervision of their airspace and the provision of air navigation control services.

In *Eurocontrol* the public-interest character of the activity is the dominant issue: Eurocontrol was behaving in the same way as a public authority. Similarly, in *Diego Cali*[36] anti-pollution supervision was considered to be a similar task. At paragraph 23 the Court states that such an activity:

constitutes a mission of general interest which is part of the essential tasks of the state relating to the environment within the public domain.

Many activities which were once the domain of the state can now be offered by non-state bodies. Here the decisive issue is whether there is a market for such activities. In *Humbel and Edel*[37] the Court ruled that the creation and maintenance of a public education system, which is compulsory and open to all, is part of the duties of the state towards its citizens. In fulfilling this duty the state is not seeking to engage in gainful activity. Even where enrolment fees might be levied, this would not alter the *nature* of the activities. However, a Member State may create a market for activities which traditionally fall within the non-economic arena. Economic and non-economic activities may co-exist and even be provided by the same body.[38] In *Ambulanz Glöckner*[39] a provider of emergency ambulance services was categorised as an undertaking because the activity took place in a competitive market and the suppliers of the services were remunerated.

The most difficult challenge for the European Courts has been the modern role of social protection systems. The pressures from complying with EMU, the Broad Economic Policy Guidelines, alongside changes in attitude towards the welfare state at the national level have encouraged the Member States to experiment with a new mix of social protection schemes. The Court has long held the view that Community law does not detract from the powers of the Member States to organise their social security systems,[40] but the experimentation with non-state provision of social security has forced the Court to draw a clearer line between the existence of this power and its exercise. In *Poucet and Pistre*[41] the issue was whether the management of a special social security scheme was an economic activity. The Court held that:

sickness funds and the organizations involved in the management of the public social security system, fulfil and exclusively social function … based on the principle of national solidarity.

---

[36] Case C–343/95 *Diego Cali v Servizi ecologici porto di Genova SpA* [1997] ECR I–1547.
[37] Case 263/86 [1988] ECR 5365.
[38] See EC Commission, Green Paper on Services of General Interest, COM(2003) 270 final.
[39] Case C–475/99 [2001] ECR I–8089, paras 19–22.
[40] Case 238/82 *Duphar v The Netherlands* [1984] ECR 523.
[41] Joined Cases C–159/91 & C–160/91 *Poucet and Pistre* [1993] ECR I–666.

In contrast to the judgment in *Höfner*, the Court examines in detail the social objectives of the social security system, stressing the importance of the role solidarity played in the financing of the scheme and the distribution of benefits. This would appear to contradict the earlier statements in *Höfner* that the legal status and financing of the undertaking are irrelevant to the inquiry into whether or not there is an economic activity. The Court ignores the fact that the same kind of activities could, and indeed were, carried out by the private sector in competitive markets. Instead, the Court uses a number of indicators to come to the conclusion that the activity of providing social security was non-economic. The social security scheme fulfilled an exclusively social function; it was based on the principle of national solidarity; it was entirely non-profit-making; the level of benefits was determined by law; the level of benefits was not determined by the contributions paid into the fund by individuals.

Before *Eurocontrol* and *Poucet and Pistre*, the competition rules were applied to services of general economic interest unless they could be justified under Article 86(2) EC. It had to be shown that the application of the competition rules impeded in law or in fact the accomplishment of the tasks assigned to them and that the development of trade was not affected in a way which was contrary to the Community interest. Following *Eurocontrol* and *Poucet and Pistre*, a new possibility was created: the Community competition rules could simply be disapplied as regards certain activities which were in the general interest. This is the opinion of Winterstein, who argues that the Court created a new a category of state acts exempted from the EC Treaty rules:[42]

> The Court, however, has chosen a different solution. Instead of assessing insurance services according to their nature, which is undoubtedly economic, and then reviewing the special monopoly rights granted to the entities providing them under Article 86(2) EC, the Court has departed from the functional approach. It has excluded the provision of social insurance services, to which affiliation is compulsory, altogether from the ambit of Community competition law on the basis of the 'solidarity principle'. In effect, the Court has thereby added a fourth category of activity to the previously existing (1) non-economic activities involving the exercise of *imperium*, (2) economic activities fully subject to competition law, and, (3) economic activities of general interest subject to Article 82(2) EC.

The existence of a core solidarity activity is linked to the exercise of public authority. Hatzopoulos argues that the Court has avoided the application of the free market/competition rules on issues that obey a completely different logic:

⁴² A Winterstein, 'Nailing the Jellyfish: Social Security and Competition Law' (1999) 20 *ECLR* 324, 327.

In this respect, one should keep in mind that the very aim of social and healthcare policy is to balance the extreme inequalities produced by free markets and competition.[43]

Solidarity emerged as a new and flexible tool for determining not only whether Article 86(1) EC should apply, but also to determine when the activity was economic in nature and whether Article 86(2) EC was satisfied.[44] Indicators have evolved to determine the nature and degree of solidarity for a national social security scheme to be taken out of the scope of Community law, with each scheme analysed on a case by case basis.[45]

The ruling in *FFSA*[46] reveals that the principle of solidarity may be extremely limited in scope. The case involved a non-profit-making organisation which managed an old-age insurance scheme intended to supplement a basic, compulsory insurance scheme. It operated according to the principles of social solidarity and social purpose set out by the public authorities in relation to conditions for membership, contributions and benefits, and was an undertaking carrying out an economic activity for the purposes of Article 81 EC. The Court attached importance to the weak role of solidarity in determining the objectives of the social security scheme and in applying the competition rules.

In a trilogy of cases, *Brentjens, Drijvende* and *Albany*,[47] The Dutch government attempted to reduce the state provision of pensions by encouraging and facilitating occupational pension schemes which complemented and replaced part of the state scheme. A challenge was made to one of the sectoral pension schemes set up in the textile sector. The Court held that some agreements may fall outside the scope of Article 81(1) EC according to their nature and purpose. Here a collective agreement made affiliation to the supplementary pension scheme compulsory. The purpose of the agreement was social in nature, and encouraged under the EC Treaty. Thus this kind of agreement fell outside the scope of Article 81(1) EC. However, the Court found that the pension fund was an undertaking for the purposes of Articles 82 and 86 EC. The relevant factors were that membership of the fund was optional, the fund was managed in accordance with the principle of capitalisation and benefits were proportionate to contributions. The Court

---

[43] V Hatzopoulos, 'Health Law and Policy: The Impact of the EU' in G. de Búrca (ed), *EU Law and the Welfare State* (Oxford, OUP, 2005) at 157.

[44] In *Poucet and Pistre*, above n 41, and Case 238/94 *José García and others v Mutuelle de Prévoyance Sociale d'Aquitaine and others* [1996] ECRI-1673 the Court found the competition rules did not apply to a compulsory insurance scheme, whereas in Case C–244/94 *FFSA* [1995] ECR I–4013 and Case C–67/96 *Albany* [1999] ECR I–5751, Cases C–115 to C–117/97 *Brentjens* [1999] ECR I–6025; Case C–219/97 *Drijvende* [1999] ECR I–6121 and Cases C–180/98 to C–184/98 *Pavlov and others* [2000] ECR I–6451 the Court found the principle of solidarity to be limited or absent.

[45] Case C–205/03P *FENIN*, Opinion of Poiares Maduro AG, 10 Nov 2005, para 1, [2006] ECR I–6295.

[46] Case C–244/94 *Fédération Française des sociétiés d'Assurance v Ministère de l'Agriculture et de la Pêche* [1995] ECR I–4013.

[47] Above n 44.

deduced that there was an element of competition between the fund and life assurance companies operating in the private sector. Other factors, for example, the pursuit of a social objective, the fact that the fund was non-profit-making, the requirement of solidarity (but only limited solidarity because benefits accrued only to members of the fund) and the statutory restrictions on the operation of the fund were not sufficient to take the activity out of the economic sphere, but Article 86(2) EC could apply. The case is important because the pension fund was a *non-state* body and the service of general economic interest being provided was not available to the whole of the (Dutch) population.

In *Pavlov*[48] the Dutch regulation acquiescing in the request from the representative body of doctors making it compulsory for all doctors to belong to an occupational pension fund was challenged as being incompatible with the competition rules. The Court looked to see whether the representative body could be an 'association of undertakings', and whether doctors individually could be regarded as undertakings. The Court found that self-employed medical specialists offer their services on the market for remuneration and they bear the financial risks for their economic activity:

> the complexity and technical nature of the services they provide and the fact that the practice of their profession is regulated cannot alter that conclusion.[49]

However, the Court reverts back to its old approach in *Batisttello*.[50] Here the Court found that the Italian fund for occupational accidents and diseases embodied enough solidarity not to fall within the scope of the competition rules. A similar approach is seen in *Freskot v Elliniko Dimosio* where a Greek scheme for the compulsory insurance of farmers against natural disasters was tested against Article 49 EC. The Court found that a service was not involved, since the contribution was essentially in the nature of a charge imposed by the legislature, levied by the tax authority. The characteristics of the charge, including its rate, were determined by the legislature and it was for the competent ministers to decide any variation of the rate.[51]

In *FENIN*[52] pharmaceutical companies alleged that a number of Spanish bodies and organisations, including government departments, abused a dominant position by systematically paying their bills late. The EC Commission rejected the complaint, arguing that the bodies concerned were not undertakings. The CFI reverted to the principle of solidarity by finding that the health service in Spain operated according to the principle of solidarity and was funded from social security contributions. It provided a service free of charge to all its

---

[48]   Joined Cases C–180/98 to C–184/98 [2000] ECR I–6451.
[49]   Above n 44, at para 77.
[50]   Case C–218/00 [2002] ECR I–691.
[51]   Case C–355/00 *Freskot v Elliniko Dimosio* [2003 ECR I–5263.
[52]   Case T–319/99 *FENIN v Commission* [2003] ECR II–357; on appeal, Case C–205/03P, [2006] 6295.

members.[53] The CFI also held that the competition rules did not apply since the bodies were not undertakings. The same characteristics were found in the Spanish national health system as were found in the social insurance system in *Poucet and Pistre*.[54] The CFI and the Court of Justice upheld the view that purchasing activities could not be seen separately from the activities for which the goods and services were used.[55]

Although the European Courts are seen to work on a case-by-case basis, we can distil a set of criteria used to establish whether there is an *undertaking*.[56] Hatzopoulos labels the factors *faisceau d'indices*.[57] Using this idea the cases can be grouped together in a methodical way to show which factors influenced the Court in finding that solidarity was present. An important factor appears to be whether the objectives being pursued are of a social nature. A first indicator is the compulsory nature of the scheme. This was an important factor in *Poucet and Pistre* and *Freskot* and was a decisive factor in *FFSA*, but was not conclusive in the *Albany* trilogy of cases. A second indicator is the manner in which the amount of contributions is calculated. In *Poucet and Pistre, Feskott* and *Batistello* the Court found that the funds applied the law and could not influence the amount of contributions which in the last resort were fixed by the state. The degree of state control over the funds is an important factor. In *Poucet and Pistre* the contributions were determined by income but were not experience-rated, pointing to the idea of solidarity.[58] In contrast, in *Drijvende* the undertaking determined the amount of the contributions and benefits. The issue of capitalisation is also a decisive factor. If the organisation engages in active management of the fund and where the amounts received depend upon the financial results of the organisation this will be a clear indicator of economic activity.[59] If the organisation is merely limited to the redistribution of contributions received, this will indicate that solidarity principles are present. In *Poucet and Pistre* the Court placed emphasis upon the availability of cross-subsidisation within the social security fund. In contrast the competitive nature of the scheme, and the fact that it was self-sufficient, was an indicator of economic activity in *Pavlov* and *Brentjens*.

ARTICLE 86(2) EC

Article 86(2) EC is addressed to a *certain category of undertakings*, rather than the Member States. As is the case with the competition rules generally, the Treaty

---

[53] Non-members of the scheme, eg, foreigners, were charged for the services.

[54] Joined Cases C–159/91 & C–160/91 *Poucet and Pistre* [1993] ECR I–637.

[55] Cf Case C–203/99 *Henning Veedfald v Århus Amtskommune* [2001] ECR I–3569.

[56] See the Opinion of Jacobs AG in Case C–67/96 *Albany* [1999] ECR I–5751.

[57] V Hatzopoulos, 'Health Law and Policy: The Impact of the EU' in G. de Búrca (ed), *EU Law and the Welfare State* (Oxford, OUP, 2005) at 153.

[58] Also in *Poucet* and in *Batistello* benefits were given even where contributions were overdue or interrupted.

[59] See *FFSA, Albany, Brentjens Drijvende, Pavlov,* all above n 44.

does not provide a definition of the kind of undertakings which may fall within Article 86(2) EC. Deringer,[60] in 1968, provided a useful checklist as to the qualities which must be inherent in an undertaking in order to bring it within the scope of Article 86(2) EC:

— The undertaking must not receive official authority merely to carry out a service if it so chooses, but must have positive duties imposed upon it to maintain the services, which it may not arbitrarily change or discontinue;
— The nature of the services must be such that if they were not carried out by the undertaking in question they would probably be supplied by the state since they are essential for supplying a vital need of the general public or for enabling the economy to function;
— Public law must have endowed these undertakings with particular powers or with certain exclusive rights relevant to their function;
— The undertaking must not only have reserved for itself general supervision of its functions but also retained a broad power through regulations to organise its services and fix its prices;
— The prices it charges must be determined not strictly according to laws of supply and demand but influenced by social and political considerations which may require some disadvantaged sections of the population to receive free, or at a reduced cost supplies, for example, telephone/postal services in remote areas;
— The services supplied must be available to all, on a non-discriminatory basis.

In one of the earliest of the cases challenging the application of competition principles to state bodies, *Sacchi*,[61] the contested national measure was a grant of exclusive rights to a company controlled by a state holding in the TV industry. The Court confirmed that the competition rules applied to private and state controlled bodies. The Court held that Article 86 EC is a *permission*, rather than a prohibition, directed at the Member States allowing them to grant exclusive rights. In *Sacchi* the Court provided a general interpretation of Article 86 EC whereby the exception or derogation of Article 86(2) EC is highlighted. The Court points out that an undertaking entrusted with the operation of services of a general economic interest is also subject to the competition provisions of the Treaty unless these provisions are incompatible with the performance of the undertaking's tasks by reason of Article 86(2) EC.

A clearer interpretation of the relationship between Article 86(1) and (2) EC is to be found in the *Terminal Equipment*[62] case where the Court makes it clear that Article 86 EC does not presuppose that *all* special or exclusive rights are compatible with the Treaty:

---

[60] A Deringer, *The Competition Law of the European Economic Community: A Commentary on the EEC Rules of Competition* (The Hague, CCH Editions, 1968) at 248–9.

[61] Case 155/73 *Giuseppe Sacchi* [1974] ECR 409.

[62] Case C–202/88 *French Republic v Commission (Terminal Equipment)* [1991] ECR I–1272.

In allowing derogations to be made from the general rules of the Treaty on certain conditions, that provision seeks to reconcile the member states' interest in using certain undertakings, in particular in the public sector, as an instrument of economic or fiscal policy with the Community's interest in ensuring compliance with the rules on competition and the preservation of the unity of the Common Market.[63]

Article 86(2) EC is not comparable with the possibility of an *exemption* being granted by the EC Commission under the old regime of Article 81(3) EC before the introduction of Regulation 1/2003/EC. It is perhaps comparable with the new balancing process of weighing up an anti-competitive agreement against Article 81(3) EC which the national courts and regulators must use to determine the applicability of Article 81(1) EC. There is however some similarity now because Article 86(2) EC can give rise to direct effect, thereby allowing national courts to apply the exemption or engage in a balancing exercise.[64] Article 86(2) EC sits uncomfortably with Article 82 EC, where there is no Treaty-based justification, although recently the Court has developed ideas of justifications.

THE APPLICATION OF ARTICLE 86 EC TO STATE MONOPOLIES

Bodson[65] was the first case to examine the interaction of Articles 86 and 81 and 82 EC. It concerned the French practice of permitting local authorities to exercise exclusive powers to conduct funerals. Some local authorities offered the service themselves; others licensed private firms to carry out the functions. The Court defines the relationship between Articles 86 and 81 and 82 EC:

the aim of [Article 86 EC] is to specify in particular the conditions for the application of the competition rules laid down by [Articles 81 and 82 EC] to public undertakings, to undertakings granted special or exclusive rights by the member states and to undertakings entrusted with the operation of services in the general economic interest.[66]

The Court ruled that Article 81 EC did not apply to contracts for concessions between public authorities and undertakings entrusted with the operation of a

---

[63]   *Ibid*, para 12.

[64]   The direct effect of Art 86(2) EC is assumed in Case C–320/91 *Criminal Proceedings Against Paul Corbeau* 1993] ECR I–2533, drawn from a statement in Case C–260/89 *Elliniki Radiophonia Tileorassi AE v Dimotiki Etairia Pliroforissis and Sotirios Kouvelas* [1991] ECR I–2925. See M Ross, 'Article 16 E.C. and Services of General Interest: From Derogation to Obligation?' (2000) 25 *ELRev* 22. Cf K Lipstein, *The Law of the European Economic Community*, (London, Butterworths, 1974) at 242, citing Case 10/71 *Ministère Public of Luxembourg v Müller* [1971] ECR 739: '[c]learly Article [86(2)] EC is not directly applicable'.

[65]   Case 30/87 *Bodson v Pompes Funèbres des Régions Libérées SA* [1988] ECR 2479.

[66]   *Ibid*, at para 16.

public service. Article 81 EC is applicable only to *agreements between undertakings*.[67] In contrast, Article 82 EC was relevant to an evaluation of the eventual anti-competitive behaviour performed by undertakings holding concessions. The Court ruled that public authorities may not either enact or maintain in force any measure contrary to Articles 81 and 82 EC. For example, Member States may not assist undertakings holding concessions to charge unfair prices by imposing such prices as a condition for concluding a contract for a concession.[68] Whether the measure was to be condemned depended on a finding that the communes imposed a given level of prices on the concession holders as a condition for being granted a funeral concession. Once market dominance is established, artificially high prices may be incompatible with Community law. Where a *public authority* fixes the prices, it violates Article 86(1) EC read with Article 82 EC. Where a *private firm* fixes the prices then Article 82 EC applies.

The interaction of Article 86 with Article 82 EC is demonstrated in *Höfner v Macrotron*,[69] a case which is seen as the turning point in the Court's attitude towards public monopolies. As a result of the establishment of a German employment agency the activities of independent recruitment consultants were suppressed by the public monopoly. The Court held that any state measure that maintained a law under which a body was forced to violate Article 82 EC was unlawful by virtue of Article 86(1) EC. The Court found a violation of the competition rules because the German rules restricted sources of supply in circumstances where the state was unable to meet demand and prevented private companies from pursuing the activity at all. The complaint was not about exclusivity but about the *distortive effect* of the inadequate supply of labour. In order to comply with the competition principles of the EU the Court required the elimination of the exclusive reservation of employment services to the state.[70]

The Court draws a fine line between the *existence* of a state monopoly and the *exercise* of the exclusive rights granted to it. Merely by *exercising* the exclusive rights granted to it the German employment agency inevitably abused a dominant position. In the judgment the Court outlines the responsibilities of the Member States. In so doing it uses a formula similar to the general principles on the interaction of Articles 3(g), 10(2) and 81–82 EC originating from the *GB-INNO* case.[71] This is consistent in principle with the Court's jurisprudence developed in relation to Member State intervention in the economy which we discussed in Chapters 2 and 3. However, the ruling in *Höfner* is far-reaching:

---

[67]   See *ibid*, at para 18.

[68]   *Ibid*, at paras 33 and 34.

[69]   Case C–41/90 *Höfner and Elser v Macrotron* [1991] ECR I–1979.

[70]   On the impact of the *Höfner* case and the subsequent ILO Convention 181 (1997) on the supply of labour by private employment agencies in the Member States see: R Blanpain, (ed), *Private Employment Agencies, Bulletin of Comparative Labour Relations* 36 (The Hague, Kluwer, 1999).

[71]   Case 13/77 *NV GB-INNO-BM v Vereniging van de Kleinhandelaars in Tabak (ATAB)* [1977] ECR 2115.

Consequently any measure adopted by a member state which maintains in force a statutory provision that created a situation in which a public employment agency cannot avoid infringing Article 82 EC is incompatible with the rules of the Treaty.[72]

The Court states that legal monopolies may be regarded as occupying a dominant position. Merely by exercising exclusive rights, certain state monopolies cannot avoid abusing their dominant position, and trade between the Member States is likely to be affected. The state employment agency had tolerated competition in the business executives' placement sector and had therefore not taken full advantage of the legal monopoly granted to it. There was competition in the market despite the state undertaking which had been given exclusive rights. But at the end of the day this competition was not tolerated by the national law, and contracts entered into outside the placement by the employment agency could be declared void. The *Höfner* case is a signal to the Member States that they cannot hide behind the legal protection afforded to monopolies when the monopoly is not being efficient and meeting the demands of the market.

Gyselen[73] observed that in *Höfner* the Court stretched the notion of abuse of a dominant position to such a point that the granting of the exclusive rights and the abusive exercise of those rights virtually coincide. The case cannot, therefore, be seen as turning on its own facts. It is clear from subsequent case law that the Court was developing a normative rule.

In *ERT*[74] the Greek government had granted an exclusive right to a Greek television and radio undertaking to carry out its activities. DEP, a TV station, had started similar activities within a smaller geographic area. The Court ruled that in relation to ERT's activities it was for the national court to determine whether practices were compatible with Article 86 EC and to verify whether those practices, if they were contrary to the provision, may be justified by the particular needs of the particular task with which the undertaking was entrusted. With regard to the measure granting the exclusive right, the Court reiterates the general principle of the *Höfner* case:

> in that respect it should be observed that [Article 86] of the Treaty prohibits the granting of an exclusive right to retransmit television broadcasts to an undertaking which has an exclusive right to transmit broadcasts, where those rights are liable to create a situation in which that undertaking is led to infringe [Article 82] of the Treaty by virtue of a discriminatory broadcasting policy which favours its own programmes.[75]

---

[72] *Ibid*, at para 27.
[73] L Gyselen, 'Anti-Competitive State Measures Under the EC Treaty: Towards a Substantive Legality Standard' (1993) *ELRev Checklist 1993*, CC77.
[74] Case C–260/89 *ERT* [1991] ECR I–2925.
[75] *Ibid*, para 37.

Gyselen[76] points out that this case shows that the Court will not necessarily require evidence that the infringement of the competition rules has materialised. ERT had refrained, from 1975 to 1988, from broadcasting programmes from other Member States. ERT could not handle the conflict which is inherent in granting one company both the exclusive right to produce and broadcast its own programmes and the exclusive right to retransmit programmes. ERT had the exclusive right to determine entry to a market where it operated in competition with other undertakings. In his Opinion, Advocate General Lenz points out that an undertaking in a dominant position would never by itself be able to create such a situation without the help of a legal monopoly. Thus a limitation of production, within the meaning of Article 82(b) EC, was inevitably created.

Article 86(2) EC is used as a filter to exempt bodies carrying out public service obligations from the full thrust of competition law. For example, in *Deutsche Post AG* an undertaking which had been granted exclusive rights as regards the collection, carriage and delivery of mail was brought within the scope of Article 86(1) EC, but it was also regarded as performing a service of general economic interest within the meaning of Article 86(2) EC.[77] In *Ambulanz Glöckner*[78] private undertakings wishing to provide ambulance services had to obtain an authorisation from the local public authorities, which consulted with medical associations which already provided ambulance services in the market. The medical aid associations were non-profit-making associations which had been entrusted by law with providing a public ambulance service. They were financed through direct public funding which paid for the infrastructure (staff, central control units and ambulance stations) to provide the ambulance service, and user charges were made for the operational costs. The Court found that the medical aid associations were undertakings. Again the public service obligation did not deny the finding of an economic activity, but it was relevant for finding that Article 86(2) EC could be invoked to find the German legislation to be compatible with the EC Treaty.

MAKING SENSE OF THE CASE LAW

The case law on Article 86 EC has been described by Hancher as 'at first sight opaque, if not erratic'.[79] Ross also describes the Court's jurisprudence as 'a long

---

[76] See above n 73. Cf. Case C–179/90 *Merci Convenzionali Porto di Genova v Siderurgica Gabrielli SpA* [1991] ECR I–5889.

[77] Joined Cases C–147/97 & C–148/97 *Deutsche Post AG v Gesellschaft für Zahlungssysteme GmbH and , Citicorp Kartenservice GmbH* [2000] ECR I–825.

[78] Case C–475/99 *Ambulanz Glöckner v Landkreiss Südwestpfalz* [2001] ECR I–8089.

[79] L Hancher, 'Community State and Market' in P Craig and G de Búrca (eds), *The Evolution of EU Law* (Oxford, OUP, 1999) at 727.

line of complex and at times abstruse case law, with difficulties being encountered in relation to virtually all its aspects'.[80] In his Opinion in *Albany*[81] General Jacobs organises the Court's case law into three categories, and this provides a useful analytical tool to explain the case law.

The *ERT*-type Cases

This group of cases includes *ERT*,[82] *Raso*,[83] *Merci Convenzionali Porto di Genova SpA*.[84] In this set of cases it was not merely the monopoly itself which infringed Article 86(1) EC, but the monopoly *in conjunction* with additional features which made abuses very likely. Abuses of a dominant position do not have to be committed; the issue is whether the national regulatory framework leads (even hypothetically) the undertakings to commit abuses. Structural measures beyond the granting of an exclusive right led the undertakings in question to abuse their dominant position. Only then was there justification for holding the state, at least partly, responsible for the anti-competitive behaviour of the monopolist.

In *ERT*[85] it was the granting of two exclusive rights to broadcast ERT's own programmes and to retransmit foreign broadcasts which created a conflict of interest. The monopoly with these rights was led to abuse a dominant position by virtue of a discriminatory policy which favoured its own programmes. In *Raso* the Italian dock-work scheme granted companies an exclusive right to supply temporary labour to certain undertakings, but also enabled those companies to compete with undertakings which depended upon their services. A conflict of interest was inevitable since, by merely exercising the monopoly, the dock-work company could distort competition in the secondary market to its advantage. *Merci* is another case involving the Italian dock-work scheme where the national court in its questions suggests that the specific circumstances resulted in, or induced the companies with exclusive rights to demand, payment for services which had not been requested and to charge disproportionate prices.

---

[80] M Ross, 'Article 16 E.C. and Services of General Interest : From Derogation to Obligation?' (2000) 25 *ELRev* 22, 23.
[81] Case C–67/96 [1999] ECR I–5751.
[82] Case C–260/89 *ERT* [1991] ECR I–2925.
[83] Case C–163/96 *Criminal Proceedings Against Raso and others* [1998] ECR I–533.
[84] Case C–179/90 [1991] ECR I–5889.
[85] Case C–260/89 *ERT* [1991] ECR I–2925.

The *Höfner*-type Cases

This group of cases, *Höfner*,[86] *Giovanna Carra*[87] and *Job Centre*,[88] comprises employment procurement monopolies, In these cases the Court held that a Member State was in breach of Articles 86 and 82 EC when the undertaking cannot avoid abusing its dominant position when it exercises its exclusive rights. In the *Höfner* situation the particular abuse was an infringement of Article 82(b) EC where the undertaking limited the provision of placement services to the prejudice of clients/consumers wishing to use the service. The placement agency could not meet the demand for the services it was entrusted to supply; effective competition by non-state companies was rendered impossible by the use of statutory provisions which prohibited competition and rendered any employment contracts void if they were facilitated by any company other than the public monopoly.

In *Job Centre* the Italian state actively enforced a similar employment monopoly through criminal law. In this case the Court stressed the particular nature of the market for the provision of employment placement services. In these cases the state merely granted an exclusive right. The Court looked at the specific economic context of the market and the nature of the services involved. It concluded that the monopoly could not avoid abusing its dominant position by constantly limiting production, markets or technical development to the prejudice of consumers within the meaning of Article 82(b) EC.

The *Höfner* and *Job Centre* cases may seem to be exceptional situations, but the cases make very fundamental inroads into the Member States' freedom to organise their economic activities in accordance with Article 295 EC. They also create standards for public service obligations. A Member State may be in breach of its duties under Community law where a public or universal service provider is not acting in an efficient manner.

The *Corbeau*-type Cases

In this group of cases *Corbeau*[89] is linked with *Corsica Ferries France*[90] and *Sacchi*.[91] The Court does not identify *which* features of the legislation are contrary to Article 86(1) and 82 EC but, instead, reads Article 86(1) with Article 86(2) and immediately starts a balancing process on the *justification* of the *scope* of the monopoly using the principle of proportionality. In *Corbeau* the Court is

---

[86]   Case C–41/90 *Höfner and Elser v Macrotron GmbH* [1991] ECR I–1979.
[87]   Case C–258/98 *Criminal Proceedings against Giovanni Carra and others* [2000] ECR I–4217.
[88]   Case C–55/96 *Job Centre coop arl* [1997] ECR I–7119.
[89]   Case C–320/91 *Corbeau* [1993] ECR I–2533.
[90]   Case C–266/96 *Corsica Ferries France SA v Gruppo Antichi Ormeggiatori del porto di Geneva Coop. arl,* [1998] ECR I–3949.
[91]   Case 155/73 *Giuseppe Sacchi* [1974] ECR 409.

generous in its interpretation of proportionality. Today the Court might not be so generous, in the light of the partial liberalisation of postal services and the acceptance that a universal service may be provided by a variety of means, and not just cross-subsidisation. In *Corsica Ferries* the Court found that exclusive mooring rights in two Italian ports were justified under Article 86(2) EC. In *Albany*[92] the Court begins by looking at the combination of Article 86(1) and 82 EC but then switches to an analysis of Article 86(2) EC. The Court finds that the legitimate objective of Article 86(2) EC is satisfied, in that the insurance fund is performing an essential social function and the proportionality requirements are met.

JUSTIFICATIONS, DEROGATIONS AND THE 'SWITCH' RULE

The regular use of Articles 31 and 86 EC exposed a number of practical and intellectual weaknesses in the drafting of the provisions. One weakness is that, unlike for the general free movement provisions, there is no Treaty based defence or justification to a finding that a state monopoly has infringed Article 31 EC.

In infringement actions brought by the EC Commission against state monopolies in the utilities sector the Member States raised Article 86(2) EC as a defence.[93] In each case the Court found that exclusive rights granted in the utilities sector were in breach of Article 31 EC and that the EC Commission had not shown why Article 86(2) EC should not apply. In *Commission v Netherlands*[94] the Court found that exclusive import rights for electricity intended for public distribution granted under legislation were contrary to Article 31 EC. The EC Commission had argued that the rights were also contrary to Article 28 EC, but the Court did not find it necessary to consider Article 28 EC. Thus there was no discussion of the application of Article 30 EC as a justification for the measures. Advocate General Cosmos had considered that where the rights infringed Article 28 EC they could *not* be justified under the public security grounds of Article 30 EC.

The EC Commission argued that Article 86(2) EC cannot be used to justify state measures that are incompatible with the EC Treaty rules on the free movement of goods. The Court looked at the combined effect of Article 86(1) and (2) EC, and ruled that Article 86(2) EC could be used to justify the grant of exclusive rights by a Member State to an undertaking entrusted with the operation of services of general economic interest. This applied even where exclusive rights were contrary to Article 31 EC, subject to two conditions. First, the undertaking granted the exclusive rights could perform the particular tasks assigned to it only through the grant of exclusive rights. The Court held that it

---

[92] Case C–67/96 [1999] ECR I–5751.
[93] In Case C–160/94 *Commission v Spain (Spanish Electricity Monopoly)* [1997] ECR I–5851 the EC Commission failed to show that a statutory monopoly existed in the electricity sector.
[94] Case C–157/94 *Commission v Netherlands (Dutch Electricity Monopoly)* [1997] ECR I–5699.

was not necessary for there to be a threat to the financial balance or economic viability of the undertaking entrusted with the operation of a service of general economic interest. Instead the Court used a literal reading of Article 86(2) EC to ask whether it would not be possible for the undertaking to perform the particular tasks entrusted to it without the special or exclusive rights at issue. The Court also set out that the tasks should be defined by reference to the obligations and constraints to which the undertaking was subject. The Court pointed out that the undertaking must be able to carry out the service of general economic interest under economically acceptable conditions.[95]

The EC Commission had suggested other ways in which the service of general economic interest could be performed which would be less restrictive, but the Court found that the EC Commission had not taken into consideration the particular nature of the Netherlands' electricity system or considered whether the proposed alternatives would indeed be viable. The Member State did not have to prove that other less restrictive measures would not fulfil the obligations of the service of general economic interest. This has been interpreted as a generous defence to an infringement of Article 31 EC, but arguably, because the case was an infringement action, the burden of proof was with the EC Commission.

Secondly, the grant of such rights should not affect the development of trade to such an extent that it would be contrary to the interests of the Community. Again the Court found that the EC Commission had not provided evidence to show *how* the development of intra-Community trade was affected by the exclusive rights. The Court held that the EC Commission should provide a definition of Community interest in relation to which the development of trade has to be assessed. Because there was no Community energy liberalisation policy at this time, the EC Commission was under an obligation to show how the development of direct trade between producers and consumers, in parallel with the development of trade between the major networks, would have been possible, taking into account the existing capacity and the electricity transmission and distribution arrangements.

In *Commission v Italy*[96] the Italian government had argued, contrary to case law,[97] that electricity was not a 'good' within the EC Treaty definition and therefore there could be no infringement of Articles 28–31 EC. The Court held that electricity could be treated as a good and adopted the same reasoning on exclusive rights and the application of Article 86(2) EC as it had used in the Netherlands judgment.

In *Commission v France*[98] rights in gas and electricity were based upon a concession. The EC Commission held that the *exercise* of the rights led to

---

[95]   Citing Case C–320/91 *Corbeau* [1993] ECR I–2533.
[96]   Case C–158/94 *Commission v Italy (Italian Electricity Monopoly)*[1997] ECR I–5789
[97]   Case 6/64 [1964] ECR 585; Case C–393/92 *Almelo v Energiebedrijf Ijsselmij* [1994] ECR I–1477, para 28.
[98]   Case C–159/94 *Commission v France* [1997] ECR I–5815.

discrimination. Consumers in France could not choose their supplies freely, and the exclusive export rights enjoyed by EDF and GDF led to allocation of national production for gas and electricity to the national market to the detriment of demand from other Member States. The Court, referring to *Manghera*,[99] held that the objective of Article 31 EC could not be attained if the free movement of goods was not assured when a state monopoly operated on the market.

In his Opinion, Advocate General Cosmos examined the application of Articles 28 and 30 EC. France had placed emphasis upon the security of supply argument to defend exclusive rights, especially since it was dependent upon the import of gas and oil supplies. The Advocate General accepted that the exclusive import rights did not affect trade between the Member States, but could not find a justification for the exclusive rights relating to export. The Court did not consider the Article 30 EC justification.

In examining the application of Article 86(2) EC the Court looked at the particular tasks entrusted to EDF and GDF. In addition to the specific public service obligations, national environmental and regional policies were included in the concession. France argued that these tasks would be compromised if the exclusive rights were removed. The Court held that there must be a direct correlation between the public service obligations and the tasks entrusted to the undertaking with special and exclusive rights. But even the French government conceded that the undertakings concerned, EDF and EGF, did not have specific obligations as regards the environmental and regional policies. But other public service obligations entrusted to EDF, such as supplying all customers, ensuring continuity of supply and non-discrimination between customers, were part of the concession agreement. In the case of GDF this was not so apparent, but the Court accepted that under the concession it was under similar obligations. Other aspects, such as the obligation on EDF to seek the most competitive tariffs and the lowest possible costs for the community, were not attainable through the exclusive rights granted. Thus the Court held that it was possible to test the necessity of the exclusive rights against the three public service obligations which the French government had proved existed. The Court then followed its rulings in the Netherlands and Italy actions to find that the EC Commission had not proved its case.

We discovered in Chapters 2 and 3 that the justifications and defences available to a Member State found to infringe Articles 81 and 82 EC are virtually non-existent. Article 86(2) EC, therefore, plays a pivotal role in protecting state activity where services of general economic interest are at stake. This is in direct contrast to restrictions on trade between the Member States which are caught by the four economic freedoms of the Internal Market. Such restrictions may be justified by reference to the original Treaty provisions, the most generous *list* of areas which might be protected from the EC Treaty rules is found in Article 30

---

[99] Case 59/75 *Public Prosecutor v Manghera* [1976] ECR 91.

EC. This set of grounds has been expanded through the mandatory requirements doctrine set out in *Cassis de Dijon*[100] and expanded in later cases such as *Commission v Denmark*[101] and *Familiapress*.[102]

The other three economic freedoms have a limited set of Treaty based exemptions and justifications. Article 58 EC sets out the conditions in which Member States may derogate from the free movement of capital provisions contained in Article 56 EC. Articles 39(3), 46(1) and 55 EC provide a set of derogations on the grounds of public health, public policy and public security. Additionally Articles 39(4) and 45 EC provide exemptions from the free movement of workers and services provisions where employment is in the public service and activities with which the state is connected, even occasionally with the exercise of official authority. This limited set of exemptions and justifications has also been expanded through *Cassis*-style mandatory requirements being accepted in the area of free movement of workers,[103] services,[104] establishment[105] and capital.[106]

The Court has accepted that the Member States and bodies with delegated public duties have a wider set of commitments to protecting not only national interests, but also public goods and public interests.[107] The Member States were under a duty to show that the manner in which such interests were protected did not lead to arbitrary discrimination and was proportionate and necessary. The Court has accepted a wide range of new public interests such as consumer protection, the protection of the environment, unfair competition, health and safety of workers. The Court has been willing to recognise the protection of human rights and constitutional *values,* for example, the protection of human dignity,[108] freedom of expression,[109] freedom of assembly[110] and cultural pluralism.[111] Additionally the Court has recognised that bodies which have delegated

---

[100] Case 120/78 *Rewe-Zentrale AG v Bundesmonopolverwaltung für Branntwein* [1979] ECR 649.

[101] Case 302/86 [1988] ECR 4607.

[102] Case C–368/95 *Vereinigte Familiapress Zeitungsverlags-und vertriebs GmbH v Bauer Verlag* [1997] ECR I–3689.

[103] Case C–415/93 *URBSFA v Bosman* [1995] ECR I–4921.

[104] Case 205/84 *Commission v Germany* [1986] ECR 3755.

[105] Case C–442/02 *Caixa Bank France v Ministère de l'Economie, des Finances et de l'Industrie* [2004] ECR I–8961.

[106] See E. Szyszczak, 'Golden Shares and Market Governance' (2002) 19 *LIEI* 255

[107] Case C–309/99 *Wouters* [2002] ECR I–1577; Case C–519/04 P *Meca Medina Medina and Macjen v Commission* [2006] ECR I-6991. The ideas contained in *Wouters* can be traced back to the submissions of Germany in *Gebhard* (Case C–55/94 [1995] ECR I–4165) and *Gottrup-Klim e.a. Grovvareforeninger v Dans Landbrugs Grovvareselskab AmbA* (Case C–250/92 [1994] ECR I–5641), a rule of reason judgment that is seen as the predecessor of *Wouters*.

[108] Case C–36/02 *Omega Spielhallen-und Automatenaufstellungs-GmbH v Oberbürgermeisterin der Bundesstadt Bonn* [2004] ECR I–9609.

[109] Case C–71/02 *Karner v Troostwijjk* [2004] ECR I–3025.

[110] Case C–112/00 *Eugen Schmidberger, Internationale Transporte und Planzüge v Republik Österreich* [2003] ECR I–5659.

[111] Case C–288/89 *Stichting Collectieve Antennevoorziening Gouda and others v Commissariaat voor de Media* [1991] ECR I–4007.

functions may also be able to raise a public interest justification for rules and regulations which may have anti-competitive effects. In *Meca-Medina*[112] the Court found that the anti-doping rules drawn up by the IOC did not constitute a restriction of competition within the meaning of Article 81 EC since '[s]uch a limitation is inherent in the organisation and proper conduct of competitive sport and its very purpose is to ensure healthy rivalry between athletes'.[113]

One of the most problematic areas facing the Court is how to reconcile and evolve one of its early rulings in *Campus Oil*[114] where economic justifications were not permitted. The more recent cases which use the competition and free movement provisions to challenge restrictions in social welfare provision frequently raise as justifications issues of financial balance, financial coherence and budget constraints.[115]

ARTICLE 86(3) EC

Article 86(3) EC is an unusual provision in the EC Treaty. It combines a supervisory element with a legislative element. The latter enables the EC Commission to adopt Directives which by-pass the traditional legislative processes of the EU ignoring the European Parliament and the Council. Early commentators saw Article 86(3) EC as playing a central role in the enforcement of Article 86(1) EC and the application of Article 86(2) EC.[116] However, the use of the direct effect of Article 86(1) EC, combined with Article 234 EC references has eclipsed this central enforcement role for Article 86(3) EC.

The Supervisory Element

The supervisory powers under Article 86(3) EC fit into the regime of supervisory duties bestowed generally on the EC Commission. The supervisory duty exists in relation to Article 86(1) and (2) EC. The EC Commission must ensure that the *Member States* do not enact or maintain in force any measures in relation to public undertakings which are contrary to the Treaty rules. The EC Commission

---

[112] Case C–519/04 P *Meca Medina Medina and Macjen v Commission* [2006] ECR I-6991.

[113] *Ibid*, at para 45.

[114] Case 72/83 *Campus Oil v Minister for Industry and Energy* [1984] ECR 2727. In this decision the Court accepted that a state requirement that importers of oil should buy 35% of their requirements from one Irish refinery which had been established to ensure security of oil supplies in Ireland was justified by reference to public security.

[115] See, eg, Case C–385/99 *Muller-Fauré* [2003] ECR I–4509; Case C–372/04 *The Queen, on the application of Yvonne Watts v Bedford Primary Care Trust, Secretary of State for Health* [2006] ECR I-4325.

[116] A view taken from the ruling in Case 10/71 *Ministère Public of Luxembourg v Müller* [1971] ECR 739.

must also ensure that *public undertakings* do not act in a manner contrary to the EC Treaty, in particular the competition rules.[117]

Article 86(3) EC was closely linked with the liberalisation processes which emerged in the 1990s. The term *liberalisation* was linked to Article 3 EC which states that the 'activities of the Community shall include "a system ensuring that competition in the internal market is not distorted". For this purpose, Article 86(3) EC was interpreted as entrusting the EC Commission with a *specific surveillance duty* 'in the case of public undertakings and undertakings to which Member States grant special or exclusive rights'. The EC Commission must 'where necessary, address appropriate directives or decisions to Member States' which enact or 'maintain in force any measure contrary to the rules contained in the Treaty, in particular to the rules provided for in Article 12 [non-discrimination on grounds of nationality] and Articles 81 to 89 EC'.

Since 1980 the EC Commission has adopted Directives under Article 86(3) EC to render transparent the financial relations between the Member States and their public companies. It has also been used to liberalise telecommunications markets. These Directives specify the obligations of the Member States resulting from the EC Treaty in the relevant area and, in principle, do not create new substantive obligations. Where Member States do not comply with such Directives, the EC Commission can initiate infringement procedures under Article 226 EC.

Article 86(3) EC also empowers the EC Commission to adopt Decisions. The EC Commission adopted its first Decision in 1985. Since then the EC Commission has adopted 15 Decisions, covering most of the areas where the Member States granted special and exclusive rights: four decisions in the postal sector; two decisions in mobile telecommunications; three decisions in the airport sector; four decisions in the port and maritime transport sector; one Decision in insurance and one Decision in broadcasting . The last Article 86(3) EC Decision was adopted on 23 October 2001. The only two important sectors where the Commission has not (yet) adopted Decisions using Article 86(3) as a legal base are energy and railways, where the liberalisation process started more recently.

The EC Commission has examined complaints in other sectors, such as horse betting, but it has not always taken a formal Decision. Compared with Decisions taken in the field of mergers, Article 86(3) EC investigations do not always result in formal Decisions. Cases may appear unfounded or remedies may be found to solve the concerns of the EC Commission in the course of the procedure. In addition, the EC Commission is under no obligation to take Decisions under Article 86(3) EC since this provision states that it should take such Decisions only 'where necessary', leaving full discretion to the EC Commission to assess the necessity of adopting a Decision.

---

[117] The Court will also use the traditional supervisory powers under Art 226 EC. See, eg, EC Commission, 'Competition: Commission Requests Sweden to End Broadcasting Services Monopoly', Press Release IP/05/343, 21 Mar 2005.

In addition to the supervisory and regulatory powers of Article 86(3) EC, the EC Commission can adopt Decisions addressed to the Member States using its powers under Regulation 1/2003[118] to take action against undertakings granted special or exclusive rights. An example of a Decision addressed to a Member State using the old powers under Regulation 17 is the essential facilities case of *Port of Rødby*.[119]

The Legislative Element

The final part of Article 86(3) EC confers legislative competence on the EC Commission. The EC Commission is given power to control public undertakings through the use of Directives or Decisions. There is no guidance on the legislative process to be followed, and contrary to the trend found elsewhere to increase the European Parliament's legislative capacity, there is no formal role for the European Parliament. Article 86(3) EC also by-passes the traditional legislative processes of the EU found in Articles 249–252 EC. It is not surprising, therefore, that when the EC Commission has tried to exercise powers under Article 86(3) EC it has come into conflict with the Member States.

The EC Commission's powers were challenged when France, Italy and the United Kingdom brought an action for a Declaration that the Transparency Directive[120] was void.[121] The Directive was the first Directive adopted by the EC Commission using Article 86(3) EC as the legal base. It imposed far-reaching new obligations upon the Member States rather than spelling out existing obligations arising out of directly applicable EC Treaty provisions. One of the obligations under the Directive was a duty imposed upon the Member States to retain records for five years concerning public funds made available to public undertakings. The UK government argued that:

> Commission Directives are not of the same nature as those adopted by the Council. Whereas the latter may contain general legislative provisions which may, where appropriate, impose new obligations on Member States, the aim of the former is merely to deal with a specific situation in one or more Member States.[122]

A further argument was that the Directive could have been adopted by the Council using Article 89 EC since the purpose of the Directive was to monitor state aid. The EC Commission argued that it was one of its duties of surveillance under Article 86(3) EC to ensure that there was transparency in the financial

---

[118] [2003] OJ L 1/1.

[119] [1994] 5 CMLR 457.

[120] Commission Dir (EEC) 80/723 on the transparency of financial relations between Member States and public undertakings [1980] OJ L195/35.

[121] Cases 188/80 to 190/80 *France, Italy, and the UK v Commission* [1982] ECR 2545.

[122] *Ibid*, at para 5.

arrangements between Member States and public undertakings. The Court rejected the United Kingdom's argument, highlighting that:

> the limits of the powers conferred on the Commission by a specific provision of the Treaty are to be inferred not from a general principle, but from an interpretation of the particular wording of the provision in question, in this case Article [86] EC analysed in the light of its purpose and its place in the scheme of the Treaty.[123]

In rejecting the second argument the Court argued that the power:

> conferred upon the Commission by Article 86(3) ... operates in a specific field of application and under conditions defined by reference to the particular objective of that article. It follows that the Commission's power to issue the contested directive depends on the needs inherent in its duty of surveillance provided for in Article 86 and that the possibility that rules might be laid down by the Council, by virtue of its general power under Article 89, containing provisions impinging upon the specific sphere of aids granted to public undertakings does not preclude the exercise of that power by the Commission.[124]

The Court held that Article 86(3) EC was the correct legal base for the Directive, emphasising the absence of a rigid separation of powers in the Community and that the EC Treaty entrusts important powers to the EC Commission, although in the legislative field this is an exceptional situation.

Telecommunications was one of the first areas to be liberalised in the EU, using Community law powers. Telecommunications are obviously an essential part of business and trade, and having a telecommunications network based upon a national monopoly was an ineffective way to develop communications in an Internal Market. Arguably, also, lack of state funding was stifling innovation. In a fast moving industry pressure from the market also created pressures for dismantling state monopolies and liberalising markets. The Court backed the use of Article 86(3) EC to liberalise telecommunications equipment and telecommunications services in *France v Commission*.[125] France brought an action for annulment of certain provisions of the second EC Commission Directive based upon Article 86(3) EC.[126] Under this Directive the Member States were to ensure the withdrawal of special or exclusive rights where such rights had been granted to undertakings to import, market, connect or put into service telecommunications terminal equipment and/or maintain such equipment. Member States then had to ensure that economic operators had the right to import, market, connect, bring into service and maintain terminal equipment, subject to a number of

---

[123]   *Ibid*, at para 6.
[124]   *Ibid*, at para 14.
[125]   Case C-202/88 *France v Commission* (Terminal Equipment)[1991] ECR I–1223.
[126]   Commission Dir 88/301/EEC of 16 May 1988 on competition in the markets in telecommunications terminal equipment [1988] OJ L131/73.

conditions. The responsibility for creating specifications, monitoring their application and granting type approval was to be transferred away from the Member States to a body independent of public or private undertakings offering goods and/or services in the telecommunications sector. Other obligations related to consumer protection: for example, Member States were required to ensure that customers could terminate, with maximum notice of one year, leasing or maintenance contracts relating to terminal equipment which had been concluded with undertakings previously enjoying special or exclusive rights.

Advocate General Tesauro saw the Directive essentially as a planning instrument, an anomalous anticipation of the legislative process. He saw that the aim of the Directive was to lay down general, abstract rules for the sector, defining the obligations incumbent upon the Member States, and that this exceeded the scope of Article 86(3) EC, falling instead within the competence of the Council. He saw the Directive as a legislative measure which altered the balance between the Institutions of the EU since it amended the very basis for the presence of the state in a particular sector of the economy.

The Court held that Article 86(3) EC does not give the EC Commission a general legislative power, but a specific power to address state measures concerning monopolies. The Court departs from the Advocate General's Opinion, stating:

> inasmuch as it makes it possible for the Commission to adopt directives, Article 86(3) of the Treaty empowers it to lay down general rules specifying the obligations arising from the Treaty which are binding on the member States as regards the undertakings referred to in Article 86 (1) and (2).

The Court upheld parts of the Directive, but found other parts went beyond the EC Commission's powers. The Court upheld the provisions of the Directive prohibiting exclusive rights in so far as they infringed Article 28 EC. But the Directive did not specify the type of special rights which are actually involved and how they are contrary to the provisions of the EC Treaty. Thus Article 2 of the Directive was declared to be invalid in so far as it referred to special rights. The Court saw the obligation to create independent bodies justified because:

> a system of undistorted competition, as laid down in the Treaty, can be guaranteed only if equality of opportunity is secured as between the various economic operators.[127]

The Court saw that an important aim of the competition rules was to guarantee equality of opportunity between competitors. If specifications are drawn up and approvals granted by an undertaking offering competing goods there is no equality in the market. The EC Commission was acting pursuant to the EC Treaty objective of a system of undistorted competition.

---

[127] *Ibid*, at para 51.

The provision on termination of leasing/maintenance contracts was declared void because Article 86 EC conferred powers on the EC Commission only in relation to state measures. Therefore Article 86 EC was not an appropriate basis for dealing with the obstacles to competition which were purportedly created by the long-term contracts referred to in the Directive.

A further attack on the EC Commission's powers under Article 86(3) EC came in *Spain and others v Commission*.[128] Again the case concerned the attempt to introduce liberalisation into the telecommunications sector. The Directive[129] here complemented the Second Telecommunications Directive by introducing comparable obligations in the market for telecommunications services. The Court takes a similar approach to the French challenge, but also clarifies that the EC Commission may use directly applicable provisions of the EC Treaty without the need for any secondary legislation on the part of the Council to create obligations to liberalise a particular sector. Belgium had argued that the free movement of services was not as developed as the free movement of goods, and therefore the liberalising obligations contained in the Directive were not valid. The Court's ruling thus moves beyond the general principle of Article 3(f) EC to requiring a directly applicable EC Treaty provision as the basis for obligations created by Article 86(3) EC. The EC Commission has to show that an infringement of directly applicable EC Treaty rules would result from the conduct it is prohibiting.

These cases show the limits of the powers of the EC Commission. Article 86(3) EC is not a legislative power; it does not allow the EC Commission to choose between various policy options and adds little to the EC Commission's general enforcement powers against the Member States using the infringement procedure of Article 226 EC. A major weakness of Article 86(3) EC is that it cannot be used as a legal base for legislation to regulate services of general economic interest.

Addressees of an EC Commission Decision may also challenge the Decision using Article 230 EC.[130] The Court has also held, rather exceptionally, that an individual or an association representing collective interests may have standing to bring an action where the EC Commission refuses to adopt a Decision in breach of its supervisory functions set out in Article 86(1) and (3) EC.[131] This is an unusual statement, since in *Commission v T-Mobile Austria*[132] the Court held that the EC Commission's refusal to take action under Article 86(3) EC did not

---

[128]   Joined Cases C–271/90, C–281/90 & C–289/90 *Spain, Belgium and Italy v Commission* [1992] ECR I–5833.

[129]   Commission Dir 90/388/EEC of 28 June 1990 on competition in the markets for telecommunications services [1990] OJ L192/10.

[130]   Case T–54/99 *max.mobil Telekommunikation Service v Commission* [2002] ECR II–313.

[131]   Case C–107/95 P *Bundesverband der Bilanzbuchhalter v Commission* [1997] ECR I–947, para 25.

[132]   Case C–141/02 P *Commission v T-Mobile Austria* [2005] ECR I–1283.

produce binding legal effects and was not a reviewable act, and in *Bilanzbuch-halter*[133] the Court affirmed the EC Commission's wide discretion to act under Article 86(3) EC.[134]

After the telecommunications rulings the EC Commission realised that its wings were clipped, and Article 86(3) EC was used in the future to amend or recast the existing Directives and not to introduce new ones. Buendía Sierra contends, however, that Article 86(3) EC still has a residual role to play where the legislative process stagnates and could be deployed 'against resistance to liberalisation found in certain sectors'.[135]

The EC Commission, sensitive to political pressure from the Member States, realised that to get them on board with the liberalisation measures it would be sensible, diplomatically as well as democratically, to use the Internal Market legal base of Article 95 EC for future liberalisation measures. This involves the co-decision procedure of Article 251 EC.[136] The result has been gradual and partial liberalisation of certain sectors which are studied in the next chapter. The price was to introduce liberalisation gradually and often in a piecemeal manner, and to allow the Member States a continued, protected presence in the market in sensitive sectors. As we shall see, this has created new regulatory issues. Often the state wants to retain an interest in markets which have been liberalised. It may do this because it wants to protect a universal service (a public service) which the private sector would not be willing to supply, or because a particular area of the economy is sensitive and the state would not want this sector out of its political control, or in the hands of foreign ownership, or because the state wants to act on a commercial basis in the liberalised market. This has created problems because the state has a dominant position on such markets and it enjoys a 'first mover advantage'. The state also enjoys consumer familiarity and trust and has the resources and regulatory powers to protect its incumbent position. This in turn has led to litigation from competitors who want to enter partially liberalised markets. In subsequent years issues have arisen over the use of cross-subsidisation, the use of illegal state aid, and access to protected markets and networks. This in turn has generated a debate on *how* to regulate newly liberalised markets with a state-incumbent and new (and potential) entrants. Liberalised markets which are not regulated efficiently tend towards oligopoly/monopoly. This raises the question of how liberalised markets should be regulated. Should the normal competition rules apply to the liberalised sectors, or should new sector specific rules be invented? These issues are addressed in the

---

[133] Above n 131.

[134] See also the judgment of the CFI in Case T–54/99, above n 130, at paras 58–59

[135] J-L Buendia Sierra, *Exclusive Rights and State Monopolies Under EC Law* (Oxford, OUP, 1999) at 429.

[136] There are specific legal bases of Art 71 EC (for transport), and Art 80(2) EC (for air and maritime transport), which allow the Council to act alone to enact further liberalisation measures.

next chapter, which uses three case studies to examine the models of liberalisation deployed by the EU and the capacity of these models to adapt to rapidly changing markets.

5

Liberalisation

WHY LIBERALISATION?

C HAPTER 1 LOOKED AT the political and economic events which changed the perception of policy-makers towards state intervention in the market, and Chapters 2–4 have examined why and how liberalisation processes were triggered through legal processes. The case law of the Court[1] gave a special impetus to the attractions of liberalisation for inefficient and unresponsive public monopolies. This mood was tempered by the Court's more cautious rulings in other cases which hit directly at the core of public services and essential services provided or regulated by the state.[2] However competition principles have been worked into the general policies of the EU and are at the heart of the Lisbon Process. The modernisation of services was a central concern and the Lisbon European Council emphasised the importance of 'an inexpensive and world-class communications infrastructure', including the full use of the digital technologies such as the internet and mobile communications.[3] The Council also stressed the need to accelerate the process of structural reform for competitiveness and innovation, by completing the Internal Market as well as promoting 'a regulatory climate conducive to investment, innovation and entrepreneurship'.[4] Although the Lisbon Process has fallen behind its own targets the renewal of the strategy in 2005[5] and the acceptance of a Directive to liberalise some services even further in the EU[6] have continued to emphasise the role of competitive services in the globalised economy.

---

[1] Case C–41/90 *Höfner* [1991] ECR I–1979; Case C–260/89 *ERT* [1991] ECR I–2925; Case C–179/90 *Port of Genoa* [1991] ECR I–5889.

[2] Eg, the energy infringement actions, discussed in Ch 4: Cases C–157/94 *Commission v Netherlands*; C–158/94 *Commission v Italy*; C–59/94 *Commission v France*; C–160/94 *Commission v Spain*, reported at [1997] ECR I–5699, I–5789, I–5815 and I–5851 respectively; and the use of solidarity to protect core services from competition in the social security and health sectors: see, eg, Joined Cases C–159/91 & C–160/91 *Poucet and Pistre* [1993] ECR I–637; Case C–67/96 *Albany* [1999] ECR I–5751.

[3] Lisbon European Council, 23–24 Mar 2000, Presidency Conclusions , 9 available at: http://www.consilium.europa.eu/ueDocs/cms_Data/docs/pressData/en/ec/00100-r1.en0.htm.

[4] *Ibid*, 5,14.

[5] EC Commission, *Communication to the Spring Council, Working Together for Growth and Jobs: A New Start for the Lisbon Strategy*, COM(2005)24, 2 Feb 2002.

[6] Directive 2006/123/EC [2006] OJ L 376/36.

Other non-legal factors also fed into the evolution of the liberalisation and privatisation processes which spread across Europe. Demands made by consumers for new and better products and services and the need for a wider range of capital investments to fund research and development which would enable producers to compete in global markets[7] were important factors. It was believed that by shifting state assets from public-sector control to the disciplines of private ownership and the capital markets huge economic efficiencies would be unleashed and, incidentally, huge sums of money could be transferred to the state's dwindling coffers. Another factor is the distinctive form of multi-layered government found in the EU, where policy-makers and strategists interconnect at different sites. The processes of liberalisation introduced even more non-governmental stakeholders into the policy formation and implementation processes, and these interests had to be catered for in new shared-governance structures, as well as new governance concepts. This is seen in the telecommunications sector where comitology processes play a central role in the harmonisation and setting of standards, and also in the informal avenues of regulatory coordination established in the energy sector. The Florence Forum (or Florence Process) is the regulatory forum for electricity and the Madrid Forum (or Madrid Process) is the Gas Regulatory Forum. The aim is to create an EU-level platform, on a voluntary basis, for informal discussion and cooperation between government, regulators and stakeholders to find common solutions to the new regulatory challenges posed by liberalisation.[8]

It was recognised that judicial intervention on an *ad hoc,* but hierarchical, basis was not the way to proceed, and the Court's cautious approach in the energy infringement cases[9] in particular brought to the fore the need for Member State involvement in liberalisation legislation. As we saw in Chapter 1, liberalisation was often introduced through the privatisation of state assets. The privatisation of public utilities such as telecommunications and energy providers posed particular problems, since such undertakings enjoy significant market power enabling them to appropriate profits and make super-normal profits. This presents governments (and the EU) with a fundamental dilemma. If the state chooses to regulate the liberalised undertakings consumers enjoy efficiency gains, but such regulation will affect the profitability of such undertakings. But to let such firms go unregulated would lose the efficiency gains from liberalisation and damage the public interest. Thus the regulatory design of each liberalisation process has been fought over amongst a variety of stakeholders. The different sectors were nudged into liberalisation at different speeds, using different political and legal techniques and at the instigation of different institutions and

---

[7] For a discussion of competition between legal orders see H-W Sinn, *The New Systems Competition* (Oxford, Basil Blackwell, 2003) ch 8.

[8] B Eberlein, 'Regulation By Cooperation: The "Third Way" in Making Rules for the Internal Energy Market' in P Cameron (ed), *Legal Aspects of EU Energy Regulation* (Oxford, OUP, 2005).

[9] Above n 2.

political actors. There are, however, common themes to the liberalisation processes in Europe; for example, the separation of the commercial activities of the former state monopolies from public service obligations and the creation of independent regulatory bodies for the liberalised sectors.

A countervailing tendency which emerged as the enthusiasm for liberalisation swept across Europe was the question: what is the *purpose* of free markets? Initial ideas were based upon the need for European industry to be competitive at the global level alongside ideas of the need for capital investment in fast moving industries. Notions of citizenship, liberty, equality of opportunity generated by free markets also gave rise to linkages between free markets and social rights, which in turn are linked to elusive notions of social justice:

> a system of free markets seems to promise not merely liberty but equality of an important sort as well, since everyone in a free market is given an equal right to transact and participate in market arrangements.[10]

Thus claims were made for improved consumer rights, fundamental rights and basic citizenship rights as a consequence of liberalisation. However, the EU was seen as a weak institutional structure for delivering the same citizenship and redistributive polices in the same way as the traditional Member States. The result has been the introduction of Article 16 EC and the recognition of fundamental rights ideas in EC Commission soft law and the Constitutional Treaty, alongside the use of subsidiarity as a safety net to ensure that these policies are secured in the liberalisation process.

SECTOR-SPECIFIC REGULATION AND COMPETITION LAW

The United Kingdom took the lead in liberalising the networked sectors in transport, utilities and telecommunications and pushed for a similar level of liberalisation at the EU level through sector-specific regulation. This regulation, although implemented through secondary legislation, generally takes precedence over the competition law rules found in the primary (economic constitution) legislation of the EC Treaty.[11] It was recognised that competition law is not necessarily a sufficient tool to create a competitive environment, especially where

---

[10] C Sunstein, *Free Markets and Social Justice* (Oxford, OUP, 1997) at 3.
[11] Yet, according to Art 36 EC, only the agricultural sector is explicitly excluded automatically from the general competition rules of the EC Treaty. Cf Joined Cases 209–213/84 *Ministére Public v Asjes* [1986] ECR 1425 and Case 66/86 *Saeed* 1989] ECR 2512 discussed in Ch 2, where the Court rejected special pleading for the transport sector, and Case 45/85 *Verband der Sachversicherer* [1987] ECR 405 where similar special pleading for the insurance sector was denied.

there is a network industry,[12] and the design of the liberalisation processes has involved a periodic review and renewal of each process.[13]

A significant feature of the liberalisation tools deployed by the EU is the complementarity of sector-specific regulation and competition law to stimulate competition in the liberalised sector and to control abuse of market power. The EU has used a mixture of regulation and competition techniques to liberalise the networked industries and create new hybrid forms of legislation which use regulation and competition principles in the same piece of legislation.[14] The use of sector-specific regulation was initially conceived of as being merely of a transitional nature, with the idea that it could be reduced and ultimately abolished when normal competitive conditions were in place in the liberalised markets.

Sector-specific regulation is used to address issues of market failure *ex ante.* One special feature of the liberalisation processes is the use of regulation to allow access to networked industries, and the Court has indicated that this is an issue better left to regulation.[15] The EU requires the enforcement of the regulatory rules by independent agencies and, as we saw in Chapters 2 and 3, such regulatory bodies with delegated and independent powers may also run the risk of infringing Articles 81 and 82 EC. Increasingly Europe is seeing the creation of a number of sector-specific regulators at the national level.

From the 1990s onwards there has been a proliferation of national regulatory authorities (NRAs) operating alongside the national competition authorities and the EC Commission, creating the potential for jurisdictional battles as we see the increasing convergence between competition and regulation in the liberalised sectors.[16] In some Member States, for example the United Kingdom, NRAs are entrusted with the application of regulatory and competition law rules.[17]

---

[12] P Slot and A Skudder, 'Common Features of Community Law Regulation in the Network-bound Sectors' (2001) 38 *CMLRev* 87.

[13] See C Henry and A Jeunemaitre (eds), *Regulation of Networked Utilities: the European Experience* (Oxford, OUP, 2001).

[14] P Nihoul, 'Convergence in European Telecommunications A Case Study on the Relationship Between Regulation and Competition Law' (1998/99) 2 *International Journal of Communications Law and Policy* 1.

[15] Case C–7/97 *Oscar Bronner GmbH & Co KG v Mediaprint Zeitungs-und Zeitschriftenverlag GmbH & Co. KG and others* [1998] ECR I–7791. However in Case C–418/01 *IMS Health GmbH & Co OHG v NDC Health GmbH & Co. KG* [2004] ECR I–5039 the Court sets out conditions where mandatory access may be ordered. Cf EC Commission Decision *GVG/FS* 2004/33/EC [2004] OJ L11/17 and the Microsoft litigation: EC Commission Decision relating to a proceeding under Article 82 of the Treaty (Case Comp/C-3/37.792 Microsoft) C(2004) 900 final.

[16] See N Petit, 'The Proliferation of National Regulatory Authorities Alongside Competition Authorities: A Source of Jurisdictional Confusion' in D Geradin, R Munoz and N Petit (eds), *Regulation Through Agencies—A New Paradigm of European Governance* (Cheltenham, Edward Elgar, 2005)

[17] P Slot and A Johnston, *An Introduction to Competition Law* (Oxford, Hart, 2006) at 325 argue that even in the UK there is a tendency for the regulators to prefer the use of sector-specific regulation over competition law, but point out that Ofgem recently sent a letter to the EC Commission asking for

The advantages of regulation are seen in the element of certainty provided for market actors. However there are disadvantages: underpinning the initial liberalisation process in the EU was the belief that regulation should be minimal and that ultimately the market could be regulated by competition law principles. Thus, the *design* of regulation is important.[18] It should be restricted to correcting market failures in a way that does not impose unnecessary costs on the regulated firms. But nevertheless regulation may appear rigid and impede innovation. Regulation often relies upon investigation and enforcement by regulatory authorities, reducing the role of private enforcement of the law.

Competition rules are general and tend to apply *ex post*. There are elements of *ex ante* regulation in EU competition law; for example, under the old Regulation 17 undertakings could notify agreements to the EC Commission for a negative clearance or an exemption under Article 81(3) EC; the mergers and state aid rules continue to rely upon *ex ante* notification schemes. Increasingly competition law is displaying a tendency towards creating sector-specific rules alongside encouraging the regulation of undertakings through private enforcement and remedies.[19] This chapter will examine the liberalisation of the telecommunications, postal services and utilities sectors in the EU in order to explore the way in which the free market and competition rules were used to stimulate competition in these sectors and the way in which EU law has created a regulatory structure for the ensuing liberalisation processes. In this chapter, three case studies will be made to show how liberalisation has taken place in the telecommunications, postal and utilities (gas and electricity) sectors. Taking as common themes the political, economic and legal processes which led to liberalisation of each sector, the case studies examine the main actors involved in the liberalisation processes and the legal tools and framework used to establish and maintain liberalisation and competitiveness of the respective markets.

TELECOMMUNICATIONS

The tendencies towards liberalisation of the telecommunications sector, seen at the national level in the UK, Sweden and Finland, worked their way into EU policy during the 1980s. All of the Member States used monopolies with special or exclusive rights, organised along national lines, for the provision of networks

an investigation into the under-utilisation of a natural gas pipeline between the UK and Belgium in the wake of significantly high gas prices in the UK: Ofgem Press Release 256/05, 29 Nov 2005.

[18] See D Geradin and J Sidak, 'European and American Approaches to Antitrust Remedies and the Institutional Design of Regulation in Telecommunications' in M Cave, S Majumdar and I Vogelsang (eds), *Handbook of Telecommunications Economics* (Oxford, OUP, 2005), ii.

[19] See, eg, D Geradin and D Henry, 'Regulatory and Competition Law Remedies in the Postal Sector' in D Geradin (ed), *Remedies in Network Industrie—EC Competition Law versus Sector Specific Regulation* (Antwerp, Intersentia, 2004).

and services.[20] This structure fragmented the European market and prevented it from using the benefits of economies of scale which rendered the European market less competitive than the liberalised markets of Japan and the United States, as well as restricting investment in what was a fast moving research and development sector.[21] The liberalisation of telecommunications was prompted by the demand for greater and better coordinated inter-Community communications networks, as well as the increased globalisation of trade. The quantitative increase in demand for these services was matched by qualitative demands for faster and better services, especially in the growing field of data communications. The understanding that telecommunications was a natural monopoly was challenged by the inability of states to meet the demands made by a new technological environment, but the EC Treaty did not give the Community competence to regulate telecommunications. A breakthrough in the scope of Community law competence came when the Court established that the competition rules were applicable to the telecommunications sector in the *British Telecommunications* judgment,[22] but competition law was used only sporadically when cross-border issues arose. In 1984 the EC Commission addressed the development of standards and the promotion of research alongside the development of structurally backward regions in the telecommunications sector,[23] but the liberalisation process of telecommunications at the Community level is usually traced back to the EC Commission's Green Paper on the Development of a Common Market for Telecommunications in 1987.[24]

A central discussion of this period was the relationship between Article 86(3) EC and Article 95 EC. In the 1987 Green Paper the EC Commission referred to the possibility of using Article 86(3) EC as a legal base for the liberalisation of telecommunications.[25] Larouche observes that the Green Paper is not explicit about which legal base should be used for liberalisation, and argues that the EC Commission was probably waiting for the reaction of the other Institutions and of the various actors in the telecommunications sector.[26] In the ensuing *Communication on the Implementation of the Green Paper up to 1992*[27] the EC Commission proposed to use Article 86(3) EC to adopt Directives for the liberalisation of the market for terminal equipment, the opening of telecommunications services and the separation of regulatory and operational functions. Controversy continued over the correct choice of legal base and the EC Commission was obliged to

---

[20]   F Blum and A Logue, *State Monopolies Under EC Law* (Chichester, Wiley, 1979).

[21]   See R Wainwright and A Jessen, 'Recent Developments in Community Law on Telecommunications' (1991) 11 *Yearbook of European Law* 79.

[22]   Case 41/83 *Italy v Commission* [1984] ECR 873.

[23]   EC Commission, *Action Plan in Relation to the Telecommunications Sector,* COM(84) 277.

[24]   EC Commission, *Towards a Dynamic European Economy— Green Paper on the Development of the Common Market for Telecommunications Services and Equipment,* COM(87) 290 final.

[25]   *Ibid,* at points 62, 69 and 186.

[26]   P Larouche, *Competition Law and Regulation in European Telecommunications* (Oxford, Hart, 2000) at 40–1.

[27]   COM(88) 48 final.

explain the choice of legal base in greater detail in the Explanatory Memorandum for the Open Network Provision Framework Directive.[28]

The EC Commission saw the two legal bases as complementary and not alternatives. Article 86(3) EC applies more precisely when the EC Commission acts in its function as guardian of the EC Treaty to end violations of the competition provisions, and is seen as a fast track alternative to the infringement action of Article 226 EC. The EC Commission takes the view that Article 95 EC addresses harmonisation measures necessary to get rid of barriers to integration arising from national legislative measures, whereas Article 86(3) EC is the only legal base for removing special or exclusive rights or altering the institutional framework in order to separate operational and regulatory functions. The Council differed from this position, seeing Article 95 EC as the vehicle to achieve a single market in telecommunications which reflected the policy choices of the Member States. Any questions of incompatibility with the EC Treaty should be raised in infringement proceedings under Article 226 EC, and not under Article 86(3) EC which offered fewer procedural guarantees.[29] The European Parliament also called upon the EC Commission to change the legal base of the Telecommunications Directive and use Article 95 EC. But the focus of the European Parliament's concern was to protect universal services provision in the Internal Market.[30]

The first 15 years of liberalisation were intensive, with the EC Commission leading the policy with a two-pronged approach, a 'basic dualism',[31] addressing the liberalisation of telecommunications markets alongside the harmonisation of standards. The telecommunications sector in the EU was fully liberalised on 1 January 1998, and this was viewed as one of the major achievements of the EU during the 1990s.

Liberalisation Measures

The first liberalisation measure taken by the EC Commission, Directive 88/301/EEC, opened up the terminal equipment market for competition, introducing the principle of full mutual recognition of type approval for telecommunications terminal equipment.[32] Using Article 86(3) EC as the legal base special or exclusive rights for the import, marketing and connection of terminal equipment were to

---

[28] COM(88)825 final, paras 7a–8a.

[29] Council Resolution of 30 June 1988 [1988] OJ C257/1.

[30] European Parliament Resolution of 14 Dec 1989 on competition in the telecommunications sector [1989] OJ C323/118.

[31] C Koenig and E Röder, 'The Regulation of Telecommunications in the European Union: a Challenge for the Countries Acceding to the European Community' (1999) 10 *European Business Review* 333.

[32] Dir 88/301/EEC [1988] OJ L131/73.

be withdrawn by the Member States. France attempted to challenge the competence of the EC Commission to use Article 86(3) EC to adopt this type of
legislation.[33] France argued that special or exclusive rights were not illegal under
the EC Treaty and that the Directive could require the removal of such rights. The
Court stated that even though Article 86(1) EC presupposes the existence of
undertakings which have certain special or exclusive rights, it does not follow that
all the special or exclusive rights are necessarily compatible with the Treaty. The
Court's judgment in *France v Commission* is seen as a watershed, giving the EC
Commission confidence to pursue the liberalisation process using Article 86(3)
EC alongside the Internal Market legal base of Article 95 EC.[34] Larouche
describes the impact of the case:

> [it] … changed the balance of Community law as regards the relationship between
> Member State intervention in the economy and the rules concerning the internal
> market or competition.[35]

The Services Directive, 90/388/EEC,[36] was also unsuccessfully challenged before
the Court of Justice.[37] This Directive created the obligation for the Member States
to withdraw exclusive rights for telecommunications operators except for voice
telephony. Voice telephony was liberalised later in Directive 96/19/EC. The
Directive obliged the Member States to separate regulatory and commercial
functions alongside creating transparent and non-discriminatory procedures for
the admission of new telecommunications services. The Member States could
impose licensing or notification requirements only to ensure compliance with
what were narrowly defined essential requirements.

Further Directives abolished special and exclusive rights for the provision of
satellite services and equipment,[38] a Directive addressing cable television[39] and a
Mobile and Personal Communications Directive.[40] Finally the Full Competition
Commission Directive, 96/19/EC,[41] established a basic regulatory framework for
the newly competitive, liberalised market.

---

[33] France was supported by Italy, Belgium, Germany and Greece in challenging the legal base of
the Dir: Case C–202/88 *France v Commission (Terminal Equipment)* [1991] ECR I–1272.

[34] F Blum and A Logue, *State Monopolies Under EC Law* (Chichester, Wiley, 1979) at. 1–4.

[35] P Larouche, *Competition Law and Regulation in European Telecommunications* (Oxford, Hart,
2000) at 49.

[36] [1990] OJ L192/10.

[37] Spain, supported by France, Belgium and Italy, attacked the use of Art 86(3) as the legal base for
Dir 90/3888 (Cases C–271/90, C–281/90 & C–289/90 *Spain v Commission* [1992] ECR I–5833).

[38] Commission Dir 94/46/EC [1994] OJ L268/15.

[39] Commission Dir 95/51/EC [1995] OJ L256/49.

[40] Commission Dir 96/2/EC [1996] OJ Ll20/59.

[41] [1996] OJ L74/13.

Harmonisation Measures

Alongside the EC Commission's activities the Council adopted a set of harmonisation Directives. Initially the two sets of provisions were viewed as distinct but complementary. Over time the demarcation line between liberalisation and harmonisation became blurred as liberalisation and harmonisation measures began to overlap.[42] Using Article 95 EC as the legal base the Open Network Provision Directive[43] was adopted on the same day as the Services Directive. This facilitated access by private companies to the public telecommunications networks and to some telecommunications services. At its heart was the harmonisation of technical interfaces and the elimination of differences in conditions of use and tariffs. These principles were extended to leased lines[44] and voice telephony,[45] with Directive 97/51/EC[46] applying to the fully liberalised telecommunications sector. In 1997 the Council adopted Directive 97/13/EC which established a harmonised regime for licensing.[47] In the light of the debate over the protection of services of general economic interest, generated by the litigation using Article 86 EC discussed in Chapter 4, the Council adopted a specific Directive on universal services.[48]

The New Regulatory Framework

The main harmonising Directives in the telecommunications liberalisation programme contained review clauses, and in 1999 the EC Commission commenced a comprehensive review of the liberalisation programme.[49] In 2002, in readiness for enlargement, the EU introduced a new regulatory framework which replaced the mass of regulation with a smaller package integrating competition law principles. Omitted from the framework were services provided over networks such as broadcasting and digital interactive services (e-banking, games, gambling) which would continue to be regulated by general Community law rules relating to free movement and non-discrimination.[50]

Underpinning the new framework is the premise that *ex ante* regulation should apply to undertakings with significant market power (called 'SMP operators')

---

[42] See P Nihoul, 'Convergence in European Telecommunications A Case Study on the Relationship Between Regulation and Competition Law' (1998/99) *International Journal of Communications Law and Policy* 1.

[43] Council Dir 90/387/EEC [1990] OJ L295/23.

[44] Council Dir 92/44/EEC [1992] OJ L165/27.

[45] Council Dir 98/10/EC [1998] OJ L101/24.

[46] [1997] OJ L295/23.

[47] [1997] OJ L117/15.

[48] Council Dir 98/10/EC [1998] OJ L101/24.

[49] EC Commission, *Review 1999—Towards a New Framework in Electronic Communications Infrastructure and Associated Services*, COM(1999)539.

[50] See specific legislation such as the Television Without Frontiers Directive, 89/552/EEC (amended by Dir 97/37/EC) [1989] OJ L298/23 .

with a decentralised approach entrusting national regulatory authorities (NRAs) with the power to tailor the content of regulation to local situations. This approach brings to the fore the interface between regulation and competition.[51]

The earlier Telecommunications Directives had adopted a formal approach adopting regulatory techniques, for example by testing market power on market shares principles. This mirrors the ideas of determining the concept of significant market power used in competition law methodology. In the classic definition of market power the Court uses an economic approach:

> a position of economic strength enjoyed by an undertaking which enables it to hinder the maintenance of effective competition on the relevant market by allowing it to behave to an appreciable extent independently of its competitors and customers and ultimately consumers.[52]

The approach used in the new regulatory package mirrors the moves towards an economics-based approach to curbing abuses of dominant power under Article 82 EC in competition law.

The Directive also refers to complex forms of dominance, for example, the concept of joint dominance, providing examples of the kind of evidence which can be used to find joint dominance in the form of Guidelines[53] and in Annex II of the Directive. Article 14(3) of the Directive echoes the ideas of leveraging (where dominant firms expand into ancillary markets) found in the judgment in *Tetra Pak*.[54]

The new electronics communications package used the Internal Market legal base, Article 95 EC, as its legal base. The central legal tool in this package is the Framework Directive,[55] setting out the principles and objectives for regulators. The Framework Directive creates a harmonised framework for regulating electronic communications services, networks and associated facilities. The main thrust of the Directive is to clarify legal terms and definitions, but it creates convergence between regulation and competition principles. The Directive also establishes horizontal principles which apply across the new legislative package.

---

[51] 'The inclusion of antitrust principles in the new package marks a clear step away from the territorial and social dimension of regulation, in the direction of an economic dimension based on a system of effective competition': A Bavasso, 'Electronic Communications: A New Paradigm for European Regulation' (2004) 24 *CMLRev* 87, 94. De Streel calls this 'a sort of "preemptive competition law"': A de Streel, 'The Integration of Competition Law Principles in the New European Regulatory Framework for Electronic Communications' (2003) 26 *World Competition* 489, 490.

[52] Case 322/81 *Michelin v Commission* [1983] ECR 3461, 3503.

[53] Commission Guidelines on Market Analysis and the Assessment of Significant Market Power Under the Community Regulatory Framework for Electronic Communications Networks and Services [2002] OJ C165/03.

[54] Case T–83/91 *Tetra Pak International v Commission* [1994] ECR II–755, para 122.

[55] Dir 2002/21/EC [2002] OJ L108/33; J-D Braun and R Capito, 'The Framework Directive' in C Koenig, A Bartosch and J-D Braun (eds), *EC Competition and Telecommunications Law* (The Hague, Kluwer, 2002).

An innovation in the Directive is the recognition that in telecommunications there are a number of inter-dependent markets.

The Directive on the Authorisation of Electronic Communications Networks and Services replaces the licensing regime established in the old package.[56] Different licensing regimes across Europe presented barriers to entry for operators.[57] Thus the new approach creates a general authorisation regime, based upon a light touch of best practice in the Member States, limiting the use of specific rights to the assignment of radio frequencies and numbers.

The Directive on universal service and users' rights relating to electronic communications networks and services[58] sets out rules on how universal service providers can be compensated for their services alongside setting out users' rights. It also empowers the NRAs to impose common tariffs and price caps on universal services when a Member State does not achieve the objectives of the Directive set out in Article 8.

The Directive on access to, and interconnection of, electronic communications networks and associated facilities[59] is aimed at establishing harmonised regulatory framework for the market in fixed and mobile telecommunications networks, cable and terrestrial broadcasting networks, satellite networks and internet protocol networks between suppliers of networks and suppliers of services, to create sustainable competition in services with concomitant consumer benefits. Also part of the package was a Decision on a regulatory framework for radio spectrum policy in the EC,[60] a regulation on unbundled access to the local loop,[61] and a Directive on privacy and processing personal data.[62] Member States were given a short implementation period until 24 July 2003 to transpose the Directives. While the new package gave the Member States some flexibility it also contained complex ideas, without clear delimitations, between competition and regulation principles.[63]

The new package of measures was innovative in attempting to find a new role for competition and regulation principles, and to obtain the 'right' mix between the two forms of regulatory intervention in the EU. The rapid convergence of telephony, internet and broadcasting markets has led to new strategic alliances[64]

---

[56] [2002] OJ L108/21. See C Koenig, A Neumann and A Koch, 'Authorisations' in *ibid.*

[57] M Sinclair, 'A New European Communications Services Regulatory Package' (2001) *Computer and Telecommunications Law Review* 156, 161.

[58] [2002] OJ L108/21. See A de Streel, 'The Protection of the European Citizen in a Competitive eSociety: The New EU Universal Service Directive' [2003] *Journal of Network Industries* 189.

[59] [2002] OJ L108/7.

[60] Dec 676/2002/EC of the European Parliament and of the Council of 7 Mar 2002 on a regulatory framework for radio spectrum policy in the European Community (Radio Spectrum Dec) [2002] OJ L108/1.

[61] Reg (EC) 2887/2000 [2000] OJ L336/4.

[62] Dir 2002/58/EC [2002] OJ L 201/37.

[63] See P Larouche, 'A Closer Look at Some Assumptions Underlying EC Regulation of Electronic Communications' [2002] *Journal of Network Industries* 148, who argues that the new package stretches competition law beyond reasonable bounds.

[64] See Y Benkler, *The Wealth of Networks* (Yale, New Haven, Yale University Press, 2006).

and new demands from consumers. It has also had spill-over effects in the creation of a virtual information society challenging traditional sectors such as publishing, broadcasting, education services and even, to some extent, traditional services, such as medical consultation services. It is anticipated that new business models will emerge for the delivery of the next generation of communications networks which will separate out *access* to the network from *delivery* of the content. This will challenge the current vertical integration of communications business, and perhaps fragment the monopoly/duopoly/joint dominance structures which continue to exist in the telecommunications sector. It will also present challenges for the concept of universal services and how regulation will tackle issues of social (and digital) exclusion. These developments already challenge the EU e-communications regulatory structure and the EC Commission started a consultation process in June 2006 to address the reform of the electronic communications regulatory package.

POSTAL SERVICES

The Market for Postal Services

Postal services were reformed in the nineteenth century. Integral to these reforms was the idea that a universal service should be provided on the basis of a uniform price for the delivery of mail anywhere within the state. To achieve this, cross-subsidisation between low-cost areas (usually densely populated urban areas) and high-cost areas (islands, rural areas and remote areas) is seen as a necessary component of providing a universal service offered by the state. This belief in protecting a universal service has been used by the Member States to stall liberalisation in the postal sector despite the fact that competition and new technologies are creating new and different consumer demands in this sector.

Recent studies have shown that liberalisation has been painfully slow in the postal sector. The WIK Report[65] shows that the development of competition in the letter postal market has been limited, even in the most liberalised of markets in Sweden. The basic postal letter market continues to be monopolistic in the EU. Even in Sweden, which abolished the postal monopoly in the early 1990s, Swedish Post retains some 93 per cent of the letter post market. In the United Kingdom, the NRA has made efforts to introduce competition in the last two years, but the Royal Mail continues to take more than 99.5 per cent of the mail volume within the licensed area. Similarly, in Germany Deutsche Post has a market share of around 95 per cent within the licensed area and in the segment opened to competition its market share is some 85 per cent. In The Netherlands, where

---

[65] Study on the Evolution of the Regulatory Model for Postal Services, WIK-Consult July 2005, available at http://ec.europa.eu/internal_market/post/studies_en.htm, at 101.

direct mail has been liberalised, the market share of TNT in the letter post segment continues to be above 95 per cent of the market share.

Postal services are paradoxical. They display inherently global tendencies and yet at the same time are fiercely national, with many still operated by state-run monopolies, keen to protect their dominant position in the face of growing competition. The postal monopoly service claims that there are economies of scale, implying that there is a natural monopoly. This assertion can be challenged, however, as changes in technology have created new forms of communication industries, for example, telecoms, mobile telecom and the internet. These new forms of communication also have repercussions for the postal sector by changing and increasing the volume of trade, for example the growth in internet purchasing, e-Bay and other on-line auctions has increased the volume of parcel post as well as the desire to obtain purchases quickly, resulting in different forms of transport and delivery of bulky items. On the other side of the coin, the use of email to send letters, circulars and bills abroad to obtain the lowest postage rates has reduced the volume of letter mail, and internet billing and banking services could also make the postal service redundant in these areas.

Improved and new technologies allow all postal operators to increase the efficiency of their logistics processes, leading to higher flexibility, greater capacity to handle large volumes, improved performance and lower costs. This is an important factor because consumption patterns are changing at the level of corporations, small and medium-sized businesses as well as in households (for example, the growth in multiple occupancy households). As a result the postal service has become fragmented, with postal services fracturing into separate activities supplying different kinds of services for ordinary post, junk mail, pre-paid mail, bills, document delivery, express postal services, parcels, freight and specialised logistics. The traditional Post Office now offers a range of other services, from financial services to the delivery of flowers. It has become a commercial actor in its own right, acquiring competitors as well as diversifying its services.

At the same time the Member States, faced with increased competition, are questioning what *kind* of universal service they should provide for consumers and how much longer they can afford to provide and fund a universal service. There are arguments that postal services are now facing the prospect of extinction, caught in a pincer movement where new technologies are changing long-established industry standards and market liberalisation is opening up markets for new entrants who are unshackled from the infrastructure which limits the incumbents.[66]

---

[66] 'Pulling the Envelope', *The Economist*, 20 Jan 2005, print edition. Editorial, 'Stand and Deliver', *The Economist*, 24 Dec 2005.

The Political Background

Liberalisation was triggered by complaints and litigation criticising the postal monopoly as inefficient and denying consumer choice. During the 1980s and 1990s other factors such as the cost of maintaining a universal service, the development of new technologies and increased consumer demands for fast, efficient and bespoke delivery services and foreign competition also moved the liberalisation process on, albeit at a snail-mail pace. Even the EC Commission was reluctant to apply the competition and free movement rules to the state-owned and state-operated postal service providers until well into the 1990s, despite complaints from competitors who were trying to bring bespoke courier services and express mail to the closed market in Europe in the 1980s.[67]

Courier services originated in the late 1960s in North America as a means of delivering important documents in a fast, reliable style later known as 'time-sensitive' and 'door-to-door delivery'. In Europe courier services were embryonic, employing few staff, and most were personally managed by highly individualistic founders. Before the creation of international conferences in the 1980s they had little access to government or commercial lobbying.[68]

In June 1983 the EC Commission sent inquiry letters to the major private postal couriers operating in Europe, asking for their opinions on the relationship between courier services and the postal monopoly laws in the Member States. A meeting of the couriers was convened by DHL in Geneva in August 1983. The couriers were able to respond to the EC Commission's inquiry with a collective, detailed report on the role of courier services and their relationship with national monopolies. At the close of the meeting the representatives of the couriers decided to form a trade group which was later called the International Express Carriers Conference (IECC). This was the start of a coordinated strategy to influence policy decision-making in the postal sector in Europe.[69]

By 1988 the Conference was funded by DHL, TNT, Federal Express and UPS. These were the major international postal couriers challenging the national postal monopolies for a share of the postal market. However, the growth of international couriers and the creation of larger firms made policy coordination difficult, leading to a breakaway group, the Association of European Express Carriers (AEEC), established by DHL and Securicor. This was matched by a new European level association of the IECC: the European Express Association.

---

[67] J Campbell Jr, 'Couriers and the European Postal Monopolies: Policy Challenges of a Newly Emerging Industry' in R Pedlar and M van Schendelen (eds), *Lobbying in the European Union* (Aldershot, Dartmouth, 1994). See also J Campbell Jr, 'The Evolution of Terminal Dues and Remail provisions in European and International Postal Law' in D Geradin (ed), *The Liberalisation of Postal Services in the European Union* (The Hague, Kluwer, 2002).

[68] See J Campbell Jr, n 67.

[69] In addition to the couriers and the postal monopolies business users, consumer groups, postal unions and policy think tanks were involved in the policy discussions of the role of postal monopolies. Polling firms were used to canvass business operators' opinion.

At this early stage of policy coordination the focus was not so much upon the competition rules of the EC Treaty as the reliance upon the free movement rules to allow unrestricted cross-border postal services.

A major innovation in postal services developed by the couriers was the use of 'remail' which was developed in the US in the early 1980s. Large users of the mail services demanded a better service and discounts for work sharing, that is pre-sorting mail or transporting mail downstream to a post office located near addresses before handing over the mail for delivery by the post office. The efficiency of this process was enhanced by the use of computer-generated mail which could be sent abroad using the local rate of delivery, 'the last mile', and thus avoiding overseas postage rates.

In the US the postal service was required to accept the right of couriers to provide an international remail service, and this resulted in the postal monopolies having to compete in the delivery of this mail to Europe.[70] The national monopolies in Europe were not entirely effective in making the final delivery of the mail, and as remail grew in importance couriers started to develop a more efficient and cheaper final delivery service in cities. The Universal Postal Convention included a provision which discouraged mailers from taking domestic mail out of the country and posting it with a postal operator in a neighbouring state. Post offices were authorised to intercept remail and return it to the original postal territory or to charge the addressee a domestic postage rate in addition to the original international rate paid by the sender. The UK Post Office convened an *ad hoc* 'Remail Conference' where the state monopolies agreed to increase the terminal dues[71] and to refuse to forward or deliver mail supplied by couriers, as well as boycotting the couriers. It was also agreed to lower the price and improve the quality of international postal services. The monopolies persuaded the 1989 UPU Congress to ratify this policy. The monopolies also created a new postal airline system and formed a new undertaking called Unipost to provide marketing, research and consulting services for international mail. This was the start of the mixed commercial activities of both postal monopolies and the competitor courier service operators.

The public monopolies were not entirely united in their response to the competition posed by private courier services. The United Kingdom was the only Member State to permit competition from private couriers, provided that they

---

[70] See J Campbell Jr, 'Remail: Catalyst for Liberalising European Postal Markets' in G Kulenkampf and H Smit (eds), *Liberalisation of Postal Markets: Papers Presented at the 6th Königswinter Seminar, WIK Proceedings Vol 7* (Bad Honnef, WIK, 2002); U Stumf, 'Remail: Catalyst for Liberalizing European Postal Markets' in M Crew and P Kleindorfer (eds), *Regulation and the Nature of Postal Services* (The Hague, Kluwer, 1993).

[71] The large increase in terminal dues affected the couriers since they paid the full cost of the dues, whereas the Member States could cancel out the cost of the dues where they exchanged similar quantities of mail. See further J Campbell Jr, 'The Evolution of Terminal Dues and Remail Provisions in European and International Postal Law' in D Geradin (ed), *The Liberalisation of Postal Services in the European Union* (The Hague, Kluwer, 2002).

charged more than £1.00 per shipment. In contrast La Poste in France adopted aggressive tactics to stem competition from couriers,[72] and the German and Danish Post Offices started cases in the national courts arguing that the courier remail service violated national monopolies. One of the first counter tactics deployed by the organised couriers was to conduct legal research to expose the legal weaknesses in the organisation and the operation of the postal monopolies in the Member States. This, however, provided only a defence mechanism to stave off the threat of prosecution; it was not used as a sword to challenge the power of the state monopolies.

The couriers deliberately avoided a head-on confrontation with the public monopolies, realising that they could not win either legal or public sympathy. The legal strategy was also influenced by the pending appeal against the EC Commission's Decision of December 1982 to apply the competition rules to certain telex activities in the *British Telecommunications* case.[73] It was recognised that the courier services needed to be recognised as a genuine commercial activity, and thus a second strand in the organised tactics was to use independent economic consultants to identify the role of couriers in the national economies. This was a difficult task, given that the courier business was still embryonic in Europe, but it proved to be a useful policy instrument in presenting the emerging courier services as a new policy issue to consumers, politicians and governments. This was a tactic which was adopted by the state monopolies in 1991 and is part of the continuing strategy to influence policy-making.

Complaints to the EC Commission

In July 1988 the IECC filed its first formal complaint to the EC Commission arguing that eight of the postal monopolies were in breach of the competition rules of the EC Treaty. The EC Commission prevaricated and the postal monopolies captured the situation by encouraging the EC Commission to prepare a Green Paper, focusing upon the necessity to preserve a high level of universal postal service, rather than consider competition issues. By July 1990 the monopoly postal operators and the couriers were able to come together to co-finance a seminar to discuss the structure of the postal industry in the light of the impending Green Paper where it was recognised that there were strong

---

[72] In 1982 courier services were banned in the provinces. Couriers were warned that they would be prosecuted for breaking the postal monopoly and were told not to advertise their services. Newspaper articles were written, and politicians made speeches questioning the legitimacy of the couriers and warning consumers not to use their services. The coercive power of the state was also used; postal inspectors and customs officials raided couriers' offices and property and bureaucratic obstacles were put in their way, for example delays in permits and licences. La Poste also insisted on an informal tax whereby couriers signed an agreement whereby they paid a sum of money for each shipment.

[73] Case 41/83 *Italy v Commission* [1984] ECR 873.

economic arguments for the liberalisation of the postal sector. The EC Commission, while sympathetic to the complaints against the postal monopolies,[74] eventually dismissed the IECC's complaints in 1995 by accepting the undertakings of the postal monopolies to amend their agreement in the proposed REIMS agreement.[75]

This agreement did not materialise since it was contingent upon the Spanish postal monopoly joining REIMS, and this did not happen. On 15 September 1999 the EC Commission approved a revised agreement known as the REIMS II agreement which largely eliminated discrimination in the delivery charges for international and domestic mail. The agreement, came some 10 years after the initial complaint lodged by the IECC and, as Campbell Jr. points out, it allowed the postal monopolies to continue with the terminal dues agreement for at least three years after the EC Commission's Decision.[76]

The IECC challenged the EC Commission's Decision before the CFI. While upholding the EC Commission's discretion to investigate complaints, the CFI reversed a key element of the Decision by holding that neither losses resulting from non-cost-based terminal dues nor a need to circumvent the postal monopoly justified a postal interception of remail.[77] The postal monopolies could not reasonably justify interception of remail by citing imperfections in a terminal dues agreement which they had drafted. The Court rejected an appeal brought by the German Post Office on this part of the CFI decision.[78] Derenne and Stockford make the point that remail issues could be viewed as the postal equivalent of telex forwarding, over which BT was held to be impeding competition:

> The case triggered a snowballing effect in telecoms liberalisation. The Commission could be considered to have missed an opportunity to use the IECC case to induce a similar effect in the postal sector.[79]

A second complaint was made to the EC Commission against the Danish Post Office which was preventing outbound courier mail. This was a test case exposing the role of a national monopoly in the remail tactics and the involvement in the Unipost activities. A third complaint was brought before the French competition authority, and also made to the EC Commission, by SFEI (later known as UFEX) in December 1990 against La Poste. La Poste had created a private joint venture,

---

[74] In 1993 the EC Commission addressed a Statement of Objections to La Poste, Deutsche Bundespost, Postdienst, Royal Mail, Régie Belge des Postes, Finnish Post, Sweden Post and Swiss PTT recognising substantial infringements of EC competition law.

[75] EC Commission, Case IV/32.791 *Remail*; Statement of Objections 5 Apr 1993; Joined Cases T–133/95 & T–204/95 *International Express Carriers Conference (IECC) v Commission* [1998] ECR II–3645.

[76] Above n 71.

[77] Joined Cases T–133/95 & T–204/95, above n 75, paras 96–102.

[78] Case C–428/98 P *Deutsche Post AG v IECC* [2000] ECR I–3061.

[79] J Derenne and C Stockford, 'Abuse of Market Powers in Postal Services: Lessons from the Commission's Decisional Practice and Court of Justice' in D Geradin (ed), *The Liberalisation of Postal Services in the European Union* (The Hague, Kluwer, 2001) at 139, 145.

called Chronopost, with a private transport company. Chronopost was able to compete against the couriers in the domestic and the international express mail markets. It was alleged that La Poste was effectively subsiding Chronopost with commercial and logistical assistance, and this was an illegal state aid and an abuse of a dominant position. The EC Commission looked at each of the allegations separately and found that there was no breach of Article 82 EC or the state aid rules. SFEI/UFEX appealed against both Decisions. In relation to the state aid Decision the EC Commission sent a letter to the Court on 14 July 1992 stating that it would withdraw the Decision, thus making the appeal for an annulment redundant.[80]

A second Decision was adopted several years later, on 1 October 1997, when the EC Commission again concluded that there was no state aid to SFMI-Chronopost.[81] The CFI annulled this Decision, finding that the EC Commission had wrongly assessed the situation by failing to compare the prices charged by La Poste to its subsidiary with those which would have been charged by an undertaking operating outside the reserved sector.[82] The EC Commission had merely ascertained that the costs of La Poste had been covered in the charges asked of its subsidiary, and the CFI held that this was not sufficient of an investigation to rule out the presence of state aid. On appeal the Court held[83] that the test proposed by the CFI was wrong. The CFI had considered that the principle that a transaction has no state aid element if it is on normal market terms could be applied to the assistance provided by La Poste, as an arm of the state, to Chronopost, as the undertaking allegedly in receipt of state aid. Specifically, the CFI held that the relevant concept of 'normal' market terms entailed a comparison with 'a private holding company or a private group of undertakings not operating in a reserved sector'.[84] The CFI quashed the EC Commission's Decision because it failed to apply this test in order to identify whether there was state aid. On appeal the Court found that the CFI had erred in law in using a test based on comparisons with normal market conditions, because La Poste's network, built to meet non-commercial public service requirements and on the basis of a reserved sector, was too dissimilar to a commercial network to enable the comparisons in the CFI's test. At paragraph 38 the Court notes the 'absence of any possibility' of using the CFI's test. Instead, the Court held that the relevant test was whether Chronopost had been charged on an objectively rational basis for no less than the costs that its use of the network had caused. This judgment

---

[80]   Case T-222/92 *SFEI v Commission,* Order of 18 Nov 1992.

[81]   Dec 98/365 of 1 Oct 1997 concerning alleged state aid granted by France to SFMI-Chronopost [1998] OJ L164/37.

[82]   Case T–613/97 *Union française de l'express (UFEX), DHL International SA, Federal express international (France) SNC and CRIE SA v Commission* [2000] ECR II– 4055, paras 74 and 75.

[83]   Case C–83/01 P *Chronopost SA, La Poste and French Republic v Union française de l'express (Ufex), DHL International, Federal express international (France) and CRIE* [2003] ECR I–6993.

[84]   *Ibid,* at para 75.

appears to be at odds with the ruling in *Altmark*,[85] delivered only two weeks later, where the Court appears to place a heavier and more transparent duty upon the Member States to organise funding for undertakings providing a service of general economic interest in order to avoid allegations of illegal state aid. Thus some 16 years after the complaint was initiated the legal issues have yet to be resolved.[86]

In relation to the allegation that the incumbent Post Office had abused its dominant position the EC Commission also dismissed the complaint in March 1992. But in August 1992 it withdrew that Decision. UFEX challenged this withdrawal, but this followed an annulment by the Court of an Order of the CFI which considered that an action lodged in 1992 by UFEX was inadmissible.[87] The EC Commission adopted a second rejection Decision on 3 December 1992, based upon the evidence that the issue had been resolved through a merger justifying that there was no Community interest in investigating the allegation any further.

The CFI upheld the EC Commission's Decision,[88] but the Court took a different view, stating that the EC Commission should have ensured that the matters complained of no longer produced anti-competitive effects before concluding that there was no Community interest in investigating the complaint. Advocate General Colomer was particularly critical of the EC Commission's passive approach, given the size of the sector concerned.[89] The CFI eventually annulled the EC Commission's Decision,[90] criticising not only the EC Commission's methodology but also its inertia in investigating the complaint. SFEI, frustrated with the EC Commission's prevarication, had also initiated an action before the Commercial Court of Paris accusing SFMI-Chronopost of unfair practices resulting from the receipt of illegal state aid. The national court made a reference to the Court. The Court, in its ruling, explained that the idea of state

---

[85] Case C–280/00 [2003] ECR I–7747.

[86] Case T–60/05 *UFEX v Commission* pending, [2005] OJ C93/39. See also Case T–613/97 *Ufex v Commission* [2006] ECR II-1531; on appeal Case C–341/06 P *Chronopost SA v Commission*, order of 18 April 2007.

[87] Case T–36/92 *SFEI v Commission* [1992] ECR II–2479; Case C–39/93/P *SFEI v Commission* [1994] ECR I–2681.

[88] Case T–77/95 *SFEI v Commission* [1997] ECR II–1.

[89] The EC Commission took the first competition decisions against The Netherlands and Spain in the early 1990s. Both states had extended their postal monopolies to the express delivery market. The EC Commission could find no justification for this, and found the monopolist to be in breach of Article 86(1) EC in conjunction with Article 82 EC. However, the Court annulled the EC Commission decision against The Netherlands on procedural grounds: Commission Dec 90/16/EEC of 20 Dec 1989 concerning the provision in The Netherlands of express delivery services [1990] OJ L10/47; Commission Dec 90/456/EEC of 1 Aug 1990 concerning the provision in Spain of international express courier services [1990] OJ L233/19; Joined Cases C–48/90 & C–66/90 *Netherlands and PTT v Commission* [1992] ECR I–565.

[90] Case T–77/95 RV *Union française de l'express (Ufex), DHL International, Service CRIE and May Courier v Commission* [2000] ECR II–2167.

aid includes not only positive benefits but also any state measures which mitigate the charges normally borne by an undertaking which have an effect equivalent to a subsidy:

> it is for the national court to determine what is normal remuneration for the services in question. Such a determination presupposes an economic analysis taking into account all the factors which an undertaking acting under normal market conditions should have taken into consideration when fixing the remuneration for the services provided.[91]

However the EC Commission took a Decision in 1998, discussed above,[92] finding that there was no state aid. The EC Commission came to this conclusion on the basis that it was not obliged to take account the fact that La Poste held a legal monopoly. The EC Commission considered that there was no state aid if the price paid by the subsidiary was the full cost price (defined as total costs plus a mark-up to remunerate equity capital investment). The CFI annulled this Decision, arguing that the test to be applied to the pricing of the supply of services by an undertaking operating in the reserved sector is a comparison with the market price.

Perhaps the most influential case was *Corbeau*.[93] Corbeau set up a rapid delivery service, infringing the Belgian postal monopoly that granted the Régie des Postes the exclusive right to operate all postal services in Belgium. The Court recognised that postal services comprise a number and variety of markets, and some of these services may be viewed as a public service obligation: the duty to provide a service which can be used by every citizen. But other services may be value-added, for example business services. The Court accepted that a postal monopoly could infringe Article 86(1) EC where the markets granted to the monopoly were excessive and unnecessary to provide a service of general economic interest. What is important in this ruling is the recognition that cross-subsidisation is the mechanism chosen by the Member States to finance the provision of universal postal services, and this influenced the drafting of the first liberalisation Directive.

Regulation: The EC Commission's Green Paper 1992

The EC Commission's Green Paper in 1992[94] was the first official analysis of postal policy since the inauguration of the modern postal service and set out some core proposals for the future direction of postal services. Amongst these

---

[91] Case C–39/94 *SFEI v La Poste and others*[1996] ECR I–3547, para 61.
[92] Dec 98/365 of 1 Oct 1997 concerning alleged state aid granted by France to SFMI-Chronopost [1998] OJ L164/37.
[93] Case C–320/91 *Corbeau* [1993] ECR I–2533.
[94] EC Commission, Green Paper on the Development of the Single Market for Postal Services, COM(91)476.

proposals was a Community guarantee of an affordable universal service throughout the EU; the liberalisation of cross-border and direct advertising of delivery services; Community-based restraints upon the incumbent postal monopolies; the creation of independent regulators to regulate prices and services as well as the prevention of a breach of the competition rules, for example, by cross-subsidisation or the alignment of charges for delivery of intra-Community mail. The EC Commission prepared a draft Directive, using Article 86(3) EC as the legal base. These ground-breaking proposals were condemned by the European Parliament in January 1993 and the Member States continued to frustrate the attempts by the EC Commission and courier postal operators to introduce liberalisation into this sector.

The Partial Liberalisation of Postal Services

To date two partial liberalisation Directives have been adopted: Directive 97/67/ EC,[95] which was amended by Directive 2002/39.[96] Directive 97/67/EC was adopted by the Council, in accordance with the co-decision procedure, on 1 December 1997 and entered into force on 10 February 1998. It was accompanied by a Commission Notice (adopted under Article 86(3) EC)[97] and a Council Resolution. The aim of the first Directive was to increase competition and to enhance the quality of postal services. The Member States were obliged to establish an independent national regulator for postal services. One reason put forward for the slow progress in opening up the letter market to competition is the lack of strong regulators in the postal sector and the lack of independence of the postal regulators from the government in each Member State. Unlike in the telecommunications sector, the postal Directives impose only *minimal* require-ments for the institutional guarantees of the postal regulators.[98] The WIK Report points out that the Postal Directives fail to address issues such as the specific requirements to ensure independence, impartiality and transparent administra-tion of the NRA. There is no requirement of treatment of affected parties in a non-discriminatory manner and no requirement of appeal from decisions of the NRA to an appellate body or a court, or even a body which is independent of the parties involved. The NRA is not under a duty to collect information necessary for regulation, or to consult with any interested parties.[99] Thus reform of the

[95] [1998] OJ L15/14.

[96] Dir 2002/39/EC. of 10 June 2003 with regard to the further opening to competition of Community postal services [2002] OJ L176/21.

[97] [1998] OJ C39/2. The use of Art 86(3) EC as a legal base for a *Notice* is questionable.

[98] Art 22 of Dir 97/67, above n 95.

[99] *Study on the Evolution of the Regulatory Model for Postal Services*, WIK-Consult July 2005, paras 2.5, 71. available at http://ec.europa.eu/internal_market/post/studies_en.htm

NRAs, along the principles found in the duties imposed upon telecommunications regulators, is now seen as an important regulatory issue in the next phase of liberalisation of the postal sector.[100]

The Directive set out a timetable for the gradual and controlled opening up of the letter market to competition which allowed all universal service providers sufficient time to put in place the further measures of modernisation and restructuring required to bring long-term viability under market conditions. It was recognised that this was a politically sensitive issue, especially since there was a high level of employment in the postal services' sector.[101]

An important aspect of the Directive was that it contributed to the definition of a European concept of a service of general economic interest which must be provided in all Member States.[102] The Directive defined the minimum characteristics of the universal service to be guaranteed by each Member State on its territory. In so doing it set common limits for the reserved services in the universal service obligation. A timetable for further gradual and controlled liberalisation was set. The Directive also laid down the principles to govern the authorisation/licensing of non-reserved services which were to be opened up to competition. The Directive defined the tariff principles applicable to the universal service, as well as the obligation of transparency of the accounts of the universal service providers. The Directive also governed the setting of quality of service standards for national and intra-Community cross-border services, alongside creating mechanisms to encourage technical harmonisation in the postal sector through the use of CEN activities and the consultation of interested parties.

On 10 June 2002, the European Parliament and the Council adopted Directive 2002/39/EC which amended the initial Postal Directive by defining further steps in the process of gradual and controlled market opening and further limited the service sectors that can be protected from competition. Member States were able from 1 January 2003 to exempt from competition items of correspondence weighing less than 100 grammes and costing less than three times the basic tariff. It was estimated that this would lead to a 9 per cent opening up of competition in the market. From 1 January 2006 the Member States were to open up to competition mail weighing less than 50 grammes and costing less than two and a

---

[100] See D Geradin, 'Enhancing Competition in the Postal Sector: Can We Do Away With Sector-Specific Regulation?', Paper delivered at 14th Conference on Postal and Delivery Economics, Bern, June 2006, available at http://ssrn.com/abstract=909008.

[101] The Report from the Commission to the European Parliament and Council on the application of the Postal Directive, COM(2002) 632 final, 25 Nov 2002 estimated that 1.2 million people in the EU were employed by universal service obligation providers.

[102] Cf Case C–240/02 *Asociación Profesional de Empresas de Reparto y Manipulado de Correspondencia (Asempre), Asociación Nacional de Empresas de Externalización y Gestión de Envíos y Pequeña Paquetería v Entidad Pública Empresarial Correos y Telégrafos, Administración General del Estado* [2004] ECR I–2461.

half times the basic tariff. It was estimated that this would lead to an additional seven per cent of the market being opened up to competition.

All outgoing cross-border mail was to be open to competition from 1 January 2003. This was estimated to lead to an additional 3 per cent of the market being opened to competition, although exceptions were possible where these were necessary to maintain the universal service, for example, if revenue from cross-border mail was necessary to finance the domestic universal service or where the national postal service in a given Member State had particular characteristics.

The Directive sets 1 January 2009 as a possible date for the full accomplishment of the Internal Market for postal services. This deadline is to be confirmed (or changed) by co-decision procedure. The Directive requires the EC Commission to make a proposal based on a study assessing, for each Member State, the impact on universal service of further opening up of the postal market.

The Directive requires the EC Commission to submit regularly (every two years) a report on the application of the Postal Directive, including the appropriate information about developments in the sector, particularly economic, social, employment and technological aspects, as well as about the quality of service.

The Directive allows the Member States to reserve certain postal services to the universal postal service operators' accounts for a large portion of the market in postal services, even though there is a rider to this provision, in that the reservation must be to the extent necessary to ensure the operation of the universal service under financially balanced conditions. The Directive requires the EC Commission to table proposals by 31 December 2006 at the latest introducing, if appropriate, the full liberalisation of the EU postal market by 2009. The EC Commission put forward proposals for full market opening on 18 October 2006.[103]

Since partial liberalisation a number of allegations have been made that the incumbents, particularly Deutsche Post, La Poste and Poste Italiane, behave in an anti-competitive manner,[104] through cross-subsidies between the commercial liberalised arm of their operations and finances and technological support from the reserved sector, and this may be a form of illegal state aid.

---

[103] Available at http://ec.europa.eu/internal_market/post/legislation_en.htm#proposal.

[104] See, eg, Case C–340/99 *TNT Traco v Poste Italiane* [2001] ECR I–4109; Italy attempted to extend the monopoly to a non-reserved sector in breach of Art 86(1) EC: Hybrid Mail [2001] OJ L63/59; Commission Dec 2001/354 Deutsche Post AG [2001] OJ L125/27; Commission Dec 2001/892 Deutsche Post—Interception of Cross-Border Mail [2001] OJ L331/40; Commission Dec 2002/180, Deutsche Post—Leveraging and abuse of a dominant position [2002] OJ L61/32; Commission Dec 2002/180/EC Hays/La Poste [2002] OJ L61/32. See further: J-F Pons and T Luder, 'La politique européenne de la concurrence dans les services postaux hors monopole' [2001] Competition Policy Newsletter (no.3); F Diez Estella, 'Abusive Practices in Postal Services? Parts I and II' (2006) 27 *ECLR* 184, 228.

The Future of a Reserved Sector

The continuance of a reserved sector has allowed the state incumbents to control the liberalised markets,[105] an immediate concern in the liberalisation programme of postal services is to shrink the reserved sector as a means of opening up the market to more competition. The 1997 Directive liberalised 3 per cent of the market and the 2002 Directive opens up to competition a letter market which is estimated to comprise 16 per cent of postal revenues. The liberalisation Directives see cross-subsidisation as a means to continue with a service of general economic interest in postal services, but over the years liberalisation has generated debate as to whether this is the most effective way to provide and finance a universal service obligation and also about the optimum size of the reserved sector.[106] The debate centres on the gains and losses between allowing greater entry into the postal market which would yield productive and allocative efficiencies and the costs of cream skimming if entry is too free and the universal service cannot be provided.[107] The 1997 Directive provides an example of alternative ways in which a universal service obligation can be funded, in that Article 9(4) provides that a fund can be created and financed by postal service undertakings which do not provide a public service obligation. The 2002 Directive addressed the problem of abuse by the incumbents by prohibiting the cross-subsidisation of universal service obligations in Article 12. However the case law post-liberalisation shows how the postal market is distorted by the maintenance of a reserved sector in the majority of the Member States.

The original reason for the reserved sector was to fund the provision of a universal service. However, as Geradin points out:

> Funding universal service through cross-subsidization between profitable and non-profitable services is a most imprecise mechanism, which is likely to lead to over-or-under compensating the operator in charge of providing this service. It also deprives the users of services maintained in the reserved area from the benefits of liberalization.[108]

The inefficiencies of the reserved sector model have been recognised, but in order to preserve the universal service obligation regulation could be used to define the scope of the universal service and ways of funding it, using alternative methods.

---

[105]   R Geddes, Competing with the Government: Anticompetitive Behaviour and Public Enterprises (Stanford, Cal, Hoover Institution Press, 2004) chs 1 and 4.

[106]   M Griffiths, 'Failing to Install Effective Competition in Postal Services: the Limited Impact of EC Law' [2000] 21 *ECLR* 399, 400.

[107]   Cf M Crew and P Kleindorfer, 'Efficient Entry, Monopoly and the Universal Service Obligation in Postal Service' (1998) 14 *Journal of Regulatory Economics* 103, who are in favour of a reserved sector, with D Geradin and C Humpe, 'The Liberalisation of Postal Services in the European Union: An Analysis of Directive 97/67' in D Geradin (ed), *The Liberalisation of Postal Services in the European Union* (The Hague/London, Kluwer, 2002) who argue against a reserved sector in postal services.

[108]   n 100 at 6.

The universal service requirement is recognised as being of constitutional importance and, as we shall see in Chapter 7, a number of consumer and fundamental rights values are being attached to it. However, the WIK Report points out that the concept of the universal service set out in the Postal Services Directive may be unnecessarily costly[109] and the Member States should be given more discretion as to *how* to define the universal service requirement. The postal service is now complemented by a range of faster communications (fax, email, text, instant messaging) which could be part of the way the universal service requirements are met. By reducing the reserved sector competition would be allowed to develop in all segments of the postal market. It would also reduce the risk of the allegations of cross-subsidisation, as well as other forms of leveraging, from the monopoly-reserved sector to the competitive markets. This is important in the light of the deadline for completely liberalising the postal market by 1 January 2009.

Regulation could also be used to regulate the 'last mile' of the postal service, that is the delivery segment. It has become clear that this involves large economies of scale and that new entrants are not able to duplicate this segment in a competitive way. There is a monopoly in this sector, as well as a bottleneck, which are often seen as indicators that an essential facilities doctrine could be invoked in this situation.[110] Thus regulation could be used to allow mandatory access to this segment, offering more competition.[111] The US and some of the Member States have experimented with this form of access system,[112] but it is by no means necessarily welcomed across Europe. For example, de Bijl *et al*, in a study commissioned by Deutsche Post and TNT, concluded that:

> specific access regulation, on top of generic non-discrimination principles, is not needed and may be counterproductive as it may force entrants into a specific entry mode, thereby possibly limiting innovation.[113]

---

[109] *Study on the Evolution of the Regulatory Model for Postal Services*, WIK Consult July 2005, 42 available at http://ec.europa.eu/internal_market/post/studies_en.htm.

[110] Cf P de Bijl, E van Damme and P Larouche, *'Light is Right': Competition and Access Regulation in an Open Postal Sector* (Tilburg, Law and Economics Center, June 2005) at 12, who argue that it is possible to enter certain product or geographical segments of the market and barriers to entry are not high. Thus the tests for access to essential services set by the Court in Case C–7/97 *Bronner* [1998] ECR I–7797 and Case C–418/01 *IMS* [2004] ECR I–5039 would not be met.

[111] Cf Art 11 of Dir 97/67 [1998] OJ L15/14 [and the amendment to Art 12 of Dir 97/67 by Dir 2002/39 [2002] OJ L176/21. Where universal service providers apply special tariffs they cannot discriminate between third parties. Such tariffs should also take into account the avoided costs compared with the standard service offered to consumers.

[112] D Geradin and J Sidak, 'The Future of the Postal Monopoly: American and European Perspectives after the Presidential Commission and Flamingo Industries' (2005) 28 *World Competition* 161; D Geradin, 'Enhancing Competition in the Postal Sector: Can We Do Away With Sector-Specific Regulation?', Paper delivered at 14th Conference on Postal and Delivery Economics, Bern, June 2006, available at http://ssrn.com/abstract=909008.

[113] P.de Bijl *et al*, above n 110. Cf D Geradin, 'Enhancing Competition in the Postal Sector: Can We Do Away With Sector-Specific Regulation?', Paper delivered at 14th Conference on Postal and Delivery Economics, Bern, June 2006, available at http://ssrn.com/abstract=909008, who marshals a number of arguments against this position, at 9–13.

In contrast Geradin argues that regulation, which offers *ex ante* certainty, can avoid protracted litigation and sector-specific regulators are much better at addressing access issues than courts applying competition law principles. This would not deter investment by the incumbent and could be temporary in nature with features to deny inefficient access.

The postal sector suffers from a number of significant market failures suggesting that regulation alongside competition law has a central role to play in the liberalisation process. To date the focus has been upon controlling the market power of the incumbents. It is arguable that in continuing to preserve (and regulate) a reserved sector of the postal services market consumers do not enjoy either the full benefits of liberalisation or the rapid changes in technological delivery of mail. The Merger Regulation has been used to impose remedies where merger transactions would have the effect of reducing competition. UPS has been at the forefront of exposing the range of mergers and acquisitions undertaken by the major postal incumbents in Europe, a major bone of contention being whether the source of the funds used by a postal incumbent to acquire other postal operators should be taken into account in the assessment of the merger. However, the EC Commission does not consider this to be a relevant factor since the focus of its attention is directed at the *consequences* of the merger. In contrast the CFI has indicated that proof that funds used for an acquisition were generated by abusive pricing practices of the incumbent in breach of Article 82 EC may create the necessity to examine the source of funds used for an acquisition in order to determine whether the acquisition stems from the abuse of a dominant position.[114] This in turn creates a duty for tight price regulation in the reserved sector.

ENERGY

Once viewed as essentially local industries providing essential services the energy utilities sector now finds itself subject to greater cross-border trade and a growing interest by foreign capital in national utilities. From 1918 onwards ideas of international regulation of utilities have been on the international agenda, but there has also been a countervailing tendency towards national control to protect security of supply of essential facilities.[115] Such forms of protection were the creation of national monopolies, exclusive rights and concessions, legal restrictions on energy imports and exports, rules limiting foreign ownership of essential energy providers and measures favouring the procurement of domestic energy

---

[114] Case T–175/99 *UPS Europe v Commission* [2002] ECR II–1915. Note that proof that the funds came from abusive pricing practices was not established in this case. See Geradin, above n 112 for other examples.

[115] See M Roggenkamp, 'Implications of GATT and EEC on Networkbound Trade in Europe' (1994) 12 *Journal of Energy and Natural Reserves Law* 59.

resources over foreign resources. The organisation of a vital element of production along national lines, regulated by the state, created a number of adverse barriers for the European integration project. The demand for energy supplies and the need for cross-border coordination of energy policies in the post-war reconstruction of Europe is seen in the creation of the ECSC and Euratom, but the EEC Treaty did not include provisions for a common energy policy.[116] It was not until the oil crisis of the 1970s that policy-makers were aware of Europe's increased dependence upon imported supplies of energy, and this focused attention on the need for common policies as the Member States introduced even more protectionist national policies.[117]

Liberalisation in the energy sector has been much slower and more piecemeal than in the telecommunications and the postal sectors. The EC Commission did not apply the competition rules in the energy sector and attempts to liberalise this sector were met with resistance from the Member States, alongside internal squabbles within the EC Commission between the Internal Market and Competition Directorates over jurisdiction. The first stages of liberalisation took place between 1989 and 1995. The United Kingdom was the first Member State partially to privatise its electricity industry. Other Member States were reluctant to privatise, mainly because of issues of securing supplies in an essential sector. However during this initial period the idea that electricity production and distribution were a natural monopoly was turned on its head as the state electricity monopolies were divided into smaller parts, comprising electricity generation, high voltage transmission systems, local distribution systems and retail to the final consumer.

The Single European Act 1987 provided the EC Commission with a new objective and a legal base from which to pursue a Community policy on energy. The EC Commission used a Working Document[118] to set out its policies, and submitted a framework and set of common rules for the completion of the Internal Market in gas and electricity in February 1992.[119] The EC Commission identified the use of national grid networks as an obstacle to realising an Internal Market in energy.[120]

The initial liberalisation proposal used Article 86(3) EC as the legal base. The Member States were unwilling to accept these proposals, even for partial opening

---

[116] N Lucas, *Energy and the European Communities* (Oxford, OUP, 1977) at 14.

[117] See J Hassan and A Duncan, 'Integrating Energy; the Problems of Developing an Energy Policy in the European Communities' (1994) 23 *Journal of European Economic History* 159; E Schumacher, 'The Struggle for a European Energy Policy' (1964) 2 *Journal of Common Market Studies* 199.

[118] COM(88)238 final.

[119] [1992] OJ C65/04 (electricity) and [1992] OJ C65/04 (gas). These proposed the abolition of special and exclusive rights to open up markets; the unbundling or administrative separation of the functions of production, transmission, distribution and supply; a qualified, but compulsory, obligation on owners of transmission and distribution grids to offer access to third parties in return for reasonable compensation (the idea of access in a regulated manner to an 'essential facility').

[120] EC Commission, *Electricity and Natural Gas Transmission Infrastructures in the Community*, SEC(92)533 final.

up of the energy sector. They were concerned with the lack of protection for services of general economic interest and also how far they could take measures to ensure security of supply. Subsequent Treaty amendments allowed the EU to take greater control over an energy liberalisation policy. The TEU 1993 added Article 3(t) EC which lists measures in the spheres of energy, civil protection and tourism to the Community's common policies and activities, and Article 129b EC on trans-European networks. The Treaty of Amsterdam 1997, in what is Article 16 EC, recognised the role of services of general economic interest in the integration process.

The lack of an Energy Charter or Chapter in the EC Treaty is often blamed for the lack of any Community-level progress in the energy sector in the 1990s.[121] The rules of the EC Treaty apply to the energy sector,[122] but the tight reins of control at the national level left little room for opportunistic litigation to challenge the way the national monopolies were run, thus the application of the free movement and competition rules has been problematic.[123] The Member States won an important point of principle in the *Campus Oil*[124] ruling. Oil companies challenged an order requiring that at least 35 per cent of their supplies of oil should be acquired at pre-determined prices from the state-owned monopoly in Ireland. The government claimed that without this security of orders the refinery would not be viable and Ireland would be dependent upon imported supplies of oil and other petroleum products. The Court accepted that the order was contrary to Article 28 EC, but could be justified by reference to Article 30 EC. Although measures had been taken at the Community level to respond to the oil crisis of the 1970s, the Court accepted that these were not sufficient to give a Member State 'unconditional assurance that supplies will in any event be maintained at least at a level sufficient to meet minimum needs'.[125]

The Court ruled that a Member State may rely upon Article 30 EC to justify 'appropriate complementary measures' even where such measures would involve elements of economic policy not normally permitted under Article 30 EC.[126] The case was interpreted as allowing the Member States a wide latitude over securing energy supplies and protecting national industry from the full rigours of the free

---

[121]   EC Commission, For a European Union Energy Policy, COM(94)659 final; cf C-D Ehlermann, 'Role of the European Commission as Regards National Energy Policies' (1994) 12 *Journal of Energy and Natural Resources* 342, 346–7.

[122]   See, eg, L Hancher, *EC Electricity Law* (London, Chancery, 1992); L Hancher, 'EC State Aids and Energy' (1995) 2 *Oil and Gas Taxation Law Review* 62; P Slot, 'Energy and Competition' (1994) 31 *CMLRev* 511.

[123]   See, eg, the individual exemption granted under Art 81(3) EC for a restrictive agreement in which German electricity undertakings and industrial producers should purchase a specific amount of German produced coal which was supported through subsidies, and yet less expensive coal could be obtained from outside Germany [1993] OJ L50/14.

[124]   Case 72/83 *Campus Oil Ltd and others v Minister of Industry and Energy and others* [1984] ECR 2727.

[125]   *Ibid*, at para 31.

[126]   *Ibid*, at para 36.

movement (Internal Market) and competition rules. However, the Court insisted that the Member States must satisfy the proportionality principle and show why restrictive measures are necessary. As we saw in Chapter 4, the Court was willing to find that exclusive rights to import and market granted to state monopolies could infringe Article 31, and the EC Commission used this tool to bring infringement actions against energy monopolies. In *Greek Oil Monopoly*[127] the EC Commission brought an infringement action challenging the natural oil refinery monopoly and its exclusive import and commercial rights. The Court held that the Greek government had not shown that without these restrictive rights the refineries would not be able to compete on the market. Frustrated by the lack of progress towards even partial liberalisation of the energy sector the EC Commission brought infringement actions against Spain, The Netherlands, Italy and France.[128] In the case against Spain the EC Commission argued that the combination of legislative provisions conferred exclusive import and export rights on Redesa. This action was dismissed for lack of proof. The case against The Netherlands concerned the import ban on electricity; electricity intended for public distribution could be imported only by the designated company (SEP). The case against Italy concerned measures which reserved import and export of electricity to the state monopoly, ENEL. The case against France concerned the measures reserving import and export of natural gas to Gaz de France and two other concessionaires. The EC Commission alleged that the exclusive rights were contrary to Articles 28 and 31 EC.

The Court examined the application of Article 31 EC first, concluding that the rights were in conflict with this provision. It was thus not necessary to examine the application of Article 28 EC. The Court then went on to discuss the applicability of Article 86(2) EC.[129] This was a bold move since it had been assumed since the *Campus Oil*[130] judgment that Article 86(2) EC could not be read across in this way to provide a derogation from the free movement rules. The Court was generous, stating that the Member States could take national policy objectives into account when defining a service of general economic interest, and that through necessity the state monopolies must be able to perform the tasks assigned to them under economically viable conditions. These cases were seen by Slot as consistent with the 'November Revolution' series of cases of *Ohra, Meng* and *Reiff*, discussed in Chapter 2.[131] However, the threat of further

---

[127] Case 347/88 *Commission v Greece* [1990] ECR 4747.

[128] Cases C–157/94, *Commission v Netherlands,* C–158/94 *Commission v Italy,* C–159/94 *Commission v France,* C–160/94 *Commission v Spain,* reported at [1997] ECR I–5699, I–5789, I–5815 and I–5851 respectively, and discussed in Ch 4.

[129] Note that the Court does not discuss the possibility of reading across the justifications found in Art 30 EC into Art 31 EC. Cf Case C–347/88 *Commission v Greece,* above n 127.

[130] Above n 124.

[131] '{T}hese judgments—by maintaining certain monopolies—seem to herald the end of an era of progressive development towards a more market-oriented economy in the Community': P Slot, Annotation of Cases C–157/94, *Commission v Netherlands;* C–158/94 *Commission v Italy;* Case 159/94 *Commission v France;* C–160/94 *Commission v Spain;* C–189/95, *Harry Franzén;* judgments of 23

intervention by the EC Commission persuaded the Member States to adopt liberalisation Directives, using what is now Article 95 EC, the Internal Market legal base.[132]

The Liberalisation Directives

The first move to create a set of common rules liberalising the energy sector[133] allowed the Member States to liberalise their energy sectors at a different pace, resulting in an even more fragmented energy market.[134] The use of informal *fora* for regulatory coordination was a new dimension to liberalisation whereby the Electricity Regulatory Forum (The Florence Forum/Process) and the Gas Regulatory Forum (The Madrid Forum/Process) were created by the EC Commission Directorate-General in charge of energy. The gas and electricity markets evolved in different ways and are different For example, gas is a primary energy source and is capable of being stored, but is dependent upon large-scale investments in infrastructure (pipelines, for example) and the market is dominated by large, non-EU suppliers.

A new package of measures was adopted and became operational on 1 July 2004 for electricity[135] and 1 July 2006 for gas.[136] The EC Commission has also adopted a number of non-binding interpretative documents to accompany the Directives. The new package encompasses a more detailed framework for the regulation of the energy market,[137] introducing new concepts,[138] with an

October 1997, Full Court, [1997] ECR I–5699, I-5789, I–5815, I–5851, I–5909 (1998) 35 *CMLRev* 1183, 1202. See also P Slot, 'Energy (Electricity and Natural Gas)' in D Geradin (ed), *The Liberalisation of State Monopolies in the European Union and Beyond* (The Hague, Kluwer, 2000).

[132] See D Finon and A Midttun, *Reshaping European Gas and Electricity Industries* (Amsterdam, Elsevier, 2004).

[133] Dir 96/92/EC of the European Parliament and of the Council of 19 Dec 1996 concerning common rules for the internal market in electricity [1997] OJ L27/20; Dir 98/30/EC of the European Parliament and of the Council of 22 June 1998 concerning common rules for the internal market in natural gas [1997] OJ L27/20; Dir 94/22/EC of the European Parliament and of the Council on the conditions for granting and using authorisations for the prospection, exploration and production of hydrocarbons (oil and natural gas) [1994] OJ L 164/3.

[134] The use of subsidiarity was justified given the divergent resource bases, legal structure, industry structure and policy choices: see P Cameron, *Competition in Energy Markets* (Oxford, OUP, 2002; second edition 2007) and EC Commission, *Communication Completing the Internal Energy Market*, COM(2001)125.

[135] Dir 2003/54/EC of the European Parliament and of the Council of 26 June 2003 concerning common rules for the internal market in electricity and repealing Dir 96/92/EC [2003] OJ L176/37.

[136] Dir 2003/55/EC of the European Parliament and of the Council of 26 June 2003 concerning common rules for the internal market in natural gas and repealing Dir 98/30/EC [2003] OJ L176/57.

[137] Gone is the flexibility of the earlier programme. Both Dirs had to be implemented by the Member States by 1 July 2004, and by this date there had to be freedom of choice for non-domestic customers with all customers enjoying freedom of choice by 1 July 2007. There are some are derogations, but these are defined and narrow in scope.

[138] Eg, enhanced consumer protection, universal service obligations, supplier of last resort, green labelling and compliance programmes.

increased role for NRAs alongside enhanced monitoring and reporting requirements for the Member States.[139] The Directives have two main aims: to increase
quantitative market opening in order to achieve full liberalisation and to enhance
qualitative regulation to increase consumer choice through uniformity and
coordination of the Member States' energy markets.

Access to the gas and electricity networks was, and continues to be, a major
issue in the liberalisation process. In the first set of liberalisation Directives the
Member States were allowed a choice between negotiated and regulated third
party access to the networks. This did not work and the EU realised that some
Member States, such as Germany, enjoyed a strategic position in the energy trade
which distorted the liberalisation processes in other states. Now, to secure
competition in the wholesale market in the energy sector, the Member States
must ensure that third party access to transmission and distribution is based
upon published tariffs, applicable to all eligible customers, and is based upon an
objective and non-discriminatory system. The NRA must approve the tariffs (or
the methodology) in advance. Article 20(2) of Directive 2003/54/EC allows
refusal of access where there is no available capacity. But conditions are attached
to this refusal. Substantiated reasons must be given, taking into account any
public service obligations, and the Member States must ensure that the transmission system operator or distribution system operator provides relevant information on measures that would be necessary to reinforce the network. Exemptions
may also be given where there are major new infrastructure projects or significant
increases in capacity in existing interconnectors.

In contrast, in the gas sector, third party access to transmission and distribution networks is to be provided on the basis of published and regulated tariffs,
but for storage facilities access is to be on either a negotiated or regulated basis
(or both). Access to upstream pipeline networks is to be separated out and
Member States are given discretion over the arrangements adopted. Exemptions
may be given for major new gas infrastructure investments.

Unbundling of vertically integrated undertakings addresses the structural
constraints of the networks in three ways: legal unbundling, functional unbundling and accounting unbundling. *Legal unbundling* separates the transmission
system operator and distribution system operator from carrying out activities not
related to transmission and distribution. Transmission and distribution are to be
carried out by a separate network undertaking with a legal form chosen by the
vertically integrated undertaking. *Functional unbundling* involves a separation of
the transmission system operator and distribution system operator to ensure
independence from the vertically integrated undertaking. *Accounting unbundling*
provides that separate accounts should be drawn up for network activities
relating to electricity and gas.

---

[139] The Gas Dir is less interventionist, however, relying more heavily on the Madrid Forum.

A significant change in the new Directives is stronger commitments to the public service obligation. This is seen as a fundamental requirement in the Recitals to each Directive. In the Electricity Directive there is a right to a universal service, which is the right of all households[140] to be supplied with electricity of a specified quantity within the territory of the Member State at reasonable, easily and clearly comparable and transparent prices. A similar obligation is not found in the Gas Directive. Alongside the universal service requirements are strengthened consumer protection rights covering the handling of complaints, protection against misleading selling and unfair contract terms. These are analysed in Chapter 7.

Cross-border trade in the electricity sector is regulated by Regulation (EC) 1228/2003 which entered into force on 1 July 2004.[141] This is an Internal Market measure, based upon Article 95(1) EC. It builds upon the work of the Electricity Regulatory Forum to increase cross-border trade through increased harmonisation of tariffs and charges. The Regulation uses inter-transmission systems and operators' compensation mechanisms to compensate for costs incurred as a result of hosting cross-border flows of electricity on their networks. It encourages consistent charging for network access by outlawing 'pancaking'[142] and distance-related charges, thereby avoiding distortions of trade. Finally it sets out general measures to improve capacity allocation including congestion management. In contrast there is a significant amount of cross-border trade in gas, and here the regulation focuses upon third party access to networks.

The new Directives created a different regulatory culture, setting out minimum requirements and creating new obligations for regulatory bodies at the national level. Part of this new role is an obligation to coordinate horizontally, at a trans-national level, as well as at the vertical level with the EC Commission. In 2003 the EC Commission established an independent European Regulators' Group for Electricity and Gas. The Directives created regulatory committees governed by the comitology procedure. The NRAs are to ensure non-discrimination, effective competition and the efficient functioning of the market. Competition authorities may also play a role in the liberalisation process. There is a requirement in the Electricity Directive that each Member State must provide a report to the EC Commission by 31 July of each year on market dominance, predatory and anti-competitive behaviour.

---

[140] Member States have a discretion to extend this obligation for small and medium-sized enterprises. Cf Case 17/03 *Vereniging voor Energie, Milieu en Water, Amsterdam Power Exchange Spotmarket BV, Eneco NV v Directeur van de Dienst uitvoering en toezicht energie* [2005] ECR I-4983.

[141] [2003] OJ L176/37.

[142] This is the accumulation of tariffs to be paid by a shipper on energy transactions between two locations using two or more transmission system operators with their own set of tariffs.

Post-Liberalisation

In its report on the internal market for electricity and gas, adopted in November 2005, the EC Commission identified the delay in applying the 2003 Gas and Electricity Directives as one of the main causes for the shortcomings in the European internal energy market. Not all of the Member States are at fault, and in Austria, The Netherlands and the United Kingdom liberalisation is advanced. However in other states there are problems in adapting deep-seated features of the national energy market to the liberalisation process. For example, France continues to attach importance to public security issues and the provision by the state of public service obligations; in Germany *ex ante* regulation is difficult to reconcile with the preference for the market mechanism.[143] Infringement actions were taken against Estonia, Ireland, Greece, Spain and Luxembourg in 2005,[144] and in 2006 infringement proceedings were commenced against 17 Member States for failure fully to implement the energy liberalisation Directives.[145]

Within the context of the revived Lisbon Process,[146] and in response to growing concerns voiced by consumers over significant price rises in 2004 and 2005[147] and complaints from new entrants unable fully to access grids, the EC Commission launched an inquiry into the competitiveness of the EU energy sector on 13 June 2005. This was initiated by a Communication from the Commissioner for Competition (Neelie Kroes), in agreement with the Commissioner for Energy (Andris Piebalgs),[148] and the adoption of a Decision pursuant to the EC Commission's *competition* enforcement powers under Article 17 of Council Regulation (EC) No 1/2003. The preliminary findings of the inquiry were published in February 2006 with a final Report in the form of a Communication on 10 January 2007.[149] Five major obstacles to competitiveness were identified in the preliminary report.

The first obstacle was the intense market concentration, with the energy market dominated by incumbents with very few new entrants. The gas incumbents tend to control imports and/or domestic production of gas, whereas electricity incumbents control generation assets.[150] Against the background of

---

[143] See M Roggenkamp (ed), *European Energy Law Report III* (Antwerp, Intersentia, 2006).

[144] IP/06/853, 6 July 2005.

[145] IP/06/430, 4 Apr 2006; IP/06/1768, 12 Dec 2006.

[146] EC Commission, *Communication to the Spring European Council—Working Together For Growth and Jobs—A New Start for the Lisbon Agenda*, COM(2005)24, at 8, 19.

[147] See http://europa.eu.int/comm/competition/antitrust/others/sector_inquiries/energy/issues_paper15112005.p.

[148] See http://europa.eu.int/comm/competition/antitrust/others/sector_inquiries/energy/communication_en.pdf.

[149] EC Commission, *Communication from the Commission to the Council and the European Parliament on the Functioning of the Internal Market in Electricity and Gas*, COM(2005) 568 final; *Communication from the Commission – Inquiry pursuant to Article 17 of Regulation (EC) No 1/2003 into the European gas and electricity sectors (Final Report)* (SEC(2006) 1724), COM/2006/0851 final.

[150] In Apr 2005, the environmental NGO, Greenpeace, published a report, *Whose Power is it Anyway?*, available at http://www.greenpeace.org/raw/content/international/press/reports/

the structured opening up of energy markets the EC Commission has used the competition provisions to regulate the processes and to ensure that dominant firms do not enhance their market strength. For example, in Portugal electricity markets are open to competition but gas markets are moving at a slower pace. Under the Second Gas Directive Portugal benefits from a derogation. The derogation allows Portugal to begin gas liberalisation at the later date of 2007 for the opening up of the natural gas to power generators with the opening up of the gas market for non-residential customers by 2009 and for set for residential customers in 2010. On 9 December 2004 the EC Commission declared the joint acquisition of Gas de Portugal (GDP) (the incumbent Portuguese gas undertaking) by Energias de Portugal (EDP) (the incumbent electricity undertaking) and Eni SpA, an Italian energy undertaking, to be incompatible with the common market, pursuant to Article 8(3) of the Merger Regulation.[151] Despite commitments (which were made at a very late stage in the proceedings) undertaken by the parties the EC Commission concluded that the proposed concentration would strengthen EDP's dominant position on the electricity markets in Portugal, as well as GDP's dominant positions on the Portuguese gas markets from the date these markets were opened up to competition, leading to the situation where competition would be significantly impeded in a substantial part of the Common Market. EDP challenged the EC Commission's Decision under the fast track procedure of the CFI.

The CFI dismissed the challenge. The CFI confirmed the way in which the EC Commission assesses remedies by examining, first, competition concerns raised by the concentration, and then the commitments offered in relation to these concerns. The EC Commission could not within the time constraints imposed by the Merger Regulation recommence its assessment of the merger in the light of any commitments made. This would appear to be seeing the commitments as a fresh notification. Such an approach would be in conflict with the requirement of speedy decisions that characterises the aims of the Merger Regulation. In relation to the substance of the challenge the CFI considered that the EC Commission had not erred in law when it concluded that the concentration would strengthen GDP's dominant position.[152]

A second obstacle to liberalisation is the vertical foreclosure caused by the vertically integrated incumbents acting at different levels of the supply chain, from wholesale to distribution of energy products. Long-term contracts have posed problems for the state aid rules and the lack of liquidity makes access

---

WhosePower.pdf analysing the market shares of Europe's 10 largest electricity utilities (EdF, E.on, RWE, ENEL, Vattenfall, Electrabel, EnBW, Endesa, Iberdrola and British Energy), arguing that the liberalisation process has worked in favour of these large established utilities, as demonstrated by the wave of takeovers that ensued after the opening of the market. Thus new, 'green' utilities have little chance to compete on an equal footing as the 'big 10' have enough influence in the sector to control prices, especially in the electricity sector.

[151]   Case COMP/M.3440 ENI/EDP/GDP.

[152]   Case T–87/05 *EDP v Commission* [2005] ECR II–3745.

difficult for new entrants to the energy market. One problem which emerged from the opening-up of the gas sector to competition was the risk of foreclosure of the downstream market through long-term gas supply contracts between traditional suppliers and distribution companies and the industrial and commercial users. Long-term contracts inhibit consumer choice by preventing consumers from switching to alternative suppliers.

As a third obstacle the EC Commission found that there was a lack of market integration in Europe. The gas and electricity markets remain largely national. New entrants have difficulty in gaining access to what are perceived to be inadequate transmission systems.

The EC Commission found an endemic lack of transparency in the energy markets. There was, for example, a lack of information on capacity available on gas networks and the wholesale electricity market, with data being shared with affiliates, putting new entrants at a disadvantage. This lack of information undermines confidence and prevents informed choices from being made by potential entrants to the market.

Finally, the EC Commission found that prices had increased dramatically since liberalisation and questioned whether there was anti-competitive behaviour on the market. In the gas sector the EC Commission noted that long-term gas supply contracts traditionally link prices to oil or oil derivatives but do not react to changes in supply or demand. In the electricity sector consumers had alleged that prices on spot and forward wholesale markets do not result from fair competition.

In addition to commencing infringement actions against the Member States[153] the EC Commission used competition law powers to conduct a series of dawn raids on gas companies in Germany,[154] Italy, France, Belgium and Austria[155] and electricity companies in Hungary.[156]

Both the energy and gas markets display high levels of concentration, but there are differences in the different stages of liberalisation of each sector and different production structures. The sectors are interconnected since gas is increasingly used as a primary fuel for electricity generation. In the electricity sector the inquiry focuses upon price formation mechanisms on the electricity wholesale markets, electricity generation and supply issues, and factors determining generators' dispatching and bidding strategies. A special focus is directed at the issue whether electricity generators possess significant market power and can influence

---

[153] Austria, Belgium, the Czech Republic, Germany, Estonia, Spain, Finland, France, Greece, Ireland, Italy, Lithuania, Latvia, Poland, Sweden, Slovakia and the United Kingdom.

[154] A second wave of dawn raids, unconnected to the first wave, took place involving German electricity undertakings in Dec 2006: 'Competition: Commission has carried out inspections in the German electricity sector', Memo/06/483, 12 Dec 2006.

[155] The EC Commission believes the companies may be restricting access to infrastructure and dividing markets.

[156] The focus is upon long-term power purchase agreements (which are also the subject of a state aid investigation) and import contracts.

electricity wholesale prices. A further issue is the existence of entry barriers and barriers to cross-border flows, for example arising from long-term supply agreements in certain Member States and the legal and operational regimes for the interconnectors that link national electricity grids. In the gas sector the inquiry focuses on long-term import contracts, swap agreements and barriers to cross-border flows of gas. The balancing requirements for gas network users and gas storage are also being investigated, alongside downstream long-term contracts and the effects they may have on switching costs and market entry.

A new development in the liberalisation process is the increasing dependence of Western Europe upon gas supplies from Russia in the context of unstable oil prices. The EC Commission has introduced a new strand to liberalisation by developing a European strategy for sustainable, competitive and secure energy[157] which has a new external relations dimension. A Green Paper was issued on 8 March 2006 and an external energy policy paper was prepared by the EC Commission with the High Representative, Javier Solana, for the European Summit in Brussels in June 2006. The creation of a fully competitive internal energy market is now a priority, and the EC Commission proposes to create an interconnection plan to foster greater trade between the Member States in energy products. A European grid is proposed with common rules and standards. The possibility of a European regulator and a European Centre for Energy Networks is on the agenda.

CONCLUSION

The liberalisation processes in the EU have followed the classical processes seen elsewhere in European integration whereby litigation relying upon the constitutional principles of the market freedoms and competition has questioned state regulatory processes. This form of negative integration has been largely in the hands of non-state, and in some cases non-EU, litigants at the national level. The EC Commission has been cautious in intervening through the use of infringement actions or Article 86(3) EC procedures and, as we have seen in the postal sector, has occasionally been extremely passive in the face of mounting challenges to state intervention in the market. The Courts' less than sympathetic attitude towards state monopolies and state laws which shore up inefficient, uncompetitive national regulatory structures post-1992 created a need for re-regulation at the EU level. The various private interests which have been brought into this regulatory process created a new institutional design for liberalised markets,

---

[157] Council Directive 2004/67/EC of 26 April 2004 concerning measures to safeguard security of natural gas supply, [2004] OJ L 127/92; Directive 2005/89/EC of the European Parliament and of the Council concerning measures to safeguard security of electricity supply and infrastructure investment Directive 2006/32/EC, [2005] OJ L 33/22; Directive 2006/32/EC of the European Parliament and of the Council of 5 April 2006 on energy end-use efficiency and energy services and repealing Council Directive 93/76/EEC, [2006] OJ L 114/64.

which often did not coincide with national interests. The regulatory reform of the European market allowed for the emergence of new forms of power. This power may be a hybrid form of public power in the form of the host state continuing to mix commercial and public service obligation interests, and also in the sense of foreign state incumbents acting in an aggressive commercial way by expanding into new markets. Private power also takes a number of different forms. This new mix of economic power has brought challenges for the nation state and the emerging polity of the EU. State power in the market has also been challenged by an increased concentration of private economic and political power, through the rapid restructuring of markets through strategic alliances, particularly in the telecommunications sector.

A central issue in the liberalisation process has been how to accommodate services of general economic interest, but in fact it is the state aid laws which have brought the issue to prominence. The Member States' unwillingness to give up control over such services forced the EU to address the Europeanisation of such services through common themes and minimum standards. This has allowed a wider range of non-state actors, as well as non-national actors, to provide such services. Chapter 7 analyses the role of such services in Community law, drawing out the common themes in the regulation process. These services, called universal service obligations in the liberalisation process, have been given even more attention since the inclusion of Article 16 EC and are placed within the Constitutional Treaty in Article III–6. While in the postal services sector there is now a discussion as to whether such services can survive in the liberalisation process, in the energy sector the Second Liberalisation Directive of 2003 has enhanced and embedded their role in the liberalisation process.[158]

The case studies show that creating competition in newly liberalised industries is not straightforward.[159] The central concern is that in Europe the state is reluctant to give up the power of incumbents, and these dominant undertakings retain considerable market power for a number of years after liberalisation. This is seen in the telecommunications and postal sectors and recently the EC Commission has acknowledged that this is also the case in the utilities sector.[160]

Incumbents display a number of first-mover advantages; for example, they have the brand familiarity and trust of the consumer, as well as the know-how and the expertise of the particular market, and are large enough and have the scope to achieve economies of scale in exploiting these advantages. Despite the separation of the regulation and the commercial activities in the newly liberalised

---

[158]　Dir 2003/54/EC [2003] OJ L176/37.

[159]　See D Geradin, 'The Opening of State Monopolies to Competition: Main Issues of the Liberalisation Process' in D Geradin (ed), *The Liberalisation of State Monopolies in the European Union and Beyond* (The Hague, Kluwer Law International, 2000) at 181.

[160]　'The Commission takes action against Member States which have not opened up their energy markets properly', European Commission Press Release, 4 Apr 2006, IP 06/430; EC Commission, *Communication From the Commission to the Council and the European Parliament, Report on the Functioning of the Internal Market in Electricity and Gas*, COM(2005)568 final.

markets, incumbents continue to have a special relationship with the state and other public authorities. Often the state retains a shareholding interest in the liberalised undertaking. Particularly in networked industries incumbents are able to deploy barriers to entry against new and potential entrants to the liberalised market, especially in controlling access to the infrastructure of a network industry.

As a result controlling the market power of the incumbent has been a central concern of the liberalisation process.[161] This has been achieved through sector-specific regulation to address, *ex ante*, market failure, the presence of bottlenecks, access to network issues, universal service obligations, the control of mergers, combined with the *ex post* application of the competition rules, using Articles 81 and 82 EC as well as the merger and state aid rules. However rather than creating a virtuous circle of European regulation the EU is immersed in a vicious circle where the regulation of state power in the market is intertwined with new forms of hybrid public/private power of dominant firms in partially liberalised markets.

The response of the EU has been in the experimental use of conventional, new and hybrid forms of regulatory, constitutional and competition law tools to identify, regulate and create legitimacy for the newly liberalised sectors, and particularly for the continuation of the ideas of public service delivery in competitive markets. The resulting mixture of traditional, new, private law, regulatory and competition law principles has transcended the traditional public/private law divide. This reclassification of traditional legal concepts eludes a satisfactory explanation and description by legal theorists, and at a practical level creates challenges for its application at the national level by NRAs and competition authorities. At the EU level it creates a regulatory framework within which the synergy provides a new interconnectedness between competition law, regulation and free market constitutional concepts and emerging ideas of consumer rights protected by by public and private law alongside new ideas of fundamental rights and citizenship. This synergy not only is used to constrain public, private and new forms of hybrid power in the market but also is a vehicle to determine the constitutional values underpinning the liberalised sectors.

---

[161] In the telecommunications sector see D Geradin and M Kerf, *Controlling Market Power in Telecommunications: Antitrust vs. Sector-specific Regulation* (Oxford, OUP, 2003).

6

State Aid

THE DEVELOPMENT AND inter-dependence of the global economy has led to competition between different states (and regions) to attract investments which will increase wealth and employment through trade. One of the effects of the regional market integration in the EU is that, while it leads to greater cross-border trade, it also emphasises the success of efficiency in market operations, with successful firms increasing their market shares; the less efficient exiting the market.[1] Thus, one paradox of European integration is that while it potentially increases the size of the market available to each firm this has economic implications which are associated more with declining markets. There are therefore economic and political incentives for Member States to grant subsidies, reducing, and even negating, the benefits which flow from market integration. There are also political pressures for states, as well as local governments, to grant state aid to firms that are struggling against increased competition as a result of the increased global and cross-border trade.

As we have seen in Chapter 4, it was not until the 1990s that Article 86 EC was used aggressively to challenge anti-competitive practices of national monopolies, using arguments that such monopolies were inefficient, out of date and not meeting consumer demands. But consumers are often slow to take up the advantages of new foreign products and continue to demand the less efficient firms' products because of consumer inertia, sometimes seen as consumer patriotism, but also because of what are now perceived to be anti-competitive, protectionist forms of aid granted to national producers.[2] This may lead to a subsidy race between the Member States, creating an uneven playing field for competitors and potential entrants to a market. While this race results in net welfare gains for some Member States, the overall benefits of market integration are reduced, and this is the justification for EU-level regulation of state aid. However, the accession to the EU in May 2004 and January 2007 of a number of

---

[1]   J Vickers, 'Concepts of Competition' (1995) 47 (1) *Oxford Economic Papers* 1.
[2]   An example is seen in the attachment to British-produced cars, despite the increase in foreign competition and the decline of the UK motor industry. In Italy the legacy of Mussolini left manufacturers making luxury goods, which consumers did not want, or could not afford, and yet successive governments continued to pour aid into these enterprises.

economies which were less developed than the existing Member States' economies has shifted the focus of regulating state aid to looking at permissible *levels* and *forms* of state aid within the EU.

The Member States regard the control of state aid as a curtailment of their sovereign powers and the scope of their industrial and economic policies. Historically, state aid has played a central industrial policy role in the Member States and remains one of the few policy instruments left to the Member States which can be used to protect national industries in an integrated market.[3] Since the Maastricht Treaty 1991 under the Broad Economic Policy Guidelines of the Member States and the Community set out in Article 98 EC, the Member States have been under greater pressure and surveillance to curb this area of public expenditure. The constraints on national budgets, alongside the questioning of the effectiveness of state aid have increased the political pressure towards a more economics, effects-based approach to the regulation of state aid in the EU. The aim being, first, to reduce the political influences on state aid; secondly, to explore how effective state aid can be used to further the integration project.

There are instances where state aid may be a legitimate response to market failure. Externalities may cause market failure; for example the market may not want to invest in unattractive areas such as inner cities or rural areas, thus providing the classic justification for the state to provide or subsidise public services. Concerns over the levels of innovation or the environment may also be legitimate reasons for the state to provide aid where the market is unwilling to bear the costs. State aid may also be a legitimate response to the effects of the market, showing concerns about equity or wider social and political objectives that are not reflected in consumer choice. Thus the EU has a role to design and administer a system of state aid regulation which will allow competition principles to create a cost-effective way of allowing European integration to continue without alienating the Member States. The political mandate in the EU is now for 'less and better targeted State aid'.[4]

State aid expenditure has decreased since the end of the 1990s. In 2002 the overall state aid expenditure was some 49 billion euros. But state aid varies between the Member States from 0.56 per cent of GDP in the United Kingdom to 1.28 per cent in Finland. The new accession states devote a larger percentage of their GDP per capita to state aid (around 1.35 per cent of GDP) than do the older Member States of the EU (around 0.45 per cent between 2002 and 2004). In

---

[3] The effects of integration are seen very early on in the history of the ECSC. The huge price differences between the high cost of Belgian coal and the lower competitive coal from the Ruhr induced subsidies to keep the Belgian coal industry active in the newly competitive market, see L Lister, *Europe's Coal and Steel Community* (New York, Twentieth Century Fund, 1960); J Meade, H. Liesner and S Wells, *Case Studies in European Economic Integration* (London, New York and Toronto, OUP, 1962).

[4] Seen in the Presidency Conclusions of the European Council since the launch of the Lisbon Process in March 2000, and more recently in the EC Commission's *State Aid Action Plan 2005* COM (2005) 107 final (7 June 2005).

absolute terms the new Member States granted some 6.27 billion euros of state aid, compared with 42.717 billion euros from the old Member States in the period 2002–4.[5] Such figures address straightforward subsidies and do not take into account other forms of state aid which may be difficult to quantify, such as state guarantees or the controversial cross-subsidisation between public and commercial activities of undertakings. The most recent *State Aid Scoreboard* reveals that the Member States are not reducing state aid in significant amounts.[6] The total amount of state aid granted in 2005 by the 25 Member States was estimated at 64 billion euros (0.59 per cent of EU GDP), compared with some 65 billion euros in 2004 (0.61 per cent of EU GDP). However, the Member States appear to have reacted positively to the objective of 'better targeted aid': more than half of the Member States have now redirected over 90 per cent of their state aid towards horizontal objectives of common interest, such as the environment and research and development. The in-depth analysis of rescue and restructuring aid shows that this type of aid, which is potentially most prone to distorting competition, amounts to 15.5 billion euros for the period 2000–5 in the EU-15 Member States. While some Member States have frequently awarded such aid during the period under review, the majority have clearly not done so. More than 95 per cent of the total aid amount was granted by the five largest Member States (Germany, France, Italy, the United Kingdom and Spain).

Increasingly attention has focused upon the use of state aid by the Member States as a central issue in the reformulation of policy towards the objectives of state intervention.[7] The Member States, while agreeing to reduce the levels of state aid, continue to flout the EC Treaty rules. Therefore the EC Commission has focused attention on improving the procedures for the regulation of state aid and improving sanctions in the form of the recovery of illegal state aid.[8] This is complemented by the concurrent increase in actions brought by non-state actors who are affected by illegal state aid.

THE LEGAL FRAMEWORK

Article 87(1) EC states that:

---

[5] *State Aid Score Board 2006*, COM (2006) 130 final, para 11. Available at: http://ec.europa.eu/comm/competition/state_aid/scoreboard/2006/spring_en.pdf

[6] COM (2006) 761 final, 11 December 2006. This *Scoreboard* focuses upon the use of rescue and restructuring aid. Available at:
http://ec.europa.eu/comm/competition/state_aid/studies_reports/studies_reports.html

[7] P Ricard, 'Londre, Paris et Berlin veulent pouvoir continuer à verser des aides à leur regions plus pauvres', *Le Monde*, 28 Jan 2005.

[8] On the inadequacy of sanctions for breach of the state aid rules see Sir Jeremy Lever KCMG, QC, 'Some Procedural Conundrums in State Aids Law' in A Biondi *et al* (eds), *The Law of State Aid in the European Union* (Oxford, OUP, 2004).

Save as otherwise provided in this Treaty, any aid granted by a Member State or through State resources in any form whatsoever which distorts or threatens to distort competition by favouring certain undertakings or the production of certain goods shall, insofar as it affects trade between Member States, be incompatible with the common market.

Article 87(2) EC sets out a list of three areas in which state aid is compatible with the Common Market.[9] Article 87(3) EC sets out five areas where state aid *may* be considered to be compatible with the Common Market. Article 87(1)(e) EC is an expansive provision since it allows the Council, acting by a qualified majority on a proposal from the EC Commission, to adopt a Decision and add other categories of aid. Article 88 EC sets out the procedural framework for the regulation of state aid, placing the EC Commission in a central role for the monitoring and enforcement of aid. Article 89 EC allows the Council, acting by a qualified majority on a proposal from the EC Commission and after consulting the European Parliament, to make appropriate regulations for the application of Articles 87 and 88 EC.

Article 87 EC creates a two-stage approach to the control of state aid. The first stage is to establish whether there is a state aid; the second stage is to assess the compatibility of the state aid with the EC Treaty. There is a negative presumption that state aid is incompatible with the EC Treaty unless it can be justified or exempted.

WHAT IS A STATE AID?

The EC Treaty does not define state aid; indeed, a Council Presidency Paper on state aid control in 1996 suggested that an absolute definition is neither possible nor desirable on account of the constant and imaginative development of methods of assistance to industry and enterprise. State aids may not always be granted in an open and transparent or accountable manner, and it is only since 1990 that the EC Commission has published positive Decisions on state aid inquiries in the Official Journal. Thus the definition of a state aid has been developed by the day-to-day practice of the EC Commission alongside the European Courts' judgments.

The EC Commission has used four indicators to establish whether there is a state aid. The first indicator involves an inquiry as to whether there is a transfer of state resources to an undertaking(s), in the form either of a loss of revenue or a cost to the state. The second indicator looks at selectivity: do some firms gain an economic advantage? Additionally there must be evidence that the state aid distorts or threatens to distort competition, and finally that trade between Member States is affected.

---

[9]   The term 'common market' is used in the EC Treaty and was not altered by the Single European Act 1987.

The European Courts and the EC Commission consider the last two conditions as being fulfilled if a measure is selective, in terms of granting an advantage to a recipient.[10] The Court has stated that 'there is no requirement in case-law that the distortions of competition, or the threat of such distortion and the effect on intra-Community trade, must be significant or substantial'.[11] Similarly the CFI has held that:

> the Commission is not required to carry out an economic analysis of the actual situation on the relevant market, of the market share of the undertakings in receipt of the aid, of the position of competing undertakings and of trade flows of the services in question between member States, provided that it has explained how the aid in question distorted competition and affected trade between Member States.[12]

These indicators raise questions which have not always been addressed consistently by the European Courts. For example, the difference between 'aid granted by a Member State', on the one hand, and 'aid granted through State resources', on the other, was not clear in the Courts' jurisprudence. Member States are able to favour certain undertakings or the production of certain goods without transferring any financial funds which can be attributed to the state. Over time a broad and a narrow interpretation of state aid emerged. Under the broad interpretation it was seen as sufficient if the state measures selectively favoured certain undertakings. Under the narrow interpretation a literal reading of Article 87(1) EC was taken as requiring that the measure must be *directly related* to state activity. An example of the narrow interpretation is seen in *Sloman Neptun*. Here the Court stated that the distinction used in the wording of Article 87(1) EC served only:

> to bring within the definition of aid not only aid granted directly by the State, but also aid granted by public or private bodies designated or established by the State.[13]

This view was followed in a number of subsequent cases.[14] The EC Commission, in *PreussenElektra*,[15] asked the Court to reconsider such a narrow interpretation

---

[10] See the Opinion of Capotorti AG of 18 June 1980 in Case 730/79 *Philip Morris Holland BV v Commission of the European Communities* [1980] ECR 2671. Cf the EC Commission's *Vademecum: Community Rules on State Aid* (2003) at 3, which rolls up the two conditions into one, available at: http://ec.europa.eu/comm/competition/state_aid/studies_reports/vademecumen2003_en.pdf

[11] Joined Cases 296 & 318/82 *Kingdom of The Netherlands and Leeuwarder Papierwarenfabriek BV v Commission of the European Communities* [1985] ECR 809.

[12] Case T–55/99 *CETM* [2000] ECR II–3207.

[13] Joined Cases C–72/91 & C–73/91 *Sloman Neptun Schiffahrts AG v Seebettriebsrat Bodo Ziesmer der Sloman Neptun Schiffahrts AG* [1993] ECR I–887, para 19.

[14] Case C–189/91 *Petra Kirshammer-Hack v Nurhan Sidel* [1993] ECR I–6185, para 16; Joined Cases C–52/97 to C–54/97 *Epifanio Viscido and others* [1998] ECR I–2629, para 13; Case C–200/97 *Ecotrade Srl v Altiforni & Ferriere di Sevola SpA (AFS)* [1998] ECR I–7907, para 35; Case C–379/98 *PreussenElektra AG v Schleswag AG* [2001] ECR I–2099, para 58.

[15] *Ibid.*

of state aid but the Court declined to do so. In this case the Court held that levies on particular firms designed to finance environmental objectives were not state aid.

In principle, all state aids which distort competition are prohibited. However, there are some situations where state aid may be justified if it is compatible with the aims of the Common Market. These justifications are contained in Articles 87(2) and (3) EC. Although not referred to in the state aid rules, Article 86(2) EC provides a special justification for aid relating to the provision of services of general economic interest. This provision has become a central tool in regulating the way in which such services are financed through state resources.[16]

State aid may be granted by public and private bodies established and, to varying degrees, controlled by the state. *Stardust Marine*[17] concerned a complex set of financial arrangements. The Court stated that the funds of public under- takings are state resources, but the *transfer* of such funds may not automatically fall within the definition of state aid.

> Even if the State is in a position to control a public undertaking and to exercise a dominant influence over its operations, actual exercise of that control in a particular case cannot be automatically presumed. A public undertaking may act with more or less independence, according to the degree of autonomy left to it by the State. Therefore, the mere fact that a public undertaking is under State control is not sufficient for measures taken by that undertaking to be imputed to the State.

The Court demanded that an examination should take place as to whether the public authorities should be regarded as being involved in some way in the adoption of the alleged aid measures. This did not have to be a precise inquiry, but state intervention could be imputed from a set of indicators which are set out in paragraphs 55–58 of the judgment. The Court found that the EC Commission had adopted, as the sole criterion, the organic criterion according to which the public undertakings were under the control of the state, and this was found to be an erroneous method of imputing the alleged aid to the state.

The role of commodity and industrial boards, which play an important role in The Netherlands' economy, have also fallen under the scrutiny of the state aid rules. Under Dutch law they are considered to be independent of the state. In the case of *Pearle*[18] the issue of whether a board had transferred state resources amounting to state aid was answered in the negative by the Court. Pearle and other traders in optical equipment had joined a board but objected to a levy which was charged for the collective advertising of optical equipment. Pearle argued that the levies were a form of state aid. The Court argued that the levies were earmarked for an advertising campaign and those funds were not made

---

[16] See Ch 7.
[17] Case C–482/99 *France v Commission (Stardust Marine)* [2002] ECR I–4397.
[18] Case C–345/02 *Pearle BV and others v Hoofdbednjfschap Ambachten* [2004] ECR I–7139.

available to the national authorities. The costs of the advertising campaign were met in full from the levies. Referring to *Sloman Neptun*, the Court noted that 'the Board's action did not tend to create an advantage which would constitute an additional burden for the State or that body'.[19] The transfer was not imputable to the state as it was proposed by the private opticians' association, and therefore the Board served merely as a *vehicle* for levying and allocating the resources collected for a purely commercial purpose which had nothing to do with policy determination.

The judgments in both *Sloman Neptun* and *Pearle* are a tacit recognition of the need for political expediency by the Court: they send a message that the Court will not intrude into sensitive areas of national policy. If the Court had decided differently in *Pearle* the result would be to transfer a large area of the regulation of The Netherlands' economy directly into Community regulation. Intervention in the *Neptun* case would have transferred into Community competence a sensitive area of labour law *and* commercial activity.

In *Stadtwerke Schwäbisch Hall GmbH*[20] the CFI found that a German scheme of tax exemption for the reserves established by nuclear power stations was not a state aid. Nuclear power stations established in Germany are obliged by law to set up reserves to cover the costs of disposing of their irradiated fuel and their radioactive waste and also the permanent closure of their nuclear plants. The German Commercial Code states that those reserves can be counted among the liabilities of the undertaking concerned and lead to a reduction of the corresponding amount from the taxable total. In 1999 three German electricity production and distribution utilities requested the EC Commission to examine the tax exemption scheme applied to those financial reserves. They claimed that that tax exemption amounted to state aid to nuclear power stations. Following a summary examination, the EC Commission decided that the tax measure at issue did not amount to state aid. The three public utilities contested the EC Commission's decision before the CFI. The CFI found that the tax exemption amounted to an economic advantage granted through state resources in so far as the state waives its right to levy a certain amount of tax revenue. Nevertheless, the CFI considered that neither the tax exemption scheme for the reserves nor the detailed rules for the implementation by the authorities of the tax scheme in dispute granted to nuclear power stations a specific advantage inherent in the notion of state aid. The CFI also found that the public utilities did not establish that the amount of the reserves was disproportionate in the light of the scale of the expenditure that nuclear power stations necessarily incur in order to finance

---

[19] *Ibid*, at para. 36.
[20] Case T–92/02 *Stadtwerke Schwäbisch Hall GmbH, Stadtwerke Tübingen GmbH, Stadtwerke Uelzen GmbH v Commission of the European Communities* [2006] ECR II-11.

their public law obligation to dispose of their radioactive waste and to decommission their plants. The CFI held that there were no factors which should have obliged the EC Commission to initiate the formal procedure for detailed investigation of state aid.

In *Ferring*[21] a tax advantage which offset the additional costs of providing a service of general economic interest did not constitute an economic advantage for the undertakings concerned, and therefore was not a state aid. In *Altmark*[22] the Court set out specific conditions which such compensation must satisfy in order to fall outside the state aid rules. Subsequently the EC Commission has adopted specific rules for the application of the state aid regime to the financing of services of general economic interest. These issues are discussed later in this chapter in the discussion of filters for state aid and, in greater detail, in Chapter 7.

THE EFFECTS OF STATE AID

The EC Commission and the European Courts look not at the form of state intervention, but focus upon its *effects*.[23] This is consistent with the application of the competition law provisions of Articles 81 and 82 EC. The Court has stated that:

> the concept of aid is thus wider than that of a subsidy because it embraces not only positive benefits, such as subsidies themselves, but also interventions which, in various forms, mitigate the charges which are normally included in the budget of an undertaking and which, without therefore being subsidies in the strict meaning of the word, are similar in character and have the same effect.[24]

Thus tax exemptions, reductions in social security contributions and other negative forms of benefits to selective firms have been held to constitute state aid because they place certain firms in a more favourable financial situation than others.

An example where a state aid was not found is seen in *Danske Busvognmænd v Commission*.[25] In 1995 the provision of public bus transport was transferred from the Danish State Railways to an independent undertaking (which was owned by the state) called Combus. The aim was to make bus transport competitive. The state had made provision in Combus' opening account to cover the additional expenditure of pensions and paid leave of absence for state officials seconded to Combus. Later, in 1998, legislation was adopted to allow for a one-off payment to

---

[21]   Case C–53/00 *Ferring SA v ACOSS* [2001] ECR I–9067.

[22]   Case C–280/00 [2003] ECR I–7747.

[23]   Case 173/73 *Italy v Commission* [1974] ECR, para 13.

[24]   Case C–387/92 *Banco Exterior de España SA v Ayuntamiento de Valencia* [1994] ECR I–877, para 13.

[25]   Case T–157/01 *Danske Busvognmænd v Commission* [2004] ECR II–917.

change the status of some 500 officials. A complaint that these payments constituted state aid was made to the EC Commission by Danske Busvognmænd, a trade association representing over 90 per cent of Denmark's regional public bus transport undertakings. Without providing any reasoning the EC Commission found that there was no state aid present. The CFI held that the EC Commission was not obliged to give specific reasons for its Decision, given the obvious nature of the payments. The intention of the payments was only to free Combus from a structural disadvantage that it held in relation to competitors in the private sector.

Under the state aid rules it is not necessary to establish that there is discrimination on grounds of nationality.[26] State aids are seen, by definition, as discriminatory infringements of the EC Treaty, and this explains why there is a presumption that such advantages affect trade between the Member States.[27] It is the selective element of aid which creates a distortion of competition. Individual aid, quite obviously, will be selective, even when it is granted as part of a general aid scheme. The most problematic cases concern selectivity in social security contributions and taxation.[28] Selectivity can be avoided if the nature and general structure of the scheme justify the selectivity and the measures pursue a purpose which is objectively justified and do not infringe Community law. However, the EC Commission has interpreted these rules stringently.[29]

STATE AID FILTERS

If the wide definition of a state aid were applied to state activity in a rigid manner, the competition rules would paralyse the economic activity of the Member States, and result in an intolerable workload for the EC Commission. There is an inherently underlying tension between the tolerance of mixed economies in the EU by virtue of Article 295 EC and the prohibition on state aid in Article 87 EC, and over the years the EC Commission has developed a number of tests which act as filters for the use of state resources and complement the soft law processes of providing guidance for the Member States in the effective use of state resources.

---

[26] Case T–55/99 *Confedaraciòn Espanola de Transporte de Mercancias (CETM) v Commission* [2000] ECR II–3207, para 49.
[27] In Case 248/84 *Germany v Commission* [1987] ECR 4013 the Court stated that the EC Commission must show that the contested aid will have an impact upon trade between the Member States.
[28] See, eg, Case 173/73 *Italy v Commission* [1974] ECR 709.
[29] Case C–75/97 *Belgium v Commission (Maribel)* [1999] ECR I–3671; Case T–55/99 CETM [2000] ECR II–3207; Case C–308/01 *GIL Insurance and others v Commissioners of Customs and Excise* [2004] ECR I–4777.

The Hypothetical Private Investor Test

Where grants of external or internal capital are given to private or public undertakings it may be difficult to establish whether there is state aid. The EC Commission has used a 'hypothetical private investor' test[30] in order to establish whether a firm would have received the alleged state aid under the same conditions if a private investor were operating under normal market conditions.[31] The test was developed in the 1980s and has been expanded to become an important policy instrument to draw the line between lawful and unlawful state intervention in the market and has been expanded to create an element of transparency in other situations where the state is involved in complex economic transactions.

The test fits with the principle of equal treatment of public and private property ownership which is found in Article 295 EC: Member States may invest and participate in commercial operations in a competitive market provided that they seek to earn a 'normal' market return for the investments. The use of the various tests is not without criticism. Parish has argued that the tests used by the EC Commission are conceptually arbitrary, and in fact do not act as a filter but lead to protracted investigations and litigation. He argues that the hypothetical private investor test 'assumes that organs of the State exist, or can exist, with the same *modus vivendi* as a private company'.[32] The state is different from any other hypothetical investor and has (theoretically) unlimited resources, although under the Broad Economic Policy Guidelines and the Stability Pact the Member States should keep within budgetary limits.

The test does not address squarely the fact that a lot of investment is made on state guarantees and that the state has a better credit rating than other economic actors. Guarantees are seen by the EC Commission as a form of state aid and, of course, may be hard to quantify. Where there is a formal finding of a state aid based upon a guarantee it is difficult for the EC Commission to order recovery of any illegal state aid.[33] The state can also provide indirect assistance where it is hard to quantify the advantage, for example, where the state supplies services and technological assistance to private firms, or where the state acts as a buyer of privately produced services, or where the state enacts preferential legislation

---

[30] Also called the 'hypothetical market economy investor principle' or the 'informed private investor test'.

[31] Case 142/87 *Belgium v Commission* [1990] ECR 959; Gas Prices [1994] OJ C35/6. See 'Application of Articles 92 and 93 of the EEC Treaty to Public Authorities' Holdings', *Bul EC* 9–1984; Commission Dir 80/723/EEC of 25 June 1980 on the transparency of financial relations between Member States and public undertakings [1980] OJ L195/35.

[32] M Parish, 'On the Private Investor Principle' (2003) 28 *ELRev* 70.

[33] On problems with state guarantees see: P Nicolaides, 'Markets and Words: the Distortive Effect of Government Pronouncements' (2005) 26 *ECLR* 119; M Friend, 'State Guarantees as State Aid: Some Practical Difficulties' in A Biondi *et al* (eds), *The Law of State Aid in the European Union* (Oxford, OUP, 2004); L Prete, 'State Aid Reform: Some Refelections on the Need to Revise the Notice on Guarantees' (2006) 29 *World Competition* 421.

giving certain firms special advantages or, perhaps the most controversial aspect of all, where there is transfer pricing (cross-subsidies) within a state-owned or controlled undertaking.

Nevertheless, despite these criticisms, the EC Commission continues to use the test seen, for example, in the *Ryanair* Decision in 2004.[34] An airport operator (BSCA), a public undertaking controlled by the region of Wallonia, granted a number of concessions to Ryanair, a low cost airline, in consideration for Ryanair opening up new air routes to and from Charleroi airport. The deal involved start-up aid in the form of marketing contributions, incentive payments and the provision of office space; a reduction in the charges for ground handling services; the region of Wallonia reduced the landing fees for Ryanair by 50 per cent of the general tariff. In a 15-year deal, Ryanair received 250,000 euros for hotel and subsistence costs for Ryanair staff; 768,000 euros for recruiting and training Ryanair staff; and 160,000 euros for each route opened (up to a max of 1.92 million euros).

The EC Commission considered parts of this deal to be illegal state aid, since the terms were not made at arm's length on a commercial footing.[35] The EC Commission's assessment that the region of Wallonia and the airport operator BSCA had not acted as private market investors has attracted criticism; for example, start-up financing creates synergy effects, bringing other airlines and service providers to the region. After the Ryanair investment was made two other low cost airlines (Wizzair and Air Polonia) and car rental and travel companies set up economic activities at the subsidised airport.[36] However, while these may benefit the local economy the test used by the Courts is to assess the returns to the hypothetical investor. In practice the Court has demanded a high return in future profits from the investment.[37]

The EC Commission has a wide discretion to apply an economic assessment of such transactions, and the European Courts will not normally intervene to substitute their own assessments. Recently, however, the CFI has started to limit the EC Commission's discretion.[38] The private hypothetical investor test is controversial and has come under criticism because it must use as a comparator with the state a private company guided by prospects of long-term profitability.[39]

---

[34] *Charleroi Airport/Ryanair*, Dec of 12 Feb 2004 [2004] OJ L137/1.

[35] After the *Ryanair* Decision the EC Commission adopted Guidelines on State Aid for Airports with a set of 12 very strict conditions which must be satisfied before start-up aid can be approved under Art 87(3) EC: *Community Guidelines on Financing of Airports and Start-up Aid to Airlines Departing from Regional Airports* [2005] OJ C312/1, para 79.

[36] See J Callaghan, 'Implications of the Charleroi Case for the Competitiveness of EU Air Transport' (2005) 26 *ECLR* 439; U Soltesz, "The New Commission Guidelines on State Aid for Airports: a Step Too Far…" (2006) 4 *European State Aid Law* 719.

[37] See, eg, Joined Cases T–129/95, T–2/96 & T–97/96 *Neue Maxhutte v Commission* [1999] ECR II–17, para 19.

[38] See Case T–11/95 *BP Chemicals Ltd v Commission* [1998] ECR I–3235.

[39] Case T–129/95, T–2/96 & T–97/96, above n 37, at para 109; Case C–280/00 *Altmark* [2003] ECR I–7747. Cf Cases C–83/01, C–93/01 & C–94/01 P *Chronopost SA v Ufex* [2003] ECR I–6993 where the

In *Alitalia*[40] the CFI stated that a capital contribution from public funds normally satisfies the test of a private investor operating in the normal conditions of the market economy and does not imply a grant of state aid if, *inter alia*, it was made at the same time as a significant capital contribution on the part of a private investor made in comparable circumstances. In this case 90 per cent of the capital of an airline was held by the Italian state finance company, Istituto per la Ricostruzione Industriale SpA (IRI), the rest being held by private investors. It embarked upon a debt and operations restructuring programme which the EC Commission objected to. However, in *Seleco*[41] the Court held that even a significant participation by non-state private investors is not sufficient to exclude state aid.

Another example of the use of the test is the *WestLB* case which began after a complaint from the federation of private banks, BDB, in Germany. In November 2004 the EC Commission finally closed the *WestLB* case after nearly a decade of investigation and deliberation. The EC Commission and the CFI found that the contribution of certain assets by the *Land* of Nordrhein-Westfalen to WestLB, a public law banking institution, contained state aid insofar as the contribution was not remunerated at the average rate of return in the German banking industry. The transfer had not resulted in an increase in the Land's holding, but had brought a return fixed at 0.6 per cent *per annum* after tax. By a Decision of 8 July 1999 the EC Commission found that a private investor would have expected a rate of return of 9.3 per cent *per annum* after tax. The CFI rejected the contention that Article 295 EC limited the scope of the state aid rules. The CFI pointed out that in order to determine whether there is state aid the profitability, or otherwise, of the beneficiary is not in principle conclusive, but must be taken into account for the purpose of determining whether the public investor behaved in the same way as a market economy investor, or whether the beneficiary received an economic advantage which it would not have obtained under normal market conditions.

To determine whether there is an economic advantage the EC Commission may take as the criterion the average rate of return in the sector concerned. But the use of such an analytical tool does not release the EC Commission from the obligation to provide adequate reasons for its final Decision and to carry out a full analysis of all the factors that are relevant to the transaction at issue, its context and the possibility that the aid may qualify for an exemption under Article 86(2) EC. The Court found that the EC Commission had not proved sufficient grounds for the choice of two of the elements taken into account in the

Court held that where the private market investor principle is applied to a firm which is carrying out a public service the comparison should be made with the cost price of the performance of the services by that company, not with a company in the commercial sector.

[40]   Case T–296/97 *Alitalia v Commission* [2000] ECR II–3871.

[41]   Joined Cases C–328/99 & C–399/00 *Italian Republic and SIM 2 Multimedia SpA v Commission of the European Communities* [2003] ECR I–4035.

calculation of the appropriate rate of return and the increase in that rate for applying it to the particular transactions under investigation. The CFI took the view that those factors were essential in the EC Commission's Decision. The EC Commission ordered the German government to collect 3 billion euros in state aid (plus interest) which had been awarded to seven public banks in the early 1990s. *WestLB* was used as the test case; it received the most state aid (some 975 million euros).[42]

A difficult area for state aid regulation is the problem we saw in Chapter 5 where cross-subsidies are used by public undertakings holding a monopoly engaging in the provision of commercial activities *and* universal service obligations/services of general economic interest. Liberalisation in Europe has taken place gradually, with state monopolies enjoying an incumbent dominant position where they have opted to continue with providing services of general economic interest in a reserved sector as well as enjoying substantial market power on the liberalised market.

In *UFEX* the CFI stated that it is not sufficient merely to demonstrate that the public undertaking in a reserved sector is paid the full costs of the provision of logistical and commercial assistance to its subsidiary acting in a competitive sector. The EC Commission must check:

> that the payment received by La Poste was comparable to that demanded by a private holding company or a private group of undertakings not operating in a reserved sector, pursuing a structural policy—whether general or sectoral—and guided by long-term prospects.[43]

In the appeal brought by La Poste, its subsidiary and France, the Court set aside the CFI judgment. The Court argued that the *actual costs* principle should apply. When assessing whether there is state aid present the EC Commission must use objective and verifiable criteria. Any 'normal market' conditions in the reserved sector are necessarily hypothetical, because no private undertaking would ever set up the infrastructure necessary to provide the service of general economic interest. State aid is excluded:

> if, first, it is established that the price charged properly covers all the additional, variable costs incurred in providing the logistical and commercial assistance, an appropriate contribution to the fixed costs arising from use of the postal network and an adequate return on the capital investment in so far as it is used for SFMI-Chronopost's competitive activity and if, second, there is nothing to suggest that those elements have been under-estimated or fixed in an arbitrary fashion.[44]

---

[42] Joined Cases T–228/99 & T–233/99 *WestLB and Land Nordrhein-Westfalen v Commission* [2003] ECR II–435; Case C–209/00 *Commission v Germany* [2002] ECR I–11695.

[43] Case T–613/97 *UFEX and others v Commission* [2000] ECR II–1531, paras 74–75.

[44] Case C–83/01 P *Chronopost SA, La Poste, French Republic v Commission* [2003] ECR I–6993, para 40.

The Private Creditor Test

Spain has been involved in a series of cases concerning the question whether the deferment of debts owed to the state is a form of state aid. The EC Commission has used the concept of a 'private creditor' test, and this has the approval of the European Courts. In *Tubacex*[45] the Court was asked to decide what interest rates should be charged by a public creditor who re-scheduled debts relating to social security payments. The EC Commission argued that the Member State should charge a market interest rate on the debts. The Court held that:

> the interest normally applicable to that type of debt is intended to make good the loss suffered by the creditor because of the debtor's delay in performing its obligation to pay off its debt, namely default interest. If the rate of default interest applied to the debts of a public creditor is not the same as the rates charged for the debts owed to a private creditor, it is the latter rate which ought to be charged if it is higher than the former.[46]

In a later case, *Lenzing AG*,[47] the issue arose as to whether a deferment of a debt was a state aid. This was a challenge by a competitor to an EC Commission Decision finding that the deferment of a social security debt was *not* a state aid. Lenzing AG, an Austrian firm, argued that the ruling in *Tubacex* concerned the *interest rate* to be charged on late debts. It argued that the recovery of a debt is normal creditor behaviour and any deferment of a debt requires special justification. The CFI held that it had only limited judicial control over the EC Commission's discretion. But it accepted the point put forward by Lenzing AG that a private creditor 'is not inclined to allow the debtor to defer repayment, but relies directly on his or her rights, if necessary by realising the securities which it holds'.[48] The CFI annulled the EC Commission's Decision since the EC Commission had not provided any acceptable reasons why a private creditor would have acted in the same way as the Spanish social security fund.

GEA[49] was one of the leading manufacturers and sellers of porcelain and china which incurred huge losses after its privatisation in 1991. The firm received state aid in the form of guarantees and a direct subsidy which had been authorised by the EC Commission with the condition that no further aid would be granted and a restructuring plan would be followed. GEA failed to comply with tax and social security obligations; existing debts were waived by the state and an extension and re-scheduling of debt was agreed over a 10-year period. But GEA failed to comply with this arrangement. The EC Commission found that the Spanish authorities

---

[45]   Case C–342/96 *Spain v Commission (Tubacex)* [1999] ECR I–2459.
[46]   *Ibid*, at para 48.
[47]   Case T–36/99 *Lenzing AG v Commission* [2004] ECR II–3597; appeal pending: Case C–525/04P *Spain v Lenzing AG*, Opinion of Kokott AG 1 February 2007.
[48]   *Ibid*, at para 98.
[49]   Case C–276/02 *Spain v Commission (GEA)* [2004] ECR I–8091.

had failed to act as diligent private creditors by not attempting to recover at least a marginal amount of the unpaid taxes and social security contributions.

The CFI annulled the EC Commission's Decision because of factual errors. It left open the question whether the Spanish government had acted as a 'private creditor', since this is for the EC Commission to assess. In contrast Advocate General Maduro provides a fuller account of how the 'private creditor' test should apply. He argues that the diligent private creditor in a market economy is an efficient economic operator, capable of discerning and using the most appropriate means of achieving a particular result. All the factors which are relevant to the specific relationship must be taken into account. According to the Advocate General the choice of waiver must fulfil at least three conditions: *first*, it must be possible, in principle, for the firm to be made economically viable and to improve its financial position; *secondly*, everything possible must be done to prevent further credit from being obtained and new debts accumulating; *thirdly*, the state must rely upon the recovery of the debts owed within a reasonable period.[50]

The Private Purchaser Test

State aid regulation applies to public procurement. Where a public contract does not correspond to a normal trade agreement state aid may be present. This is particularly the case where the purchase of goods and services has not been preceded by a sufficiently advertised open tender. The EC Commission has indicated that the use of open tender procedures is one way in which a Member State can avoid the application of state aid rules, since the use of such procedures is seen as a means of showing that a Member State was not attempting to grant an advantage to a selected undertaking.[51] Where a state purchases goods and services for a market price when it does not have an actual need for the goods and services, the CFI and the Court of Justice have ruled that this is not a normal market transaction.[52]

The Private Vendor Test

The rise in privatisations across Europe during the 1990s brought about the question whether a state may be providing state aid when it sells off state assets at below the market price. The state may do this in order to keep the previously state owned/public companies in the hands of national capital, and also it may be a way of paying back political favours. The issue arises: did the state act in the way

---

[50] *Ibid*, at paras 36–40.
[51] See also the discussion of *Altmark*, below.
[52] Joined Cases T–116/01 & T–118/01 *P&O European Ferries (Vizcaya) SA and Diputación Foral de Vizcaya v Commission* [2003] ECR II–2957, para 117; on appeal Case C–442/03 P *P&O European Ferries (Vizcaya) SA and Diputación Foral de Vizcaya v Commission* [2006] ECR I-4845.

a private vendor would act? From the *1991 Report on Competition Policy XXI* onwards the EC Commission has been consistent in its Annual Reports and practice in stating that there would *not* be state aid present when state assets were sold to the highest bidder in an open and unconditional bidding procedure. The EC Commission published a Communication in 1997 relating to the sale of public land. Again the EC Commission emphasises the use of a tendering procedure to avoid state aid:

> Following a sufficiently well-publicised, open and unconditional bidding procedure, comparable to an auction accepting the best or only bid is by definition at market value and consequently does not contain State aid.[53]

Where a bidding procedure or independent valuation does not take place the sale must be notified to the EC Commission in order for the EC Commission to determine what the sale price would be under normal market conditions.[54]

If such a tender procedure does not occur an independent valuation must take place, using independent asset valuers. Such valuations must establish the market value of the assets on the basis of generally accepted market indicators and valuation standards. This must take place prior to the sale. In *Valmont Nederland BV v Commission*[55] the CFI held that where the EC Commission examines experts' reports drawn up after the sale of the assets it is bound to compare the sale price actually paid with the price suggested in the experts' reports. It can then determine whether the sale price diverges sufficiently to justify there being a benefit which could constitute state aid.

The Market Economy Operator Test

A final filter which has developed is the notion of the state or an undertaking controlled by the state acting as a rational operator in a market economy. The EC Commission or a competitor must be able to show that the contract or other relationship entered into by the state exceeds the bounds of normal commercial transactions between two private operators. In *Linde*[56] a subsidy granted at a higher rate to a privatised undertaking allowing it to build a carbon monoxide production facility which complemented its existing activities was declared by the EC Commission to be an illegal state aid, but the CFI held the subsidy to be an essential part of the commercial arrangement that led to a decrease in the exposure to future losses which the German public bodies would normally have

---

[53] Communication 97/c 209/03 on state aid elements in sales of land and buildings by public authorities [1997] OJ C209/3, pt II.1.

[54] See, eg, Commission Dec, *Koninklijke Schelde Groep* [2001] OJ L14/56, para 79; Commission Dec, *Gothaer Fahrzeugtechnik GmbH* [2002] OJ L314/62, para 30.

[55] Case T–274/01 *Valmont Nederland BV v Commission* [2004] ECR II–3145, para 45.

[56] Case T–98/00 *Linde AG v Commission* [2002] ECR II–3961, paras 49 and 52.

had to bear. In another example, the EC Commission declared aid given for the construction of a five-star hotel at a tourist resort in Austria to be compatible with the EC Treaty because it fell within the meaning of Article 87(3)(c) EC as aid intended to facilitate the development of certain economic areas. This was possible because the construction project included a reciprocal five-year agreement between the proposed hotel operator and the local Loipersdorf Spa (a public commercial undertaking) under which the Spa undertook to reserve 50 bedrooms per day for three years (creating an occupancy rate of 16.7 per cent) at a price equal to the average price for bedrooms let at the hotel. The Spa undertook to enlarge its facilities, reserving reclining beds for the Hotel guests and excluding rival hotels from direct access to the Spa before 1 January 2003. The Decision was challenged by four operators of four-star hotels in the locality, arguing that the EC Commission had failed to take into account that the commitment by the Spa to reserve the 50 bedrooms per day was a form of public subsidy which amounted to illegal state aid. The Court concluded that:

> The applicant's argument does not permit the conclusion that the stipulations agreed between the Siemens Hotel and Loipersdorf Spa exceed the bounds of a normal commercial transaction between two private operators.[57]

Financing Services of General Economic Interest

A different kind of filter developed by the European Courts relates to compensation for services of general economic interest. Both the central state and local authorities provide funding and/or other advantages for undertakings which provide such services, and now the liberalisation of markets has opened the way for such services to be provided on a competitive basis.[58] This in turn has led to the recognition that such services should be provided in an effective, cost efficient and transparent way. One way of achieving this is for such services to be opened up to tendering procedures. In *Altmark*[59] the Court sets out criteria which can be used by the Member States in order to avoid the application of the state aid rules. The *Altmark* ruling uses a benchmarking exercise where the operations of a public service obligation provider are assessed against a 'typical well run company'. This is different from the hypothetical private investor test, discussed above, which focuses upon the question whether state funds are made available to

---

[57] Case T–158/99 *Thermenhotel Stoiser Franz Gesellschaft mbH & Co KG and others v Commission* [2004] ECR II–1, para 112.

[58] See E Szyszczak, 'Public Service Provision in Competitive Markets' (2001) 20 *Yearbook of European Law* 35.

[59] Case C–280/00 *Altmark Trans GmbH* [2003] ECR I–7747. See: F Louis and A Vallery, '*Ferring* Revisited: the *Altmark* Case and State Financing of Public Services Obligations' (2004) 57 *World Competition* 53; A. Biondi and L Rubini, 'Aims, Effects and Justifications: EC State Aid Law and Its Impact on National Social Policies' in M Dougan and E Spaventa (eds), *Social Welfare and EU Law* (Oxford, Hart, 2004).

a comparable private investor operating under market conditions at the same time and in comparable circumstances.[60] The EC Commission followed the ruling in *Altmark* with a Framework and a Decision.[61]

AID WHICH IS COMPATIBLE WITH THE COMMON MARKET

Article 87(2) EC states that the following types of aid *shall* be allowed:

a. aid having a social character, granted to individual consumers, granted without discrimination related to the origin of the product concerned;

b. aid to make good the damage caused by natural disasters or exceptional circumstances, and

c. aid granted to compensate certain areas of Germany for the economic advantages caused by its division into East and West.[62]

Whereas Article 87(3) EC states that the following types of aid *may* be compatible with the Common Market:

a. aid to promote economic development of areas with abnormally low standards of living and serious unemployment;

b. aid to promote an important project of common European interest, or to remedy severe disturbances in the economy of a Member State;

c. aid to facilitate the development of certain economic activities or certain areas where the aid does not adversely affect trading conditions to an extent contrary to the common interest;

---

[60]   Case C–209/00 *Commission v Germany* [2002] ECR I–11695.

[61]   Commission Framework (adopted on 13 July 2005) for state aid in the form of public service compensation [2005] OJ C297/4; Commission Dec of 13 July 2005 on the application of Art 86(2) of the Treaty to state aid in the form of public service compensation granted to certain undertakings entrusted with the operation of services of general economic interest [2005] OJ L312/67. Ch 7 discusses these measures in detail.

[62]   This provision is limited in scope. In Case C–156/98 *Germany v Commission* [2000] ECR I–6857 the Court held that this provision refers to the economic disadvantages caused by the division of Germany in 1948; for example, breaks in communication links, loss of markets as a result of the breaking off of commercial relations between the two parts of Germany. Aid which had been granted to offset the economic backwardness of the East German *Länder* after unification did not fall within Art 87(2)(c) EC. Under Art III–167 of the Constitutional Treaty this provision may be repealed 5 years after the Constitutional Treaty comes into force by the Council acting on a proposal from the EC Commission.

d. aid to promote heritage and culture conversation where the aid does not adversely affect trading conditions and competition to an extent contrary to the common interest, and

e. such other categories of aid as may be specified by the European Council.

Over the years the EC Commission has used soft law processes, as well as adopting Guidelines and Communications and Regulations, to provide guidance on what *type* and *level* of aid are likely to be acceptable.[63] In a number of cases the CFI has held that the EC Commission is bound by these measures.[64] The Court and Advocate General Lenz have argued that the Member States are bound by these Guidelines if they have agreed to the contents.[65] The Court has recognised that the EC Commission must maintain flexibility to amend its decision-making practice. Where the Guidelines are based upon Article 88(1) EC they are but one element of the regular and periodic cooperation where the EC Commission, in cooperation with the Member States, must keep existing systems of aid under constant review.[66] The Courts will examine whether the EC Commission has followed its own Guidelines and will also assess whether the Guidelines and their practical application are compatible with Community law.[67]

Generic *horizontal* rules and Guidelines may apply to specific types of firms, for example, small and medium-sized undertakings,[68] or to activities across the whole EU economy, for example employment and training aid.[69] There are special horizontal Guidelines in the form of the Framework and Decision for funding services of general economic interest.[70] *Specific* Guidelines apply to

---

[63] See M Cini, 'The Soft Law Approach: Commission Rule-making in the EU's State Aid Regime' (2001) 8 *Journal of European Public Policy* 192.

[64] Case T–380/94 *AIUFASS and AKT v Commission* [1996] ECR II–2169, para 57; Case T–149/95 *Etablissements J. Richard Ducross v Commission* [1997] ECR II–2031; Case T–16/96 *Cityflyer Express Ltd. v Commission* [1998] ECR II–757, para 57; Case T–214/95 *Het Vlaamse Gewest (Flemish Region) v Commission* [1998] ECR II–717, para 89; Joined Cases T–129/95 & T–2/96 *Neue Maxhütte Stahlwerke GmbH and Lech-Stahlwerke GmbH v Commission* [1999] ECR II–17, para 150.

[65] Case C–313/90 *CIRFS and others v Commission* [1993] ECR I–1125.

[66] See also Art 18 of Reg 659/99 [1999] OJ L 83/1 where Guidelines may be one way of covering proposals for appropriate measures. Under Art 19 a Member State will be bound only if it has accepted the proposed guidelines and has informed the Commission of this fact.

[67] Case T–27/02 *Kronofrance SA v Commission* [2004] ECR II–4177; Case C–91/01 *Italy v Commission (Solar Tech)* [2004] ECR I–4355 and Case T–137/02 *Pollmeier Malchow GmbH & Co. KG v Commission* [2004] ECR II–3541.

[68] Community guidelines on state aid for small and medium-sized enterprises (SMEs) [1996] OJ C213/4; Commission Recommendation 96/280/EC of 3 Apr 1996 concerning the definition of small and medium-sized enterprises [1996] OJ L107/4 + Annex.

[69] Guidelines on aid to employment [1995] OJ C334/4; Commission Notice on monitoring of state aid and reduction of labour costs [1997] OJ C 1/10; Framework on training aid [1998] OJ C343/10.

[70] Commission Framework (adopted on 13 July 2005) for state aid in the form of public service compensation [2005] OJ C297/4; Commission Dec of 13 July 2005 on the application of Art 86(2) of the Treaty to state aid in the form of public service compensation granted to certain undertakings entrusted with the operation of services of general economic interest [2005] OJ L312/67.

rescue and restructuring activities,[71] regional aid[72] and aid to deprived urban areas.[73]

Rescue and restructuring aid poses particular problems for the EU, often bringing the EC Commission in direct conflict with a Member State over national policy. Guidelines in the form of a *Communication*[74] have been introduced to allow the Member States to assist undertakings that are in crisis. The EC Commission has imposed strict limits to this kind of aid, since it can be anti-competitive, ineffective and inefficient. It has the potential to keep inefficient firms in the market, and this is why the aid can be granted only after a feasible, coherent and far-reaching plan has been drawn up involving at least the reorganisation and rationalisation of the undertaking's activities, usually involving withdrawal from loss-making activities. The plan may also include plans for diversification towards new and viable activities. Another aspect involves financial restructuring, addressing the causes of loss-making activities. The EC Commission's Guidelines walk a tight line between balancing the anti-competitive effects of rescue and restructuring aid and the benefits which flow from the undertaking's survival in the market. The loss of the undertaking may alter the competitive structure of the market and social and regional cohesion issues may emerge where unemployment results from the closure of a local firm.

Rescue aid can be granted only to stem serious social difficulties, and must not have serious spill-over effects on other Member States. Rescue aid must be limited to loans or loan guarantees. In both rescue and restructuring aid the EC Commission applies a 'one time, last time principle'. Thus aid may be granted to an undertaking only once in a 10-year period. Rescue aid must be of a temporary nature, its aim being to keep an undertaking in difficulty afloat, to give it a breathing space to decide on a rescue or a liquidation plan. Because it is in the nature of a loan, any rescue aid must be repaid. In the light of the Lisbon Process the EU has had to adapt state aid policy to enable aid to be given in areas which are a priority, for example, the European Employment Strategy, as well as reconsidering which forms of aid might improve competitiveness.

---

[71] Community guidelines on state aid for rescuing and restructuring firms in difficulty [1994] OJ C368/12; Commission communication concerning extension of the guidelines on state aid for rescuing and restructuring firms in difficulty [1998] OJ C74/31; Commission communication concerning the extension of the Guidelines on state aid for rescuing and restructuring firms in difficulty [1999] OJ C67/11; Community Guidelines on state aid for rescuing and restructuring firms in difficulty (Notice to Member States including proposals for appropriate measures) [1999] OJ C288/2; Corrigendum to the Community guidelines on state aid for rescuing and restructuring firms in difficulty [2000] OJ C121/29.

[72] Guidelines on National Regional Aid 2007-2013, OJ 2006 C54/13.

[73] Guidelines on state aid for undertakings in deprived urban areas [1997] OJ C146/6; Commission notice on the expiry of the guidelines on state aid for undertakings in deprived urban areas (notified under document number C(2002) 1806) [2002] OJ C119/21.

[74] Communication from the Commission, *Community Guidelines on State Aid for Rescuing and Restructuring Firms in Difficulty* [2004] OJ C244/02.

Additionally there are specific *sectoral* rules which adapt Community Guidelines and rules to take account of sectoral features in the audiovisual,[75] postal services,[76] public service broadcasting,[77] electricity,[78] transport,[79] agriculture and fisheries,[80] shipbuilding,[81] steel,[82] synthetic fibres[83] and coal[84] sectors.

A Member State may also ask for direct assessment of a proposed state aid under Article 87(3) EC if it is unsure if its proposals fall squarely within a Block Exemption or Guideline.

The plethora of policy rules has led to a jungle of official communications and soft and hard law governing the procedure and substance of state aid regulation in the EU. A central aim of the *State Aid Action Plan*, therefore, is to simplify and rationalise this *ad hoc* growth of soft law guidance.

Block Exemptions

The EC Commission's use of soft law has prepared the way for more detailed and binding Regulations to be used in the areas where there is consensus on the most appropriate form of state intervention in sensitive areas of the Member States' economy. Article 89 EC allows the Council to make appropriate regulations for the application of Articles 87 and 88 EC, in particular, to determine the

---

[75] Communication from the Commission to the Council, the European Parliament, the Economic and Social Committee and the Committee of the Regions on the follow-up to the Commission Communication on certain legal aspects relating to cinematographic and other audiovisual works (Cinema communication) [2004] OJ C123/1; Communication from the Commission to the Council, the European Parliament, the Economic and Social Committee and the Committee of the Regions on certain legal aspects relating to cinematographic and other audiovisual works [2002] OJ C43/6.

[76] Notice from the Commission on the application of the competition rules to the postal sector and on the assessment of certain State measures relating to postal services [1998] OJ C39/2.

[77] Available at:
http://eur-ex.europa.eu/LexUriServ/LexUriServ.do?uri=CELEX:52001XC1115(01):EN:NOT.

[78] Commission Communication relating to the methodology for analysing State aid linked to stranded costs, Commission letter, SG(2001)D/290869 of 6 Aug 2001.

[79] See http://ec.europa.eu/dgs/energy_transport/state_aid/transport_en.htm.

[80] See http://ec.europa.eu/agriculture/stateaid/index_en.htm.

[81] Commission Communication concerning the prolongation of the Framework on State aid to shipbuilding [2006] OJ C260/7.

[82] Communication from the Commission: Rescue and restructuring aid and closure aid for the steel sector, OJ 2002 C 70/21; An aid prohibition for investment projects in the steel industry [2002] OJ C70/8; Communication from the Commission concerning certain aspects of the treatment of competition cases resulting from the expiry of the ECSC Treaty [2002] OJ C152/5.

[83] Previously, several sensitive industrial sectors have been subject to specific, stricter rules on state aid, eg, *a Code on aid to the synthetic fibres and Community framework on State aid to the motor vehicle industry*. Rules in sensitive industrial sectors have been included within the multi-sectoral framework on regional aid for large investment projects through its latest revision. Sectors where serious structural problems prevail have been specified in the following Communication modifying the framework: *Commission Communication on the modification of the multi-sectoral Framework on regional aid for large investment projects (2002) with regard to the establishment of a list of sectors facing structural problems and on a proposal of appropriate measures pursuant to Article 88 paragraph 1 of the EC Treaty, concerning the motor vehicle sector and the synthetic fibres sector* [2003] OJ C263/3.

[84] See http://ec.europa.eu/dgs/energy_transport/state_aid/energy_en.htm.

conditions for when Article 88(3) EC applies and the categories of aid exempted from this procedure. The Council has delegated this power to the EC Commission in Regulation 994/98/EC[85] enabling the EC Commission to adopt block exemptions in relation to small and medium-sized undertakings (SMEs), environmental protection, employment and training.

DEROGATION FROM THE STATE AID RULES FOR TRADE IN ARMS AND WAR MATERIAL

In 1957 the Member States recognised that they should retain sovereignty over a number of matters which concerned national defence and security. Article 296(1)(b) EC subjects the production of and trade in arms, munitions and war materials to special rules. A list of the materials covered by this Article was drawn up by the Council on 15 April 1958 and is referred to in Article 296(2) EC. The Member States enjoy a wide discretion in assessing which matters of national defence and security should be protected by this provision.[86]

Article 296 EC is part of the final provisions of the EC Treaty and is therefore capable of affecting all of the general EC Treaty provisions, including the rules on competition and free movement. A Member State is not required to notify to the EC Commission any measures which are covered by Article 296(2) EC. The EC Commission has the power to ensure that the measure does not adversely affect the conditions of competition in the Common Market in relation to any products which are not intended specifically for military purposes. A special procedure is set out in Article 298(1) EC whereby the EC Commission must work with the Member State to see how any measures which distort competition can be adjusted.

THE ROLE OF THE EC COMMISSION

The EC Commission plays a central role in the control of state aid in the EU. Under powers granted to the EC Commission by Article 88(3) EC the Member States must notify proposed state aid which does not fall within the EC Treaty exemptions or the block exemptions or the EC Commission Decision relating to aid to Services of General Economic Interest to the EC Commission in advance for approval. Any aid which is put into operation without notification is unlawful *per se* and must be repaid with interest. Until 1999 the procedures for notifying state aid were not officially formalised. This allowed for flexibility and a certain amount of diplomatic negotiation between the EC Commission and the Member State, but also created problems for legal certainty. Now detailed rules on

---

[85]   [1998] OJ L142/1.
[86]   Case T–26/01 *Fiocchi Munizioni SpA v Commission* [2003] ECR II–3951, para 58.

notification and other procedural issues codified from the European Courts' case law are set out in Council Regulation (EC) 659/1999[87] and Commission Regulation (EC) 794/2004.[88]

The last sentence of Article 88(3) EC gives rise to direct effects giving national courts a role in enforcing state aid. This may exist concurrently with an EC Commission investigation.[89] For example, national courts can grant injunctions and award damages where there is unlawful state aid.[90] Recently the Court has indicated that Article 88(3) EC must be interpreted as meaning that national courts should safeguard the rights of individuals against possible disregard, by the national authorities, of the prohibition on putting aid into effect before the EC Commission has adopted a Decision authorising that aid. In doing so, the national court must take the Community interest fully into consideration and must not adopt a measure which would have the sole effect of extending the circle of recipients of the aid.[91] A failure to follow this obligation could give rise to a *Francovich* liability for the national court.

The EC Commission has the power to order the recovery of illegal state aid with interest.

DIFFERENT CLASSIFICATIONS OF AID

Existing Aid

Existing aid comprises aid which was granted before the entry into force of the EEC Treaty, or aid applied by a Member State before accession to the EU, or aid which has been authorised by the EC Commission. Under Article 88(1) EC the Member States are under a duty to keep existing aid under constant review. Existing aid cannot be challenged in the national courts, but a complaint can be brought before the EC Commission. It is for the EC Commission to propose measures for amendment or withdrawal of the aid if it is no longer compatible with the Common Market.[92] If the Member State contests the proposals the EC Commission may start a formal examination of the aid under Article 88(2) EC.

---

[87]   [1999] OJ L83/1.

[88]   [2004] OJ L140/1.

[89]   Case C–39/94 *SFEI* [1996] ECR I–3547. See *Commission Communication on the cooperation between national courts and the Commission in the field of State aids* [1995] OJ C312/8; M Ross, 'State Aids and National Courts: Definitions and Other Problems—a Case of Premature Emancipation?' (2000) 37 *CMLRev* 401.

[90]   Case C–354/90 *Fedération Nationale du Commerce Extérieur des Produits Alimentaaires and Syndicat National des Négociants et Transformateurs de Saumoin v France* [1991] ECR I–55053.

[91]   Case C–368/04 *Transalpine Ölleitung in Österreich GmbH, Planai-Hochwurzen-Bahnen GmbH, Gerlitzen-Kanzelbahn-Touristik GmbH & Co. KG v Finanzlandesdirektion für Tirol, Finanzlandesdirektion für Steiermark, Finanzlandesdirektion für Kärnten* [2006] ECRI-9957.

[92]   Art 18 of Reg 659/99/EC [1999] OJ L 83/1.

New Aid

New aid is aid granted after the EEC Treaty came into force and after accession for new Member States. It also covers amendments to existing aid. This may create uncertainty about which procedural rules apply. New aid should be notified to the EC Commission, except where it falls within the block exemptions[93] or is safely covered by one of the filter tests described above. New aid must be notified to the EC Commission before it can be put into operation.[94] Given that it can take up to 22 months for an EC Commission Decision to materialise, Member States must carefully plan their state aid proposals.

The EC Commission must conduct an initial examination of the aid and decide whether it is compatible with the Common Market or open a preliminary examination procedure.[95] This operates as a standstill mechanism; the aid cannot be put into operation until the EC Commission has taken a final Decision. The EC Commission must act within two months. If it makes a positive decision that the aid is compatible with the Common Market the Member State may proceed with the aid. If the Decision is negative the Member State may appeal the Decision to the CFI. The EC Commission can buy more time by opening the procedure set out in Article 88(2) EC. The Member State may also contest this Decision using Article 230 EC.[96]

Under Article 88(2) EC there is a wider inquiry as to the potential effects of the proposed aid. Thus competitors and others who will be affected by the aid, as well as interest groups (environmentalists, consumers, for example) have a right to make comments. By doing so the interested parties may create *locus standi* to challenge a negative Decision by the EC Commission.[97] The EC Commission must adopt a final Decision within 18 months. Where the EC Commission fails to act, the Member State may call upon the EC Commission to act within two months. The EC Commission's Decision is subject to judicial review by the CFI, with an appeal on a point of law to the Court of Justice.

Accession Aid

The enlargement of the EU on 1 May 2004 created new problems for state aid control because eight out of the 10 Accession States have only recently become market economies. There is still a political tendency for these states to look to state intervention in the market as an economic, political and social policy tool.

---

[93]   Although to ensure that the EC Commission can monitor all aid the Member State must send a summary outline of the aid to the EC Commission.

[94]   Reg 794/2004 [2004] OJ L 140/1 sets out the notification form.

[95]   Arts 88(3) and 4 EC.

[96]   Case C–312/90 *Spain v Commission* [1992] ECR I–4117; Case C–47/91 *Italy v Commission* [1992] ECR I–4145.

[97]   See, eg, Case C–367/95 P *Commission v Chambre Syndicale (Sytravel)* [1998] ECR I–1719.

When Austria, Finland and Sweden acceded to the EU their state aid had been subject to the EFTA Surveillance Authority, and therefore the 2004 Accession required a different approach. The EU used a system of close monitoring of state aid in the Accession Reports which took place in the run up to the enlargement in 2004. Under the Europe Agreements, which were the bilateral framework agreements between the EU and each candidate country establishing the legal framework for the adaptation of national legislation to the *acquis communautaire*, each Accession State had to adopt and implement a national state aid law and a national authority responsible for state aid.

The EC Commission approved a series of transitional state aids to address particular problems associated with accession. In particular aid was needed to support the financial sector, coal, steel, agriculture, and the new Accession States continue to direct aid towards particular sectors, rather than implementing the Lisbon and Stockholm objectives of directing aid towards *horizontal projects*. Additionally many Accession States use incentive measures, such as tax breaks, to encourage inward investment.

Procedures were put in place to deal with the special problems posed by the Accession States.[98] Where state aid was identified as incompatible with the Common Market the Accession States had to adapt or abolish the aid. In order to prevent incompatible state aid continuing after enlargement a new surveillance mechanism covering all sectors, except for transport and agriculture, was introduced, known as the 'existing aid' mechanism. In transport and agriculture measures could be counted as existing aid provided that they were notified to the EC Commission by 31 August 2004. These measures enjoy the protection of a sunset clause, which allows the new Member States a longer period of time, until April 2007, to ensure the compatibility of the measures with Community law.

During the first phase of this surveillance mechanism in 2002 some 222 measures were approved by the EC Commission and listed in the Treaty of Accession. During the second phase a new mechanism called the 'interim procedure' approved some 278 measures as existing aid. New state aid measures were notified to the EC Commission until 30 April 2004 and a number of state aid measures from this period continue to be assessed by the EC Commission. There was an incentive for the Accession States to bring their state aid into effect before 1 May 2004. Any state aid granted after that date becomes new aid. The total state aid granted by the Accession States in the four years before 1 May 2004 was some 5.7 billion euros per year. Three Accession States, Poland, the Czech Republic and Hungary, accounted for 86 per cent of this aid.

The Treaty of Accession uses the distinctions between 'existing aid' and 'new aid' which are found in the EC Treaty. The EC Commission will not necessarily approve aid which was approved by national authorities prior to accession.

---

[98] J Kankanen, 'Accession Negotiations Brought to Successful Conclusion', *Competition Policy Newsletter* No. 1 (2003); G Roebling, 'Existing Aid and Enlargement', *Competition Policy Newsletter* No. 1 (2003), available at http://europa.eu.int/comm/competition/publications/cpn/.

Existing aid is aid which existed prior to entry into force of the Accession Treaty and has not changed materially in the interim. Such aid also embraces aid which has been authorised by the EC Commission or the Council (or is deemed so authorised) or is aid which has been paid prior to the 10-year limitation period set out in Article 15 of Regulation 659/1999. This aid was listed in Annex IV, Chapter 3 to the Accession Treaty.

To be included in Annex 4, the measure had to have been reviewed and approved by the national authority, and the EC Commission did not object to the measure in the framework of the information and consultation mechanisms established by the Europe Agreements. Annex 4 was closed on 1 November 2002. From November 2002 until 1 May 2004 a transitional period was in operation and a second list of approved existing aid measures was to be adopted. Aid granted prior to 10 December 1994 is deemed to be existing aid *per se*.

THE *DE MINIMIS* PRINCIPLE

The effect of state aid on competition and trade is relatively under-explored in the European Courts' jurisprudence. Indeed where state aid has been granted in breach of the procedural rules of the EC Treaty, the EC Commission does not have to provide an exact economic analysis of *how* trade and competition are affected, since to require this would confer procedural advantages upon the Member States.[99] The selectivity of aid is sufficient to draw the conclusion that competition will be distorted. Operating aids are deemed to always distort competition. The Court has not been willing to apply a *de minimis* principle, and therefore even a small distortion of competition law will bring into play the state aid rules. Similarly the effect on trade does not have to be appreciable. For example, in the *Altmark*[100] case it was argued that the alleged aid involved only local operations, and yet the Court dismissed the use of a *de minimis* principle.[101] In contrast, the EC Commission recognises the *de minimis* principle, believing that small amounts of aid may be beneficial and have a negligible impact on trade between Member States. This policy has developed from Guidelines and a Notice to a piece of hard law, Regulation 69/2001.[102] This Regulation was revised in December 2006 by Regulation 1998/2006 which came into operation on 1 January 2007.[103] The Regulation exempts small subsidies from the obligation to notify; aid of up to 200,000 euros granted over any period of three years will not be considered state aid. Loan guarantees will also be covered to the extent that the guaranteed part of the loan does not exceed 1.5 million euros. In order to avoid

---

[99]   Case T–214/95 *Het Vlaamse Gewest (Flemish Region) v Commission* [1998] ECR II–717.

[100]   Case C–280/00 *Altmark* [2003] ECR I–7747.

[101]   Case C–351/98 *Spain v Commission* [2002] ECR I–8031, para 51.

[102]   Commission Reg (EC) 69/2001 of 12 Jan 2001 on the application of Arts 87 and 88 of the EC Treaty to *de minimis* aid [2001] OJ L10/30.

[103]   [2006] OJ L 379/5.

abuses, forms of aid for which the inherent aid amount cannot be calculated precisely in advance ('non-transparent' aids) and aid to firms in difficulty have been excluded from the Regulation. In 2003 the then Commissioner, Mario Monti, indicated that the EC Commission would focus upon major state aid cases and issued two proposals for allowing small amounts of state aid to be used without notification to the EC Commission.[104] These ideas were incorporated into the reform of state aid in the *State Action Plan* and are implemented through Regulation 69/2001.

A *de minimis* approach is used under the package of measures to regulate payments for the provision of services of general economic interest.[105] Compensation which is less than 30 million euros *per annum* paid to undertakings with an annual turnover of less than 100 million euros, or is paid to hospitals, social housing undertakings or certain small air or maritime undertakings, airports and posts providing a service of general economic interest does not have to be notified to the EC Commission. Larger amounts of compensation must be notified to the EC Commission, and the Framework sets out the conditions under which Article 86(2) EC may apply. Under Article 86(2) EC the rules on state aid apply to services of general economic interest only to the extent that the rules do not obstruct the performance of the services, in law and in fact. Even when Article 86(2) EC can apply, the development of trade must not be affected to an extent that would be contrary to Community interests.

PORTUGUESE PIGS AND THE BATTLE FOR COMPETENCE

Article 88(2) EC is an unusual provision, giving the Member States limited access, by way of a *derogation* from the EC Commission's competence, to regulating state aid. On the application of a Member State concerned by a state aid measure the Council may use a unanimous vote to decide that a state aid is compatible with the Common Market if such a decision is justified by *exceptional* circumstances. Although the provision is little used, since it can apply only in exceptional situations,[106] the EC Commission will usually challenge any resort to Article 88(2) EC in order to exert its central position in the regulation of state

---

[104] These covered a limited amount of state aid (LASA) and a limited effect on trade (LET) but were criticised because of the complexity of the rules surrounding the way in which the aid could be given.

[105] Commission Framework (adopted on 13 July 2005) for state aid in the form of public service compensation [2005] OJ C297/4; Commission Dec of 13 July 2005 on the application of Art 86(2) of the Treaty to state aid in the form of public service compensation granted to certain undertakings entrusted with the operation of services of general economic interest [2005] OJ L312/67.

[106] Statistics can be found in the Opinion of Cosmos AG in Case C–122/94 *Commission v Council* [1996] ECR I–881. There were no decisions between 1960 and 1967; 14 between 1967 and 1983 and 23 between 1984 and 1994.

aid. The provision is used mainly in the agricultural sector, although in recent years it has been used in ancillary areas linked to the agricultural sector[107] and also in the transport sector.[108]

In the *Portuguese Pigs* case the Court limited the role of the Council under Article 88(2) EC. The facts concerned a Decision adopted by the Council on 21 January 2002, authorising Portugal to pay a group of pig farmers state aid which was equivalent to an aid they had already received under what the EC Commission had deemed to be an illegal state aid scheme.[109] The Council accepted that there were exceptional circumstances since the economic viability of a number of pig farmers was threatened by the withdrawal of the aid. This would have social effects in certain regions because 50 per cent of the pig farming was concentrated in less than 5 per cent of the geographical area of Portugal. The Court agreed with the Advocate General and the EC Commission that Article 88(2) EC could not be used to declare compatible with the Common Market aid which the EC Commission had deemed to be incompatible. Similarly the Court held that Article 88(2) EC cannot be used to declare compatible with the Common Market *new aid* which was designed to compensate the beneficiaries of unlawful aid to cover the cost of repaying the illegal state aid. The Court was concerned to secure the effectiveness of state aid regulation, a task entrusted to the EC Commission under Articles 87 and 88 EC.[110]

TIME LIMITS FOR RECOVERY OF ILLEGAL STATE AID

There are no time limits set for recovery of illegal state aid in Regulation 659/1999. Article 14(3) of the Regulation requires recovery to be effected without delay and in accordance with procedures under national law. The EC Commission duplicates this language in its recovery Decisions, adding a rider that the Member State should inform the EC Commission within two months of the

[107] Council Dec of 16 July 2003 on the compatibility with the common market of an aid that the Italian Republic intends to grant to its milk producers [2003] OJ L184/15 and Council Dec of 16 July 2003 on the granting of aid by the Belgian Government to certain coordination Centres established in Belgium [2003] OJ L184/17. These coordination centres were subject an Order of the President of the Court of 26 June 2003 in Joined Cases C–182/03 R & C–217/03 R *Belgium and Forum 187 ASBL v Commission* [2003] ECR I–6887, paras 51–52.

[108] Council Dec 3 May 2002 on the granting of a national aid by the authorities of the Kingdom of The Netherlands in favour of road transport undertakings [2002] OJ L131/12; Council Dec of 3 May 2002 on the granting of a national aid by the authorities of the Italian Republic in favour of road transport undertakings [2002] OJ L131/14; Council Dec of 3 May 2002 on the granting of aid by the French government for road transport undertakings [2002] OJ L131/15.

[109] Case C-110/02 *Commission Council* [2004] ECR I-6333. Commission Dec 2000/200/EC [2000] OJ L66/20; Commission Dec 2001/86/EC [2001] OJ L29/49.

[110] See also Joined Cases 102/03 & 207/03 *Belgium v Commission* [2006] ECR I-5479 where the Court annulled an EC Commission decision for failing to set out a transitional period for the authorisation of tax co-ordination centres.The case involved a Council Decision taken under Art 88(2) EC after the EC Commission had taken a final Decision finding the aid in question to be incompatible with the Common Market.

notification of the Decision of the measures taken to comply with it. The Court has held that this form of wording obliges the Member States only to inform the EC Commission within two months of the measures already taken, and measures planned to recover the illegal aid. It does not impose a duty upon the Member States to implement the measures within two months.[111] In addition to the recovery of the illegal aid interest at the customary market rate must be levied on the aid from the time of its grant to repayment. The EC Commission's *State Action Plan*, alongside studies commissioned,[112] reveals that this is weakness in the enforcement of the state aid rules.

THE ROLE OF THE EUROPEAN COURTS

The European Courts have contributed to the procedural rules where Decisions or inaction on the part of the EC Commission are challenged. Where a Member State is the addressee of a Decision it will have *locus standi* to challenge the Decision under Article 230(1) EC. In recent years there has been a significant rise in individual, third party complaints where the applicant must satisfy the rigorous conditions of Article 230(4) EC. Under individual aid schemes beneficiaries always have *locus standi*. The beneficiary may also challenge an initiation EC Commission Decision which characterises a measure as new, aid since the Member State must then suspend the implementation of the aid until a final Decision has been taken. In *Forum 187 I* [113] the CFI held that an initiation Decision which recognises that the measure is existing aid cannot be challenged separately because the legal position of the beneficiary is not affected until the EC Commission issues a final negative Decision declaring the aid to be incompatible with the Common Market.[114]

Competitors may bring an action against an EC Commission Decision not to initiate a formal investigation where the EC Commission has concluded that the measure is not a state aid or, if it is, it is compatible with the Common Market.[115] A direct competitor[116] will have similar rights where state aid has been approved.[117] This is because the procedural rights of the competitor, as well as its

---

[111] Case C–499/99 *Commission v Spain* [2002] ECR I–6031.
[112] Available at: http://ec.europa.eu/comm/competition/state_aid/studies_reports/studies_reports.html.
[113] Order in Case T–276/02 *Forum 187 ASBL v Commission* [2003] ECR II–2075.
[114] See Art 18 of Reg 659/1999 [1999] OJ L 83/1.
[115] Case C–367/95 *Commission v Chambre Syndicale nationale des entreprises de transport de fonds et valuers (Sytravel) and Brink's France SARL* [1998] ECR I–1719, para 62.
[116] Case T–69/96 *Hamburger Hafen-und Lagerhaus Aktiengesellschaft Zentralverband der Deutschen Seehafenbetriebe eV and Unternehmensverband Hafen Hamburg eV v Commission* [2001] ECR II–1037; Order in Case T–41/01 *Rafael Pérez Escolar v Commission* [2003] ECR II–2157 and Order in Case C–379/03 P *Rafael Pérez Escolar v Commission* 1 October 2004 [2005] OJ C19/10.
[117] Case T–11/95 *BP Chemicals Ltd. v Commission* [1998] ECR II–3235, paras 78–81.

economic position, are affected by the EC Commission's Decisions. The competitor has the burden of showing *how* its position is affected[118] and must show the adverse effect of the aid on its competitive position, showing a causal link between the aid and the adverse effect. The competitor does not have to show that trade between the Member States is affected by the (alleged) state aid[119] In *Cook*[120] Advocate General Tesauro argued that an applicant contesting an EC Commission Decision to raise no objections to an aid under Article 88(3) EC has limited information, and therefore the onus of proving that it was a competitor competing genuinely and not marginally with the firm receiving the aid was not as onerous as normal rules for third party rights to *locus standi* normally required under Article 230 EC.

Competitors have also been given rights to challenge an approval of state aid after a formal investigation, but have a higher hurdle to leap in order to show *locus standi*:[121]

> not only the undertaking in receipt of the aid but also the undertakings competing with it which have played an active role in the procedure opened pursuant to Article 88(2) EC in respect of an individual aid have been recognised as being individually concerned by the Commission decision closing that procedure, provided that their position on the market is substantially affected by the aid which is the subject of the contested decision.[122]

Here the firm must show a more individualised effect of the EC Commission's Decision, for example, its participation in the investigation or a substantial effect of the decision on its position on the market.

Where general state aid schemes are concerned the test for individual concern to establish *locus standi* is even stricter, even where the applicant has made an initial complaint to the EC Commission.[123] In *ADL and Hapag Lloyd*[124] standing was denied to beneficiaries of a tax scheme where the EC Commission had taken a Decision prohibiting the scheme. Hapag Lloyd had actively participated in the formal investigation procedure but could not show that it was sufficiently individualised from other beneficiaries of the tax scheme.[125] In contrast the CFI held that it was sufficient that the applicant:

---

[118] Case T–188/95 *Waterleiding Maatschappij 'North-West Brabant' NV v Commission* [1998] ECR II–3713, paras 62–64.

[119] Case T–158/99 *Thermenhotel Stoiser Franz Gesellschaft mbH & Co KG and others v Commission* [2004] ECR II–1, paras 75–76.

[120] Case C–198/91 *William Cook plc v Commission* [1993] ECR I–2487.

[121] Case T–11/95 *BP Chemicals Ltd v Commission* [1998] ECR II–3235, paras 78–81; see also: Order of the President of the Court in Case T–358/02 *Deutsche Post AG and DHL v Commission*, [2004] ECR II–1565, paras 34 ff.

[122] Case 169/84 *Cofaz SA and others v Commission* [1986] ECR 391, paras 24–25.

[123] Case T–398/94 *Kahn Scheppvaart BV v Commission* [1996] ECR II–477.

[124] Case T–86/96 *Arbeitsgemeinschaft Deutscher Luftfahrt-Unternehmen and Hapag-Lloyd v Commission* [1999] ECR II–179.

[125] Cf Case C–313/90 *CIRFS and others v Commission* [1993] ECR I–1125.

played an active part in the formal review procedure which led to the adoption of the decision and in the informal discussions relating to its implementation, doing so in many different active ways and producing scientific reports in support of its case.[126]

Here it was held that the applicant influenced the decision-making process and was a useful source of information. There are arguments that the European Courts should look for a consistent approach to standing, not differentiating between whether the Decision was taken before or after the formal investigation procedure.[127]

Where the state aid has been granted under a general aid scheme and the EC Commission has made a recovery order the beneficiaries are individually concerned and have standing to challenge the EC Commission's Decision.[128] The CFI has also allowed an interest group to bring such an action.[129] Where individuals are successful in their action the annulment of the EC Commission's Decision is applicable only to the applicant. Thus it is administratively more practical for a Member State to bring an annulment action where, if successful, the Decision would be annulled *vis-à-vis* all beneficiaries of the general aid scheme.

Action for Failure to Act: Article 232(3) EC

Where the EC Commission initiates the preliminary procedure but fails to adopt a Decision within a reasonable period of time, the complainant and any other interested parties to the formal investigation procedure may bring an action for failure to act under Article 232(2) EC. The same hurdles for standing apply. A series of cases concerning complaints by private broadcasters challenging state aid awarded to public broadcasters reveal the limitations of giving the EC Commission a central role in the monitoring and enforcement of state aid.[130] As we shall see in the next chapter, public service broadcasting is a sensitive political issue where there are allegations that the financing of public service broadcasters infringe the state aid rules. The EC Commission was reluctant to act on these complaints, and over six years elapsed from the initial complaints made by the competitors of the public service broadcasters. The EC Commission eventually stated that on the information available it could take no action as it was unsure if the aid was new aid or existing aid. The competitors brought an action under

---

[126] Case T–114/00 [2002] ECR II–5121, para 66.
[127] Cf Case C–78/03P *Commission v ARE* [2005] ECR I–10737, where the Court explains the difference between the preliminary stage of the EC Commission's investigation and the formal stage.
[128] Joined Cases C–15/98 & C–105/99 *Italy, Sardegna Lines and Servizi Maritimi della Sardegna SpA v Commission* [2000] ECR I–8855.
[129] Case T–55/99 *CETM v Commission* [2000] ECR II–3207.
[130] Case T–95/96 *Gestevision Telecinco SA v Commission* [1998] ECR II–3407; Case T–17/96 *TF1 v Commission* [1999] ECR II–1757 (appeal dismissed in Joined Cases C–302/99 P & C–308/99 P *Commission and France v Télévision française 1 SA* [2001] ECR I–2125.

Article 232 EC and the CFI upheld the complaint.[131] Even after the CFI judgment the EC Commission failed to take action, and therefore another action was taken against the EC Commission for failure to act. The EC Commission eventually informed the competitors that it had taken a decision to investigate certain state aid measures paid to the public broadcaster, RTP. In a formal Decision taken in April 2002 the EC Commission stated that the aid measures could be justified under Article 86(2) EC, provided they did not over-compensate for the costs of providing a public service by the public broadcaster, RTP. A formal investigation was commenced but this did not cover the annual compensation measures paid to the public broadcaster. Instead the EC Commission avoided classifying the annual compensation scheme as a new aid by requesting information from Portugal under Article 10(3) of Regulation 659/1999, publishing this request in the Official Journal, even though the Regulation does not require such a publication.[132] The Article 232 EC action continued, but the CFI ruled that the EC Commission had been called upon to act, and had acted; thus the action was devoid of purpose.[133]

CONCLUSION

During the 1990s the state aid provisions of the EU were transformed from the Cinderella of competition law to a significant tool in controlling state intervention in the economy. State aid enforcement continues to be politically motivated, and some firms continue to be reluctant to challenge state aid, fearing economic and political reprisals. However, the cross-border effects of state aid have motivated the EC Commission to take a closer look at the distortive effects of illegal aid, and liberalisation has also motivated foreign firms to scrutinise their competitors' finances, especially where there is an incumbent operating in the market.

Attempts have been made by the EC Commission and the European Courts to get to grips with illegitimate forms of state aid which will hamper the integration process, and to draw brighter lines for the use of intelligent state aid which may contribute to meeting the targets set for the Lisbon Process. Thus enforcement priorities have changed. Loans or capital injections in failed companies are no longer seen as acceptable, and other forms of aid are subject to greater scrutiny, particularly in the areas of state guarantees, subsidies for services of general economic interest, tax measures, social contributions and the legitimacy of alleged research and development or regional aid. However, the state aid tools have also become the central policy tool around which the provision of services of general economic interest in liberalised and competitive markets has been mediated, allowing them to modernise and continue to operate.

---

[131]   Joined Cases T–297/01 & T–298/01 *SIC SA v Commission* [2004] ECR I–743.
[132]   [2002] OJ C98/2.
[133]   Above n 131.

As we saw in Chapter 1, state aid is still a sensitive political issue and has become a significant concern in the Lisbon Process. State aid has been subjected to greater proceduralisation and transparency, and it is no longer the preserve of the EC Commission. Recently competitors, consumers, interest groups and NGOs have sought to gain standing to challenge the EC Commission's monitoring and enforcement powers. During the 1990s the EC Commission was able to introduce a number of policies in the field of state aid and obtained the Member States' approval for these by the use of soft law processes. Aid for sensitive social issues has been mediated through EC Commission Guidelines, and eventually a framework for granting aid to provide services of general economic interest was possible. The result of these processes is that now there is a plethora of rules, hard and soft, and the EC Commission is now consolidating these new policy directions in a modernisation programme.

7

Services of General Economic Interest

DEFINITIONS

THE TERM 'SERVICES of general economic interest' is used in the EU to describe a myriad of services, traditionally provided by the state and/or public and private bodies, which are delivered within the territory of each state for the use of individuals, public bodies and commercial entities. The term finds expression in the EC Treaty in Articles 16 and 86(2) EC but it is not defined. Within the EU, in soft law, hard law and case law, the term often embraces, and is interchangeable with, other ideas of 'services of general interest', 'universal service obligations' and 'public service obligations'[1] and, as they are known in the United Kingdom, 'public services'.[2] The term 'services of general economic interest' refers to services of an *economic* nature which the Member State and/or the EU subjects to specific *public service obligations* by virtue of a general interest criterion. A better definition of the term would be the provision of 'economic services which are in the general interest'. Such services may include the traditional services provided by network utility industries, broadcasting, education, social and healthcare sectors. Newer ideas of such services involve access to financial services and internet services. A new term, 'services of general interest'. has emerged in the Community soft law discourse. This is a broad term and refers to any activity which the public authorities classify as being of general interest and subject to specific public service obligations.[3] Such goods and services are either regulated or provided by the public sphere.

---

[1] For a discussion of the various terms see EC Commission, Green Paper on Services of General Interest, COM(2003) 270 final, 21 May 2003, and Communication From the Commission to the European Parliament, The Council, The European Economic and Social Committee and the Committee of the Regions White Paper on Services of General Interest, COM(2004)374 final, 12 May 2004. In the light of the Council agreement on a Directive liberalising services in Europe, the Socialist Group of the European Parliament, in May 2006 put forward a proposal for a Community definition of services of general interest. See http://www.socialistgroup.eu/gpes/policydetail.do?lg=en&id=594.

[2] According to the EC Commission, the use of the term 'public service' is too imprecise and may cause confusion: see The White Paper, *ibid.*

[3] *Ibid*, at 9.

In economic terms public goods are somewhat different from services of general economic interest. Public goods are non-rivalrous in that the consumption of the goods by one person does not reduce the possibilities of others using or consuming the good. Examples of public goods are street lighting, or defence or some kinds of preventive medicine. Economists argue that it is difficult, or impossible, to exclude anyone from using the goods, and hence making a consumer pay for the goods. Thus, as a result, public goods are not normally provided by the market but are provided publicly and justify some form of state intervention. However, in the light of the liberalisation and privatisation processes a number of core services of general economic interest are now provided by the private sector and under market conditions. These markets are often tightly regulated.

The EU has forced a new institutional design upon the regulation of such services at the national and the EU level. In the light of these changes various pressure groups,[4] non-governmental organisations and the European Parliament[5] have called upon the EU to create a Charter for Services of General Economic Interest, particularly in relation to issues of accessibility and quality of such services. The response of the EU has been *ad hoc* and resulted in fragmentation with different regulatory models, bound by a set of loose common themes and principles.[6]

CITIZENSHIP

Services of general economic interest play an important role in the lives of the citizens of Europe, non-Member State nationals living and working within the

[4] See, *inter alia*, ETUC, 'Towards a Framework Directive on Services of General Economic Interest', available at http://www.etuc.org/a/2477; Social Platform, Declaration on Services of General Interest and the European Convention, available at http://www.socialplatform.org/module/FileLib/DeclarationENfin.doc; CELSIG, available at http://www.celsig.org/indexGB.htm.

[5] See the Resolution on the Communications from the Commission on services of general interest in Europe: 'The European Parliament considers that services of general interest are based on the principles of continuity, solidarity, equal access and treatment for all users, overall economic efficiency, concern for long-term needs and the management of non-renewable or rare resources. It points out that these services give rise to constraints for the operators in the sectors concerned, and for the regulatory authorities. It welcomes the Commission communication, which expresses for the first time full recognition of public services in their European dimension. Parliament calls on the Commission to define the scope and nature of services of general interest, the principles that underpin them, and the level of services needed to reach the objectives of the European Union. It calls for the drawing up of an action plan, accompanied by a timetable, for translating Treaty objectives into policy. It also calls on the Commission to draw up a Charter of the principles governing services of general economic interest, containing their justification and principles, the type of missions and rights to be given to operators and a list of sectors where the notion should apply.' COM(96)443, C4-0507/96, A4-0357/1997), available at: http://www.europarl.europa.eu/comparl/libe/elsj/charter/default_en.htm

[6] For an analysis of the role of services of general economic interest see: *Services of General Economic Interest Opinion Prepared By the State Aid Group EACP*, 29 June 2006, available at http://ec.europa.eu/comm/dgs/competition/sgei.pdf.

EU and also commercial businesses operating within its territory. Indeed, somewhat paradoxically, while services of general economic interest are moving towards a closer conceptual understanding of their links with Citizenship in the EU, at the national level services of general economic interest are often valuable safety nets for non-citizens of the EU who are denied benefits under the Community law free movement provisions.

Increasingly services of general economic interest have come under attack from litigation using the competition and Internal Market provisions of the EC Treaty. The litigation exposes the fact that the EU lacks a clear strategy on *how* to promote and defend the role of such services in the newly liberalised, competitive economy. Article 86(2) EC is a central legal provision which allows for mediation between traditional state duties towards citizens and the demands of competitive markets. It has its limitations in that it is traditionally seen as a *derogation* from the fundamental economic freedoms and competition law, and therefore should be interpreted strictly. Additionally, Article 16 EC recognises that such services have a role to play in the future constitutional shape of Europe,and this EC Treaty provision is enhanced by the recognition of a right of *access* to services of general economic interest as one of the fundamental rights of the EU in Article 36 of the Charter of Fundamental Rights of the Union.[7] While of constitutional importance, neither provision provides a legal base to develop the role of public services in Europe. Yet in the EC Commission's various soft law communications on services of general economic interest it is emphasised that they constitute 'a key element in the European Model of Society'[8] and that 'general interest services are at the heart of the European Model of Society'.[9] It is recognised that such services may have far-reaching consequences, particularly in their redistributive effects, and this explains a tendency towards respecting the territorial nature of such services. However, the increasing impact of the EU on major social institutions and market regulation, as well as the level of public expenditure, economic, social and monetary policies in the Member States, alongside growing ideas of an EU notion of solidarity, has led Baquero Cruz to describe the EU regulation of services of general economic interest as 'contributing to the basic structure of a society of societies'.[10]

The White Paper on Services of General Interest claims that such services 'were also the subject of intense debate within the Convention on the future of

---

[7] Now forming Art II–36 of the Treaty establishing a Constitution for Europe 2004. At the time of writing, Dec 2006, the Treaty remains unratified.

[8] *Communication on Services of General Interest in Europe* [2001] OJ C17/4.

[9] *Services of General Interest in Europe* [1996] OJ C281/3.

[10] J Baquero Cruz, 'Beyond Competition: Services of General Interest and European Community Law' in G de Búrca (ed), *EU Law and the Welfare State In Search of Solidarity* (Oxford, OUP, 2005) at 169.

Europe',[11] but the issue of competence in the area of services of general economic interest was not seen as a priority. The Working Group on Social Europe could not agree on whether Article 16 EC should be amended to provide a legal base for EU level legislation on services of general economic interest,[12] and the resulting amendment to Article 16 in the Treaty establishing a Constitution for Europe, Article III–6, emphasised that services of general interest were subject to European law but did not provide the legal means for the enactment of such laws, opening up the possibility that the EU could be in breach of its fundamental duty to respect the role of such services in competitive markets in Europe.

The EC Commission has used a soft law discourse to promote a more clearly defined working relationship between the *aims* of services of general economic interest and the *operation* of the Internal Market in order to secure a clearer understanding of the constitutional foundations of the economic and political constitution of Europe.[13] This process has been interrupted by a series of attacks upon the provision of services of general economic interest using Article 86 EC and the state aid provisions in the national courts. The issue of whether financing of services of general economic interest can and should be regulated at European level has dominated the European political agenda throughout the 1990s and eventually has turned out to be the motivating factor for the EC Commission to introduce a limited form of regulation in this area. The sensitivity of the issue, combined with fundamental disagreements between the Member States, has stalled progress towards an acceptable comprehensive regulatory regime.[14] Yet, at the same time, services of general economic interest have been brought within the competence of Community law, largely as a result of negative integration processes when litigants challenge the anti-competitive effects of the national regulation of services of general interest, highlighting a regulatory gap in European integration described by Scharpf as 'the political decoupling of economic integration and social protection issues which has characterised the real process of European integration from Rome to Maastricht'.[15]

---

[11] *Communication From the Commission to the European Parliament, The Council, The European Economic and Social Committee and the Committee of the Regions White Paper on Services of General Interest,* COM(2004) 374 final, 12 May 2004, para 1.

[12] Final Report of Working Group XI on 'Social Europe', CONV 516/03. See Baquero Cruz, above n 10.

[13] *Commission Communication on Services of General Interest in Europe* [1996] OJ C281/3; *Commission Communication on Services of General Interest in Europe* [2001] OJ C17/4; *Commission Report to the Laeken European Council, Services of General Interest,* COM(2001)598 final.

[14] See *Communication From the Commission to the European Parliament, The Council, The European Economic and Social Committee and the Committee of the Regions White Paper on Services of General Interest,* COM(2004) 374 final, 12 May 2004, at para 4.1.

[15] F Scharpf, 'The European Social Model' (2002) 40 *Journal of Common Market Studies* 645, 646.

CULTURAL PERCEPTIONS OF SERVICES OF GENERAL ECONOMIC INTEREST

Historically services of general economic interest have been provided in different ways and are culturally specific.[16] They are an evolving concept, particularly as many of the traditional duties of the state have been liberalised and privatised, and it is acknowledged that some core services of general economic interest can be provided by both public and private operators. Similarly developments in the commercial sector may be deemed to be services of general economic interest which must be made available on accessible terms and prices to all users. One example is the issue of access to financial services. Another example is the use of the internet by governments as a tool of regional, social and education policy, through subsidisation of the instalment and use of this service. Services of general economic interest are also used to provide cohesion and stability to a society and play an important role in a state's social policy reflecting its political views and a society's values. In addition to access and availability of public services, continuity of supply is also a central theme in the delivery of services of general economic interest and, in the post 9/11 world, there is increased awareness of the need to protect essential services of general economic interest from terrorist attacks.[17]

Services of general economic interest can be grouped into broad families. France, the fiercest opponent of a competition-centred model of services of general economic interest has entrenched such services legally, institutionally and culturally. Other Member States, for example, Germany, Spain and Italy, use administrative law to regulate these services but have not entrenched them into constitutional law. Other Member States, most notably the United Kingdom, have been at the forefront of privatisation and opened up services of general economic interest markets to liberalisation, competition and privatisation, imposing few constraints on the application of the law of the market, as well as creating new hybrid forms of financing the provision of such services and their delivery. Today the issue of how much competition should be allowed in the provision of services of general economic interest is a political rather than a legal question, reinforced by the presence of Article 295 EC.

The creation of a European *idea* of services of general economic interest has largely been as a result of negative integration processes. In particular the use of Article 86(1) EC to attack public monopolies through the national courts and the use of Article 86(2) EC to defend services of general interest from the full rigour of the competition and free market rules. Within this process the European

---

[16] See T Prosser, *The Limits of Competition Law: Markets and Public Services* (Oxford, OUP, 2005); P Nebbia, *Unfair Contract Terms in European Law* (Oxford, Hart, 2007) ch 6.

[17] The vulnerability of services of general economic interest to attack by political groups (in the form of strikes) and terrorist groups is a recurring theme of European history. For a recent example of Community regulation see Reg (EC) No. 725/2004 of the European Parliament and of the Council of 31 Mar 2004 on enhancing ship and port facility security [2004] OJ L129/6.

Courts have created ideas of *how* services of general economic interest should be regulated and how they should perform in competitive markets. The EC Commission, through soft law processes, has built up a concept of a European idea of services of general economic interest, attempting a balance between national and EU competence. Legislative intervention has been through the use of concepts such as public service obligations and universal service obligations in the liberalisation processes, and more recently in finding ways in which the state may fund services of general economic interest that are compatible with the new attitudes towards state aid in the EU.

Thus we have only a partial concept of services of general economic interest at the EU level, complemented by national models. However, the litigation and debate over the role of services of general economic interest form part of a wider debate over the future economic and social constitution of Europe and the political battle over competing visions of the European Social Model.[18]

THE ROLE OF ARTICLE 86(2) EC

Article 86(2) EC states that undertakings entrusted with a service of general economic interest are subject to the rules of the EC Treaty in so far as those rules do not obstruct the provision of the service.[19] This provision has direct effect. Baquero Cruz has pointed out how the provision differs from other exemptions or justifications found in the EC Treaty and classifies Article 86(2) EC as a 'binary or switch-rule' that sets out the conditions when the normal, fundamental economic freedoms and competition rules of the EC Treaty should not be applied. The idea that Article 86(2) EC is an autonomous provision throws new light upon its interpretation, since the traditional view is that Article 86(2) EC is an exception to or derogation from fundamental economic clauses of the EC Treaty and should therefore be interpreted strictly as well as according to the principle of proportionality.[20] As we discovered in Chapter 4, Article 86 EC enjoyed a quiet life, with little litigation or academic interest in the provision until the 1990s. Then Article 86(2) EC became the battleground where the role of services of general economic interest was fought over. Paradoxically, this has elevated Article 86(2) EC from being a derogation in the EC Treaty to what Baquero Cruz describes as a 'judicially enforceable constitutional norm'.[21]

---

[18] A Sapir, 'Globalisation and the Reform of European Social Models', *bruegel policy brief*, Nov 2001, 1; C Boutayeb, 'Une récherche sur la place et les fonctions de l'intérêt général en droit communautaire' [2003] *Revue Trimestrelle de Droit Européen* 587, 607–8.

[19] A fuller discussion of Art 86 EC can be found in Ch 4.

[20] Case C–157/94 *Commission v Netherlands* [1997] ECR I–5699, para 37. See also: P Pescatore, 'Public and Private Aspects of European Community Competition Law' (1987) 10 *Fordham International Law Journal* 398; J Buendia Sierra, *Exclusive Rights and State Monopolies Under EC Law* (Oxford, OUP, 1999) at 300–36.

[21] J Baquero Cruz, *Between Competition and Free Movement: the Economic Constitutional Law of the European Community* (Oxford, Hart, 2002) at 76–80.

Article 86(2) EC is aimed at *undertakings* entrusted with the operation of a service of general economic interest. This may include non-state owned undertakings which have been entrusted with the task of providing a service of general economic interest.[22] It may also be used to justify state measures which are contrary to Article 86(1) EC.[23] Article 86(2) EC also applies to a revenue producing monopoly.

The concept of a service of general economic interest is a Community law concept and is capable of a wide definition, embracing the provision of goods as well as services.[24] In the Courts' case law the following have been found to be services of general interest: a river port; a public telecommunications network, water distribution, television services, electricity distribution, transport, employment recruitment, basic postal services, regional development and a supplementary pension fund.

The Member States have the discretion to decide which services of general economic interest they wish to promote. The Court has used the concept of an 'economic' activity as one of the screening devices for the application of the EC Treaty rules,[25] and thus the idea of a service of general economic interest may vary from Member State to Member State and may vary over time. The advent of privatisation has meant that in some Member States some services of general economic interest no longer exist, and changes in technology also show that at the national and the EU level the concept is a dynamic, and evolving, idea.[26] While much of the case law on Article 86(2) EC has turned upon the concept of economic activity[27] it is proportionality of the measures taken by the Member State which has proved, in recent years to be at the real heart of Article 86(2) EC.

The proportionality test is the fulcrum around which the application of Article 86(2) EC is balanced. Some Member States argued that the European Courts had applied the competition rules strictly when applying Article 86(2) EC, and this

---

[22] Case 127/73 *Belgische Radio en Televisie et société belge des auteurs, compositeurs et éditeurs v SV SABAM et NV Fonior (BRT II)* [1974] ECR 51, para 20; Case 172/80 *Gerhard Züchner v Bayerische Vereinsbank AG (Züchner)* [1981] ECR 2021, paras 6–7.

[23] Case 66/86 *Ahmed Saeed* [1989] ECR 853, paras 54 ff; Case C–41/90 *Höfner* [1991] ECR I–2017, paras 24–26;Case C–179/90 *Port of Genoa* [1991] ECR I–5926, paras 8–24; Case 18/88 *RTT* [1991] ECR I–5980, paras 21, 22 and 36; Case C–320/91 *Corbeau* [1993] ECR I–2568, paras 13 ff; Case C–159/94 *French Gas and Electricity Monopolies* [1997] ECR I–5815. The CFI has also confirmed this in Case T–106/95 *FFSA v Commission* [1997] ECR I–229.

[24] See A Deringer, 'Equal Treatment of Public and Private Enterprises. General Report' *Equal Treatment of Public and Private Enterprises* (Copenhagen, FIDE Congress, 1978).

[25] See, eg, Case C–364/92 *SAT Fluggesellschaft v Eurocontrol* [1994] ECR I–43 and Joined Cases C–264/01, C–306/01, C–354/01 & C–355/01 *AOK Bundesverband* [2004] ECR I–2493.

[26] Eg in Case 18/88 *RTT* [1991] ECR 5979, para 16 the Court states '[a]t *the present stage of development of the Community* [a] monopoly, which is intended to make a public telephone network available to users, constitutes a service of general economic interest within the meaning of [Article 86(2)] of the Treaty' (my emphasis). See also the EC Commission soft law discourse cited above in n 1.

[27] For a thorough analysis of the case law see J Buendia Sierra, *Exclusive Rights and State Monopolies Under EC Law* (Oxford, OUP, 1999), Pt III, ch 8.

justified the introduction of Article 16 EC to redress the balance in favour of the social dimension to services of general economic interest.

This is certainly true of the early case law.[28] The Court appears to argue for a necessity test to be satisfied, alongside assessing the proportionality of the restrictive measures.[29] *Corbeau* is seen as a decisive case by Advocate General Darmon since, instead of 'repeating the things which States are prohibited from doing in relation to the grant of exclusive rights, specifies what they can do'.[30] In the later infringement action against The Netherlands concerning exclusive rights in the utilities sector the Court begins by stating that, as a provision which is a derogation from the EC Treaty rules, Article 86(2) EC should be interpreted strictly. The Court also states that the aim of Article 86(2) EC is to reconcile the Member States' interest in using certain undertakings, in particular in the public sector, as an instrument of economic or fiscal policy with the Community interest in ensuring compliance with the rules of competition and the preservation of the unity of the Common Market.[31] The Court did not agree with the EC Commission that there were alternative ways of providing the service of general economic interest which interfered less with competition, and it was not necessary to show that the survival of the undertaking would be threatened if the exclusive rights were not granted.

In *Albany*[32] the Court also rejected the argument that the Member State had to adopt the least restrictive of competition option and instead affirmed that the Member States have a discretion to choose from a number of policy options which may be necessary to achieve a legitimate aim in providing a service of general economic interest.

In analysing the case law Baquero Cruz[33] argues that the Court has used a less restrictive objective necessity test, rather than a strict application of the proportionality test, when balancing the different concerns addressed by Article 86(2) EC. This does not necessarily lead to a prioritisation of social concerns over competition law concerns. His conclusion is that the Court has established a mechanism which can be used by the courts, national as well as European, for balancing the different concerns which are recognised in Article 86(2) EC.

---

[28] Case 155/73 *Sacchi* [1974] ECR 409; Case 66/86 *Ahmed Saeed Flugreisen and Others v Zentrale zur Bekämpfung unlauteren Wettbewerbs* [1989] ECR 803. See M van der Woude, 'Article 90: Competing for Competence' [1992] *ELRev Checklist* 1991, 60.

[29] These tests are continued in some of the later case law. See Case C–203/96 *Chemische Afvalstoffen Dusseldorp BV and Others v Minister van Volkshuisvesting, Ruimtelijke Ordening en Milieubeheer* [1998] ECR I–4075, para 67; Opinion of Léger AG in Case C–309/99 *Wouters* [2002] ECR I–1577; and Opinion of Léger AG in C–438/02 *Hanner* [2005] ECR I–455, paras 140–141.

[30] Opinion of Darmon AG in Case C–393/92 *Almelo* [1994] ECR I–1477, paras 144–146.

[31] Case C-157/94 *Commission v Netherlands* [1997] ECR I-5699, at paras 38–39.

[32] Case C–67/96 [1999] ECR I–5751.

[33] J Baquero Cruz, 'Beyond Competition: Services of General Interest and European Community Law' in G de Búrca (ed), *EU Law and the Welfare State In Search of Solidarity* (Oxford, OUP, 2005).

CONSTITUTIONAL AND FUNDAMENTAL RIGHTS

The first EC Treaty amendment to address the issues raised by the case law on Article 86 EC was Article 16 EC, introduced by the Treaty of Amsterdam 1997. The wording of Article 16 EC, its legal status and its precise aim have given rise to much speculation. Duff has argued that 'there is no more stark exposure in the Treaty of the division ... between those who wish to regulate to protect public utilities and those who wish to make them competitive'.[34] Article 16 EC states:

> Without prejudice to Articles 73, 86 and 87, and given the place occupied by services of general economic interest in the shared values of the Union as well as their role in promoting social and territorial cohesion, the Community and the Member States, each within their respective powers and within the scope of application of this Treaty, shall take care that such services operate on the basis of principles and conditions which enable them to fulfil their missions.

A Declaration states that this Treaty provision:

> shall be implemented with full respect for the jurisprudence of the Court of Justice, inter alia as regards the principles of equality of treatment, quality and control of such services.

Commentators have delivered a range of interpretations on Article 16 EC. Flynn[35] has described Article 16 EC as a response to the growing intrusion of liberalisation and privatisation into the traditional sphere of services of general economic interest in Europe. He sees Article 16 EC as a reflexive response by some Member States to the encroachment of the market: a protectionist measure.

In contrast Ross[36] argues that Article 16 EC may be seen as a declaration of a new, modern, endorsement of social objectives shielding certain public service provision from the free market and competition rules. One interpretation which could be placed upon Article 16 EC is that it reinforces the regulatory development of a European concept of services of general economic interest by creating a *communautaire* obligation to support services of general interest beyond the purely competition law context. In this respect, Ross argues, Article 16 EC shifts the focus of Community law from seeing services of general economic interest merely as a *derogation,* to realising that the promotion of such services are an *obligation* in Community law.

---

[34] A Duff, *The Treaty of Amsterdam* (London, The Federal Trust, Sweet and Maxwell, 1997) at 84.

[35] L Flynn, 'Competition Policy and Public Services in EC Law After the Maastricht and Amsterdam Treaties' in D O'Keeffe and P Twomey (eds), *Legal Issues of the Amsterdam Treaty* (Oxford, Hart, 1999).

[36] M Ross, 'Article 16 E.C. and Services of General Interest: From Derogation to Obligation?' (2000) 25 *ELRev* 22.

Buendia Sierra, on the other hand, has argued that Article 16 EC 'does not modify Article 86(2) EC but rather reaffirms the logic behind the provision'.[37] However Article 16 EC does go further in that, while it is accepted that it may not give rise to direct effect, it has a teleological value. It obliges the Member States and the EU to ensure the achievement of the objectives it has set. Prosser argues that Article 16 EC reinforces a growing recognition that the values associated with public services do have an important role as limits on the scope of competition values and the positive value of services of general economic interest as expressions of citizenship rights;[38] whereas in contrast Szyszczak argues that Article 16 EC is part of the new institutional design to create European ideas of services of general economic interest which can be delivered through competitive markets.[39]

Maresca has made the radical suggestion that a violation of the commitment to services of general economic interest in Europe could rise to liability in damages.[40] Szyszczak has argued, for example, that it could be used in a judicial review, where it is alleged that EU policy and legislative measures infringe the aims and purpose of Article 16 EC.[41] The reformulation of Article 16 EC in Article III–6 of the Constitutional Treaty opens up the possibility that the EU may be in breach of its fundamental duty to respect the role of services of general economic interest in the competitive markets of Europe.

Since 1997 there have been few judicial clues as to the role Article 16 EC should play. Advocate General Jacobs refers to Article 16 EC and Article 36 of the Charter of Fundamental Rights of the EU in his Opinion in *GEMO*[42] but offers no further clarification of their roles.

However, in *Eschirolles*[43] national court called into question previous case law of the Court because of subsequent amendments to the general part of the EC Treaty. The Court held that new provisions defining general objectives of the Community 'must be read in conjunction with the provisions of the Treaty designed to implement those objectives'. If directly applicable provisions have *not* been amended, then the European Courts' interpretation cannot be called into question. Using this ruling to interpret Article 16 EC, it would seem that the previous case law on Article 86(1) and (2) EC case law should continue to apply.

---

[37] J-L Buendia Sierra, *Exclusive Rights and State Monopolies Under EC Law* (Oxford, OUP, 1999) at 313.

[38] T Prosser, *The Limits of Competition Law. Market and Public Services* (Oxford, OUP, 2005) at 161.

[39] E Szyszczak, 'Public Services in Competitive Markets' (2001) 21 *Yearbook of European Law* 35, 64.

[40] M Maresca, 'The Access to the Services of General Interest (SGIs), Fundamental Right of European Law, and the Growing Role of Users' Rights', Paper delivered at the 10th Conference of International Consumer Law, Lima, Peru, 2–6 May 2005.

[41] E Szyszczak, 'Financing Services of General Economic Interest' (2004) 67 *MLR* 982.

[42] Case C–126/01 *Ministère de l'Economie, des Finances et de l'Industrie v GEMO SA* [2003] ECR I–13769.

[43] Case C–9/99 *Echirolles* [2000] ECR I–8207, para 24.

In hindsight, and in the light of the Constitutional Treaty, Article 16 EC fits the pattern of the move within the EU from a purely *economic* community of Member States to the idea found in Article I–3.3.of the Constitutional Treaty of a community of Member States *and* Citizens 'in a highly competitive social market economy' where national interests are recast as interests to be addressed at the trans-national level.[44]

THE CONSTITUTIONAL TREATY 2004

Under the heading, 'Access to Services of General Economic Interest' and placed in Chapter IV (which is entitled 'Solidarity', Article 36 of The Charter of Fundamental Rights of the EU states that:

> The Union recognises and respects access to services of general economic interest as provided for in national laws and practices, in accordance with the Treaty establishing the European Community, in order to promote the social and territorial cohesion of the Union.

This provision has been included as Article II–96 of the Constitutional Treaty. Article 36 is seen as a programmatic provision and does not create any new rights.[45] In the Explanations provided on the Charter by the Council of the EU in December 2000 it is stated that Article 36 fully respects Article 16 EC:

> It merely sets out the principle of respect by the Union for the access to services of general economic interest as provided for by national provisions when those provisions are compatible with Community legislation.

By including a right of *access* to services of general economic interest as a fundamental right the debate on the role of such services moves into a wider domain. Issues of rights to services of general economic interest have traditionally focused upon the liberalised sectors (the networked industries and postal services). Now there are new discussions as to whether other forms of services of general economic interest are necessary. For example, in order to participate in the modern economic world access to financial services, is an indispensable part of exercising economic citizenship in the EU.

In the Constitutional Treaty Article 16 EC becomes Article III–122 and is modified slightly by the addition of a new sentence:

---

[44] A Hertier, 'Market Integration and Social Cohesion: the Politics of Public Services in European Regulation' (2001) 8 *Journal of Public Policy* 825; M Ross, 'Article 16 E.C. and Services of General Interest: From Derogation to Obligation?' (2000) 25 *ELRev* 22.

[45] Art II–112(7). Information, including national constitutional provisions, international law, Community case law and legislative provisions which form the background to this right can be found at http://www.europarl.europa.eu/comparl/libe/elsj/charter/art36/default_en.htm.

European Laws shall define the principles and conditions on the basis of which services of general interest operate without prejudice to the competence of the Member States, in compliance with the Constitution, to provide, to commission and to fund such services.

This was proposed by the Working Group on Social Europe,[46] providing for the first time a general legal base for defining services of general economic interest at the EU level.

Article III–166(3), which is the revised Article 86(3) EC, makes it clear that the EC Commission does not have power to enact legislation under this provision, but only administrative measures of a general or individual nature. This is a legislative enactment of the case law discussed in Chapter 4, where the Court imposed limits on the EC Commission's powers.

The Working Group also proposed a new provision allowing the EC Commission to take action, including the initiation of infringement proceedings if measures based on Article III–122 had the effect of distorting the conditions of competition in the Internal Market.[47] This was not incorporated into the Constitutional Treaty.

CREATING A COMMUNITY *CONCEPT* OF PUBLIC SERVICES THROUGH THE STATE AID RULES

The state aid rules have moved to the centre of the European regulatory debate in defining and regulating services of general economic interest. When the state finances activities which are non-economic in nature,[48] such activities are *not* caught by the EC Treaty rules on competition and the Internal Market. When the state finances activities of an economic nature, the direct finance, or other benefits,[49] may be a state aid which must be approved and monitored by the EC Commission. The EC Commission and the European Court of Justice initially took the view that such payment (or advantage) for providing public services was *compensation* for providing the service, and where the payment (or advantage) was not excessive, it fell outside the scope of the state aid regime.[50] However, the

---

[46] CONV 516/1/03 of 4 Feb 2003, para 32.

[47] R Rodrigues, 'Vers une loi européenne des services publics' (2003) *Revue du Marché Commun et de l'Union européenne* 503.

[48] Eg, security, justice, social security, health and education. The Court and the EC Commission stress that Member States are free to determine their public services. The question whether such services are bound by the EC Treaty rules is essentially a question of Community law: see *Communication From the Commission to the European Parliament, The Council, The European Economic and Social Committee and the Committee of the Regions White Paper on Services of General Interest*, COM(2004) 374 final, 12 May 2004, para 4.2.

[49] Eg, special tax, social security rules, state guarantees, special or exclusive rights, tariff averaging, contributions by market participants and solidarity based financing.

[50] Case 240/83 *Procureur de la République v Association de défense des brûleurs d'huiles usagées (ADBHU)* [1985] ECR 531; *Disposal of German Waste Oils* [1969] *Bull EC II* 9/10, at 35–6. In the light

EU has not maintained a consistent approach, and over time the EC Commission and the European Courts have oscillated between a state aid and a compensation approach. The ruling in *Altmark* [51] attempted to settle the issue by setting out a set of prescriptive conditions whereby Member States could finance a public service obligation without falling foul of the state aid rules. This could have heralded a new regulatory approach towards the provision and financing of services of general economic interest in Europe, settling differences of opinion between the Member States, the EC Commission, the Advocates General, the Court of First Instance (CFI) and the Court of Justice as to whether payments for public services are caught by the state aid rules of the EC Treaty. However, the conditions set in *Altmark* did not match the way most Member States financed public service obligations, in addition to setting out tough compliance criteria.

A STATE AID APPROACH

The question whether payments for public services can amount to state aid arises because of the wide definition given to the concept of a state aid by the European Courts and the focus upon the *effects* of a measure, rather than its categorisation by a Member State. Payments for public services are not always easy to quantify according to market principles, and the effect on trade between Member States and distortion of competition may be difficult to assess.

The issue of the application of state aid rules to public services was raised in the *Spanish Banks* case,[52] but the Court did not address the issues fully. In two later cases the CFI took the view that finance for services of general economic interest fell within the ambit of the state aid regime.[53] This approach brings a number of procedural obligations for the Member States: existing state aid must be monitored by the EC Commission, new state aid cannot be implemented until it has been notified and been approved by the EC Commission.[54] A failure to notify new state aid, or an attempt to implement the state aid before approval of the aid has been received, renders the aid illegal. Member States are under a duty to recover illegal state aid, with interest, from the recipients of the aid.[55]

---

of subsequent case law it may be hard to separate out state aid from revenues earned by the undertaking supplying the service, since in the light of the ruling in *PreussenElektra* such revenues would be deemed not to have come from state sources and would not be classified as state aid: Case C–379/98 [2001] ECR I–2099.

[51] Case C–280/00 *Altmark Trans GmbH and Regierungspraesidium Magdeburg* v *Nahverkehrsgesellschaft Altmark GmbH* [2003] ECR I–7747.

[52] Case C–387/92 *Banco Exterior de España* v *Ayuntamiento de Valencia* [1994] ECR I–877.

[53] Case T–106/95 *FFSA* [1997] ECR II–229; Case T–46/97 *SIC* [2000] ECR II–2125.

[54] See Arts 87 and 88 EC and Reg 659/99 [1999] OJ L83/1. Special rules exist for state aid in the Accession States.

[55] Art 14(1) of *ibid*; Case C–390/98 *HJ Banks & Co Ltd* v *Coal Authority* [2001] ECR I–6117, para 74.

A state aid approach towards the financing of public services brings greater accountability and transparency to public finances and is in keeping with the approach taken by the EC Commission in the Transparency Directive towards openness in public finances.[56] This approach has consonance with the political commitment of the Member States in the Lisbon Process to reduce the amount of state aid and move towards greater use of horizontal state aid.[57] For the Member States the move to a state aid approach implied greater planning for the financing of public services and a time lag before such aid could be implemented. For the EC Commission it entailed a greater workload, but also the incentive to address the regulation of services of general economic interest in the Internal Market.

A difficulty with the state aid approach is the question whether national courts may take into account Article 86(2) EC. As we have seen in Chapter 4, in some applications of Article 86(1) and (2) EC, for example the *Corbeau* case,[58] the Court of Justice has taken a balancing approach. It is arguable that a similar balancing approach can be taken in the application of Articles 87(1) and 86(2) EC. But even if Article 86(2) EC does apply, it raises the issues whether the measure should be notified in the first instance to the EC Commission. Member States are not allowed to self-assess the application of the derogations/ exemptions to the state aid rules and, given the EC Commission's central role in the regulation of state aid, the answer should be in the affirmative: the EC Commission should continue to assess the compatibility of *any* state aid with the Internal Market. In the *Spanish Banks*[59] case and in *France v Commission*[60] the Court indicates that notification and compliance with the procedural state aid rules are necessary, but there are suggestions that the state aid regime could be relaxed, allowing Member States to implement notified aid to public providers of services of general interest, but not be subject to the standstill provisions.[61]

A COMPENSATION APPROACH

Where funds or other advantages are granted by the state to compensate for costs derived from public service obligations, the Court has ruled that such payments

---

[56] Commission Dir 80/723/EEC [1980] OJ L195/35, as amended by Dir 85/413/EEC [1984] OJ L229/20; Dir 93/84/EC [1993] OJ L254/16; Dir 2000/52/EC [2000] OJ L193/75.

[57] Stockholm Presidency Conclusions 2001. The Member States agreed to the use of new forms of economic governance, particularly the use of a State Aid Score Board, as additional forms of monitoring the use of state aid. This fits with the governance tools of the Internal Market and the open method of coordination, of using greater transparency, accountability, peer pressure and learning from best practice as new ways of enforcing and coordinating EU objectives.

[58] Case C–320/91 [1993] ECR I–2533.

[59] Above n 52.

[60] Case C–332/98 [2000] ECR I–4833, paras 27–32.

[61] Opinion of Tizzano AG in Case C–53/00 *Ferring v ACOSS* [2001] ECR I–9067; Second Opinion of Léger AG, paras 70–73 in *Altmark*, above n 51.

(or advantages) are not state aids. *Ferring*[62] concerned a tax exemption granted to wholesale distributors of pharmaceutical products. Council Directive 92/25/EEC[63] allowed the Member States to impose public service obligations on wholesale distributors where public health requirements demanded this and the public service obligation was proportionate to such requirements. To balance the public service obligation French law imposed a tax on sales of medicinal products, exempting wholesalers who, it was argued, were at a competitive disadvantage when compared with outlets not under a duty to provide a public service obligation (for example, pharmaceutical laboratories). A pharmaceutical company challenged the French tax, arguing that the special exemption for the wholesalers providing a public service obligation was a form of illegal state aid.

The Court of Justice, following the Opinion of Advocate General Tizzano, took the view that a difference in treatment between undertakings did not automatically imply the existence of an advantage for the purposes of the definition of a state aid under Article 87(1) EC. There was no advantage where the difference in treatment was justified by reasons relating to the logic of the Member State's tax system. Secondly, the Court found that the pharmaceutical wholesalers had to bear additional costs as a result of performing the public service obligation. Provided that the tax on direct sales imposed upon the pharmaceutical laboratories was equivalent to the additional costs borne by the wholesalers there was no state aid. The Court goes further by demanding that there is a necessary connection between the tax exemption and the additional costs incurred, so that the wholesalers could not be deemed to enjoy any real advantage. This issue was to be determined by the national courts.

Where the tax exemption (or, more generally, compensation provided for a public service obligation) was in *excess* of the additional costs incurred in providing the public service obligation then a particular undertaking could be enjoying an advantage which could be a state aid. The issue, then, was whether such aid could be justified by reference to Article 86(2) EC. Given that Article 86(2) EC is a derogation from fundamental EC Treaty obligations it should be applied narrowly and according to the principle of proportionality. It is incumbent upon the Member State pleading Article 86(2) EC that the conditions for application of the Treaty provision are fulfilled.[64] While it is arguable that the Court has taken a softer line on proportionality when interpreting Article 86(2) EC,[65] a Member State would have difficulty justifying how compensation in *excess* of the additional public service obligation costs was necessary and proportionate.

---

[62]   Case C–53/00, above n 61.

[63]   [1992] OJ L113/1.

[64]   These conditions have been set out by Léger AG in his Opinion in Case C–309/99 *Wouters and Others* [2002] ECR I–1577, paras 157–166 and also Case C–438/02 *Åklagaren v Krister Hanner* [2005] ECR I–455 paras 135–144.

[65]   This appears to be the case after the energy infringement actions: Joined Cases C–157/94 *Commission v Netherlands* [1997] ECR I–5699; Case C–158/94 *Commission v Italy* [1997] ECR I–5789;

Difficulties with the Compensation Approach

Advocate General Léger criticised the compensation approach in his first Opinion in *Altmark* on 19 March 2002. In his view there were flaws with the *Ferring* approach, since it conflated the two-step approach which was required under state aid rules of, first, categorising the measure and, secondly, looking to see if it could be justified. In *Ferring*, it was argued that the Court had focused upon the *aims* of the measure, not its *effects*. A second criticism of *Ferring* was that it deprived Article 86(2) EC of its essential role of reconciling competing interests in the Community law framework, since excess compensation for a public service obligation would not satisfy the tests of necessity and proportionality. Thirdly, the compensation approach risked undermining the effectiveness of the EC Commission's supervisory powers in the field of state aid.

Disquiet with *Ferring* was expressed also by Advocate General Jacobs in his Opinion of 30 April 2002 in *GEMO*,[66] where he offers an alternative quid pro quo approach and by Advocate General Stix-Hackl in her Opinion of 7 November 2002 in *Enirsorse*.[67] Post-*Ferring* the EC Commission was rigorous in its scrutiny of financing of public services, referring to its *Communication on Services of General Economic Interest*. [68] The EC Commission took the view that a tax exemption in favour of joint stock companies established by Italian municipalities to provide a number of local services did not satisfy the principles of neutrality and proportionality, did not assign specific public service obligation providers or set out the amount of compensation and the net extra costs involved in providing a public service obligation.[69] In another Decision involving Deutsche Post the EC Commission found that a rebate scheme did not match the public service obligation and was not necessary, thus finding that there was illegal state aid.[70]

There are a number of other legal and economic criticisms which can be directed against the compensation approach. In *Ferring* there is the assumption that the only advantage gained from payment for services of general economic

---

Case C–159/94 *Commission v France* [1997] ECR I–5815 and Case C–160/94 *Commission v Spain* [1997] ECR I–5851. These cases can be viewed as extraordinary, as they were infringement actions concerning a sensitive sector which the Member States were reluctant to open up for liberalisation. Cf L Soriano, 'How Proportionate Should Anti-competitive State Intervention Be?' (2003) 28 *ELRev* 112; the debate in Germany, cited at fn 31 in A Bartosch, 'Clarification or Confusion? How to Reconcile the ECJ's rulings in *Altmark* and *Chronopost*?', Working Paper 02, *clasf Working Paper Series*, available at http://www.clasf.org.

[66] Case C–126/01 [2003] ECR I–13768.

[67] Case C–34/01 [2003] ECR I–14243.

[68] *Communication on Services of General Interest in Europe* [2001] OJ C17/4.

[69] An indication of the EC Commission's strong feelings is to be found in an article by an EC Commission official which is cited at fn 6 of the Second Opinion of Léger AG, 14 Jan 2003: D Grespan, 'An Example of the Application of State Aid Rules in the Utilities Sector in Italy' (2002) 3 *Competition Policy Newsletter* 17.

[70] Commission Dec 2002/753/EC of 19 June 2002 on measures implemented by the Federal Republic of Germany for Deutsche Post AG [2002] OJ L247/27.

interest is the financial one. This ignores the fact that a number of other direct and indirect, tangible and intangible, benefits may accrue by the taking on of a public service obligation. EC Commission Decisions and the Courts' case law reveal problems in the liberalisation process where incumbents provide a public service obligation alongside other commercial market activities.[71] For example, where there are common costs there may be risks of cross-subsidisation between the finances of the public service obligation and the commercial activities, despite the requirements of the Transparency Directive for the separation of accounts.[72] There is the difficulty of separating out the fixed costs of providing commercial activities alongside public service obligation activities and the extra, variable costs associated with providing the public service obligation.[73] As a result the EC Commission has imposed stringent conditions upon Deutsche Post[74] and the German public banks to ensure that any relationship between the commercial and public service obligation operations are conducted at arm's length.[75]

A more fundamental criticism of the compensation approach is that the Court does not address the question of what the market would have provided in the absence of the tax exemption. This is a necessary question in order to estimate

---

[71] The liberalisation of postal services is a good example: see Ch 5.

[72] In 2000 the EC Commission amended the Transparency Dir requiring undertakings entrusted with a public service obligation which were also exposed to competition to draw up separate accounts. But this obligation does not apply where the public service obligation has been awarded through an open, transparent and non-discriminatory procurement procedure: Art 4(2) of Commission Dir 80/723/EEC of 25 June 1980 on the transparency of financial relations between Member States and public undertakings [1980] OJ L195/35, amended by Dir 2000/52/EC of 26 July 2000 [2000] OJ L193/75. See P Nicolaides, 'Distortive Effects of Compensatory Aid Measures: A Note on the Economics of the *Ferring* Judgment' (2002) 23 *ECLR* 313; C Rizza, 'The Financial Assistance Granted by Member States to Undertakings Entrusted with Operation of a Service of General Economic Interest' in A Biondi *et al* (eds), *The Law of State Aid in the European Union* (Oxford, OUP, 2003). Cf the German Landesbanken cases where the 'balance sheet effect' was used. The unlimited guarantee to the public service obligation providers reduced borrowing costs of the competitive operations. This would now be dealt with by the requirement for accounting segregation between the public service obligation activities and commercial activities in Art 2(d) of the Transparency Dir (Joined Cases T–228/99 & T–233/99 *Westdeutsche Landesbank Girozentrale and Land Nordrhein-Westfalen. v Commission* [2003] ECR II–435; Case C–209/00 *Commission v Germany* [2002] ECR I–11695), discussed in Ch 6.

[73] In *Ferring* there was no obligation to provide a universal service, which is the requirement for the special treatment afforded to public service obligations in the regulated liberalisation programmes of the EU. Thus there were advantages for the wholesalers to locate in, and supply, urban areas over rural areas.

[74] EC Commission Dec 2001/354 [2001] OJ L125/27. See also EC Commission Dec 2002/180/EC *Hays/La Poste* [2002] OJ L61/32 where the EC Commission found the French incumbent in breach of Art 82 EC where the reserved sector (public service obligation) used persuasive methods to force business to business customers for Hays' DX service to change to La Poste's DX service by threatening to withdraw preferential postal rates offered to such customers in the separate (reserved) business to consumer postal market.

[75] Commission Dec 2001/354/EC of 20 Mar 2001 [2001] OJ L125/27. See S Moser, N Pesaresi and K Soukup, 'State Guarantees to German Public Banks: a New Step in the Enforcement of State Aid Discipline to Financial Services in the Community' (2002) 2 *Competition Policy Newsletter* 1. See also Commission Dec 2002/180/EC *Hays/La Poste* [2002] *ibid.*

the need for a marginal subsidy to pay for the public service obligation. In *Ferring* would the wholesalers have provided the service without the subsidy?

There may be advantages in the financing of a public service obligation which cannot be measured purely in financial terms. Taking on the extra pharmaceutical stocks in *Ferring* may have provided economies of scale. This in turn may increase or reinforce a dominant position. The reinforcement may be less tangible and hard to quantify immediately in purely financial terms, but a *commercial* market position may be enhanced through the award of a public service obligation merely by the association of the public service obligation products and services with the commercial activities of the provider, consumers identifying a particular brand with certain qualities which can be trusted. The consumer may be induced, intentionally or unintentionally, to buy the commercial products and services as a result of the association with the public service obligation. Admittedly poor performance in the provision of the public service obligation may lead to the opposite behaviour.

ALTMARK

The preliminary ruling in *Altmark*,[76] decided by the Full Court, offered the opportunity to reconcile the different approaches. Altmark Trans had received a subsidy from the German public authorities to operate a passenger bus service in the Stendal region. A competing bus company challenged the licences granted on the ground that Altmark Trans was not economically viable and would not survive in the competitive market without the public subsidy, which, the competitor argued, was a form of illegal state aid. The German authorities had chosen not to apply the sectoral rules, therefore the residual state aid rules came into play. Even though only *local* bus services were involved the Court ruled that trade between Member States could be affected, given the liberalised transport market in the EU since 1995.[77]

In a *Non-Paper on Services of General Economic Interest* issued in November 2002 the EC Commission[78] remained neutral as to whether the Court of Justice should adopt the compensation approach offered by the Court of Justice, the state aid approach offered by the CFI or the *quid pro quo* approach offered by Advocate General Jacobs in his opinion in *GEMO*. The German and Spanish governments supported the compensation approach but the Danish, French, United Kingdom and Netherlands governments opted for the *quid quo pro*

---

[76]   Case C–280/00 *Altmark Trans GmbH and Regierungspraesidium Magdeburg* v *Nahverkehrsgesellschaft Altmark GmbH* [2003] ECR I–7747.

[77]   *Ibid*, at para 81. The Court's endorsement of the 'no *de minimis*; approach is repeated in Joined Cases C–34/01 to C–38/01 *Enirsorse SpA v Ministero delle Finanze* [2003] ECR I–14243, para 28.

[78]   Available at http://ec.europa.eu/comm/competition/state_aid/others/sieg_en.pdf.

approach. Against this lack of consensus the Court opted for the compensation approach, citing *ADBHU*[79] and *Ferring*,[80] but providing four conditions to be met:

first, the recipient undertaking must actually have public service obligations to discharge which have been clearly defined;

secondly, the parameters of the basis on which compensation is calculated must be established in advance and in an objective and transparent manner, to avoid conferring an economic advantage which may favour the recipient undertaking over competing undertakings;

thirdly, the compensation must not exceed what is necessary to cover all or part of the costs incurred in the discharge of public service obligations, taking account of the relevant receipts and the reasonable profit for discharging those obligations;

finally, where there is no public tendering system to choose the public service provider the level of compensation must be determined by an analysis of the costs a typical undertaking, well run and adequately provided for to meet the necessary public service requirements, would have incurred in discharging those obligations, taking into account the relevant receipts and the reasonable profit for discharging the obligations.

All four conditions must be satisfied for the measure not to constitute state aid. The first condition follows established case law[81] and the EC Commission's soft law Communications.[82] The second condition introduces a new standard which is harder to satisfy than the use of Article 86(2) EC to justify state aid for public service obligations. Conditions 3 and 4 take a new direction in the financing of services of general interest and are not without difficulty in interpretation and application.[83] Condition 3 is a clarification of the proportionality rule used in the application of Article 86(2) EC. The fact that a public service obligation may make a reasonable profit acts as an inducement for private sector undertakings to

---

[79] Case 240/83 *ADBHU* [1985] ECR 531.

[80] Case C–53/00 *Ferring v ACOSS* [2001] ECR I–6639.

[81] See Case 127/73 *BRT v SABAM* [1974] ECR 313, para 20; Case 66/86 *Ahmed Saeed Flugreisen* [1989] ECR 803, para 55.

[82] Available at: http://ec.europa.eu/comm/competition/state_aid/studies_reports/studies_ reports. html.

[83] Note the defence of *Altmark* by Bartosch (A Bartosch, 'Clarification or Confusion? How to Reconcile the ECJ's rulings in *Altmark* and *Chronopost*?', Working Paper 02, *clasf Working Paper Series*, available at http://www.clasf.org), where he argues that the 4 criteria are no less problematic than the criteria which have evolved in the application of Art 86(2) EC. See, however, Case C-451/03 *Servizi Ausiliari Commercialisti Srl v Giuseppe Calafiori* [2006] ECR I-2941 where the Court states that conditions 3 and 4 of the *Altmark* test are questions of fact for the national court to decide (paras 69 and 70) but then in para 71 states that the national court does not have jurisdiction to decide whether a state aid is compatible with Community law.

take on public service obligations.[84] Condition 4 introduces a new benchmarking element into the assessment of the funding of public service obligations.

In his Opinion in *GEMO*,[85] Advocate General Jacobs stressed that the issue at stake was the EC Commission's supervisory role in the state aid sphere. His Opinion offers a new dimension to the debate, in that he contextualises the direction the discourse on the provision of services of general interest should take in the light of Article 16 EC and Article 36 of the Charter of Fundamental Rights of the EU. Advocate General Jacobs argued that the polarisation of *either* a compensation approach *or* the state aid approach was not the correct solution. To him the crucial aspect is the *link* between the financing of the public service obligation and the duties imposed. He argued that where the finance was intended as the *quid pro quo* for clearly defined public service obligations the link between state finance and the public service obligation was direct and manifest, and then the compensation approach of *Ferring* should apply. But where the link between the state finance and the public service obligation was not clearly defined then the state aid approach should apply.

Positive Features of *Altmark*

A number of features of the *Altmark* ruling can be judged in a positive light. It provides for greater transparency in the assignment of public service obligations and greater legal certainty as to how the financing of public service obligations should be assessed. The Court appears to be endorsing the EC Commission's regulatory approach to the regulation of services of general economic interest.[86] The fourth condition, excludes from state aid regulation public service obligations which have not been awarded by a procurement process. This fits with EC Commission policy stated in in decisions and soft law communications[87] as well as the Transparency Directive.[88] Ensuring competition for the market is seen as an important objective of competition policy in the case of services of general economic interest where competition after the award of the public service obligation is limited due to very high fixed costs. A tendering scheme helps to ensure that the undertaking chosen is the operator which can carry out the task

---

[84]   This is a new element. The idea was raised by Lenz AG in Case 240/83 *ADBHU* [1985] ECR 531, but the Court did not rule on the point.

[85]   Case C–26/01 [2003] ECR I–13769.

[86]   See E Szyszczak, 'Governance' (2003) 3 *ERA-Forum* 130.

[87]   Commission Dec of 29 Sept 1999 State Aid No NN 88/98 United Kingdom Financing of a 24-hour advertsing-free News Channel Out of the Licence Fee by the *BBC Report* SG(1999) D/10201; Report *of the Commission to the Council of Ministers: Services of General Economic Interest in the Banking Sector* of 17 June 1998, para 3.2.; Commission Notice on *Services of General Interest* [2001] OJ C17/4. Presumably the EC Commission sees open tendering as a process relieving it of investigative work.

[88]   See Commission, *Communication on Services of General Economic Interest*, 2001 at 26, *ibid.* See also Case C–31/03 *Consorzio Aziende Metano (Coname) v Comune di Cingia de'Botti, intervener Padania Acque SpA* [2005] ECR I–7287.

efficiently, and competition for the award of the tender will ensure that the undertaking is not excessively over-compensated. However, the only justification for EU intervention can be where the market for the public service obligation has a cross-border element, that is where there are competitors for the service from another Member State. This is a new departure, and not only introduces a new form of benchmarking but also sends clear messages to the EC Commission and the Member States about the need for new approaches towards good governance in the operation of public service obligations.[89] However, it is argued that a tendering system is not a substitute for *ex post* checks on the accounts and quality of a public service obligation provider, particularly where an incumbent is capable of deriving profits over and above the costs of providing the public service obligation.[90]

Member States have some leeway and some autonomy in choosing what should be a public service obligation and how it is awarded and financed, provided these processes conform to Community law.[91] In *Analir* the Court grants the Member States a wide discretion to create public service obligations provided that in exercising that discretion the award:

> must be based on objective, non-discriminatory criteria which are known in advance to the undertakings concerned, in such a way as to circumscribe the exercise of the national authorities' discretion.[92]

In a later judgment the Court established further guidance, in that the direct award of a concession must, on the basis of Articles 43 and 49 EC, comply with transparency requirements in order for undertakings from another Member State to have access to the necessary information to place them in a position to apply for the concession.[93] The use of the principle of transparency does not, however,

---

[89] Complex public–private partnerships introduced by tender are under scrutiny for the possibility of state aid. For other examples see A Bartosch, 'The Relationship Between Public Procurement and State Aid Surveillance: The Toughest Standards Applies?' (2002) 39 *CMLRev* 551, 554–5; C Bovis, 'Financing Services of General Interest in the EU: How Do Public Procurement and State Aids Interact to Demarcate Between Market Forces and Protection?' (2005)11 *ELJ* 79. In a post-*Altmark* ruling the CFI was prepared to look behind a public tendering privatisation process to examine whether there was illegal state aid: Case T–157/01 *Danske Busvognmænd v Commission* [2004] ECR I–917.

[90] 'Services of General Economic Interest Opinion Prepared by the State Aid Group of EAGCP', 29 June 2006, available at: http://ec.europa.eu/comm/competition/state_aid/studies_reports/studies_reports.html.

[91] Case C–458/03 *Parking Brixen GmbH v Gemeinde Brixen* [2005] ECR I–8612 is a useful reminder of the residual role of the Internal Market rules when the specialised procurement rules do not apply.

[92] Case C–205/99 *Asociatión Profesional de Empresas Navieras de Líneas (Analir) and ors v Administración del Estado* [2001] ECR I–1271.

[93] Case C–231/03 *Consorzio Aziende Metano (Coname) v Comune di Cingia de' Botti* [2005] ECR I–7287.

imply an obligation to grant the public service obligation through a tender. This, however, is at odds with the fourth criterion of the *Altmark* judgment and also the *Brixen* ruling.[94]

This fourth condition also indicates that the Court is suggesting to the EC Commission that it should take a closer look at the efficiency of the way in which services of general interest are run. A negative aspect of this scrutiny process is that some public service providers could be under-funded in the future. What the Court seems to imply is that the EC Commission and the Member States should scrutinise the way in which some public service obligations have been gold-plated in the past without sufficient economic justification.[95] This is in line with the attitude taken towards the provision of universal obligations, a good example being the conditions set out in the Notice on the Postal Sector,[96] and the greater emphasis being placed upon the evaluation of services of general economic interest.[97]

The ruling in *Altmark* can be squared with the political commitment towards greater transparency in state aid processes post-Stockholm. All compensatable costs must be identified and costed before the public service obligation is taken up. The ruling in *Altmark,* while resonating with the Commission's Transparency Directive obligations, would also seem to go further than the Directive's obligations in the need to establish *in advance* the criteria for financing public service obligations.[98]

Continuing Problems with *Altmark?*

The four criteria contain a number of vague phrases which may lead to further litigation about their precise meaning. For example, the fourth condition raises many new questions involving legal and economic discussion.[99] An immediate question is whether the *Altmark* ruling can be reconciled with the ruling of the

---

[94]   Above n 91.

[95]   Cf Commission Dec of 12 Mar 2002 on the aid granted by Italy to Poste Italiane SpA (formerly Ente Poste Italiane) [2002] OJ L282/29.

[96]   [1998] OJ C39/2.

[97]   *Communication from the Commission: A Methodological Note for the Horizontal Evaluation of Services of General Economic Interest,* COM(2002) 331 final, 18 June 2002. The White Paper, COM(2004) 374 final, 12 May 2004, at para 45, promised a horizontal evaluation of services of general interest in 2004. See *Commission Staff Working Paper: Horizontal Evaluation of the Performance of Network Industries Providing Services of General Economic Interest 2004 Report,* SEC(2004)866/1.

[98]   Case C–280/00 *Altmark Trans GmbH and Regierungspraesidium Magdeburg* v *Nahverkehrsgesellschaft Altmark GmbH* [2003] ECR I–7747. Additionally the EC Commission itself has gone further in its Decs against Deutsche Poste and the negotiations with the German banks discussed above at nn 73 and 33, demanding the structural separation of the commercial and public service obligations activities.

[99]   Cf, eg, the discussion of the price to be paid for a service which is not a public service obligation in the ruling by the CFI shortly after *Altmark* in Joined Cases T–116/01 & T–118/01 *P&O European Ferries (Vizcayaa) SA and Diputación Foral de Vizcaya* v *Commission* [2003] ECR II–2957; on appeal Case C–442/03 P ECR I-4845.

Court delivered just a couple of weeks earlier in *Chronopost*.[100] In the latter judgment the Court annulled the judgment of the CFI on the ground that the private market investor test was an inappropriate test to use for an undertaking operating in a reserved sector. The Court criticised the CFI's purely commercial approach, arguing that there was no market for the provision of services linked to a universal postal network such as the one provided by La Poste. This would seem to be at odds with the fourth criterion of *Altmark* which looks to a typical comparator undertaking, well run and adequately provided for, to assess the costs of providing the public service obligation. This suggests some conceptual confusion about *how* public service obligations are to be provided in competitive markets. On the one hand *Chronopost* is suggesting that public service obligations are subject to special non-market rules, but, on the other hand, *Altmark* suggests that public service obligations should *not* be given any special privileges when they have not been subject to a public tender.

Bartosch[101] provides a technical way of distinguishing the cases by arguing that *Altmark* is concerned with establishing how a *general framework* can be established to take compensation for public service obligations out of the state aid regime. In contrast in *Chronopost* there was no market as there was only one operator offering services linked to a universal postal network, and thus there was no market to act as a benchmark for the services provided.

The ruling in *Altmark* allows the Member States to experiment with selection processes without having to notify and suspend the finance under the state aid rules. Draganic[102] takes a more extreme view and argues that the proportionality test deployed by the *Altmark* criteria is looser than the proportionality requirements of Article 86(2) EC and leans in favour of national services of general economic interest. *Altmark* certainly respects the principle of subsidiarity, giving the Member States leeway in the organisation of their public service obligations, but it is also *prescriptive*. Member States must adhere to a new set of regulatory criteria if they wish to take advantage of not having to notify measures to the EC Commission.

A disappointing aspect of the *Altmark* ruling is its failure to address the legal situation where a Member State does not satisfy the four conditions. If the public service obligation is efficient and performs below the costs projected it will be deemed to have received state aid. This does not provide incentives for the public

---

[100] Joined Cases C–83/01 P, C–93/01 P & C–94/01 P *Chronopost SA, La Poste and French Republic v Union française de l'express (Ufex), DHL International, Federal express international (France) and CRIE* [2003] ECR I–6993. *Altmark* is consistent with the EC Commission's investigation into the spill-over effects of funding a public service obligation in *TV2 Denmark* [2003] OJ C59/2, discussed below. The EC Commission argues that price dumping of advertising on a commercial market should be determined by reference to an 'efficient' operator.

[101] See A. Bartosch, 'Clarification or Confusion? How to Reconcile the ECJ's rulings in *Altmark* and *Chronopost*?', Working Paper 02, *clasf Working Paper Series*, available at http://www.clasf.org.

[102] I Draganic, 'State Aid or Compensation for Extra Costs: Tuning the Test of Proportionality in EC Competition Law' (2006) 4 *European State Aid Law Quarterly* 683.

service obligation and could lead to under-finding of public service obligations merely to avoid the state aid procedures. The Member State authorities may miscalculate costs, or there may be a change in the economic climate, or an emergency/crisis where the state has to intervene in order to ensure that public services continue to exist. Presumably there is no relaxation in the state aid procedures and the Member State is under an obligation to notify the aid,[103] suspend it and wait for EC Commission clearance.

Altmark provides no guidance on the justification of the state aid, how Article 86(2) EC may apply[104] and whether, if there is litigation in the national court, Article 86(2) EC has direct effect. Advocate General Tizzano in *Ferring*[105] suggested that national judges could apply Article 86(2) EC. This idea is criticised by Rizza,[106] who argues that such an approach would virtually nullify the procedural rules of the state aid provisions in relation to public service obligations. In contrast Advocate General Léger in *Altmark*[107] argued that the national courts should *not* have the power to apply Article 86(2) EC in state aid assessments.

Altmark does not provide guidance on the situation where the Member State departs from the parameters set in advance for the financing of the public service obligation. For example, where there is an unexpected change in the economic situation, a crisis or a simple miscalculation of the parameters of how the public service obligation should be financed. Presumably the state aid procedures come into play. This not only makes the notification procedures cumbersome but can cause complicated problems where non-notified aid has been paid and becomes illegal, with the consequent duty to be recovered from the recipient(s).

---

[103] In the *Spanish Banks* case (Case C–387/92 *Banco Exterior de España v Ayuntamiento de Valencia* [1994] ECR I–877) the Spanish government had argued that if the measure was a state aid there was still no duty to notify the aid under the normal procedures. In Case C–332/98 *France v Commission* [2000] ECR I–4833 the Court indicates that notification and compliance with the procedural state aid rules is necessary. Thus Art 86(2) EC has a more limited role to play in the second stage of the justification of a measure, and this would seem to deny a role for a rule of reason in state aid law for services of general economic interest.

[104] But if conditions 1 and 3 are not met there is no room for application of Art 86(2) EC. The Court was generous in its interpretation of Art 86(2) EC in the infringement actions concerning the utilities sector cited above, in n 20. But given the stern approach the EC Commission takes towards state aid and the Member States' commitments post-Stockholm to reduce the overall amount of state aid we cannot take for granted the assumption that the case law of Art 86(2) EC will automatically apply. This view is reinforced in the second Opinion of Léger AG in *Altmark*, where he states that Art 86(2) EC should take direct effect in the national courts.

[105] Case C–53/00 *Ferring v ACOSS* [2001] ECR I–6639.

[106] C Rizza, 'The Financial Assistance Granted by Member States to Undertakings Entrusted with Operation of a Service of General Economic Interest' in A Biondi *et al* (eds), *The Law of State Aid in the European Union* (Oxford, OUP, 2003).

[107] Case C–280/00 *Altmark Trans GmbH and Regierungspraesidium Magdeburg v Nahverkehrsgesellschaft Altmark GmbH* [2003] ECR I–7747.

Thus, the *Altmark* ruling leaves a number of unanswered questions which have not been answered by subsequent rulings,[108] and the EC Commission has adopted a different approach in decisions taken post-*Altmark*.[109] Exacerbating this uncertainty was the fact that the *Altmark* litigation put the EC Commission's strategy towards creating a coherent normative framework for services of general interest on hold.[110]

A REGULATORY APPROACH

Eventually the EC Commission adopted a package of measures using an EC Commission Decision and a Framework drawn up as part of the State Aid Action Plan.[111] These measures rely upon *de minimis* principles. Where the *Altmark* conditions are not met then the Commission Decision[112] and Framework[113] apply. If neither applies, the residual state aid rules may still be used, including the reading across of Article 86(2) EC to justify a state aid measure.

Under the EC Commission decision there is the use of a *de minimis* principle. Public service compensation that amounts to state aid is permitted (that is, it falls within Article 86(2) EC and does not need to be notified to the EC Commission) if it is less than 30 million euros *per annum* paid to undertakings with an annual turnover of less than 100 million euros, or is paid to hospitals or social housing undertakings or certain small air or maritime undertakings, airports and ports carrying out a service of general economic interest. There must be an official act (for example, a statutory rule) specifying the undertaking's precise public service obligation, the parameters for calculating, controlling and reviewing the public service obligation and the arrangements for avoiding over-compensation. The amount of public service compensation should not exceed the costs involved in

---

[108] See Case C–126/01 *GEMO* [2003] ECR I- 13769 and Joined Cases C–34/01 to C–38/01 *Enirisorse SpA* v *Ministero delle Finanze* [2003] ECR I–14243.

[109] Compensation given to Italian, Portuguese and Spanish broadcasters was found not to meet the *Altmark* criteria and was deemed to be state aid. But in so far as the compensation did not exceed the net additional costs of the public service obligation it was justified under Art 86(2): 'Commission decides on public TV financing in Italy and Portugal', EC Commission Press Release IP/03/1399, 15 Oct 2003.

[110] EC Commission, *Services of General Interest*, COM(2003) 270 final, 21 May 2003, especially para 4.2.

[111] See http://ec.europa.eu/comm/competition/state_aid/overview/sar.html. See: L Svane, 'Public Service Compensation in Practice: Commission Package on State Aid for Services of General Economic Interest' (2005) 3 *Competition Policy Newsletter* 34, available at http://europa.eu.int/comm/competition/publications/cpn/cpn2005_3.pdf.

[112] Commission Dec of 13 July 2005 on the application of Art 86(2) of the Treaty to state aid in the form of public service compensation granted to certain undertakings entrusted with the operation of services of general economic interest [2005] OJ L312/67.

[113] Commission Framework for state aid in the form of public service compensation [2005] OJ C297/4.

performing the public service obligation; taking into account relevant receipts and a reasonable profit; the compensation is only used for the service of general economic interest concerned.

A public service obligation which does *not* satisfy the *Altmark* criteria or the EC Commission Decision must be notified to the EC Commission in the usual way. The Framework addresses when Article 86(2) EC will apply. The Framework is identical to the Decision, except for the fact that where state aid falls within the Decision it does not have to be notified to the EC Commission. The EC Commission is obviously concerned with larger amounts of state aid and wants the opportunity to scrutinise it, and may impose conditions on the grant of the aid. Where the public service obligation does not fall under the conditions of *Altmark*, the Decision or the Framework, the residual state aid rules may still apply. But in the light of the stringent attitude towards state aid in the Lisbon Process it is likely that only in exceptional circumstances would such aid receive the EC Commission's approval.

SERVICES OF GENERAL ECONOMIC INTEREST AFTER *ALTMARK*

Public Service Broadcasting: A Special Case?

The regulation of public service broadcasting is a contentious area. The Court of Justice in *Sacchi*[114] confirmed that the provisions of the EC Treaty applied to the transmission of television signals, and in later cases broadcasting has been held to be an economic activity falling within the scope of the EC Treaty. The application of the EC Treaty rules to public broadcasters led to the Member States adopting Protocol 27 on the System of Public Broadcasting in the Member States in the Amsterdam Treaty 1997. This states that:

THE HIGH CONTRACTING PARTIES,

CONSIDERING that the system of public broadcasting in the Member States is directly related to the democratic, social and cultural needs of each society and to the need to preserve media pluralism,

HAVE AGREED UPON the following interpretative provisions, which shall be annexed to the Treaty establishing a Constitution for Europe:

The provisions of the Constitution shall be without prejudice to the competence of Member States to provide for the funding of public service broadcasting insofar as such funding is granted to broadcasting organisations for the fulfilment of the public service remit as conferred, defined and organised by each Member State, and insofar as such

---

[114] Case 155/73 *Sacchi* [1974] ECR 409.

funding does not affect trading conditions and competition in the Union to an extent which would be contrary to the common interest, while the realisation of the remit of that public service shall be taken into account.

The EC Commission has recognised that public service broadcasting is a service of general interest: a service which 'the Member states subject to specific public service obligations by virtue of a general interest criterion'.[115] Nevertheless, and despite the Protocol, the defence of the Member States' specific regulation of the general interest is subject to Community law. It is recognised that the general interest is based upon common values. These have been tested and developed in the Court's case law as well as finding expression in Community legislation.[116] In the EC Commission's Communication, *Services of General Interest in Europe,*[117] the common values are identified as 'freedom of expression and the right of reply, pluralism, protection of copyright, promotion of cultural and linguistic diversity, protection of minors and of human dignity, consumer protection'.

The EC Commission's Communication makes it clear that the competition rules will be applied to this sector for the benefit of consumers, not citizens. It is also clear that Community interests will prevail over national interests. The EC Commission is entrusted:

> with the task of preventing anticompetitive behaviour to the detriment of the consumers, notably the abuse of dominant positions and, on the basis of merger control, the creation of oligopolistic or monopolist market structures.[118]

Both the Protocol and the Communication place constraints on the remit and the modalities of public service broadcasting by the insistence on compliance with the state aid provisions of the EC Treaty. These rules demand that the public funding of public service broadcasters is in proportion to the public service remit which has been defined by the Member State. The Communication refers to a number of complaints received by the EC Commission from commercial broadcasters, particularly concerning the use of commercial advertising and its compatibility with public service aims.[119]

Public service broadcasters are under pressure throughout Europe, facing scrutiny in the way in which they operate and the way in which they are financed.

---

[115] Annex II to the *Communication from The Commission on Services of General Interest in Europe,* 20 Sept 2000.

[116] See L Woods and J Scholes, 'Broadcasting: the Creation of a European Culture or the Limits of the Internal Market?' (1997) 17 *Yearbook of European Law* 47; K-H Ladeur, 'European Media Law: A Perspective on the Challenge of Multimedia' in F Snyder (ed), *The Europeanisation of Law* (Hart, Oxford, 2000); J Holmes, 'Communicating Culture in the European Union: The Media, Language, and Education' in R Craufurd Smith (ed), *Culture and European Union Law* (Oxford, OUP, 2004).

[117] COM(2000)580 final 3, 35.

[118] *Ibid.*

[119] See the EC Commission's XXIXth *Report on Competition Policy* 1999, SEC(2000)720 final, at 89 ff; Case T–266/97 *VTM v Commission* [1999] ECR II–2329.

All the Member States recognise, to varying degrees, the fact that public broadcasting plays an important role in the functioning of a democratic society and in the development and transmission of social, educational and cultural values.[120] The Member States also recognise that television and access to multimedia communications constitute the main sources of information sharing. This raises issues of how a public service obligation can be reconciled with the commercial value of broadcasting and also whether public broadcasting duties can be placed upon private operators. Issues are also raised as to how far private operators should be asked to subsidise public broadcasting.

Public service broadcasting as a service of general economic interest has been mediated through the use of the state aid rules. Public broadcasting poses special problems which have been resolved through soft law and special pleading at the political level. It is organised in different ways throughout the EU, with some states such as France and Italy creating state-owned undertakings that perform public service broadcasting tasks, while other states allow several undertakings with a mixture of public and private ownership to perform the tasks. In The Netherlands, for example, almost 20 independent private undertakings perform public service broadcasting duties. Until the 1980s broadcasting in general was a monopolistic market in which only public service broadcasters, financed by the state, operated. State finance takes many forms ranging from tax breaks, levies set on TV-set buyers, compulsory licence fees,[121] capital injections, debt write-offs and direct subsidies. As the Member States opened up broadcasting to competition the financing of public service broadcasting from state resources was ring-fenced and a fine balance was drawn between EU and national competence. Community law allows the Member States to retain the task of striking a balance between values and non-economic aims (for example, quality in broadcasting), but Community law retains the ultimate power to decide whether the balance has been taken correctly through the use of the principle of proportionality.[122]

---

[120] See D Goldberg, T Prosser and S Verhulst (eds), *Regulating the Changing Media: A Comparative Study* (Oxford, Clarendon Press, 1998).

[121] Compulsory levies and licence fees raise questions of whether there is an advantage or transfer from *state* resources in order for such forms of compulsory revenue-raising to be a form of state aid: cf Case C–379/98 *PreussenElektra* [2001] ECR I–2099, para 58. The EC Commission sees such forms of mandatory regulation as state funds within the meaning of Article 87(1) EC: Case NN 70/98 Kinderkanal and Phoenix [1999] OJ C 238/3. In NN 631/01 BBC Licence *Fee*, para 20, supra n 88, the EC Commission referred to the fact that the mandatory TV licence fee was authorised by a Government Minister; 'on this ground, the licence fee constitutes a mandatory fee imposed by the state, and, therefore, the funds thereby obtained constitute state funds within the meaning of Article 87(1) of the Treaty'. The distinguishing features appeared to be to be the state control over the revenues, an important point raised also by Jacobs AG in *PreussenElektra* at para. 165. Licence fees are akin to parafiscal charges. See also the Public Broadcasting Communication, [2001] OJ C 320/4, para 17, which was adopted *after* the *PreussenElektra* ruling.

[122] See R Craufurd-Smith, 'Re-thinking European Union Competence in the Field of Media Ownership: the Internal Market, Fundamental Rights and European Citizenship' (2004) 29 *ELRev* 652.

Broadcasting has undergone radical technological changes and, as with the liberalisation of telecommunications, the abolition of national monopolies was in response to these developments which created new demands for investment, research and marketing. This in turn has led to the greater commercialisation of broadcasting.

The Member States are given a wide leeway to determine the scope of public service broadcasting within their territory. Such forms of broadcasting usually include news and culture programmes, as well as sport and entertainment, and quite often the whole programme spectrum of the broadcaster is considered to be within the remit of the public service obligation. More recently public service broadcasters have engaged in commercial activities, selling their programmes abroad, selling advertising and selling spin-offs from programmes such as books and toys through commercial merchandising. In the wake of increased competition in the market, this broadening of commercial activities has created tensions as to whether the remit of the public service broadcaster, supported entirely or in part, by state funds, should be limited and/or opened up to tender.[123] In the early 1990s the new commercial broadcasters from Spain, France and Portugal began lodging complaints with the EC Commission alleging that the state financing of public service broadcasters was a form of state aid which was incompatible with the EC Treaty under Article 87(1) EC.

The competitors pointed out that the programmes of public broadcasters did not differ in content from the commercial rivals' programmes, and indeed the latter were often limited in what they could broadcast through Member States' licensing regulation. State financing of broadcasting did not meet any of the criteria for justification or exemption under Article 87(2) or (3) or Article 86(2) EC. State financing of public broadcasters often went beyond the costs of providing a public service and were not proportionate. It was also alleged that public service broadcasters held incumbent dominant positions in the broadcasting markets and abused that position, particularly in selling advertising, since public broadcasters did not have to cover the full cost of production.[124]

There are parallels with the complaints made in the postal sector which are discussed in Chapter 5. The EC Commission was aware of the political sensitivity of the issues and could not adopt a position.[125] Therefore, the broadcasters brought actions against the EC Commission before the CFI for failure to act

---

[123] Analogies are drawn with the telecommunications monopolies. For support of a tendering system see: C Giles, 'The Public Challenges for Communications Sector Over the Next 10 Years: Contestable Public Service Funding' in E Richards, R Foster and T Kiedrowski (eds), *Communications the Next Decade: A Collection of Essays Prepared for the UK Office of Communications* (London, Ofcom, 2006). At the time of writing (Dec 2006) the book was available at http://www.ofcom.org.uk/research/commsdecade/.

[124] There is a useful summary of the history and legal position in *Communication from the Commission on the application of State aid rules to public service broadcasting* [2001] OJ C320/5.

[125] See Case T–17/96 *TF1 v Commission* [1999] ECR II–1757, paras 60–68.

under Article 232 EC.[126] In *TF1* and *Gestevisión Telecinco* the complaint was upheld, the complaint forcing the EC Commission to start taking a position on the financing of public broadcasters.

On 17 October 2001 the EC Commission adopted a Communication[127] in which it recognised the importance of public broadcasting in European society and the recognition of this role in the EC Treaty. The Communication sets out the circumstances in which financing of a public broadcaster amounts to state aid and the conditions for the application of Article 86(2) EC. Of significance is the international nature of the ownership of broadcasters and the international markets in which broadcasters compete where state aid may distort competition and trade between Member States.[128] In some cases the effects on trade may be indirect. For example in the Decision on aid to local television stations in the French Community in Belgium[129] the EC Commission argued that the market for the sale and acquisition rights for programmes might be neglected since the local TV stations would focus on programmes of local interest. The local operators were not active in the international markets, but it was argued that their mere presence diverted audiences away from competitors operating at the international level, reducing the advertising revenue of the competitors.

The EC Commission argued that where there is no public tendering process for a public service obligation the transfer of public funds is a state aid.[130] In *BBC 24-Hour News* the EC Commission stated:

> any State measure capable of putting an undertaking in a more favourable position than its competitors and having an effect on trade between member States has to be regarded as falling under the ban in Article 87(1) EC.[131]

In both instances the national authorities had argued that the payments were to cover the costs of providing a public service obligation. In *SIC v Commission* the CFI annulled the Decision on procedural grounds but confirmed that compensation payments to the public service broadcaster were a form of state aid. After *Ferring*[132] the EC Commission, in a decision relating to the BBC funding of nine digital channels, looked at the proportionality of the payments to find that the

---

[126] Case T–231/95 *SIC v Commission*, removed from the Register, 4 July 1997; Case T– 17/96 *Télévision française 1 SA (TF1) v Commission* [1999] ECR II–1757; Case T–95/96 *Gestevision Telecinco SA v Commission* [1998] ECR II–3407.

[127] *Communication of the Commission on the Application of the State Aid Rules to Public Service Broadcasting* [2001] OJ C320/4.

[128] NN 631/01 *BBC Licence Fee*, para 22, supra 88; *State Financing of Danish Public Broadcaster TV2* [2003] OJ C 59/2. para 52.

[129] NN 548/01 *Aid to Local Television Stations in the French-speaking Community in Belgium* [2002] OJ C150/7.

[130] Case NN 70/98 *Kinderkanal and Phoenix* [1999] OJ C 238/3.

[131] NN88/98 *BBC 24-Hour News Channel* [2000] OJ C78/6, para 24.

[132] Case C–53/00 *Ferring v ACOSS* [2001] ECR I–6639.

funding did not amount to a real advantage to the recipients.[133] In *SIC* the Court of First Instance applied the derogation of Article 86(2) EC.[134]

The Broadcasting Communication sets out the criteria for applying Article 86(2) EC.[135] The service in question must be a service of general economic interest and clearly defined as such by the Member State; the undertaking must be explicitly entrusted by the Member State with the provision of that service; and the ban on state aid does not obstruct the performance of the particular tasks assigned to the undertaking and trade between Member States must not develop in a way which would be contrary to the interests of the Community. The EC Commission applied Article 86(2) EC in a series of decisions post-*Altmark* arguing that the European Court ruling had not changed the applicability of Article 86(2) EC when applied to state aid. The EC Commission asserted that the *Altmark* ruling provided support for the EC Commission's practice of applying Article 86(2) EC to public service broadcasting situations. In RAI,[136] RTP,[137] France 2 and France 3[138] the EC Commission declared that the European Court had 'implicitly confirmed' in its *Altmark* ruling that state aid under Article 87(1) EC can be compatible with the Common Market if it satisfies the conditions of Article 86(2) EC.[139] The EC Commission refers to paragraph 57 of the Broadcasting Communication where proportionality is established if state aid, including all direct and indirect revenues derived from the public service obligation, does not exceed the net costs of the obligation. Thus the net benefit that non-public service activities derive from the public service activity is taken into account in assessing the proportionality of the aid. In *BBC Digital Curriculum*[140] the EC Commission was confronted with a public broadcaster providing services not only through traditional television programmes but also through the internet.

---

[133] NN 631/01 *BBC Licence Fee* [2000] OJ C78/6, para 54.

[134] Case T–46/97 *SIC v Commission* [2000] ECR II–2125 See also in *Kinderkanal/Phoenix*, above n 130; *BBC 24-Hour News supra* n 131.

[135] Commission communication on the application of state aid rules to public service broadcasting [2001] OJ C 320/4, para 29.

[136] Commission Dec of 15 Oct 2003 on the measures implemented by Italy for RAI SpA [2004] OJ L119/1.

[137] Commission Dec of 15 Oct 2003 on *ad hoc* measures implemented by Portugal for RTP [2005] OJ L142/1.

[138] Commission Dec of 10 Dec 2003 on State Aid implemented by France 2 and France 3 [2004] OJ L361/21.

[139] Contrast E Szyszczak, 'Financing Services of General Interest' (2004) 67 *MLR* 982; A Sinnaeve, 'State Financing of Public Services: The Court's Dilemma in the *Altmark* Case' (2003) *European State Aid Law Quarterly* 351; N Lindner, 'The Impact of the Decision of the European Court of Justice in *Ferring* on European State Aid Law' (2003) 9 *European Public Law* 359 and the Opinion of Léger AG in Case C–280/00 *Altmark Trans and Regierungsprasidium Magdeburg* [2003] ECR I–7747, para 79. Under the *Ferring/Altmark* compensation approach state financing is limited to compensating for the provision of a public service obligation. If there is over-compensation it is unlikely that the proportionality requirement of Art 86(2) EC will be met.

[140] Commission Dec of 1 Oct 2003 on State Aid No N 37/2003, *United Kingdom, BBC Digital Curriculum* C (2003) 3371 final. See also C Koenig and G Husi, 'Public Funding of Digital Broadcasting Under EC State Aid Law' (2004) 4 *European State Aid Law Quarterly* 605.

Licence fees were used to finance internet educational services providing interactive learning materials free to homes and schools. The EC Commission found *new* state aid present but it could be justified under Article 86(2) EC as a service of general economic interest in education. It could be argued that educational facilities were part of the old state aid regime, and it was only the *way* in which these were delivered that was different. This Decision raises a number of issues for the Member States on whether to notify new ways of delivering a public service, the separation of accounts and the calculation of the costs of providing new modes of delivery of traditional public services.

In a second case involving internet services, *TV2/Danmark,* the EC Commission found for the first time that the criteria for applying Article 86(2) EC were not met in the financing of a public service broadcaster and ordered the recovery of the funding.[141] Together with letters sent to The Netherlands, Germany and Ireland in March 2005,[142] this Decision indicates that new concerns are raised as to the proportionality and cost-calculation of financing public service broadcasting, especially where the public service broadcaster is engaging in commercial activity. The EC Commission is concerned to ensure more transparency between public service obligations and commercial activity to avoid illegal cross-subsidisation between the two activities. The EC Commission found that TV2 enjoyed a number of financial advantages, for example, licence fee resources, transfer of resources from a TV2 fund, corporation tax exemptions, interest and instalment-fee establishment loans, state guarantees for operating loans, free transmission frequency with national coverage and a must-carry status. These advantages were not available to commercial television stations. TV2 also engaged in commercial internet services. The EC Commission found that the second and fourth conditions of *Altmark* were not met for the funding to be seen as public service obligation compensation. As in the Decisions in *RAI, RTP* and *France 2* the EC Commission preferred to see the financing as state aid under Article 87(1) EC and conduct an investigation into the proportionality of the measures, using Article 86(2) EC as the legal base.

The EC Commission decided that the financing had exceeded the net costs of TV2 by some 84.3 million euros, and therefore TV2 had been over-compensated for what was a legitimate public service obligation, entrusted to it through a legislative act. The EC Commission rejected the private investor argument put forward by the Danish government where it argued that it had behaved in the same way as a private investor would in re-investing TV2's annual profit and the profit was a reasonable return on TV2's activities. The EC Commission did not

---

[141] Commission Dec of 19 May 2004 on measures No C 2/2003 (ex NN 22/02) implemented by Denmark for TV2/Danmark C (2004) 1814 final. Letters were also sent to the governments of Germany, Ireland and The Netherlands in which the EC Commission preliminary findings drew the conclusion that the funding of the public service broadcaster did not conform to the state aid rules.

[142] For a discussion of the content of these letters see N Sumrada and N Nohlen, 'Control of State Aid for Public Service Broadcasting: Analysis of the European Commission's Recent Policy' (2005) 4 *European State Aid Law Quarterly* 609.

accept the Danish government's argument that TV2 needed the capital surplus as a reserve against fluctuations in advertising income, finding that holding the surplus was not necessary for TV2 to function properly. The EC Commission also investigated whether TV2 had depressed prices in commercial markets, for example, the advertising market, by aiming to reduce the revenue of competitors. The EC Commission could not find sufficient evidence to determine whether the advertising prices of TV2 were high enough to enable an efficient commercial operator to cover its stand alone costs, taking into account TV2's rebate policy. But the EC Commission did find that any loss of TV2's income from advertising did not exceed the level of over-compensation for the public service obligation.

THE LIBERALISATION PROCESS

The ring-fencing of services of general economic interest was a central feature of the Member States' acceptance of the liberalisation programmes in the sectors of telecommunications, utilities and postal services discussed in Chapter 5. The appeal to the general interest demanded by the Member States works also in the Community's interest in the integration process. It serves two distinct functions: according to the *nature* of the general interest, it allows the Community legislator to ascertain the legitimacy of intervention at the EU level *and* also gives the EU legitimacy by responding to a clearly identified and especially selected *collective need*. The general interest becomes a *condition* of legality for the Community's legislative intervention; a passive legislative function. The appeal to the general interest allows the Community to show its citizens that it is responsive to individual and collective needs, thus giving the Community democratic legitimacy, and the Community is established alongside the national legislator as guardian and guarantor of the general interest.

The link reconciling the liberalisation process and the defence of public services is made in the use of a new Community law concept of 'universal service' developed through soft law processes of the EC Commission[143] and integrated into the liberalisation Directives. Although the definition of a universal service differs between the liberalised sectors there are two motivating factors driving the concept: justice and equal opportunities. Universal service obligations are portrayed as having a role to play in the redistributive tasks of the state, allowing for wealthier providers and consumers to cross-subsidise poorer consumers of public services. This in turn has contributed to the idea of citizenship rights derived

---

[143] EC Commission Communication, *Services of General Interest in Europe* [1996] OJ C281/03; *Communication From the Commission Services of General Interest in Europe*, COM(2000) 580 final, at 3; E Szyszczak, 'Public Service Provision in Competitive Markets' (2001) 20 *Yearbook of European Law* 35.

from universal service obligations. One aspect of liberalisation is that consumers of universal services are often placed in a better legal position to assert rights on the quality of public services.

The new institutional design for public services in the liberalisation process places the consumer in a special contractual relationship with the public/private provider of a universal service. For the provider this makes a number of inroads into the freedom to contract and has attracted criticism from Teubner, who describes the use of universal service obligations in the privatisation process of Community law as a strange phenomenon whereby arcane principles discarded from medieval law obligations are suddenly transposed into the private law relationships of competitive markets.[144] However, the liberalisation process is a gradual movement towards introducing full competition in markets, and the role of universal services may not always fit into the model of a competitive market.

COMMON THEMES FOUND IN UNIVERSAL SERVICE OBLIGATIONS

In the EU liberalisation processes the state continues to act as a guarantor of the provision of public services, and a number of common themes underpin the relationship between the provider and the consumer of such services. The White Paper[145] assumes that liberalised markets will automatically make services of general interest more cost efficient and consequently more affordable. But in recent years the EC Commission has intervened to regulate liberalised markets to intensify competition and improve consumer choice and the affordability of such services. The state provides the legal and regulatory framework which sets out consumer rights and remedies and the provider's obligations, organised around a number of themes.[146]

Access and Affordability

A first theme is the idea that universal services guarantee access to all, irrespective of the economic, social or geographical situation, at a specified quality and an

---

[144] G Teubner, 'After Privatization? The Many Autonomies of Private Law' (1998) 51 *Current Law Problems* 393, 411.

[145] Communication From the Commission to the European Parliament, The Council, The European Economic and Social Committee and the Committee of the Regions White Paper on Services of General Interest, COM(2004) 374 final, 12 May 2004.

[146] See: P Nebbia, *Unfair Contract Terms in European Law* (Oxford, Hart, 2007) ch 6; P Rott, 'A New Social Contract Law for Public Services?—Consequences from Regulation of Services of General Economic Interest in the EC' (2005) 3 *European Review of Contract Law* 324; D Tambini, 'What Citizens Need to Know. Digital Exclusion, Information Inequality and Rights' in E Richards, R Foster and T Kiedrowski (eds), *Communications The Next Decade: A Collection of Essays Prepared for the UK Office of Communications* (London, Ofcom, 2006); D Puttman, 'The Continuing Need to Advance the Public Interest' in Richards *et al.*.

affordable price. As Sauter notes, it is not only geographical penetration but also social penetration that is demanded.[147] In the 1993 *Communication on the Consultation on the Review of the Situation in the Telecommunications Services Sector*[148] the EC Commission identified three principles upon which the universal service obligation rested: continuity, equality and affordability. The incorporation of a universal service obligation was a central aspect of securing the liberalisation of the telecommunications sector.[149] Directive 97/33/EC defined a universal service as:

> a defined minimum set of services of specified quality which is available to all users independent of their geographical location and, in the light of specified national conditions, at an affordable price.'

In the new electronic communications package there is now a specific Directive, Directive 2002/22, addressing universal service obligations.[150]

Individual access to services of general interest is another dimension of universal services in the network industries. It will be recalled that this is a fundamental right recognised in Article 36 of the Charter of Fundamental Rights of the EU. For example, an individual consumer needs an installation in his/her home or place of business for telecommunications and energy supplies. Thus Article 4 of Directive 2002/22/EC states that the Member States shall ensure that all *reasonable* requests for connection at a fixed location to the public telephone network and for access to publicly available telephone services at a fixed location are met by at least one undertaking. The connection provided shall be capable of allowing end-users to make and receive local, national and international telephone calls, facsimile communications and data communications at data rates that are sufficient to permit functional internet access, taking into account prevailing technologies used by the majority of subscribers and technological feasibility. However the increased convergence and complexity of digital communications networks may make such rights illusory, even within the next decade.

Ideas of affordability and equality of access are seen also in the definition of a universal service in the postal sector as set out in the Postal Services Directive, 97/67/EC.[151] In the reserved sector the state must provide a permanent postal service of a specified quality at all points in the territory at affordable prices for

---

[147] W Sauter, 'Universal Service Obligations and the Emergence of Citizens' Rights in European Telecommunications Liberalization' in M Freedland and S Sciarra (eds), *Public Services and Citizenship in European Law* (Oxford, OUP, 1998).

[148] COM(93)159 final, at 21.

[149] *Communication from the Commission to the Council and the European Parliament on the Consultation of the Review of the Situation in the Telecommunications Sector,* COM(93)159 final.

[150] Dir 2002/22/EC on universal service and users' rights relating to electronic communications networks and services (Universal Service Directive) [2002] OJ L08/51.

[151] [1998] OJ L15/14, as amended by Dir 2002/39/EC [2002] OJ L176/21. See also the Postal Notice [1998] OJ C39/2. See D Geradin (ed), *The Liberalisation of Postal Services in the European Union* (The Hague, Kluwer, 2002).

all users. Users have the right to a universal service in the shape of a minimum of one clearance and one delivery to the home or premises of every natural or legal person every working day and not less often than five days a week. Collection and delivery points must be accessible. The universal service applies to sorting, transport and distribution of postal items in the reserved sector. The Postal Notice addresses the fact that postal service liberalisation was partial, leaving incumbents as dominant players in the newly liberalised markets. The EC Commission was concerned that postal operators granted special or exclusive rights could let the quality of the universal service decline or not provide incentives to improve the quality of the service. The case law of the Court of Justice provided a guarantee of the *quality* of the universal service; by failing to address the quality of services provided, a Member State could be breach of Articles 86 and 82 EC.[152]

The Electricity Directive borrows from the telecommunications sector using the concept of 'the price to beat' by placing competitive pressure on pricing supply offers through the obligation to supply electricity a reasonable, easily and clearly comparable and transparent prices.[153] The Gas and Electricity Directives place obligations upon the Member States to ensure that there are adequate safeguards to protect vulnerable consumers, including appropriate measures to help such consumers to avoid disconnection.[154] A Member State can decide whether the consumer is at fault or whether he/she is unable to pay for the service as a result of what Wilhelmsson[155] has coined *social force majeure,* and find solutions to the problem in cooperation with public authorities.

The liberalisation Directives provide a *minimum* set of contractual elements which must be present. For example, the Directives restrict termination and disconnection of the services. Article 3(5) of Directive 2003/54 provides that:

> Member States shall take appropriate measures to protect final customers, and shall in particular ensure that there are adequate safeguards to protect vulnerable customers, including measures to help them avoid disconnection.

There are rules relating to pre-contractual and contractual information which enable consumers to make an informed choice. In Article 6 of the Postal Services Directive, for example, Member States are obliged to:

> take steps to ensure that users are regularly given sufficiently detailed and up-to-date information by the universal service providers regarding the particular features of the

---

[152]   Case C–41/90 *Höfner & Elser v Macrotron GmbH* [1991] ECR I–1979; Case C–179/90 *Port of Genoa* [1991] ECR I–5889.

[153]   Art 3(3) of Dir 2003/54/EC [2003] OJ L 176/37.

[154]   Art 3(5) of *ibid* and Art 3(3) of Dir 2003/55/EC [2003] OJ L176/57.

[155]   T Wilhelmsson, 'Services of General Interest and Private Law' in C Rickett and T Telfer (eds), *International Perspectives on Consumers' Access to Justice* (Cambridge, CUP, 2003) at 165.

universal services offered, with special reference to the general conditions of access to these services as well as to prices and quality standard levels. This information must be published in an appropriate manner.

Article 12 of the Postal Services Directive, 97/67/EC, states that prices must be set so that all users have access to the services provided. The Annexes to the Gas and Electricity Directives specify in detail the consumer protection measures needed to allow consumer choice to be a realistic decision. The Green Paper,[156] refers to the obligations of the Member States to use their public welfare systems to help needy consumers who are unable to pay for services of general economic interest.

The EC Commission continues to insist that the definition of universal services and public service obligations is a task for the public authorities at the relevant level.[157] This division of competence is eroded, in that the liberalisation Directives set some *standards* for services of general interest. Indeed, in the telecommunications sector these standards are quite detailed. Directive 2002/22/EC[158] provides that consumers have the right to a single narrowband network connection. The Member State may restrict the end-user's primary location or residence, but may not restrict access to the Integrated Services Digital Network (ISDN). Telephone directories must be made available and updated at least once a year. Article 5 relates to operator assistance and to directory enquiry services, and Article 25 refers to the availability of free itemised billing services.

In the postal services sector a number of minimum standards are set out. The universal service provider guarantees, every working day, a delivery and clearance service to the home or premises of every natural or legal person. Eighty-five per cent of the postal items of the fastest standard category shall be delivered within three days after the day of deposit, and 97 per cent of the postal items within five days.[159] The definition of a universal service includes a number of minimum facilities: the clearance, sorting, transport and distribution of postal items weighing up to two kilogrammes; the clearance, sorting, transport and distribution of postal packages up to 10 kilogrammes; services for registered items and insured items.[160] The Member States are allowed to take into account specific situations in their territory, for example, the density of network postal agencies.

In addition to the political objectives of ensuring equity, participation, cohesion and solidarity there are also economic efficiency considerations behind the guarantee of access to universal services. In the case of postal services and telecommunications there are network externalities: the utility of the network

---

[156] Communication From the Commission to the European Parliament, The Council, The European Economic and Social Committee and the Committee of the Regions White Paper on Services of General Interest, COM(2004) 374 final, 12 May 2004, para 21.

[157] *Ibid*, at 5.

[158] Dir 2002/22/EC of 7 Mar 2002 on universal service and users' rights relating to electronic communications, networks and services (Universal Service Directive) [2002] OJ L108/51.

[159] Annex A of Dir 97/67/EC [1997] OJ L 15/14.

[160] Art 3(4) of *ibid*.

service to each user increases with the number of other users of the service. Another user of the service will exert a positive externality on all other users of the service.

Paying for Services of General Economic Interest

Many services of general economic interest cannot be provided without some form of subsidy. A common reason for the state to intervene to provide a service of general economic interest is market failure. As we have seen in the last section network externalities may increase the use of a service of general economic interest in a networked sector, and since the private benefit of using a postal or telecommunications service is lower than the social benefit there are good reasons for the state legitimately to subsidise the use of such service, especially for consumers who would not otherwise have access to a networked service. There are also political reasons for subsidising a service of general economic interest, for example, in the interests of social inclusion and territorial cohesion.

In order to meet the obligations contained within Community law the state may be obliged to subsidise or cross-subsidise such services.[161] The Court has recognised that cross-subsidisation between economically viable and non-viable services may be a legitimate form of state intervention in certain sectors.[162] Similarly in the Green Paper[163] the EC Commission states that it is a core responsibility of public authorities to ensure that basic collective and qualitative needs are met and that services of general interest are preserved when market forces cannot achieve this, whether the services are performed by the state or non-state bodies. However, competition issues relating to cross-subsidisation emerge where a former public provider of a service of general economic interest is also present in the liberalised market.[164] The Court in *Altmark*[165] has set out the conditions under which state subsidisation of services of general economic

---

[161] There are differing views on whether Art 16 EC obliges the state to subsidise services of general economic interest: C Bovis, 'Financing Services of General Interest in the EU: How do Public Procurement and State Aids Interact to Demarcate between Market Forces and Protectionism?' (2005) 11 *ELJ* 79, 94 ff; V Karayannis, 'Le service universel de télécommunications en droit communautaire: entre intervention publique et concurrence' [2002] *Cahiers de droit européen* 315, 333.

[162] Case C–320/91 *Corbeau* [1993] ECR I–2533.

[163] *Communication From the Commission to the European Parliament, The Council, The European Economic and Social Committee and the Committee of the Regions White Paper on Services of General Interest*, COM(2004)374 final, 12 May 2004.

[164] Cf L Hancher and J Buendia Sierra, 'Cross-subsidisation and EEC Law' (1998) 38 *CMLRev* 901 with G Abbamonte, 'Cross-subsidisation and Community Competition Rules: Efficient Pricing versus Equity' (1998) 23 *ELRev* 414.

[165] Case C–280/00 *Altmark Trans GmbH and Regierungspraesidium Magdeburg* v *Nahverkehrsgesellschaft Altmark GmbH* [2003] ECR I–7747..

interest can be made without bringing the state aid rules into play,[166] and these decisions were reinforced by the EC Commission's package of measures in July 2005.[167]

Regulating universal service obligations in such a way introduces the notion of providing consumers with a defined service which can only be provided at net cost, which an operator could and might want to avoid but for the universal obligation. The very existence of universal obligations implies that the services would not be provided under normal market conditions since such services would not be profitable.[168] Community law has, therefore, engaged with the issue of financing universal obligations. The traditional means of financing a universal obligation is through cross-subsidisation between loss-making and profitable activities within an integrated public monopoly, and in *Corbeau*[169] the Court accepted that this was a legitimate means of ensuring a core universal service. Liberalisation reduced the possibilities of cross-subsidisation, but, as we saw in Chapter 5, somewhat paradoxically in the post-liberalisation era cases have been brought alleging the reverse process, where the incumbent charged with providing a universal service obligation uses its inherent market power to cross-subsidise the commercial arm of its operations.

Continuity

The EC Commission has defined continuity in the Green Paper as placing an obligation upon the provider of the service to ensure that it is supplied without interruption.[170] A far-reaching obligation is seen in Article 3(1) of the Postal Services Directive[171] where the state is to ensure the permanent provision of a postal service. Postal services cannot be interrupted or cease, except in situations of *force majeure.* Under Article 23 of the Universal Service Directive, 2002/22/EC, Member States are obliged to take all necessary steps to ensure the integrity of the public telephone network at fixed locations. If there is a network breakdown or *force majeure* situation, the Member States must ensure the availability of the

---

[166] See also Case C–379/98 *PreussenElektra* [2000] ECR I–2099.

[167] Commission Dec of 13 July 2005 on the application of Art 86(2) of the Treaty to state aid in the form of public service compensation granted to certain undertakings entrusted with the operation of services of general economic interest [2005] OJ L312/67 and Commission Framework for state aid in the form of public service compensation [2005] OJ C297/4.

[168] See also the finding by the Court of Justice in a case of alleged state aid in the French postal sector in Joined Cases C–83/01P, C–93/01P & C–94/01P *Chronopost SA, La Poste and French Republic v Ufex and others* [2003] ECR I–6993. The CFI should not have used a test to determine whether there was illegal state aid using comparisons based upon normal market conditions, because La Poste's network, built to meet non-commercial public service requirements and on the basis of a reserved sector, was too dissimilar to a commercial network to enable such comparisons.

[169] Case 66/86 [1989] ECR 803.

[170] See also *Green Paper Towards a European Strategy for the Security of Energy Supply,* COM(2000)769 final.

[171] Art 5(1) of Dir 97/67.

public telephone network and publicly available telephone services at fixed locations. Member States must also ensure that undertakings providing publicly available telephone services at fixed locations take all reasonable steps to ensure uninterrupted access to emergency services.

Consumer Law and State Liability

The EC Commission's White Paper pursues the idea of a *rights-based* approach towards services of general economic interest. The idea of a universal service 'establishes the right of everyone to access certain services considered as essential'.[172]

The intervention at the EU level of setting standards for services of general economic interest alongside the ideas of universal access for such services raises an important question: who is liable if these obligations and standards are not met? The idea that remedies may be available for failure to provide traditional public services in accordance with Community law standards creates issues of enforcement using Community and national consumer law and contract law, as well as public law principles of state liability.

Community law has established a general principle that national law must provide effective remedies which are enforceable through judicial proceedings.[173] The state is under a duty to provide a legal framework that allows for effective control mechanisms for individuals to pursue rights against a service provider and to receive effective remedies. The state may be at fault for failing to create the infrastructure necessary to maintain services of general economic interest at a satisfactory level. The state does not necessarily have to provide an infrastructure for services of general interest but must ensure that one is in place. This may involve financial support for private service providers and subsidisation. It may also be jointly liable with a non-state service provider in failing to meet the expectations of Community law. From *Francovich*[174] onwards the Court has set out the conditions for state liability: the rule of law infringed must be intended to confer rights on individuals; the breach of the law must be sufficiently serious; and there must be a direct causal link between the breach of the state's obligations and the loss and/or damage suffered by the individual concerned.[175]

Article 16 EC may be used as a teleological tool for interpretation, but is unlikely to give rise to direct effect. The fundamental right of *access* to a service of

---

[172] Communication From the Commission to the European Parliament, The Council, The European Economic and Social Committee and the Committee of the Regions White Paper on Services of General Interest, COM(2004) 374 final, 12 May 2004, at 8.

[173] W van Gerven, 'Bridging the Gap Between Community and National Laws: Towards a Principle of Homogeneity in the Field of Legal Remedies?' (1995) 32 *CMLRev* 679, 679 ff and 'Of Rights, Remedies and Procedures' (2000) 37 *CMLRev* 501.

[174] Cases C–6 & C–9/90 *Francovich and Bonifaci v Italy* [1991] ECR I–5537.

[175] See C Vajda QC, 'Liability for Breach of Community Law: A Survey of the ECJ Cases Post *Factortame*' (2006) 17 *EBLR* 257.

general economic interest will also provide teleological guidance on *how* access to such services is provided, although, as Ross[176] points out, an individual right to services of general economic interest calls for a differentiated response. Consumer and user rights protection is a predominant theme.[177] For example, under the sectoral Directives the *aim* of the regulation of the services of general economic interest is to promote consumer (or user) rights. See, for example, Recital 3 of the Universal Service Directive, 2002/22/EC, which refers directly to the consumer protection competence of Article 153 EC, or Recitals 11, 12 and 14 of the Postal Services Directive, 97/7/EC, which refer to user rights.

However, in order to give rights which are enforceable in national courts, the conditions for direct effect must be present. Many of the provisions refer to *specific* contractual rights of the consumer, for example, the right to switch suppliers, and pre-contractual rights, for example, rights to information under Article 3 with Annex A of the Electricity Directive, 2003/54/EC, and the right to terminate the contract in case of a price alteration or any unilateral change to the contract terms under Annex A lit b) of Directives 2003/54/EC and 2003/55/EC.

Community law refrains from regulating in detail issues such as affordable price or the minimum quality of services. Affordable price will depend upon specific national conditions, for example consumer prices and income.[178] The regulatory standard is very general, for example, Article 1(2) of the Universal Service Directive, 2002/22/EC, refers in general terms to:

> rights of end-users and the corresponding obligations on undertakings providing publicly available electronic communications networks and services..

A similar general standard is set in the Postal Services Directive:

> Member States shall ensure that users enjoy the right to a universal service involving the permanent provision of a postal service of specified quality at all points in their territory at affordable prices for all users.[179]

The EC Commission envisages that national contract law will govern the obligation to contract, the control of the content and the price of services, restrictions on the contract provider in terminating the contract, extended rights for the consumer to terminate the contract and to switch provider, and pre-contractual and contractual information. However, the increasing trends towards the need for EU level harmonisation of certain aspects of private law, alongside the EU obligations set out in the liberalised sectors, creates a tendency towards convergence of these principles at the EU level.

---

[176] M Ross, 'The Europeanization of Public Services Supervision: Harnessing Competition and Citizenship?' (2004) 23 *Yearbook of European Law* 489.

[177] White Paper on Services of General Interest, COM(2004) 374 final, 9.

[178] See Arts 1(2) and 9(1) of Dir 2002/22/EC.

[179] Art 3(1) Dir 97/67/EC.

CONCLUSION

The original EEC Treaty and the current EC Treaty do not address the provision or the organisation or the financing of services of general economic interest as an objective of European integration. However, Articles 16 and 86(2) EC show that the EU respects the role these services play in the social and territorial cohesion of the EU. As a result of liberalisation of markets, the attacks upon public monopolies in the national courts using Article 86(1) EC, alongside changing consumer expectations of services of general economic interest, and the provision and regulation of such services have increasingly been Europeanised from the 1990s onwards. The tensions between public service values and the provision of goods and services through competitive markets have been mediated through a variety of European policy tools.

The process was started through typical negative integration techniques using Article 86(1) EC, with the partial re-regulation of such services at the EU level using Community-based concepts of the way in which services of general economic interest should be delivered in competitive markets. This has occurred from case law which has moved from being permissive of certain state intervention to address perceived market failures towards a prescriptive approach, seen especially in the ruling in *Altmark*.[180] This ruling reveals how the financing of services of general economic interest and the relationship of state subsidies with the state aid rules has centred the discourse on services of general economic interest around the state aid rules. *Altmark* also places the public procurement of services of general economic interest as a central and crucial legal tool in assuring the competitiveness of such services. This in effect is part of a process of creating public markets where both the state and private commercial operators may provide services of general economic interest which are responsive to market conditions and consumer needs.

These developments have brought transparency to the award of public service obligations. They recognise that providers of public services which may also be engaged in commercial activities, and that profit motives are not inconsistent with the public interest. The case law has been reinforced through soft law, the use of the open method of coordination, as well as specific sectoral rules relating to universal service obligations. Thus the Member States are under new obligations to ensure the quality and the consistency of the delivery of services of general economic interest. More recently, the fundamental rights and citizenship nature of these services have been developed in the provisions of the Constitutional Treaty, and the EC Commission in the White Paper[181] has used the idea

---

[180]   Case C–280/00 *Altmark Trans GmbH and Regierungspraesidium Magdeburg* v *Nahverkehrsgesellschaft Altmark GmbH* [2003] ECR I–7747.

[181]   *Communication From the Commission to the European Parliament, The Council, The European Economic and Social Committee and the Committee of the Regions White Paper on Services of General Interest*, COM(2004)374 final, 12 May 2004, at 4.

that access to affordable high quality services of general interest is an essential component of European citizenship and necessary to allow citizens to enjoy their fundamental rights.

As a result, the EU has created its own reforming agenda which is at odds with the policies of the Member States. Although we can discern common themes and common underlying concepts in the liberalisation programmes, the regulatory reform of the European public services market in general has resulted in the fragmentation of the regulatory approach towards services of general economic interest. The state aid rules are taking over from Article 86 EC as the main focus for the reform of the provision of services of general economic interest, with an increasing emphasis upon efficiency and *consumer* rights which may be at odds with the traditional social and citizenship rights previously linked to the provision of services of general economic interest.

8

Conclusion

THE EEC TREATY tolerated a view that the Member States were free to choose the mix between the public and private provision of goods and services in the market.[1] At this time large sectors of the economy were controlled directly by the state and the Treaty provisions attempted to steer a compromise between free markets and state intervention in markets. The Treaty addressed only extreme forms of state intervention, such as state aids and state monopolies.

The analysis in this book shows how, with limited legal tools, national courts, regulatory bodies, the European Courts and the EC Commission have played a crucial role in determining, defining and shaping the scope of legitimate state intervention in the market. A recurring theme throughout the book is the accepted role of law in this process and the manner in which the European Courts have played a pivotal role in elevating the competition law provisions, alongside the free movement provisions of the Treaty, into an economic constitution. A prominent feature of this constitution is that it governs the relationship between the various actors, the roles and levels of government and their relationship with the market. A second feature of the modern economic constitution is the way in which it mediates the apparent tensions between the use of markets to provide a wide range of goods and services to citizens *and* the preservation of traditional values, alongside the creation of new values in the delivery of such goods and services.

The chapters of this book show how the EU, using traditional Community law processes and new forms of economic governance, has developed a far-reaching control of state intervention in the market with limited legal tools. The basic legal toolkit of the EEC Treaty, particularly the free movement and competition rules, is not easy to apply in the context of Article 295 EC which supports a mixed economy in the EU. The EEC Treaty rules were a compromise: they refused to address directly the issue of state intervention in competitive markets and did not provide guidance for the complex economic and political task of weeding out legitimate state intervention in the economy from legitimate forms of state

---

[1] Case 6/64 *Costa v ENEL* [1964] ECR 585.

intervention which were necessary and also could be beneficial for European integration. Instead the Treaty addresses only a narrow area, protecting services of general economic interest from the full rigour of the market in Article 86(2) EC. Even this has proved to be an insufficient compromise, with the liberalised sectors creating more detailed sector-specific rules and the protection and promotion of such services in competitive markets highlighted in new constitutional provisions such as Article 16 EC and Article 36 of the Charter of Fundamental Rights of the EU.

The European Courts were aware of the need to limit the scope for the exercise of public economic authority by the Member States, and since the late 1980s the Courts have struggled to differentiate between typical state activities where there is an exercise of public power and economic activity where the state may disrupt normal commercial activities because of its unusual authority in a commercial market.[2] Some clear bright lines can be drawn; for example in the discussion in Chapter 4, we see where the Court has separated out instances when the state is exercising powers of *imperium* or where social protection schemes display a sufficient degree of solidarity, taking such activities outside the scope of Community law.

Chapters 2, 3 and 4 show that a key jurisdictional legal tool deployed by the EC Commission and the European Courts is to ask whether the state, or a state-regulated body, is acting as an undertaking.[3] The very broad and functional test for an undertaking, as set out in *Höfner*[4] at first sight appears to be circular, with the concept of economic activity becoming the central issue. However, despite these limitations, Winterstein[5] observes that a functional approach has allowed an activity neither to lose its economic nature because it is exercised by the state (or a state body), nor to become economic because it is performed by a non-state body. This allows the state to contract out typical state activities. Additionally, the Courts have introduced a number of safety nets by excluding certain activities (for example, education, healthcare and pensions) from the concept of economic activity in order to avoid a finding that there is an undertaking and have deployed the use of a broad concept of solidarity in order to rule out economic activity.

The difficulty of drawing bright lines between state public and state commercial activity is seen in the relationship between national regulatory powers and the economic activity of the state, explored in case law relating to Articles 81, 82

---

[2]   L Montana and J Jellis, 'The Concept of an Undertaking in EC Competition Law and its Application to Public Bodies: Can You Buy Your Way into Article 82?' (2003) 2 *Competition Law Journal* 110; J van de Gronden, 'Purchasing Care: Economic Activity or Service of General (Economic) Interest' (2004) 25 *ECLR* 88.

[3]   V Louri, '"Undertaking" as a Jurisdictional Element for the Application of the EC Competition Rules' (2002) 29 *Legal Issues of European Integration* 143.

[4]   Case C–41/90 [1991] ECR I–1979.

[5]   A Winterstein, 'Nailing the Jellyfish: Social Security and Competition Law' (1999) 20 *European Competition Law Review* 324, 327.

and 10 EC in Chapters 2 and 3.[6] The initial stance of the Court appeared capable of imposing severe constraints on the economic policy of the Member States.[7] The use of the *effet utile* doctrine led to the assumption that state measures could infringe the competition rules of the Community where the state imposed regulations which facilitated the conclusion of, or reinforced the effects of, restrictive agreements and where it delegated to undertakings the responsibility to take measures of economic policy.

There was strong support for this policy,[8] but also criticism. The 'November Revolution' rulings of the Court in 1993[9] brought limitations to this expansive reasoning by requiring clear links between state regulation and the alleged anti-competitive conduct. This approach draws a sharp line demarcating national economic policy as a form of public law, independent of private agreements. It is a long period between the successful use of the formula in a preliminary ruling in *Ahmed Saeed*[10] to the use of the principle in the rulings in *CNSD*[11] and *CIF*.[12] Yet, in the more recent rulings, the Court shows that it continues to be attached to the *principle* of state liability under the competition rules.[13] There has yet to be a finding that a state measure may be in violation of Article 82 EC *per se*. The idea of state liability under Article 82 EC has gained currency only when applied in conjunction with Article 86 EC.

This was also the period where Article 28 EC came to play an expansive role in breaking down state regulatory barriers to trade, even where such regulation appeared to regulate the national market. In the early period of the development

---

[6] L Gyselen, 'State Action and the Effectiveness of the EEC Treaty's Competition Provisions' (1989) 26 *CMLRev* 33.

[7] Case 229/83 *Leclerc v Au Blé Vert* [1985] ECR 1; Case 267/86 *Van Eycke v ASPA* [1988] ECR 4769.

[8] R Joliet, 'National Anti-competitive Legislation and Community Law' (1989) 12 *Fordham International Law Journal* 172; J-F Verstrynge, 'The Obligations of the Member States as Regards Competition in the EEC Treaty' in B Hawk (ed), *Annual Proceedings of the Fordham Corporate Law Institute* (New York, Fordham Corporate Law Institute, 1988).

[9] Joined Cases C–267 & C–268/91 *Keck and Mithouard* [1993] ECR I–6097; Case C–2/91 *Criminal Proceedings Against Wolfgang Meng* [1993] ECR I–5751; Case C–185/91 *Bundesanstalt für den Güterfernverkehr v Gebrüder Reiff GmbH & Co KG* [1993] ECR I–5801. Cf B van der Esch, 'The System of Undistorted Competition of Article 3(f) of the EEC Treaty and the Duty of Member States to Respect the Central Parameters Thereof (1998) 11 *Fordham International Law Journal* 409.

[10] Case 66/86 *Ahmed Saeed* [1989] ECR 803.

[11] Case C–35/96 *Commission v Italy* [1998] ECR I–3851.

[12] Case C–198/01 [2003] ECR I–8055.

[13] Cf R Wainwright and A Bouquet, 'State Intervention and Action in EC Competition Law' in B Hawk (ed), *International Anti-trust Law and Policy Fordham Corporate Law 2003* (New York, Juris, 2004) at 539 who argue that the modern principle is reduced in importance. In comparison with the United States' approach, which it is argued is much weaker, the EU appears to take a tougher stance on the regulation of state intervention in the market: see E Fox, 'State Action in Comparative Context: What if Parker v. Brown were Italian?' in *ibid*; M Marques Mendes, 'State Intervention/State Action—A U.S. and EC Perspective from Cassis de Dijon to Altmark Trans and Beyond: Trends in the Assessment of State Intervention by the European Courts' in *ibid.*; T Muris, 'State Intervention/State Action—A US Perspective' in *ibid*. T Zywicki *et al*, *Report of the State Action Task Force* (Washington, DC, Office of Policy Planning, Sept 2003), available at http://www.ftc.gov/os/2003/09/stateactionreport.pdf.

of an economic constitution the Court chose to develop Article 28 EC over the competition rules. However, the examination of the cases in Chapters 2 and 3 shows how the Court was not always clear, or structured, in its thinking over the interaction of the free movement and competition rules. It has been suggested in this book that one reason which may explain *why* the Court chose to develop Article 28 EC over the competition rules is because Article 30 EC (and, later, the mandatory requirements doctrine of *Cassis de Dijon*[14]) allowed the Member States a justification for state measures, whereas Articles 81 and 82 EC did not contain a public interest justification for the Member States to raise. Over the years a generic public interest justification has been stretched across the other fundamental free movement provisions. Given the wider application of the competition rules to state activity it therefore seemed logical to open up the availability of a public interest justification when the competition rules are being applied to the state, as well as delegated authorities within the state and autonomous regulatory bodies. As a result a generic public interest justification has emerged which satisfies the needs of non-state bodies in the Internal Market and the competition policy field in a series of cases from *Reisebüro Broede* [15] through *Wouters*[16] to *Meca-Medina*.[17]

Chapters 2 and 3 show how the modern discourse on the legitimate role of state intervention in the market has been dependent upon individual or private litigation in the national courts. It is puzzling why greater use has not been made of Article 97 EC since this provides for a procedure for combating distortions caused by laws, regulations or administrative rules of the Member States by the EC Commission.[18] The answer can be found in Chapter 5, where we see that, despite a number of complaints brought to the EC Commission alleging abuse of market power by state monopolies, the EC Commission trod a cautious path and was reluctant to take decisive action, even when faced with direct complaints from competitors (and potential competitors) in markets closed to competition. A second answer lies in the significance of the direct effect of Articles 81, 82 and 86 EC and the absence of direct effect of Article 97 EC. The absence of the opportunity to raise this Article in the national courts deprived it of any role in determining the boundaries between acceptable and unacceptable state intervention in the market.

Article 86 EC emerged as the legal provision delimiting the acceptable amount and form of legal state intervention in the market during the 1990s. Chapter 4

---

[14]   Case 120/78 *Rewe-Zentral v Bundesmonopolverwaltung für Branntwein* [1979] ECR 649.

[15]   Case 3/95 *Reisebüro Broede v Gerd Sandker* [1996] ECRI-6511.

[16]   Case C–309/99 [2002] ECR I–1577.

[17]   Case C–519/04 [2006] ECR I-6991. See E Szyszczak, 'Competition and Sport' (2007) 32 *ELRev* 95.

[18]   Eg, Slot and Johnston argue that '[t]he *PreussenElektra* case (Case C–379/98 *PreussenElektra AG v Schleswag AG* [2001] ECR I–2099) could be cited as a candidate for the application of this provision': P Slot and A Johnston, *An Introduction to Competition Law* (Oxford, Hart, 2006) at 339, fn 150.

shows how the Court has drawn a line between the exercise of public authority and the exercise of economic activity.[19] Article 86 EC has thus played a central role in the specific application of Article 10(2) EC. It has been used to reconcile the fundamental economic freedoms of the Internal Market and the competition rules of the EC Treaty with the existence of a public sector. As we have seen, it is a complex legal provision. Article 86 EC requires an investigation into which areas of public intervention fall within the remit of Article 86(1) EC. Where the EC Treaty rules apply, the scope of the derogation in Article 86(2) EC and the use of the principle of proportionality determine the balance between the social and the economic dimension of the Internal Market and the balance of competence between Member States' policies and the economic drivers of European integration. The competence of the EC Commission to enact Directives and Decisions under Article 86(3) EC has been eroded by the political weight of the Member States. This has had an impact upon the way in which liberalisation has been implemented in the EU. Article 86(3) EC gives the EC Commission competence to act independently immune from the usual political EC Treaty legislative processes. However, attempts by the EC Commission to use Article 86(3) EC as a tool to further a Community liberalisation policy have been curtailed by the political power of the Member States and less than sympathetic treatment by the Court.

As Chapter 5 shows, paradoxically, the partial liberalisation of sensitive sectors has allowed the state to enhance its authority and to exercise power, directly and indirectly, in the liberalisation processes in competitive markets. Thus, in the liberalisation process clear distinctions between traditional or typical functions of the state and new commercially orientated activities of the state have evaporated as the state has called upon the private sector to deliver traditional state goods and services in competitive markets. Consequently the state continues to have a significant influence on the market and competitive relations *within* the market. The liberalisation processes have evolved in different ways and at different speeds. Chapter 5 explores the new institutional designs of these processes and reveals how the restructuring of markets, alongside rapid technological developments, has brought the use of competition law principles to prominence in the regulation of new forms of economic power in the liberalised markets. The major challenge now for the EU is how to address the rise in consumer power which can determine how goods and services are provided in competitive markets.

A challenge for the future is that while the Member States are compelled to, and indeed some Member States want to, withdraw from *direct* intervention in the economy and give way to competition in the market, the EU is unable to replace the void left by the interventionist state, particularly its public welfare

---

[19] See Case C–41/90 *Höfner v Macrotron* [1991] ECR I–1979. See also the EC Commission, *23rd Competition Report 1993*, COM(94)161, 211.

role, since the EU's powers for intervention and redistribution are limited. Chapter 7 therefore examines the impact on EU public services of Article 16 EC and Article 36 of the Charter of Fundamental Rights and the introduction of a set of EU-based values into the liberalisation processes. We see how these values are often crafted in vague and generalised terms, leaving room for greater specificity to be provided by the Member States. Alongside these traditional values, modern constitutional ideas also place value on market efficiency, consumer choice and control of market power as part of a new package of citizens' *rights*: consumers, alongside competitors, are seen as the beneficiaries of the liberalisation processes.

The use of universal service obligations to protect essential public services in the liberalisation processes serve as a reminder of the limits of the market to guarantee these values, but also an indicator of how the market can improve the quality of these values. Chapters 4, 6 and 7 show how the only Treaty justification for state anti-competitive activity, Article 86(2) EC, has been read across into other Treaty provisions. This limited justification, relating to services of general economic interest, has proved to be the centre of a much wider discourse on how to balance market freedoms against fundamental notions of citizenship and solidarity. The limitations of the Treaty model are remedied in the more detailed liberalisation measures where the EU takes over a prescriptive model, setting out minimum conditions for the maintenance of a universal service in the liberalised sectors. These standards have an important role to play in the integration project, since they have the potential to create convergence, with the Member States moving towards a harmonised approach to the provision of services of general economic interest using techniques of good governance transparency and accountability.

Bibliography

ABBAMONTE, G, 'Cross-subsidisation and Community Competition Rules: Efficient Pricing versus Equity' (1998) 23 *European Law Review* 414.

ALTER, K and MEUNIER-AITSAHALIA, S, 'Judicial Politics in the European Community—European Integration and the Path-breaking *Cassis de Dijon* Decision' (1994) 26 *Comparative Political Studies* 535.

AMATO, G, *Antitrust and the Bounds of Power. The Dilemma of Liberal Democracy in the History of the Market* (Oxford, Hart, 1997).

BACH, A, Annotatation Case 185/91, *Bundesanstadlt für den Güterfernverkehr v Gerbrüder Reiff GmbH & Co KG*; Case C–2/94, *Meng*; Case 245/91, *OHRA Schadeverzekeringen NV* (1994) 31 *Common Market Law Review* 1358.

BACON, K, 'State Regulation of the Market and EC Competition Rules: Articles 85 and 86 Compared' (1997) 18 *European Competition Law Review* 283.

BAQUERO CRUZ, J, *Between Competition and Free Movement* (Oxford, Hart, 2002).

—— 'Beyond Competition: Services of General Interest and European Community Law' in G de Búrca (ed), *EU Law and the Welfare State In Search of Solidarity* (Oxford, OUP, 2005).

BARTOSCH, A, 'The Relationship Between Public Procurement and State Aid Surveillance: The Toughest Standards Applies?' (2002) 39 *Common Market Law Review* 551.

—— 'Clarification or Confusion? How to Reconcile the ECJ's Rulings in *Altmark* and *Chronopost*?', Working Paper 02, *clasf Working Paper Series*, available at http://www.clasf.org.

BAVASSO, A, 'Electronic Communications: A New Paradigm For European Regulation' (2004) 41 *Common Market Law Review* 87.

BENGOETXEA, J, *The Legal Reasoning of the European Court of Justice* (Oxford, Clarendon Press, 1993).

BENKLER, Y, *The Wealth of Networks* (Yale, New Haven and London, Yale University Press, 2006).

BIONDI, A and RUBINI, L, 'Aims, Effects and Justifications: EC State Aid Law and Its Impact on national Social Policies' in M Dougan and E Spaventa (eds), *Social Welfare and EU Law* (Oxford, Hart, 2004).

BISHOP, M and KAY, J, 'Privatization in the United Kingdom: Lessons From Experience' (1989) 17 *World Development* 643.

BLACK, J, 'Decentring Regulation' (2001) *Current Legal Problems* 103.

—— 'Enrolling Actors in Regulatory Systems: Examples From the UK Financial Services Regulation' [2003] *Public Law* 63.

BLANPAIN, R (ed), 'Private Employment Agencies', *Bulletin of Comparative Labour Relations* (The Hague, Kluwer, 1996) 36.

BLUM, F and LOGUE, A, *State Monopolies Under EC Law* (Chichester, Wiley, 1998).

BOYLE, T, 'Barriers to Contested Takeovers in the European Community' (1991) 12 *Company Law* 163.

BOUTAYEB, C, 'Une recherche sur la place et les fonctions de l'intérêt général en droit communautaire' [2003] *Revue Trimestrielle de Droit Européen* 587.

BOUTCHKOVA, M and MEGGINSON, W, 'The Impact of Privatisation on Capital Market Development and Individual Share Ownership' (2000) 29 *Financial Management* 67.

BOVIS, C, 'Financing Services of General Interest in the EU: How Do Public Procurement and State Aids Interact to Demarcate Between Market Forces and Protection?' (2005) 11 *European Law Journal* 79.

BRAUN, J-D and CAPITO, R, 'The Framework Directive' in C Koenig, A Bartosch, and J-D Braun (eds), *EC Competition and Telecommunications Law* (The Hague, Kluwer, 2002).

BRITTAN, SIR LEON, *Competition Policy and Merger Control in the Single European Market* (Cambridge, Grotius, 1991).

BUENDIA SIERRA, J, *Exclusive Rights and State Monopolies Under EC Law* (Oxford, OUP, 1999).

BULMER, S, 'Institutions and Policy Change in the European Communities: the Case of Merger Control' (1994) 72 *Public Administration* 423.

BUTLER, S, 'Privatization for Public Purposes' in W T Gormley, Jr (ed), *Privatization and Its Alternatives* (Madison, Wisc, University of Wisconsin Press, 1991).

CAMERON, P, *Competition in Energy Markets* (Oxford, OUP, 2002).

CAMPBELL JR, J, 'Couriers and the European Postal Monopolies: Policy Challenges of a Newly Emerging Industry' in R Pedlar and M van Schendelen (eds), *Lobbying in the European Union* (Dartmouth, Aldershot, 1994).

—— 'The Evolution of Terminal Dues and Remail Provisions in European and International Postal Law' in D Geradin (ed), *The Liberalisation of Postal Services in the European Union* (The Hague, Kluwer, 2002).

—— 'Remail: Catalyst for Liberalising European Postal Markets' in G Kulenkampf and H Smit (eds), *Liberalisation of Postal Markets: Papers Presented at the 6th Königswinter Seminar*, WIK Proceedings Vol 7 (Bad Honnef, WIK 2002).

CAPUTI JAMBRENGHI, P, '"Creating A Level Playing Field" in the Italian Retail Distribution Market: The Use of EC Law and the Role of the Italian Anti-trust Authority' (1996) 17 *European Competition Law Review* 189.

CHALMERS, D, 'Free Movement of Goods Within the European Community: an Unhealthy Addiction to Scotch Whisky?' (1993) 42 *International and Comparative Law Quarterly* 269.

—— HADJIEMMANUIL, C, Monti, G, and Tomkins, A, *European Union Law, Text and Materials*, (Cambridge, CUP, 2006).

CHUNG, C-M, 'The Relationship Between State Regulation and EC Competition Law: Two Proposals for a Coherent Approach' (1995) 16 *European Competition Law Review* 87.

CINI, M, *From Soft Law to Hard Law?: Discretion and Rule-making in the Commission's State Aid Regime* (Florence, Robert Schumann Centre for Advanced Legal Studies, EUI, 2000).

—— 'The Soft Law Approach: Commission Rule-making in the EU's State Aid Regime' (2001) 8 *Journal of European Public Policy* 192.

COLLIARD, C, 'L'obscure clarité de l'article 37' [1964] *Dalloz* Ch. XXXVII 263.

CRAUFURD-SMITH, R, 'Re-thinking European Union Competence in the Field of Media Ownership: the Internal Market, Fundamental Rights and European Citizenship' (2004) 29 *European Law Review* 652.

CREW, M and KLEINDORFER, P, 'Efficient Entry, Monopoly and the Universal Service Obligation in Postal Service' (1998) 14 *Journal of Regulatory Economics* 103.

DE BIJL, P, van Damme, E, and Larouche, P, *'Light is Right': Competition and Access Regulation in an Open Postal Sector* (Tilburg, Tilburg Law and Economics Center, June 2005).

DE JONG, H, 'Concentration in the Common Market: a Comment on a Memorandum of the EEC Commission' (1966–67) 4 *Common Market Law Review* 166.

DELLA CANANEA, G, 'Administration by Guidelines: The Policy Guidelines of the Commission in the Field of State Aids' in I Harden (ed), *State Aid: Community Law and Policy* (Cologne, Bundesanzeiger, 1993).

DERENNE, J and STOCKFORD, C, 'Abuse of Market Powers in Postal Services: Lessons from the Commission's Decisional Practice and Court of Justice' in D Gerdain (ed), *The Liberalisation of Postal Services in the European Union* (The Hague, Kluwer, 2001).

DERINGER, A, *The Competition Law of the European Economic Community: A Commentary on the EEC Rules of Competition* (The Hague, CCH Editions, 1968).

—— 'Equal Treatment of Public and Private Enterprises. General Report', *Equal Treatment of Public and Private Enterprises* (Copenhagen, FIDE Congress, 1978).

DE STREEL, A, 'The Integration of Competition Law Principles in the New European Regulatory Framework for Electronic Communications' (2003) 26 *World Competition* 489.

DEVROE, W, 'Privatizations and Community Law: Neutrality versus Policy' (1997) 34 *Common Market Law Review* 268.

DIEZ ESTELLA, F, 'Abusive Practices in Postal Services? Parts I and II' (2006) 27 *European Competition Law Review* 184.

DOUGAN, M and SPAVENTA, E, "Wish You Weren't Here ..." New Models of Social Solidarity in the European Union' in M Dougan and E Spaventa (eds), *Social Welfare and EU Law* (Oxford, Hart, 2005).

DRAGANIC, I, 'State Aid or Compensation for Extra Costs: Tuning the Test of Proportionality in EC Competition Law' (2006) 4 *European State Aid Law* 683.

DUFF, A, *The Treaty of Amsterdam* (London, Federal Trust, Sweet and Maxwell, 1997).

EBERLEIN, B, 'Regulation By Cooperation: The "Third Way" in Making Rules for the Internal Energy Market' in P Cameron (ed), *Legal Aspects of EU Energy Regulation* (Oxford, OUP, 2005).

EDWARD, D and HOSKINS, M, 'Article 90: Deregulation and EC Law. Reflections Arising from the XVI Fide Conference' (1995) 32 *Common Market Law Review* 160.

EHLE, D, 'State Regulation under United States Antitrust State Action Doctrine and under E.C. Competition Law: a Comparative Analysis' (1998) 6 *European Competition Law Review* 380.

EHLERMANN, C-D, 'The Contribution of EC Competition Policy to the Single Market' (1992) 29 *Common Market Law Review* 257.

—— 'Managing Monopolies: The Role of the State in Controlling Market Dominance in the European Community' (1993) 14 *European Competition Law Review* 61.

EHLERMANN, C-D, 'Role of the European Commission as Regards National Energy Policies' (1994) 12 *Journal of Energy and National Resources* 342.

ELHAUGE, R, 'The Scope of Antitrust Process' (1991) 104 *Harvard Law Review* 668.

FENGER, N and BROBERG, P, 'National Organisation of Regulatory Powers and Community Competition Law' (1995) 16 *European Competition Law Review* 365.

FINON, D and MIDTTUN, A, *Reshaping European Gas and Electricity Industries* (Amsterdam, Elsevier, 2004).

FLYNN, L, 'Competition Policy and Public Services in EC Law After the Maastricht and Amsterdam Treaties' in D O'Keeffe and P Twomey (eds), *Legal Issues of the Amsterdam Treaty* (Oxford, Hart, 1999).

FOREMAN-PECK, J and MILLWARD, R, *Public and Private Ownership of British Industry 1820–1990* (Oxford, Clarendon Press, 1994).

FOX, E, 'State Action in Comparative Context: What if Parker v. Brown were Italian?' in B Hawk (ed), *International Anti-trust Law and Policy Fordham Corporate Law 2003* (New York, Juris, 2004).

FREEMAN, J, 'Private Parties, Public Functions and the New Administrative Law' (2000) 52 *Administrative Law Review* 813.

FRIEND, M, 'State Guarantees as State Aid: Some Practical Difficulties' in A Biondi *et al* (eds), *The Law of State Aid in the European Union* (Oxford, OUP, 2004).

GAGLIARDI, A, 'What Future for Member States' Monopolies?' (1998) 23 *European Law Review* 371.

—— 'United States and European Union Antitrust versus State Regulation of the Economy: Is There a Better Test?' (2000) 25 *European Law Review* 367.

GARDNER, A, 'The Velvet Revolution: Article 90 and the Triumph of the Free Market in Europe's Regulated Sectors' (1995) 16 *European Competition Law Review* 78.

GEDDES, R, *Competing With the Government: Anticompetitive Behaviour and Public Enterprises* (Stanford, Cal, Hoover Institution Press, 2004).

GERADIN, D, 'The Opening of State Monopolies to Competition: Main Issues of the Liberalisation Process' in D Geradin (ed), *The Liberalisation of State Monopolies in the European Union and Beyond* (The Hague, Kluwer, 2000).

—— (ed), *The Liberalisation of Postal Services in the European Union* (The Hague, Kluwer, 2002).

—— 'Enhancing Competition in the Postal Sector: Can We Do Away With Sector-specific Regulation?', Paper delivered at 14th Conference on Postal and Delivery Economics, Bern, June 2006, available at http://ssrn.com/abstract=909008.

—— and HENRY, D, 'Regulatory and Competition Law Remedies in the Postal Sector' in D Geradin (ed), *Remedies in Network Industries—EC Competition Law versus Sector Specific Regulation* (Antwerp, Intersentia, 2004).

—— and HUMPE, C, 'The Liberalisation of Postal Services in the European Union: An Analysis of Directive 97/67' in D Geradin (ed), *The Liberalisation of Postal Services in the European Union* (The Hague/London, Kluwer, 2002).

—— and KERF, M, *Controlling Market Power in Telecommunications: Antitrust vs. Sector-specific Regulation* (Oxford, OUP, 2003).

—— and PETIT, N, 'La politique industrielle sous les tiers croises de la mondialisation et du droit communautaire de la concurrence', Working Paper, 2006, available at: http://www.ieje.net/fileadmin/IEJE/Pdf/Mondialisation_politique_industrielle_e_.pdf.

—— and SIDAK, J, 'European and American Approaches to Antitrust Remedies and the Institutional Design of Regulation in Telecommunications' in M Cave, S Majumdar and I Vogelsang (eds), *Handbook of Telecommunications Economics, Vol 2* (Oxford, OUP, 2005).

—— and —— 'The Future of the Postal Monopoly: American and European Perspectives after the Presidential Commission and Flamingo Industries' (2005) 28 *World Competition* 161.

GERBER, D, 'Constitutionalizing the Economy: German Neo-liberalism, Competition Law and the "New" Europe' (1994) 42 *American Journal of Comparative Law* 25.

—— *Law and Competition in Twentieth Century Europe. Protecting Prometheus* (Oxford, Clarendon Press, 1998).

GERSTENBERGER, O, 'Expanding the Constitution Beyond the Court: The Case of Euro-Constitionalism' (2002) 8 *European Law Journal* 172.

GILES, C, 'The Public Challenges for the Communications Sector Over the Next 10 Years: Contestable Public Service Funding' in E Richards, R Foster and T Kiedrowski (eds), *Communications the Next Decade: A Collection of Essays Prepared for the UK Office of Communications* (London, Ofcom, 2006). At the time of writing (December 2006) the book was available at http://www.ofcom.org.uk/research/commsdecade/.

GOLDBERG, D, Prosser, T and Verhulst, S (eds), *Regulating the Changing Media: A Comparative Study* (Oxford, Clarendon Press, 1998).

GONZÁLEZ-ORÚS, J, 'Beyond the Scope of Article 90 of the EC Treaty: Activities Excluded From the EC Competition Rules' (1999) 5 *European Public Law* 387.

GORMLEY, L, 'Actually or Potentially, Directly or Indirectly? Obstacles to Free Movement of Goods' (1990) 15 *Yearbook of European Law* 197.

GRAHAM, C, 'All that Glitters ... Golden Shares and Privatised Enterprises' (1988) 9 *Company Law* 23.

—— and PROSSER, T, *Privatising Public Enterprises* (Oxford, Clarendon Press, 1991).

GRESPAN, D, 'An Example of the Application of State Aid Rules in the Utilities Sector in Italy' (2002) 3 *Competition Policy Newsletter* 17.

GRIFFITHS, M, 'Failing to Install Effective Competition in Postal Services: the Limited Impact of EC Law' (2000) 21 *European Competition Law Review* 399.

GYSELEN, L, 'State Action and the Effectiveness of the EEC Treaty's Competition Provisions' (1989) 26 *Common Market Law Review* 33.

—— 'Anti-Competitive State Measures Under the EC Treaty: Towards a Substantive Legality Standard' [1993] *European Law Review Competition Checklist 1993* CC78.

HANCHER, L, *EC Electricity Law* (London, Chancery, 1992).

—— 'EC State Aids and Energy' (1995) 2 *Oil and Gas Taxation Law Review* 62.

—— 'Community State and Market' in P Craig and G de Búrca (eds), *The Evolution of EU Law* (Oxford, OUP, 1999) 727.

—— and BUENDIA SIERRA, J, 'Cross-subsidisation and EEC Law' (1998) 38 *Common Market Law Review* 901.

HARDEN, I, 'The Approach of English Law to State Aids to Enterprise' (1990) 11 *European Competition Law Review* 100.

HASSAN, J and DUNCAN, A, 'Integrating Energy; the Problems of Developing an Energy Policy in the European Communities' (1994) 23 *Journal of European Economic History* 159.

HATZOPOULOS, V, 'Health Law and Policy: The Impact of the EU' in G de Búrca (ed), *EU Law and the Welfare State* (Oxford, OUP, 2005).

HAWK, B, 'The EEC Merger Regulation: the First Step Toward One-Stop Merger Control' (1990) 59 *Antitrust Law Journal* 195.

HENRY, C and JEUNEMAITRE, A, (eds), *Regulation of Networked Utilities: the European Experience* (Oxford, OUP, 2001).

HERTIER, A, 'Market Integration and Social Cohesion: the Politics of Public Services in European Regulation' (2001) 8 *Journal of Public Policy* 825.

HOFFMAN, A, 'Anticompetitive State Legislation Condemned Under Articles 5, 85 and 86 of the EEC Treaty: How Far Should the Court Go After *Van Eycke*?' (1990) 15 *European Competition Law Review* 1.

HOLMES, J, 'Communicating Culture in the European Union: The Media, Language, and Education' in R Craufurd Smith (ed), *Culture and European Union Law* (Oxford, OUP, 2004).

HOOD, C, Scott, C, James, O. and Travers, T, *Regulation Inside Government* (Oxford, OUP, 2000).

ICHIKAWA, Y, 'The Tension Between Competition Policy and State Intervention: the EU and US Compared' (2004) *European State Aid Law Quarterly* 555.

JANS, J, 'Proportionality Re-visited' (2000) 27 *Legal Issues of Economic Integration* 239.

JOLIET, R, 'National Anti-competitive Legislation and Community Law' (1989) 12 *Fordham International Law Journal* 172.

KARAYANNIS, V, 'Le service universel de télécommunications en droit communautaire: entre intervention publique et concurrence' [2002] *Cahiers de droit européen* 315.

KAY, J and THOMPSON, D, 'Privatization: A Policy in Search of a Rationale' (1986) 96 *Economic Journal* 18.

KOENIG, C and HUSI, G, 'Public Funding of Digital Broadcasting Under EC State Aid Law' (2004) 4 *European State Aid Law* 605.

—— NEUMANN, A and KOCH, A, 'Authorisations' in C Koenig, A Bartosch and J-D Braun (eds), *EC Competition and Telecommunications Law* (The Hague, Kluwer, 2002).

—— and RÖDER, E, 'The Regulation of Telecommunications in the European Union: a Challenge for the Countries Acceding to the European Community' (1999) 10 *European Business Law Review* 333.

KOUTRAKOS, P, 'Healthcare as an Economic Service under EC Law' in M Dougan and E Spaventa (eds), *Social Welfare and EU Law* (Oxford, Hart, 2005).

KULENKAMPF, G and SMIT, H (eds), *WIK Proceedings Vol 7* (Bad Honnef WIK, 2002).

KUZNETSOV, I., 'The Legality of Golden Shares Under EC Law' (2005) 1 *Hanse Law Review* 22, available at http://www.hanselawreview.org/pdf/Vol1No1Art3.pdf.

LADEUR, K-H, 'European Media Law: A Perspective on the Challenge of Multimedia' in F Snyder (ed), *The Europeanisation of Law* (Oxford, Hart, 2000).

LANDES, D, *The Wealth and Poverty of Nations* (London, Abacus, 1998).

LAROUCHE, P, *Competition Law and Regulation in European Telecommunications* (Oxford, Hart, 2000).

—— 'A Closer Look at Some Assumptions Underlying EC Regulation of Electronic Communications' [2002] *Journal of Network Industries* 148.

LENAERTS, K, 'Constitutionalism and the Many Faces of Federalism' (1990) 38 *American Journal of Comparative Law* 205.

LEVER, SIR JEREMY, KCMG, QC, 'Some Procedural Conundrums in State Aids Law' in A Biondi *et al* (eds), *The Law of State Aid in the European Union* (Oxford, OUP, 2004).

LINDNER, N, 'The Impact of the Decision of the European Court of Justice in *Ferring* on European State Aid Law' (2003) 9 *European Public Law* 359.

LIPSTEIN, K, *The Law of the European Economic Community* (London, Butterworths, 1974).

LISTER, L, *Europe's Coal and Steel Community* (New York, Twentieth Century Fund, 1960).

LOOZEN, E, 'Professional Ethics and Restraints of Competition' (2006) 31 *European Law Review* 28.

LOUIS, F and VALLERY, A, '*Ferring* Revisited: the *Altmark* Case and State Financing of Public Services Obligations' (2004) 57 *World Competition* 53.

LOURI, V, '"Undertaking" as a Jurisdictional Element for the Application of the EC Competition Rules' (2002) 29 *Legal Issues of European Integration* 143.

LUCAS, N, *Energy and the European Communities* (Oxford, OUP, 1977).

MAHBOOBI, I, *Recent Privatisation Trends* (Paris, OECD, 2002).

MAJONE, G, *Deregulation or Regulation? Regulatory Reform in Europe* (London, Pinter, 1990).

—— 'Paradoxes of Privatization and Deregulation' (1994) 1 *Journal of European Public Policy* 54.

MARENCO, G, 'Public Sector and Community Law' (1983) 20 *Common Market Law Review* 505.

—— 'Pour une intérpretation traditionelle de la notion de mesure d'effet equivalent à une restriction quantitative' [1984] *Cahiers de Droit Européen* 291.

—— 'Competition Between National Economies and Competition Between Business—A Response to Judge Pescatore' [1987] 11 *Fordham International Law Journal* 420.

—— 'Government Action and Antitrust in the United States: what lessons for Community Law?' (1987) 14 *Legal Issues of European Integration* 1.

MARESCA, M, 'The Access to the Services of General Interest (SGIs), Fundamental Right of European Law, and the Growing Role of Users' Rights', Paper delivered at the 10th Conference of International Consumer Law, Lima, Peru, 2–6 May 2005.

MARQUES MENDES, M, 'State Intervention/State Action—A U.S. and EC Perspective from Cassis de Dijon to Altmark Trans and Beyond: Trends in the Assessment of State Intervention by the European Courts' in B Hawk (ed), *International Anti-trust Law and Policy Fordham Corporate Law 2003* (New York, Juris, 2004).

MCGOWAN, L and CINI, M, 'Discretion and Politicization in EU Competition Policy: the Case of Merger Control' (1999) 12 *Governance* 175.

MEADE, J, Liesner, H and Wells, S, *Case Studies in European Economic Integration* (London, New York and Toronto, OUP, 1962).

MONTANA, L and JELLIS, J, 'The Concept of an Undertaking in EC Competition Law and its Application to Public Bodies: Can You Buy Your Way into Article 82?' (2003) 2 *Competition Law Journal* 110.

MONTI, G, 'Article 81 EC and Public Policy' (2002) 39 *Common Market Law Review* 1057.

MORTELMANS, K, 'Article 30 of the EEC Treaty and Legislation Relating to Market Circumstances: Time to Consider a New Definition' (1991) 28 *Common Market Law Review* 115.

MOSER, S, Pesaresi, N and Soukup, K, 'State Guarantees to German Public Banks: a New Step in the Enforcement of State Aid Discipline to Financial Services in the Community' (2002) 2 *Competition Policy Newsletter* 1.

MURIS, T, 'State Intervention/State Action—A US Perspective' in B Hawk (ed), *International Anti-trust Law and Policy Fordham Corporate Law 2003* (New York, JURIS, 2004).

NEBBIA, P, *Unfair Contract Terms in European Law* (Oxford, Hart, 2007).

NEERGAARD, U, *Competition and Competences The Tension Between European Competition Law and Anti-competitive Measures by the Member States* (Copenhagen, DJØF, 1998).

—— 'State Action and the Competition Rules: A New Path?' (1999) 6 *Maastricht Journal* 380.

NICOLAIDES, P, 'Distortive Effects of Compensatory Aid Measures: A Note on the Economics of the *Ferring* Judgment' (2002) 23 *European Competition Law Review* 313.

—— 'Markets and Words: the Distortive Effect of Government Pronouncements' (2005) 26 *European Competition Law Review* 119.

NIHOUL, P, 'Convergence in European Telecommunications A Case Study on the Relationship Between Regulation and Competition Law' [1998/99] 2 *International Journal of Communications Law and Policy* 1.

OSBORNE, D and GABLER, T, *Reinventing Government: How the Entrepreneurial Spirit is Transforming the Public Sector* (Reading, Mass, Addison-Wesley, 1992).

PAPPALARDO, A, 'State Measures and Public Undertakings: Article 90 of the EEC Treaty Revisited' (1991) 12 *European Competition Law Review* 29.

PARISH, M, 'On the Private Investor Principle' (2003) 28 *European Law Review* 70.

PESCATORE, P, 'Public and Private Aspects of Community Competition Law' [1987] *Fordham Corporate Law Institute* 381.

PETIT, N, 'The Proliferation of National Regulatory Authorities Alongside Competition Authorities: A Source of Jurisdictional Confusion' in D. Geradin, R. Muñoz and N. Petit (eds), *Regulation Through Agencies—A New Paradigm of European Governance* (Cheltenham, Edward Elgar, 2005).

PETRETTO, A, 'The Liberalization and Privatization of Public Utilities and the Protection of Users' Rights: The Perspective of Economic Theory' in M Freedland and S Sciarra (eds), *Public Services in European Law* (Oxford, OUP, 1997).

POIARES MADURO, M, 'Reforming the Market or the State? Article 30 and the European Constitution: Economic Freedom and Political Rights' (1997) 3 *European Law Journal* 51.

—— *We the Court* (Oxford, Hart, 1997).

—— 'Europe's Social Self: The Sickness Unto Death' in J Shaw (ed), *Social Law and Policy in an Evolving European Union* (Oxford, Hart, 2000).

PONS, J-F, and Luder, T, 'La politique européenne de la concurrence dans les services postaux hors monopole' [2001] *Competition Policy Newsletter* (no.3).

PRETE, L, 'State Aid Reform: Some Reflections on the Need to Revise the Notice on Guarantees' (2006) 29 *World Competition* 421.

PROSSER, T, *The Limits of Competition Law. Market and Public Services* (Oxford, OUP, 2005).

PUTTMAN, D, 'The Continuing Need to Advance the Public Interest' in E Richards *et al* (eds), *Communications: The Next Decade: A Collection of Essays Prepared for the UK Office of Communications* (London, Ofcom, 2006).

RAWLINGS, R, 'The Euro-law Game: Deductions from a Saga' (1993) 20 *Journal of Law and Society* 309.

REICH, N, 'The "November Revolution" of the European Court of Justice—*Keck, Meng* and *Audi* Revisited' (1994) 31 *Common Market Law Review* 459.

RIZZA, C, 'The Financial Assistance Granted By Member States to Undertakings Entrusted With the Operation of a Service of General Economic Interest' in A Biondi *et al* (eds), *The Law of State Aid in the European Union* (Oxford, OUP, 2003).

RODRIGUES, R, 'Vers une loi européenne des services publics' [2003] *Revue du Marché commun et de l' Union européenne* 503.

ROGGENKAMP, M, 'Implications of GATT and EEC on Networkbound Trade in Europe' (1994) 12 *Journal of Energy and Natural Reserves Law* 59.

—— (ed), *European Energy Law Report III* (Antwerp, Intersentia, 2006).

ROSS, M, 'Art. 37—Redundancy or Reinstatement' (1982) 7 *European Law Review* 285.

—— 'Keck: Grasping the Wrong Nettle' in A Caiger and D Floudas (eds), *1996 Onwards* (Chichester, John Wiley, 1996).

—— 'State Aids and National Courts: Definitions and Other Problems—a Case of Premature Emancipation?' (2000) 37 *Common Market Law Review* 401.

—— 'Article 16 E.C. and Services of General Interest: From Derogation to Obligation?' (2000) 25 *European Law Review* 22.

—— 'The Europeanization of Public Services Supervision: Harnessing Competition and Citizenship?' (2004) 23 *Yearbook of European Law* 489.

ROTH, W-H, 'Joined Cases C–267 and C–268/91 Bernard Keck and Daniel Mithouard; C–292/92 Ruth Huenermund et. al. v Landesapothekerkammer Baden-Wuerttemberg' (1994) 31 *Common Market Law Review* 845.

ROTT, P, 'A New Social Contract Law for Public Services?—Consequences from Regulation of Services of General Economic Interest in the EC' (2005) 3 *European Review of Contract Law* 324.

SAPIR, A, 'Globalisation and the Reform of European Social Models', *bruegel policy brief,* November 2001, 1.

SAUTER, W, *Competition Law and Industrial Policy in the EU* (Oxford, Clarendon Press, 1997).

—— 'Universal Service Obligations and the Emergence of Citizens' Rights in European Telecommunications Liberalization' in M Freedland and S Sciarra (eds), *Public Services and Citizenship in European Law* (Oxford, OUP, 1998).

SCHARPF, F, 'The European Social Model' (2002) 40 *Journal of Common Market Studies* 645.

SCHEPEL, H, 'Delegation of Regulatory Powers to Private Parties Under EC Competition Law: Towards a Procedural Public Interest Test' (2002) 39 *Common Market Law Review* 31.

SCHINDLER, P, 'Public Enterprises and the EEC Treaty' (1970) 7 *Common Market Law Review* 57.

SCHUMACHER, E, 'The Struggle for a European Energy Policy' (1964) 2 *Journal of Common Market Studies* 199.

SCOTT, C, 'Analysing Regulatory Space: Fragmented Resources and Institutional Design' [2001] *Public Law* 32.

SINCLAIR, M, 'A New European Communications Services Regulatory Package' [2001] *CTLR* 156.

SINN, H-W, *The New Systems Competition* (Oxford, Basil Blackwell, 2003).

SINNAEVE, A, 'State Financing of Public Services: The Court's Dilemma in the *Altmark* Case' (2003) *European State Aid Law* Quarterly 351.

SLOT, P, 'Energy and Competition' (1994) 31 *Common Market Law Review* 511.

—— ANNOTATION OF CASES C–157/94, *Commission v Netherlands*; C–158/94 *Commission v Italy*; Case 159/94 *Commission v France*; C–160/94 *Commission v Spain*; C–189/95, *Harry Franzén*; judgments of 23 October 1997, Full Court, [1997] ECR I–699, 5789, I–5815, I–5851, I–5909 (1997) 34 *Common Market Law Review* 1183.

—— 'Energy (Electricity and Natural Gas) in D Geradin (ed), *The Liberalisation of State Monopolies in the European Union and Beyond* (The Hague, Kluwer, 2000).

—— and JOHNSTON, A, *An Introduction to Competition Law* (Oxford, Hart, 2006).

—— and SKUDDER, A, 'Common Features of Community Law Regulation in the Network-bound Sectors' (2001) 38 *Common Market Law Review* 87.

SOAMES, T, 'An Analysis of the Principles of Concerted Practice and Collective Dominance: A Distinction Without A Difference?' (1996) 17 *European Competition Law Review* 24.

SOLTESZ, U, 'The New Commission Guidelines on State Aid for Airports: a Step too far...' (2006) 4 *European State Aid Law* 719.

SORIANO, L, 'How Proportionate Should Anti-competitive State Intervention Be?' (2003) 28 *European Law Review* 112.

STEINER, J, 'Drawing The Line: Uses and Abuses of Article 30 EEC' (1992) 29 *Common Market Law Review* 749.

STUMF, U, 'Remail: Catalyst for Liberalizing European Postal Markets' in M Crew and P Kleindorfer (eds), *Regulation and the Nature of Postal Services* (Boston, Mass, Kluwer, 1993).

SUMRADA, N and NOHLEN, N, 'Control of State Aid for Public Service Broadcasting: Analysis of the European Commission's Recent Policy' (2005) 4 *European State Aid Law* 609.

SUNSTEIN, C, *Free Markets and Social Justice* (Oxford, OUP, 1997).

SVANE, L, 'Public Service Compensation in Practice: Commission Package on State Aid for Services of General Economic Interest' (2005) 3 *Competition Policy Newsletter* 34.

SZYSZCZAK, E, 'Free Trade as a Fundamental Value' in K Economides, L Betten, J Bridge, V Shrubsall and A Tettenborn (eds), *Fundamental Values* (Oxford, Hart, 2000).

—— 'The Evolving European Employment Strategy' in J Shaw (ed), *Social Law and Policy in An Evolving European Law* (Oxford, Hart, 2000).

——, 'Public Services in Competitive Markets' (2001) 21 *Yearbook of European Law* 35.

—— 'Golden Shares and Market Governance' (2002) 29 *Legal Issues of Economic Integration* 255.

—— 'Governance' (2003) 3 *ERA-Forum* 130.

—— 'Financing Services of General Economic Interest' (2004) 67 *Modern Law Review* 982.

—— 'State Intervention in the Market' in T Tridimas and P Nebbia (eds), *EU Law for the 21st Century: Rethinking the New Legal Order Volume 2* (Oxford, Hart, 2004).

—— 'The Regulation of Competition' in N Shuibhne (ed), *The Regulation of the Internal Market* (Cheltenham, Edward Elgar, 2006).

—— 'Experimental Governance: The Open Method of Co-ordination' (2006) 12 *European Law Journal* 486.

—— 'Competition and Sport' (2007) 32 *European Law Review* 95.

TAMBINI, D, 'What Citizens Need to Know. Digital Exclusion, Information Inequality and Rights' in E Richards, R Foster and T Kiedrowski (eds), *Communications The Next Decade: A Collection of Essays Prepared for the UK Office of Communications* (London, Ofcom, 2006).

TEMPLE LANG, J, 'Article 5 of the EEC Treaty: The Emergence of Constitutional Principles in the Case Law of the Court of Justice' (1987) 10 *Fordham International Law Journal* 503.

—— 'Community Constitutional Law: Article 5 EEC Treaty' (1990) 27 *Common Market Law Review* 646.

—— 'The Duties of Cooperation of National Authorities and Courts Under Article 10: Two More Reflections' (2001) 26 *European Law Review* 84.

TEUBNER, G, 'After Privatization? The Many Autonomies of Private Law' (1998) 51 *Current Legal Problems* 393.

TORGERSEN, O-T, 'The Limitations of the Free Movement of Goods and Freedom to Provide Services—in Search of Common Approach' (1999) 10 *European Business Law Review* 371.

VAJDA, QC, C, 'Liability for Breach of Community Law: A Survey of the ECJ Cases Post *Factortame*' (2006) 17 *European Business Law Review* 257.

VAN DE GRONDEN, J, 'Purchasing Care: Economic Activity or Service of General (Economic) Interest' (2004) 25 *European Competition Law Review* 88.

VAN DER ESCH, B, 'The System of Undistorted Competition of Article 3(f) of the EEC Treaty and the Duty of Member States to Respect the Central Parameters Thereof' (1998) 11 *Fordham International Law Journal* 409.

—— 'Anticompetitive State Measures in the EEC and EEC Competition Policy and Enforcement' in B Hawk (ed), *Annual Proceedings of the Fordham Corporate Law Institute* (New York, Fordham, 1989).

VAN DER WOUDE, M, 'Article 90: Competing For Competence' [1991] *European Law Review Supplement (Competition Law Check List)* 60.

VAN DEN BOGGAERT, S, 'Horizontality' in C Barnard and J Scott (eds), *The Law of the Single Market* (Oxford, Hart, 2002).

VAN GERVEN, W, 'Bridging the Gap Between Community and National Laws: Towards a Principle of Homogeneity in the Field of Legal Remedies?' (1995) 32 *Common Market Law Review* 679.

—— 'Of Rights, Remedies and Procedures' (2000) 37 *Common Market Law Review* 501.

VAN MIERT, K, 'Liberalization of the Economy of the European Union: The Game is Not (Yet) Over' in D Geradin (ed), *The Liberalization of State Monopolies in the European Union and Beyond* (The Hague, Kluwer, 2000).

VENIT, J, 'The 'Merger' Control Regulation: Europe Comes of Age ... Caliban's Dinner' (1990) 40 *Common Market Law Review* 7.

VERHOEVEN, A, 'Privatization and EC law: Is the European Commission "Neutral" With Respect to Public Versus Private Ownership of Companies?' (1996) 45 *International and Comparative Law Quarterly* 27.

VERSTRYNGE, J-F, 'The Obligations of Member States As Regards Competition in the EEC Treaty' in B Hawk (ed), *Annual Proceedings of the Fordham Corporate Law Institute* (New York, Fordham, 1989).

VICKERS, J, 'Concepts of Competition' (1995) 47(1) *Oxford Economic Papers* 1.

——and YARROW, G, 'Economic Perspectives on Privatization' (1991) 5 *Journal of Economic Perspectives* 111.

VON DER GROEBEN, H, *The European Community: The Formative Years. The Struggle to Establish the Common Market and Political Union (1958–66)*, European Perspectives Series (Luxembourg, Office for Official Publications of the European Communities, 1985).

WAINWRIGHT, R and JESSEN, A, 'Recent Developments in Community Law on Telecommunications' (1991) 11 *Yearbook of European Law* 79.

—— and BOUQUET, A, 'State Intervention and Action in EC Competition Law' in B Hawk (ed), *International Anti-trust Law and Policy Fordham Corporate Law 2003* (New York, Juris, 2004).

WEATHERILL, S, 'After *Keck*: Some Thoughts on How to Clarify the Clarification' (1996) 33 *Common Market Law Review* 885.

—— 'Recent Case Law Concerning The Free Movement of Goods: Mapping The Frontiers of Market Deregulation' (1999) 36 *Common Market Law Review* 53.

—— 'The EU Charter of Fundamental Rights and the Internal Market', Francisco Lucas Pires Working Papers Series on European Constitutionalism, Working Paper 2003/03, Facudade de Direito da Universidade Nova de Lisboa.

WEILER, J, 'The Transformation of Europe' (1991) 100 *Yale Law Journal* 2403.

—— 'Journey to an Unknown Destiny' (1993) 31 *Journal of Common Market Studies* 417.

—— 'The Constitution of the Common Market Place: Text and Context in the Evolution of the Free Movement of Goods' in P Craig and G de Búrca (eds), *The Evolution of EU Law* (Oxford, OUP, 1999).

—— (ed), *The EU, the WTO and the NAFTA Towards a Common Law of International Trade* (Oxford, OUP, 2000).

WHISH, R, 'Collective Dominance' in D O'Keeffe and M Andenas (eds), *Liber Amicorum for Lord Slynn* (The Hague, Kluwer, 2000).

—— *Competition Law*, 4th edn (London, Butterworths, 2004).

WHITE, E, 'In Search of the Limits of Article 30 of the EEC Treaty' (1989) 26 *Common Market Law Review* 235.

WILHELMSSON, T, 'Services of General Interest and Private Law' in C Rickett and T Telfer (eds), *International Perspectives on Consumers' Access to Justice* (Cambridge, CUP, 2003) 165.

WILKS, S, 'The Metamorphosis of European Competition Law' in F Snyder (ed), *European Community Law, Vol 1.* (Aldershot, Wiley, 1993).

WILS, W, 'The Search for the Rule in Art.30 EEC: Much Ado About Nothing' (1993) 18 *European Law Review* 475.

—— 'The Undertaking as Subject of E.C. Competition Law and the Imputation of Infringements to Natural or Legal Persons' (2000) 25 *European Law Review* 99.

—— 'Should Private Antitrust Enforcement Be Encouraged?' (2003) 26 *World Competition* 473.

WINTER, J, 'Re(De)fining the Notion of State Aid in Article 87(1) of the EC Treaty' (2004) 41 *Common Market Law Review* 475.

WINTERSTEIN, A, 'Nailing the Jellyfish: Social Security and Competition Law' (1999) 20 *European Competition Law Review* 324.

WOODS, L and SCHOLES, J, 'Broadcasting: the Creation of a European Culture or the Limits of the Internal Market?' (1997) 17 *Yearbook of European Law* 47.

WOOLDRIDGE, F, 'Some Recent Developments Concerning Article 37 of the EEC Treaty' (1979) 1 *Legal Issues of European Integration* 120.

YARROW, G, 'Privatization in Theory and Practice' (1986) 2 *Economic Policy* 324.

Index